MW00814227

What the industry Experts are Saying

"This wonderful guide is the first I've seen that takes the user through the entire process of creating and designing their own documents, stationery, financial tables . . . even forms . . . and sets the stage for the readers future productivity in Word. Marianne's book is a wonderful addition to the growing collection of computer literature and a must-have for any Mac Word user looking to maximize the program's myriad capabilities."

Ron Lockhart
General Manager
Electronic Directions

"Marianne Carroll's new book is a great primer for business users of Microsoft Word 5.0. Its unique task-oriented format is easy-to-read and loaded with visuals, making it an excellent alternative to the run-of-the-mill tutorial/references on Word 5.0."

Corey Sherman
Anderson Consulting
Arthur Andersen & Co.

"A great book! Useful for beginner and expert—for executive and knowledged worker—for anyone who is more concerned with results than with tools."

Jim Young
Assistant to the Chairman, EDS
President, MacIS

Marianne Carroll's Super Desktop Documents

Marianne Carroll

New York   London   Toronto   Sydney   Tokyo   Singapore

Brady Publishing

Published by Brady Publishing
a Division of Prentice Hall
Computer Publishing
15 Columbus Circle
New York, New York 10023

Manufactured in the United States of America

2   3   4   5   6   7   8   9   10

Library of Congress Cataloging-in-Publication Data

ISBN 0-13-964156-4

Acknowledgments

Deep within the contained silence of writing this book, the faces, gestures and voices of those people who were there somewhere along the path to its creation surface in my consciousness. And so, I'd like to acknowledge my mother, who first said, "Why don't you learn to type so you can get a job?" and my father, with his careful attention to detail, who both gave me my early start in the work force. I'd like to thank the countless clients, students, friends (find yourself in this book!) and supportive network of "family" whose inquisitive minds and fearless—even fear-full—approach to the computer have helped me to search ever deeper for inventive ways to explain and empower them to discover their own document solutions in Microsoft Word. I would not have given birth to this book if Lou Giacalone hadn't planted the seed by steering me to my agent, Matt Wagner, at Waterside Productions who then connected me with Tracy Smith, my editor at Brady Publishing, and whose unwavering belief in this book kept me going. With deep appreciation and gratitude to Leslie Koch and David Pearce at Microsoft Corporation for championing and supporting, not only a great software product for the Macintosh, but also the work I've done with it. Thank you to The Cobb Group—their publications on Word continue to be an invaluable resource. Major thanks to my fellow consultants and friends in the Macintosh Consultants Network[sm] who sponsored my "word debut" at their conferences and brought me to the attention of Microsoft. Thanks to Apple Computer, Inc., their Consultant Relations program, the folks at the New York Market Center, MacWorld Expo and MacUser for continuing to expose me. To *Exposure Pro* from Baseline Publishers—thanks for the timesaving screen shot utility without which I could not have executed this book on schedule, and equal thanks to Mainstay for their great desk accessory, *ClickPaste*, which gave me finger-tip viewing access to the hundreds of screen shots you'll see. For centering my thoughts, guiding my spirit, and supporting me with the sheer joy of their laughter, thanks to Club WICCA and The War Council. A special thank you to Michael Hanes for his patient understanding and loving support along the way. And thanks to the Universe—for having me be a part of the "word" process.

****

This book is dedicated with love to my brother David,
with the hope that he might some day be able to read it.

Trademarks

PostScript is a regular trademark of Adobe Systems, Inc.

Apple is a registered service mark; AppleShare, AppleTalk, Finder, ImageWriter, LaserWriter, Mac, Macintosh, MultiFinder, and Quickdraw are registered trademarks and TrueType is a trademark of Apple Computer, Inc.

DeskWriter™ is a registered trademark of Hewlett-Packard Company.

Microsoft, Microsoft Word, Microsoft Excel and Microsoft Windows are registered trademarks of Microsoft Corporation. U.S. Patent No. 4974159.

ITC Zapf Dingbats font, Copyright© International Typeface Corporation 1991. All rights reserved.

Courier is a registered trademark of Smith-Corona Corporation.

Helvetica, Times and Palatino are registered trademarks of Linotype AG and/or its subsidiaries.

StyleWriter is a registered trademark of Carolina Engineering Laboratories.

MacPaint, MacWrite and FileMaker Pro are registered trademarks of Claris Corporation.

Trademarks of other products mentioned in this book are held by the companies producing them.

Limits of Liability and Disclaimer

The author and the publisher of this book have used their best efforts in preparing this book and the programs contained in it. These efforts include the development, research, and testing of the theories and programs to determine their effectiveness. The author and publisher make no warranty of any kind, expressed or implied, with regard to these programs or documentation contained in this book. The author and publisher shall not be liable in any event for incidental or consequential damages in connection with or rising out of the furnishing, performance, or use of these programs.

Contents at a Glance

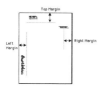

Chapter 8

Expense Reports and Financial Tables 333

Chapter 9

Long Document Structuring and Management 395

Chapter 10

Productivity Solutions for Your Word Processing Environment 485

Index 531

Table of Contents

Chapter 2 **How to Use Your Letterhead Document to Write a Letter   55**

Chapter 3   **How to Format a Two-Page Letter for Preprinted Letterhead Stationery   105**

Chapter 4   **How to Make Lists of Items   117**

Chapter 5   How to Format Envelopes for Printing   179

**Chapter 6   How to Mail Merge (You Need to Send Something
to a Lot of People Right Away...)   199**

Chapter 7   **Forms Generation   261**

INTRODUCTION

Background

The computer industry has revolutionized the way business is conducted in the late 20th century so that those who have a Macintosh computer on their desktop are likely to utilize some form of a word processing application to assemble and communicate their business ideas. It is rare, indeed, that a Mac ever leaves the dealer's premises without a word processing application installed on its hard disk.

The process of capturing "words" on a computer that can then be electronically reproduced on a printed page has gone far beyond the faithful old IBM Selectric typewriter's capabilities. With the growing sophistication of "word" processing applications, one might view this phenomenon to be more aptly described as "document" processing. Sitting in front of choices for hundreds of fonts, graphics, borders, shading, tables, pagination, section formatting, spell checking, grammar checking and countless other functions, shaping your thoughts with a "word" processor has now become an adventure into the more complex world of document formatting.

Corporations and small businesses in the '90s are having to "do more with less." Smaller staffs and less time for more business are probably the reasons why people purchase a computer in the first place. Technology is the answer to greater efficiency in the workplace. With the implementation of powerful technology, the simple generation of a fax, memo or quick business letter is not always left to the administrative assistant, secretary or word processing pool.

More and more, business executives, managers and directors are finding they want to control the initial formulation of their ideas. They create their own documents electronically and then "mail" them across the network to the administrative and/or secretarial assistants for revisions and content formatting.

Intuitive as the Macintosh and many functions of word processing might seem, few people really have the time in their business day to explore the more advanced uses of the very tool which could lead to more efficient—and more effective—document production tasks.

If only there were documents that came "pre-formatted" for quick text entry or even if there were 15 extra minutes in a day where you could learn a good technique that really meets your specific needs. Only then might you be able to recoup hours of valuable document revision time where everyone's schedules would benefit.

Who is This Book For?

This book was written for anyone who needs to create documents for use in the daily business of running a company and who doesn't have time to waste figuring out how to achieve the specific results they need—now. It's for those who struggle with or without the help of manuals to attempt to make a simple letter fit attractively on a single page, who try to position someone's address correctly on an envelope for printing, or who need to format an important business plan, financial table or invoice. It's for anyone who's wanted to be more efficient with the basic word processing knowledge they retained from their initial 3–6 hours of whirlwind hands-on training.

This book is specifically written for anyone who can visualize how they want text to appear on the page but can't figure out—for the life of them—what Microsoft calls "it" so they can look "it" up in the manual's index or by accessing the Help Window. It's also for anyone who has managed to figure out what the names of the processes are, but the manual doesn't seem to show enough examples that illustrate what their unique problem might be and how to achieve the results they want. It's for anyone who wants a clear, step-by-step handbook for documents real people create in real business situations.

In short, this book is for anyone who needs to communicate on paper with the business world and has chosen Microsoft Word 5.0 for the Macintosh as their tool for executing the documents that speak for them.

Assumed Knowledge

In order to create a book that will meet the needs of the widest audience of users for the least amount of paper, I have had to assume a basic level of knowledge on the behalf of the reader. By outlining here those concepts and processes you will need to know before you begin using this book, I hope to reduce the frustration level on your part for what I do not explain.

Subjects that will not be addressed in this book are:

Basic Macintosh skills such as cut, copy, paste, click, press, and drag; knowing which version of Macintosh system software you are operating; differences between Macintosh system software for System 6.0.x and System 7.0; what the difference is between MultiFinder and the Finder; how to navigate file folders and locate documents within the Finder as well as the Open dialog boxes within Microsoft Word; storing, copying, deleting and backing up of files; initialization of floppy disks and any hardware utility functions; how to install and launch Microsoft Word and other applications (such as Microsoft Excel and FileMaker Pro); how to use Microsoft Excel or FileMaker Pro (to create tables, graphs or databases); installation and management of fonts; installation and selection of printers and printer drivers; and how to use basic graphics tools for programs such as MacPaint or MacDraw that apply to the new Edit Picture function in Microsoft Word.

In essence, to use this book you should have received training in Macintosh basics as well as Microsoft Word basics. This book is **not** a substitute for an introductory hands-on Microsoft Word class or the Getting Started manual that ships with Microsoft Word.

A number of word processing functions such as Spell Checking and dictionaries, Word count, indexing, Find and Replace, Publish and Subscribe, Voice Annotations, graphics management, Hyphenation, file conversion, equations, Microsoft Mail, the Thesaurus and Grammar Checker, Footnotes and every keyboard shortcut possible within Microsoft Word will not be addressed within the contents of this book.

Rather than serve as a reference for the multitudinous functions available within Microsoft Word, this book is a resource for the kinds of business documents you want to execute with your Macintosh, and the specific steps you take and techniques you would use in Microsoft Word 5.0 to produce them.

Point of View

Much of the information we receive every day comes through our eyes—television, magazines, billboards, advertising. We live in a visual world. "A picture is worth a thousand words." As an active participant in this visual world, my favorite reading material has always been comic books. I interpreted "black dots on the page" to produce music on my violin in an orchestra. I was drawn to the study of Egyptian hieroglyphs—hundreds of sophisticated graphics that represent sounds of an unspoken language. I immersed myself in the study of sign language to see how "shaped" actions communicated ideas, thoughts and feelings. I interpret astrological symbols to gain insight into the forces that shape my world.

Though the computer industry speaks of "the graphical user interface" (or GUI), no one seems to write "graphical user" books (or GUBs). When reading manuals, you are often left to "picture" what it is that the author is talking about. I've read more software manuals in the last seven years than I have comic books. A voice inside me has always cried, "Show me a visual reference of what you mean so I can understand what you are telling me!" Somehow, I feel that I am not alone. For this reason, I set out to write *Super Desktop Documents* as the first "comic book" approach to word processing.

Albert Fuller, a dear colleague, musician, and friend, always comments on the art of musical performance: "They see you before they hear you." This book has been written so that you, the reader, can "see" what is about to be discussed before you "hear" the written word. Circles, arrows, and boxed text within the picture itself are there as a form of "balloon" dialog to help you rapidly understand and know what will be discussed in more detail below. The numbered figures are referenced within the text at the point where a second, more-informed look back to the illustrated figure will add another layer of understanding.

The 769 figures in this book are also there so you can quickly find your way to the part of the book that addresses your most immediate needs or document formatting problems. Hopefully, the figures will guide you to solutions for successfully producing "something that looks like this..." The first half of the book was written as more of a "step-by-step" guide for the execution of basic document production tasks.

At the beginning of each chapter there is a short overview of the kinds of word/document processing tasks you'll be learning. There are also specific examples of documents and situations you might encounter which are addressed in greater detail within each section. In all, there are over 100 different document examples contained within this book.

If you understand and practice the techniques in the first half of the book, you'll have a firm foundation for attempting the more complex kinds of documents discussed in the second half of the book. Once a concept has been introduced, I do not explain the reasons behind using the formatting technique every time it appears throughout the book. For instance, you won't get an explanation of why you should use the Paragraph dialog box to apply space before a paragraph every time you see an instruction such as, "Choose Paragraph from the Format menu and enter 18 pt in the Before edit bar."

The first part of the book makes greater use of "Steps"—a single process is explained in fuller detail. The second half of the book may have many tasks described within a single example. Menu items, functions and format settings are displayed in bold type so that your eye can quickly grasp the actions your hands need to execute. Standard Microsoft Word keyboard commands are presented in context where they help to expedite the given process more efficiently.

Throughout the book, I've tried to imagine your questions—your "but what if I want to do this..." responses—by providing italicized "Notes" as "asides" along the way. My years of training users of all kinds and levels of experi-ence—children, the hearing and visually impaired, secretaries, engineers, corporate executives, writers, musicians, artists, businessmen, business-women, and even computer "nerds"—have given me the unique advantage of observing common stumbling blocks everyone has with word processing concepts and document production needs.

I hope this book will serve to empower your usage of Microsoft Word so that you will have the confidence to explore and discover your own solu-tions for added efficiency in your everyday document production environment.

How to do something that looks like this...

CHAPTER 1

How to Create Your Own Letterhead

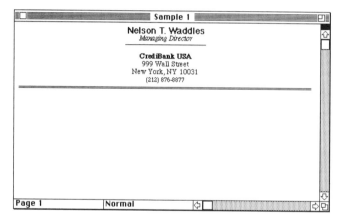

Figure 1.1

Overview

You might have started a new business, changed your phone number, or moved to a new address and are hesitant to make that expensive investment in printed letterhead stationery just yet. Or, perhaps you might want to print out a letter on inexpensive laser copier paper to send as a fax and save your quality stationery for direct mail.

Working with Microsoft Word, you can choose from the variety of fonts and type styles on your Macintosh to give your correspondence a professional look. In what follows, you'll learn how to use Word's various formatting capabilities for fonts, borders, spacing, and margins to achieve the appearance you desire. You'll also learn how to save time when creating more letters by setting an automatic date, formatting your document so it can track multiple pages, and saving it in a "stationery" format for repeated use.

Once you've created your letterhead, you'll move on to explore ways you can add further customization to your letter formatting. You'll also learn timesaving tips for adjusting your document to fit on a single page. These will be covered in Chapter 2: "How to Use Your Letterhead Document to Write a Letter." When you're familiar with these techniques, you can then concentrate on the content of your letter and know you can easily make formatting adjustments where necessary.

Setting Up Your Working Environment

Y ou'll find that you can use the Ribbon and Ruler to apply many kinds of text and paragraph formatting with a simple click of the mouse. You'll also reduce the amount of mouse dragging you would do from the Font, Format, and other menus when applying and changing text formatting. More important, the Ribbon and Ruler give you an immediate "reading" on what formats have been applied to the text you're currently working with.

Before you get started, make sure you've got Word set up to work with these timesaving tool bars. If you don't have a blank Untitled document on the screen in front of you, go to the **File** menu and choose **New**.

STEP ONE

Move your pointer into the **View** menu and hold the mouse button down. If Ribbon and Ruler have check marks next to them, you're ready to move on. If not, select the **Ribbon** and the **Ruler** from the **View** menu. Your objective is to have the Ribbon and Ruler displayed just under the name "Untitled" in the document window as shown in Figure 1.2.

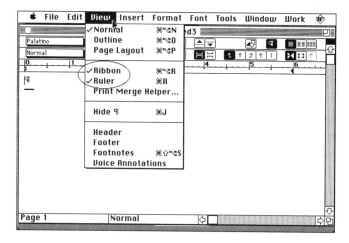

Figure 1.2

NOTE: *If ever you want to turn the Ruler or Ribbon off, simply choose the item from the View menu again. The check mark will disappear, as will the Ruler or Ribbon in your document window.*

STEP TWO

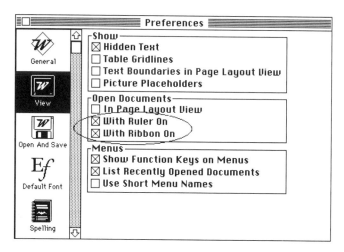

Figure 1.3

> **NOTE:** *Preferences can be set so that your word processing environment is consistent every time you launch Word.*

You'll probably want to view the Ribbon and Ruler for every document you work with. To avoid having to select the Ribbon and Ruler from the View menu for each document you open, you're going to adjust your working environment Preferences so that Word sets these document views automatically.

Go to the **Tools** menu and choose **Preferences**. Click on the **View** icon. If the box next to **With Ruler On** or **With Ribbon On** is blank, then click once inside the box so there is an X (Figure 1.3). This X indicates the option is selected or "turned on."

> **NOTE:** *When you are more proficient with Word, viewing the Ribbon and Ruler when opening documents might not be your personal preference. To change this, choose Preferences from the Tools menu and click the X in the box next to With Ruler On or With Ribbon On to turn the option off. The box would then be left blank.*

STEP THREE

Click in the Preferences close box (the upper left corner) to return to your document. From now on, every time you open a document or create a new one, the Ruler and Ribbon will be displayed.

Formatting Your Name and Address

You probably have a fair idea of how you want your letterhead to look. You might also want to experiment with a variety of options and decide as you go along. You're going to explore how the Ribbon and Ruler, plus a few other formatting choices, can help you produce the results you're after.

The initial example will familiarize you with the ease of executing formats with the Ribbon and Ruler. Once you're familiar with these tools, you will know how to create the other letterhead formats suggested at the end of this chapter.

Entering Text

STEP ONE

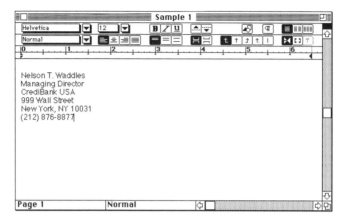

Figure 1.4

Although you'll be referring to example text in the figure displays as you're working through these steps, you should enter your own letterhead information now. Type your name and then press the **Return** key to begin each new line for your title, company, and address. For the moment, don't worry if the font you are working with doesn't match what you see in the example (Figure 1.4).

Displaying Spaces in Your Document

STEP TWO

You're going to be formatting each line of text separately. Though it doesn't look like it, each one of these lines is a different paragraph. How Microsoft Word defines a paragraph is more easily explained if you execute the following step.

Place your pointer in the **Ribbon** and click on the ⁊ icon (Figure 1.5).

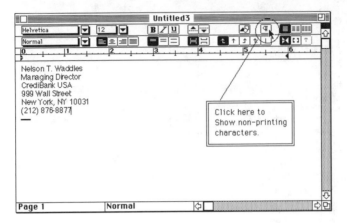

Figure 1.5

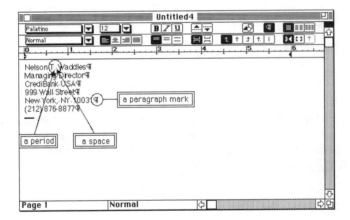

Figure 1.6

This action displays nonprinting characters in your document window. These nonprinting characters give you an "inside look" at your document to see how many spaces you have between words, when you've pressed the Tab and Return keys, and other kinds of text formats. In order to quickly assess spacing and cursor placement, you'll want to work with the Show ¶ icon turned on.

Between each word is a space. Note the difference between a space and a period (Figure 1.6). A nonprinting space character is displayed slightly higher than a period and sits above the baseline of your text.

After each line is a paragraph mark (¶). A paragraph occurs whenever you press the Return key. It can be a single line of text, multiple lines, or even a blank line. Microsoft Word defines a paragraph as any amount of text or graphics followed by the nonprinting paragraph mark.

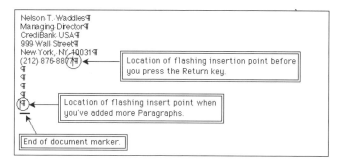

Figure 1.7

Add a few blank paragraphs to the end of your address by pressing the **Return** key several times in a row (Figure 1.7). If you didn't have Show ¶ turned on, you'd never know there were blank paragraphs in your document. Often stray paragraph marks can cause pagination, spacing, and other problems. With Show ¶ you can easily identify the source of the problem and quickly resolve it.

Whenever you want to see how your document text will look when it prints out, simply click the [¶] icon to turn off the nonprinting characters.

> **NOTE:** *There are advantages and disadvantages to adding space to your document by pressing the Return key. When to use the Return key for appropriate document spacing is discussed in Chapter 2.*

Selecting Text

STEP THREE

You're going to center the text you've just entered. However, before you can center anything, you have to select what it is that you want centered. The Macintosh principle of "select and do" is critical to all the text and paragraph formatting you'll be executing.

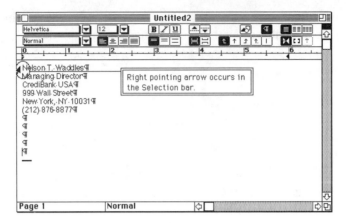

Figure 1.8

You may be surprised to know that in Microsoft Word there are over 20 different techniques you can use just for selecting text! To save time and avoid confusion, you're going to use the most efficient method for the kind of text selection you want to expedite in the steps that follow.

Move the mouse to the very beginning of the first line of text. Now watch carefully. Your mouse pointer should become a right-pointing arrow when it passes over the narrow blank strip between the edge of the document window and the beginning of your text (see Figure 1.8). This area is called the Selection Bar.

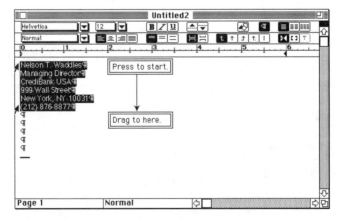

Figure 1.9

The Selection Bar is unique to Microsoft Word and is an extremely handy tool for selecting large amounts of text. With the pointer located in the Selection Bar, press the mouse button down. You'll notice the entire line becomes selected. Keep the mouse button pressed and drag down to the bottom of your name and address to select it (Figure 1.9).

Centering Text

STEP FOUR

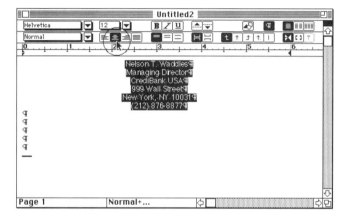

Figure 1.10

Now that your text is selected, move your mouse pointer into the Ruler and click on the Centering icon as shown in Figure 1.10. The text should now be centered.

Applying Font, Size, and Bold Format

STEP FIVE

Move the mouse pointer next to the first line of text. Notice that the "real estate" area of the Selection Bar has been extended to include all the blank space to the immediate left of the text (Figure 1.11). Whenever you move text away from the 0 point of your ruler (by centering or changing indents), the area is adjusted for where your pointer becomes a right-pointing arrow. Click once with the right-pointing arrow to select the entire line.

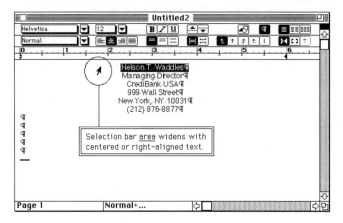

Figure 1.11

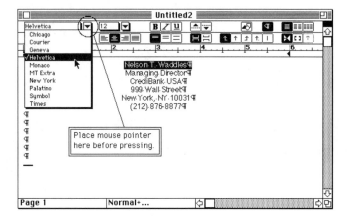

Figure 1.12

You're going to use the Ribbon to change this text to Helvetica 14 point Bold. Place the mouse pointer on the selection arrow (Figure 1.12) next to the font name. Pressing the mouse causes a list of fonts to drop down. Simply press and drag to apply the Helvetica font.

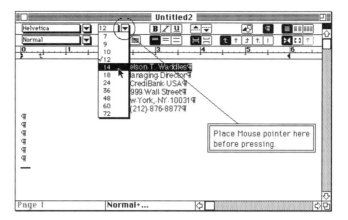

Figure 1.13

Press and drag on the selection arrow for font size (Figure 1.13) to apply 14 point.

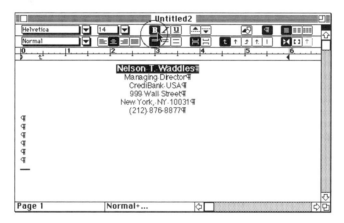

Figure 1.14

Next, click on the **Bold** icon as shown in Figure 1.14.

Alternate Formatting Techniques with the Ribbon

STEP SIX

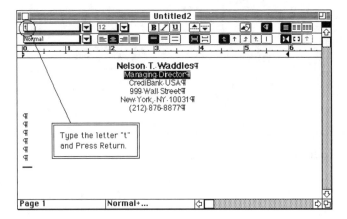

Figure 1.15

You're going to apply **Times 11 point Italic** to the second line of text—your title—and explore some alternate ways to do formatting with the Ribbon. Select the title line by clicking next to it with the right-pointing arrow in the Selection Bar area.

In addition to selecting a font from a drop down list in the Ribbon, you can also type the font name from your keyboard. To do this, click once in the font name box in the Ribbon. The box will become highlighted.

You only need to type the first few characters of the font name or the just first character if there is no other font that begins with that same letter. So, type a **t** for Times (Figure 1.15), and then press the **Return** key. Your text will have Times applied to it, and the Times font name should also appear in the Ribbon.

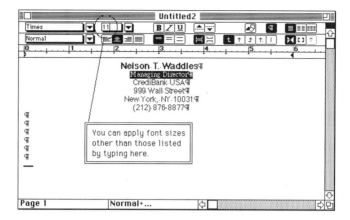

Figure 1.16

Next, you're going to make this text 11 point. Move your pointer into the Ribbon and look at the drop down list of font sizes. You'll see that 11 point is not listed there as a choice. Similar to what you did to apply a font name in the previous step, click inside the Ribbon's font size box to highlight its contents.

Type the number **11** to replace the highlighted text and then press the **Return** key (Figure 1.16).

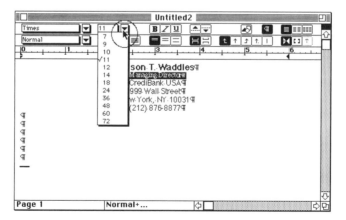

Figure 1.17

Your text is formatted as 11 point and the number 11 is now displayed in the drop down list (Figure 1.17).

NOTE: *Font sizes that are not the typical installed screen font sizes (i.e., 11, 15, 23, 32, etc.) will appear in the drop down Ribbon list only under certain circumstances: either the text formatted with the font size is selected or the flashing insertion point is located within a text block formatted with the abnormal font size.*

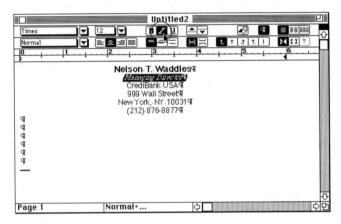

Figure 1.18

Finally, click on the **Italic** icon in the Ribbon as shown in Figure 1.18.

Applying Decorative Borders

STEP SEVEN

The sample letterhead at the beginning of this chapter has a thin decorative line dividing the name and title from the rest of the address. Microsoft Word calls these lines Borders. In order to create a border, you will use the Border dialog box located in the Format menu.

Keeping the second line of text selected, go to the **Format** menu and choose **Border**.

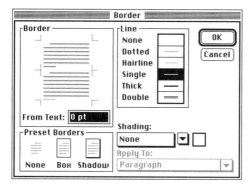

Figure 1.19

The **Border** dialog box has a number of formatting options. On the upper left is a diagram of how the border will look when it is placed around, beside, or under your paragraph text. It is important for you to understand that borders are applied to entire paragraphs of text, not to individual lines of text within a paragraph.

From a designer's viewpoint, you should place a bit of space between your text and the border so that the text can "breathe." To achieve this, you'll make an entry in the **From Text** edit bar.

Press the **Tab** key on your keyboard. This highlights the contents of the From Text edit bar so you can replace them (Figure 1.19). Type the number **3**. You are applying 3 points (pt) of space—don't worry about typing the **pt**. Microsoft Word formats any numerical entry in this box as points.

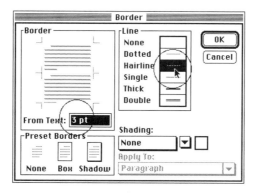

Figure 1.20

Next, choose **Hairline** from the list of Line types by clicking in the box next to it (Figure 1.20). When you click there, notice that the From Text edit bar remains highlighted and "pt" is added after the number 3.

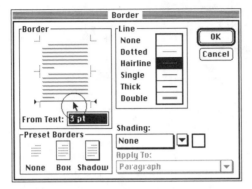

Figure 1.21

Finally, click once at the bottom of the border diagram to apply the line (Figure 1.21). A line will appear with triangular selection markers on either side of it. Click the **OK** button and the title text in your document will now display a border beneath it.

Resizing Border Length for Centered Text

STEP EIGHT

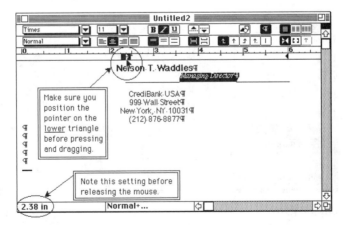

Figure 1.22

Borders extend to the edges of your margins. However, you might want to shorten the length of the border so that it's about the same size as the text for your name. To do this, you're going to work with the indent icons in the Ruler.

Position your pointer in the Ruler on top of the **lower** part of the left indent triangle, as shown in Figure 1.22. This grabs the entire left indent marker. Press and drag the left indent marker so that it aligns to a point inside the first two letters of your name. If you have a longer title than the example text, you might want to place the left indent marker further to the left of your name.

As you're moving the left indent, notice the number of inches displayed in the lower left status bar of the window. Though many people rely on the Ruler settings, the number displayed in the status bar is a more exact and efficient way to obtain correct settings—especially for centered text. It's important that you remember or jot this number down as soon as you release the mouse button. You'll use the same number to set the right indent marker.

When you have released the mouse button, you will see your text jump. The border has adjusted itself to start at the position of the left indent marker; however, your text is formatted as centered and will now appear misaligned (Figure 1.22).

Centering occurs between the left and right indent marker positions. Therefore, the center point for your text has now been altered to somewhere around the 4-inch mark. Next, you're going to adjust the right indent marker and bring that center point back in line with the rest of your text.

Figure 1.23

Position the mouse pointer in the Ruler over the right indent marker. The right indent is one solid marker, so you don't have to be as cautious as you were with the left indent. Press and drag the marker over to the left. Look carefully in the lower left status area of the document window—it is circled in Figure 1.23—and you will see the number of inches the right indent marker is moved in from the right margin. When you see the status bar display the same number as for the left indent, release the mouse button. What you've just executed is an **equal** indent on the left and right, so the text is centered properly to what comes before and after it.

> **NOTE:** *Whenever you move the left or right indent marker, the number of inches you are moving away from the margin is always displayed in the lower left status bar area.*

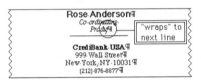

Figure 1.24

You might want to use the letterhead stationery you create for yourself as a model for someone else's letterhead. Or, better yet, you might need to revise your own letterhead when your title is changed because of a promotion or career move. Depending on the length of the title, you should know how to make the proper readjustments for the border length.

In Figure 1.24, the title text was selected and a new title was entered to replace it. Because the indent settings were shorter than the new title length, text wrapped to the next line.

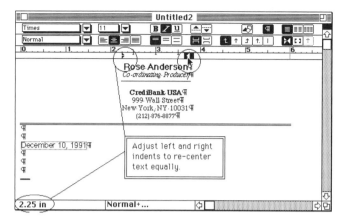

Figure 1.25

To make the adjustment, you would need to move the left and right indent markers. Just remember that in order to keep your text centered, you will need to place the left and right indent markers an equal distance from the left and right margins. There is no set rule for determining what these settings will be—you'll have to use the trial-and-error method to see how the text behaves and what is most pleasing to you. However, use the numbers displayed in the lower left status area to help you set the indents equally.

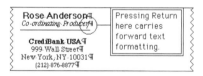

Figure 1.26

Instead of having one long title line, you might also decide to break the title up into two lines of text. Either press the **Return** key at the end of the first half of your title (if you have entered it in total) or at the end of the paragraph (if you have just entered part of it) as shown in Figure 1.26. All your text formatting will be carried forward to the next line.

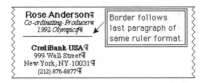

Figure 1.27

You might be perplexed that the border at the bottom of the title paragraph moves forward to the next line (Figure 1.27). Borders set for the bottom of a paragraph will occur after the last paragraph of the same format.

Adding Space Above Formatted Text

STEP NINE

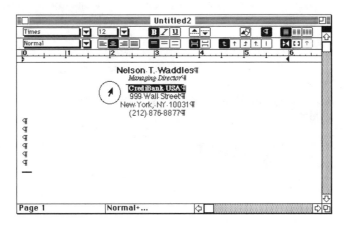

Figure 1.28

Next, you'll apply formatting to the paragraph with your company name. Using the Selection Bar and the right-pointing arrow, click once to select the company. Use the format tools in the Ribbon to apply `Times 12 point Bold` (Figure 1.28).

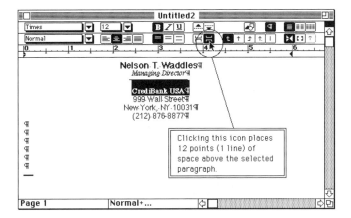

Figure 1.29

You might want to put some distance between your company's name and your own name and title. To do this, you would want to apply space above the company paragraph. With the company text still selected, click on the **Open Space between paragraphs** icon in the Ruler, as shown in Figure 1.29. The **Open Space** icon is the easiest and fastest way to place 12 points (1 line) of space above a paragraph.

The button on the left is the **Closed Space between paragraphs** icon. To remove the spacing above a paragraph, you would click the **Closed Space** icon. It is usually the icon that is selected when you first enter text in a document.

> **NOTE:** *Rather than pressing the Return key twice between paragraphs of body text, the Open Space between paragraphs icon is a handy tool that automatically spaces the text for you.*

More Format Variations

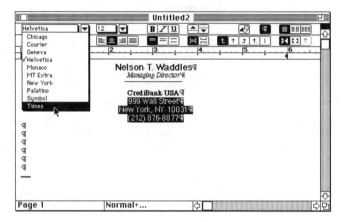

Figure 1.30

You're going to apply the Times font to the remaining three lines of text. Using the right-pointing arrow in the Selection Bar, press and drag to select all three lines; then apply the **Times font 12 point** from the **Ribbon** (Figure 1.30).

Often a phone number can be printed at a smaller font size, making the address information stand out more clearly. To format the phone number, first select the phone number by clicking next to it with the pointer in the Selection Bar. Apply **10 point** format from the **Ribbon**.

STEP ELEVEN

As a final step you might want to place another decorative border at the bottom of your letterhead information. This time the border will fall beneath the phone number, so keep the paragraph with the phone number selected. Go to the **Format** menu and choose **Border**. Press the **Tab** key on your keyboard once to highlight the **From Text** edit bar. Type the number **6**. This time you'll be adding 6 points of space between the phone number and the border (Figure 1.31).

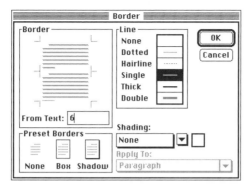

Figure 1.31

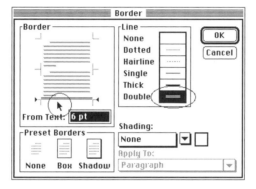

Figure 1.32

Next, click beside the word **Double** to select the **Double Line** format. Click at the bottom of the border diagram to apply the border (Figure 1.32); then click on the **OK** button.

You've just executed a handful of formatting techniques using the **Ruler**, **Ribbon**, and **Border** dialog boxes. Though this suggested letterhead format may not be what you had in mind, you now have a basic understanding of how these tools can quickly help you format text.

You might want to explore other fonts, formats, and border options before continuing. However, you should save your work to avoid the loss of what you've accomplished so far. Once your document is saved, you might want to look at other letterhead format examples at the end of this chapter.

Saving a Stationery Document

Microsoft Word 5.0 has a special file format called Stationery. What exactly is a Stationery document? It's a type of document that serves as a template for the creation of other documents. When you save a document in a stationery format, it protects the original, master document. Each time you open a stationery document, you are actually opening a copy of the stationery to work with. It's like having a fresh sheet of preformatted paper (letterhead stationery!) each time you want to write a letter.

STEP ONE

To save your document in the stationery format, go to the **File** menu and choose **Save**.

STEP TWO

You may want to create a new folder for your stationery document or place it in a correspondence folder you have already created on your hard disk. If you are working with System 7.0, you can create a new correspondence folder by clicking on the **New Folder** button. If you are working in System 6.0.x, navigate to the folder on your hard disk in which you want to save your stationery documents.

STEP THREE

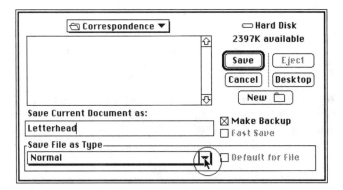

Figure 1.33

Name the document Letterhead. However, before you click on the **Save** button, there is one more step necessary. Position the mouse over the downward arrow, as shown in Figure 1.33, and press.

STEP FOUR

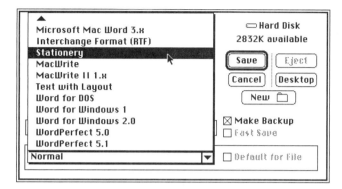

Figure 1.34

A list of file format types will pop up. Select the **Stationery** format (Figure 1.34) and release the mouse. Now your document is saved as a Stationery file type, and you can click on the **Save** button. Don't be alarmed, however, that when you return to your document window the title bar still says "Untitled." Remember, you never work with the original document when you are working with stationery documents.

You may be saying, "But what if I want to make changes to my original Letterhead stationery document?" You can and you will. In fact, you're going to make some more changes and save those changes in the following section.

Setting Margins

Typically, when you work with letterhead stationery, the letterhead information is fairly close to the top edge of the printed page. You're going to view your document from another perspective and see where the letterhead is positioned relative to the edge of the paper it will print on. Once in this view, you can easily make adjustments for the top margin setting.

Working in Print Preview

STEP ONE

Go to the **File** menu and choose **Print Preview**.

STEP TWO

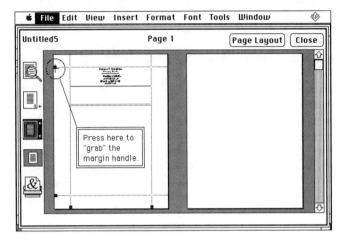

Figure 1.35

Print Preview is a bird's-eye view of your entire document as it will print on your printer. You're going to set the top margin for your document here.

There are four dotted lines surrounding the inner part of the text. Each line has a square box on one end called a "handle." These represent the margin placements for your entire document. You're going to work with one of the margin handles to reset the top margin.

Position the pointer over the top left handle. As you move over the handle, the pointer arrow will change to a cross hair (Figure 1.35).

Press the mouse button and drag upwards to change the margin. As you move the margin handle, its position relative to the top edge of the printed page is displayed in the Print Preview window (Figure 1.36). Release the mouse button when "0.50 in" is displayed. In a few moments, the screen display will refresh itself with the newly positioned text in place.

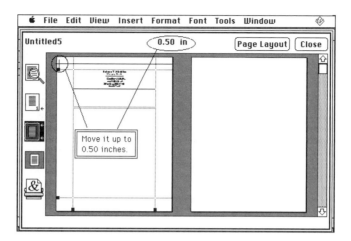

Figure 1.36

Magnifying Text in Print Preview

STEP THREE

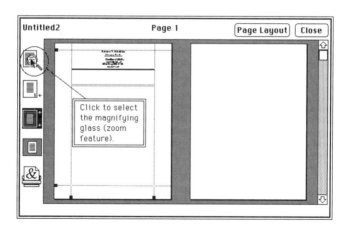

Figure 1.37

Though this repositioned top margin may seem to be satisfactory, you'd probably like to have a closer look to see if it's what you wanted. While in Print Preview, you can zoom in on your document. Click once on the magnifying glass icon to select the magnifying tool (Figure 1.37).

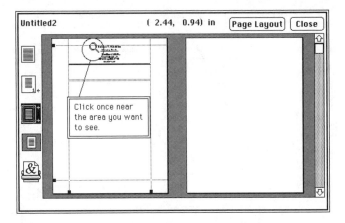

Figure 1.38

Position the magnifying tool over the area you want to look at (the top of your document) and click once (Figure 1.38). Your document will be zoomed to 100 percent. However, you can't alter or edit any of the document contents; it's a "look only" mode.

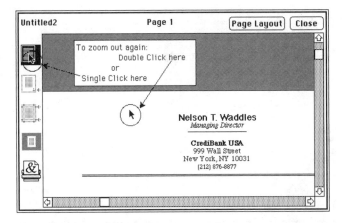

Figure 1.39

To zoom back out, you can use either of two methods: 1) Click once on the highlighted icon in the upper left; or 2) double-click with the mouse pointer anywhere within the document (Figure 1.39).

> **NOTE:** *You can also zoom in on any part of a document in Print Preview simply by pointing to the area you want to view and double-clicking.*

If you are satisfied with your margin settings, click on the **Close** button in the upper right corner of the Print Preview window to return to your document.

Alternate Ways to Set Margins

You can also adjust your document margins without visiting Print Preview by choosing **Document** from the **Format** menu.

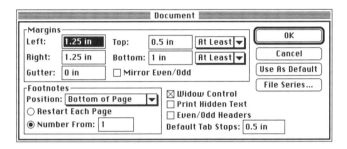

Figure 1.40

As you will see, the **Document** dialog box reflects any margin changes you may have made while in Print Preview. The Top margin (0.5 in) reflects the alteration you might have made earlier.

The **Document** dialog box (Figure 1.40) has edit bars for the **Left**, **Right**, **Top**, and **Bottom** margins. You can press the **Tab** key on your keyboard to high-light and advance to the next edit bar. By simply typing, you can replace the edit bar contents with the measurement you want. Margins are in inches so that you need only type the number without the "in" indication (e.g., 1.5), and Microsoft Word will still register the margin setting correctly. Click on the **OK** button to return to your document.

Automating the Date of Your Correspondence

Microsoft Word has a function that will automatically insert the current date from your Macintosh control panel into your document. Not only does this save time, it takes the guess work out of determining what today's date actually is.

> **NOTE:** *The Insert Date function inserts the date for when you actually print out your letter. The use of the automatic date function may cause problems if you want to review the letter at some point in the future and refer to the date the letter was actually executed. Whenever a document containing the Insert Date entry is opened, the date will be updated to the current date set by the control panel of your computer. You may decide not to use the automatic date in your correspondence for this reason.*

STEP ONE

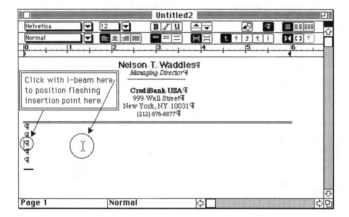

Figure 1.41

Before you insert the date, you'll need to place the flashing insertion point at the position where the date will appear in your letter. The date should be placed a few paragraphs under your letterhead text. Move the pointer— which is now the shape of an I-beam—into the white space near the third blank paragraph mark. Click once (Figure 1.41).

STEP TWO

Go to the **Insert** menu and choose **Date**.

STEP THREE

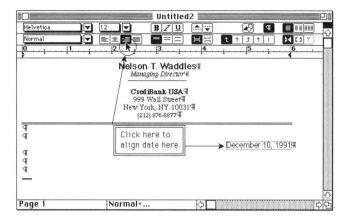

Figure 1.42

Once you've got the date information in your document, you may prefer a certain placement of the date on the page. Perhaps you want it align to the right margin. Here is where a simple click on the Ruler paragraph alignment icons will help you decide which looks best.

Click on the right-aligned icon (Figure 1.42) to align the date to the right.

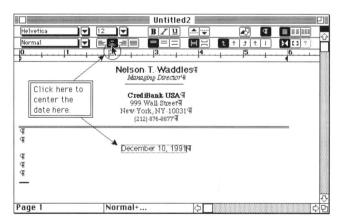

Figure 1.43

Click on the center-aligned icon for a centered date (Figure 1.43).

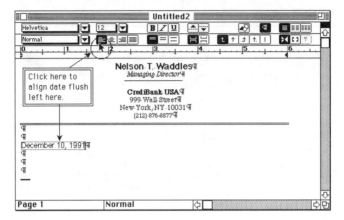

Figure 1.44

If you want to return to the original left-aligned placement, click on the left-aligned icon (Figure 1.44).

Each one of these clicks on the ruler alignment icons quickly adjusts the position of the date for you. However, remember that in order to position the date, you must have the blinking insertion point located somewhere within the paragraph or have the paragraph line selected.

> **NOTE:** *You may want to align the date with a closure (for instance, Yours truly) and a signature line that is neither centered nor right-aligned. To do this requires the placement of a tab marker and is covered in the next chapter, "How to Use Your Letterhead Document to Write a Letter" (the section, "Moving the Position of the Date and Closure").*

Saving Changes to the Stationery Document

Before you put the finishing touches to your stationery, you need to save the changes you've just made. Remember, you are working with an Untitled stationery document; however, the procedures for updating the master document are fairly straightforward.

STEP ONE

Go to the **File** menu and choose **Save**.

STEP TWO

You should be located in the same folder as when you first named and saved your Letterhead document. In fact, you should see the Letterhead document grayed out in the folder window.

Type the name "**Letterhead**." Be attentive that you type the word "Letterhead" accurately, as you are going to replace the existing Letterhead document.

Select **Stationery** from the **Save File as Type** list.

STEP THREE

Click on the **Save** button.

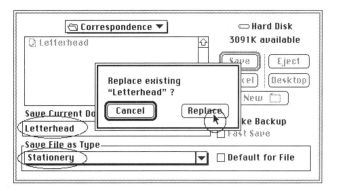

Figure 1.45

A dialog box will ask you if you want to replace the existing Letterhead document (Figure 1.45). Click on the **Replace** button. Once you've completed this step, you'll return once again to an Untitled document. Remember, the changes you just saved have been made to your master Letterhead document, which is retained on your hard disk.

Recovering from Accidents

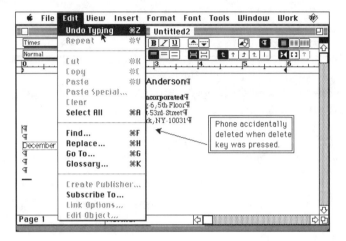

Figure 1.46

Whenever you have text highlighted, you are working in a "keyboard-sensitive" state. If, by accident, you press the delete key or any other key while a paragraph of text is still highlighted, the entire paragraph will disappear or the text will be replaced by the stray character you might have touched.

You can restore the highlighted text to your document if you execute the following step IMMEDIATELY. This must be your very next step or you will lose what you just deleted. Go to the **Edit** menu and choose **Undo Typing** (Figure 1.46).

> **NOTE:** *The Undo function is something you will want to remember for the future, so make a note of it!*

Formatting Your Letterhead for Multi-Page Letters

The Letterhead stationery you've created is effective for brief, one-page letters. But what if you want to produce a more substantial letter that flows on to two or more pages? There are some formatting issues that need to be clarified for the successful execution of longer letters.

In the steps you followed for setting up your letterhead, you might have set the top margin for the Letterhead document to 0.5 inch. This is an appropriate setting for the positioning of your letterhead information. However, when text of your letter flows over to the second page, text appearing 0.5 inch from the top of the second page hugs the edge rather closely. The overall document doesn't "breathe" properly and will look badly formatted. Of course, if this is of no concern to you, you can ignore this entire section and work with your letterhead document as it is currently formatted.

The word-processing concept you are going to address in this section involves the flow of text from one page to another. Microsoft Word has an automatic pagination feature that takes the actual guess work out of planning page breaks. However, there are some formatting consequences with pagination that you will need to accommodate for your overall letterhead page setup scheme.

> **NOTE:** *In the General Preferences settings, you can set an option so that repagination is performed automatically in the background as you work with your documents.*

Typically, regular body text should start 1 inch from the top edge of the paper. However, in an area known as a "header" (which occurs at the top of every page following the first page), you might want to place information containing the date, page number, and perhaps the name of the addressee.

What follows are the steps you would take to create that extra space at the top of the page, starting with the second page. You'll also learn how to place automatic page numbers and other information in the top of your document (the header) or at the bottom of your document in an area called the "footer."

Creating a Different First Page

STEP ONE

In order to work with a header that contains the spacing and information mentioned above, the header should be separate from anything that appears on the first page. Therefore, you need to format your document to ensure the first page remains different. You'll do this with a simple click of a button.

Go to the **Format** menu and choose **Section**.

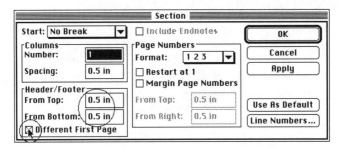

Figure 1.47

The Section dialog box contains various settings for columns and page and line numbering which do not apply to your formatting concerns at this time. What you want to set is the header and footer information for pages that follow the first page. Simply click in the box next to **Different First Page** (Figure 1.47) so that there is an X in the box. Also, note that the actual information contained in a header or footer will be positioned 0.5 inch from the edge of the page.

STEP TWO

Creating a Header

In order to work with your header, you select **Header** from the **View** menu. Make sure that you are working in **Normal** view (i.e., there is a check mark next to the word **Normal** in the **View** menu). If you are not, simply go to the **View** menu and choose **Normal**.

The Ribbon and Ruler views are not automatically presented when you work in a header. Go to the **View** menu and choose **Ruler**. You might also want to view the Ribbon. Using the Ruler and/or Ribbon tools will help to make the formatting of your header easier to accomplish.

To give yourself more working space, you might also want to click in the **Zoom** box on the upper right to expand the header area.

STEP THREE

Inserting Header Elements

Typical header elements for a letter contain the addressee's name, the date the letter was written, and the page number. Header information helps in the management of a document once it is printed should the letter pages become separated or misplaced.

In the steps that follow, there are examples of several ways you might choose to arrange this information.

Three Lines of Data

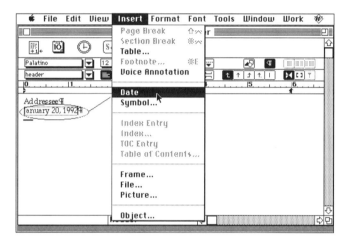

Figure 1.48

Type the word "**Addressee**" which will serve as placeholder text for when you actually execute the letter. Press the **Return** key for a new line and then go to the **Insert** menu and choose **Date** (Figure 1.48). By choosing **Insert Date**, your letter will automatically have the same date that appears on the first and each subsequent page. Press the **Return** key for a new line.

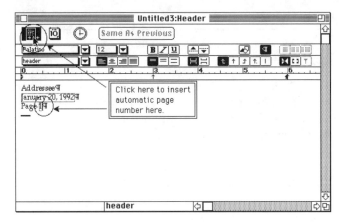

Figure 1.49

Type the word **Page** followed by a **space**. Next, you will insert an automatic page number. Like the automatic date feature, the automatic page number keeps track of the correct page numbers for your document and adjusts itself for each page you print out. To insert an automatic page number, click on the page number icon in the header ruler area (Figure 1.49).

The automatic page number will begin numbering your pages from the second page, even though the header window displays the number 1. You can verify the accuracy of your page numbering, once you have executed a two-page letter and examine the document in either the **Page Layout** or **Print Preview** views.

The other icons in the header ruler area are for the date and time your document is printed, and are useful for tracking printed versions of long reports that go through multiple revisions.

Last, press the **Return** key for a new line (Figure 1.50). This line will be left blank to provide breathing space between the header text and the main text of your letter. Click in the **Close box** on the upper left to close the Header window and return to your document.

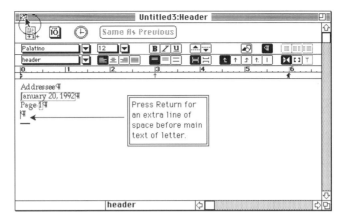

Figure 1.50

A Single Line Across the Top of the Page

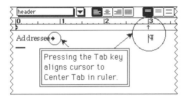

Figure 1.51

You might prefer to have your header information on a single line, spaced across the top of your document. In order to format this information, you're going to take advantage of some automatic formats already programmed into your header.

Type the word **Addressee** which will serve as placeholder text for when you actually execute the letter. Press the **Tab** key on your keyboard. This will position the flashing insertion point directly beneath a centered tab marker, preset by Microsoft Word, which appears on the ruler. This kind of tab will center the text at the 3-inch mark (Figure 1.51).

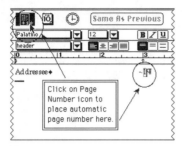

Figure 1.52

Type a **dash**, followed by a **space**; then click on the automatic page number-ing icon in the ruler (Figure 1.52). The automatic page number will begin numbering your pages from the second page, even though the header window displays the number 1. You can verify the accuracy of your page numbering, once you examine the document in either the Page Layout or Print Preview views.

When the automatic page number is inserted, type another **space** followed by a **dash**. You should notice that the text centers itself to the 3-inch mark as you type.

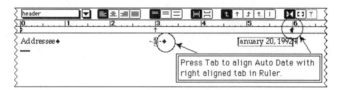

Figure 1.53

To enter the last piece of information, press the **Tab** key on your keyboard once more. There is another type of preset tab marker placed in the ruler that is somewhat difficult to see as it lies directly beneath the right indent marker. This tab mark will align text to the right indent of your document. Go to the **Insert** menu and choose **Date**. When the date is inserted, it will be aligned on the right beneath the right indent marker (Figure 1.53).

Since this variation spreads all the header information out on one line across the top of your document, some extra formatting has to be applied to allow for space beneath the header. You might recall that when you ex-ecuted Step 1 (you chose Format Section to create a different first page) you were asked to take note of the header setting at 0.5 inch from the top of the page.

If you want to have the main text of your letter begin at 1 inch from the top of your document, you have to adjust the space that follows your header information. Since the header begins at 0.5 inch, you need the header to occupy 0.5 inch of space for a total of 1 inch.

Here's how you accomplish that in one easy step. Go to the **Format** menu and choose **Paragraph**.

Figure 1.54

Press the **Tab** key on your keyboard once to highlight the contents of the second edit bar next to the word **After**. You are going to place extra space after this paragraph to bring the total space from the top of the page to 1 inch. Type the number **24** (for 24 points) and click **OK** (Figure 1.54). When you've finished, click in the header **Close box** in the upper left corner.

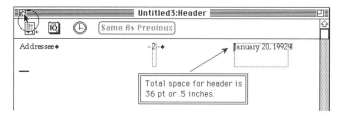

Figure 1.55

Here's an explanation for why you needed to execute the preceding step. One inch of space equals 72 points. The main text (the body of the letter) should begin at 1 inch from the top of the document. The top of the header begins at 0.5 inch from the edge of the page. You need to account for another 0.5 inch, or 36 points, of space before the main text of the letter begins.

A single line of text typically occupies 12 points of space. By adding another 24 points of space after the header paragraph (which happens to be a single line), you will have a total of 36 points of space (the necessary 0.5 inch) (Figure 1.55).

Page Number Only

This variation takes into consideration the explanation given above regarding spacing of header text. Your personal preference might be to have no header text whatsoever and merely place a page number at the top right corner of each page.

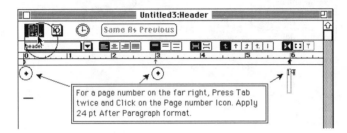

Figure 1.56

After choosing **Header** from the **View** menu, press the **Tab** key twice to advance the blinking insertion point to the tab setting on the far right. **Click** on the Page Numbering icon (Figure 1.56). Go to the **Format** menu and choose **Paragraph**. Press the **Tab** key once to highlight the contents in the After edit bar. Type the number **24** to apply 24 points of space after the paragraph, as shown in Figure 1.54.

Breathing Space with No Text

This final variation allows for proper spacing with no text in the header whatsoever. As explained in Figure 1.55, the header must contain 36 points of space for the main body of your letter to begin at 1 inch.

Figure 1.57

While the Header view is open, go to the **Format** menu and choose **Paragraph**. Press **Tab** to move to the **After** edit bar and type **24**, as shown in Figure 1.57. Click on the **OK** button.

STEP FOUR

Inserting Footer Elements

It may be your personal preference to place in a footer the same information that would have appeared in the headers described previously. If you plan to use footers for pagination information, be sure to also format the header with the Paragraph spacing outlined in the example in Figure 1.58.

Go to the **View** menu and choose **Footer**.

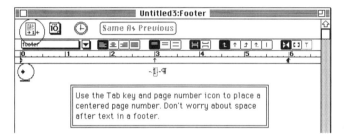

Figure 1.58

To center the page number in a footer, press the **Tab** key once. This aligns the blinking insertion point at the 3-inch mark, just under the preset center-aligned tab mark. Press the **hyphen** key, followed by a **space**. Click on the Page Number icon in the ruler. Then press the **spacebar** once and insert another hyphen. The automatic page number will begin numbering your pages from the second page, even though the header window displays the number 1. You can verify the accuracy of your page numbering once you have executed a two-page document and examine the document in either the Page Layout or Print Preview views.

You might want to model your footer after the setups explained for headers shown in the second amd third examples above. However, do not apply the 24 points of space after the paragraph. It's not necessary to have space after a footer, as the bottom of your page does not require this.

Save Your Formatting Changes

Once you've decided on the header or footer format for your stationery, save the changes to your Letterhead stationery document as outlined in the steps for Figure 1.45.

Additional Letterhead Ideas

Because of Microsoft Word's ability to convert and insert graphics files (PICT, PICT2, EPS, TIFF, MacPaint files), you might want to consider having your company logo scanned at a graphics service bureau. You could then place the logo in your first page header. However, graphics (especially PostScript) dramatically increase the size of your documents and require additional hard disk space. If you place a graphic in your letterhead stationery, each time you create a new letter you are carrying disk space storage overhead for the graphic.

For simple reverse type, boxes, shading, and bitmapped graphics, you might want to use Microsoft Word's built-in graphics tools and borders to dress up your letterhead. Though EPS graphics print out much cleaner on a laser printer, letterhead documents you've created with Microsoft Word graphics should be suitable for a fax-transmitted letter or a memo.

Before showing you a few samples of letterhead ideas, you should know that you can also place letterhead information in the First Header of your document. Deciding on whether to place your letterhead information in a header or at the top of your normal document window is often a matter of personal preference, individual work habits or the nature of your letterhead information.

Placing Letterhead Information in the First Header

You might prefer to move your letterhead information that currently appears at the top of your stationery document into the First Header area. This would then cause the flashing insertion point to be positioned at the top of a new Untitled document where you could immediately enter the addressee information (Figure 1.59).

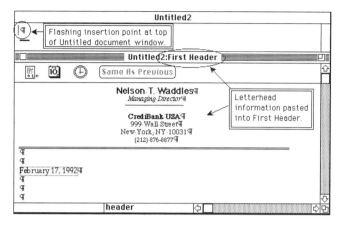

Figure 1.59

To Transfer Letterhead Information

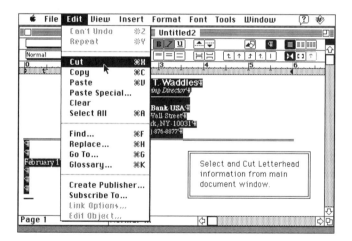

Figure 1.60

1. Open your Letterhead stationery (an Untitled document should appear in the window).

2. Select the letterhead information and choose **Cut** from the **Edit** menu (Figure 1.60).

3. Go to the **View** menu and choose **First Header**.

4. Go to the **Edit** menu and choose **Paste**.

5. Click in the **Close box** of the First Header window.

6. **Save** the changes to your letterhead stationery.

Using Reverse Type

Figure 1.61

Normally, text you enter in your document is formatted as the color black, since it typically prints out on white paper. For added contrast, you might want to consider using reverse type—or white text against a black background. This is often done for a company name or to a block of information for added emphasis. To create white text, you will select the color **White** from the **Character** dialog box.

The example letterhead in Figure 1.61 places information in both a First Header and a First Footer. You might decide to place your company name and address information at the top of your document stationery and telephone and fax information at the bottom.

As with all paragraph borders created in Microsoft Word, the length of the border is determined by the position of the left and right indent markers. The distance the border extends beyond all sides of the text is set from within the **Border** dialog box using the **From Text** setting.

To Create Reverse Type with a Border

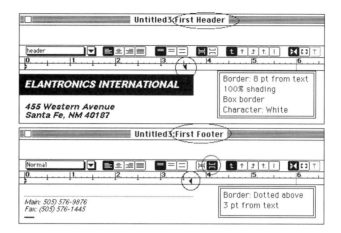

Figure 1.62

1. Enter your text. You may want to use a slightly larger bold font (Figure 1.62 uses 14 point Helvetica Black font).

2. Go to the **Format** menu and choose **Border**.

3. Press the **Tab** key and enter the number **8** in the **From Text** edit bar.

4. Select the **Single Line** width and click on the **Box** Preset Border.

5. Choose **100%** from the **Shading** list box.

6. Click **OK**.

7. Select your text and go to the **Format** menu and choose **Character**.

8. Choose **White** from the **Color** list box and click **OK**.

9. Move the **Right Indent** marker in the Ruler to a position that is close to the last letter of your text line, but does not cause it to wrap to a new line.

NOTE: *Don't be deceived by what may appear in the Normal or Page Layout views of text that has 100 percent shading applied to it. These views will always display reverse text as white against a black background if Show ¶ is turned on. Only when you are viewing your document with Show ¶ turned off or from Print Preview will you see how your document will print the final text format. Use Print Preview (or turn off Show ¶) to double-check for those circumstances in which you may have forgotten to format the text in the shaded border area as White. Print Preview will always display any unformatted text (which is black) in a shaded box as a solid black box.*

In the Figure 1.62 example, the First Footer information has a dotted border at the top of the first line of telephone information. To create space between the text and the dotted border, there is a 3 point From Text setting applied with the Border dialog box. In addition, the right indent marker has been moved over so that it aligns with the shaded First Header information.

Notice there is a slight difference in the right indent settings between the First Header and the First Footer. This is an adjustment for the difference in the From Text border settings (reverse type header has 8 point and dotted footer border has 3 point).

Using Graphics

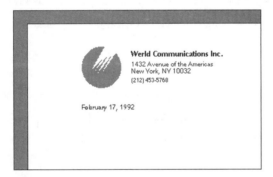

Figure 1.63

You can use the **Insert Picture** function or you can click on the **Graphics** icon in the Ribbon) to create simple, yet effective, bitmapped graphics for your letterhead. You can then insert and align text with your graphic, right from within the Edit Picture window.

When using different font sizes and formats (such as **bold** or *italic*), you will be restricted to only those choices currently displayed in the Font and Format menus. For this reason, you might want to add to the Format or Font menus any formats you plan to use that don't regularly appear there. Use the **Commands** command from the **Tools** menu to do this prior to inserting your graphic.

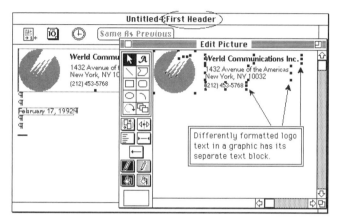

Figure 1.64

One of the difficulties in text formatting from within the Edit Picture window is the application of various fonts, sizes, and formats. The entire block of text will assume the format you select. To have differently format-ted text for, say, your company name and address, you will have to create and align different text blocks for each line. With a little practice, moving and aligning text blocks in the Edit Picture window shouldn't be too difficult to master for you to produce a graphically pleasing letterhead logo.

Using Graphics and Text in Tables

Figure 1.65

You may want to explore the use of tables to help align both text and graphics for your letterhead information. There also might be a special kind of border that you would like to have extend down the left or right side of the page. A table will help you to keep all the information as a single unit while also giving you the flexibility to move and align individual parts of your text and graphics.

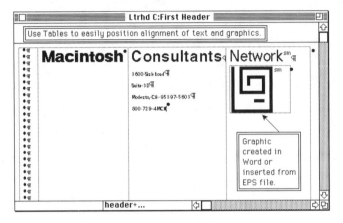

Figure 1.66

In the example shown in Figure 1.66, a table was inserted into the First Header of the document and text was placed in each of four separate cells. The far left column was used to create a dotted border along the left side of the document. The dot was created by pressing the **Option** key and typing the number **8** (• is often called a "bullet"). The **Return** key was pressed for a bullet on each new line.

The space between each bullet was controlled by using the Line spacing edit bar in the Paragraph dialog box. The entire column was selected and a line spacing of 10 point was entered and the Exactly line spacing option chosen.

On the far right column, a graphic was created for the logo beneath the first paragraph of text using Microsoft Word's graphics tools (click on the **Graphics** icon located on the Ribbon).

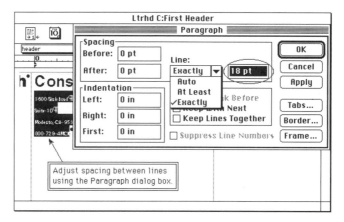

Figure 1.67

Once the graphic was created and scaled to size, the text in the column to the left of the logo was entered. Space was placed between each line of text using the Line spacing edit bar from the **Paragraph** dialog box (Figure 1.67).

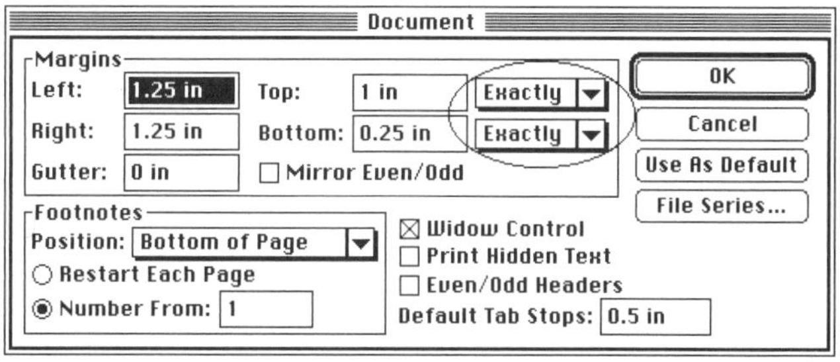

Figure 1.68

You might plan to format your letterhead with text or a border like the example shown in Figure 1.66. In order for this text to print alongside the regular body text of the letter, you will need to reset the margins for your document. Go to the **Format** menu and choose **Document**. Next to the Top margin edit bar is a drop down list. Choose the **Exactly** setting for both the Top and Bottom margins (Figure 1.68). This will prevent your header information from displacing regular text in your document.

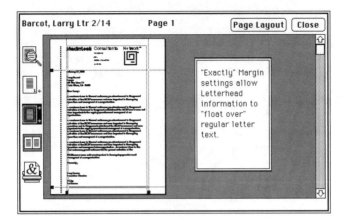

Figure 1.69

When you view your document in Page Layout view, don't be confused if all your header information is not displayed. Print Preview is the only view that can accurately display this kind of header information when margins have an Exactly setting (Figure 1.69).

How to Use Your Letterhead Document to Write a Letter

In Chapter 1 you created a letterhead template to streamline the formatting procedures for executing a letter. However, there are a number of additional formatting concerns you might need answers to when you generate the actual letter. For instance, how do you make adjustments for body text with a first line that is indented? How do you manipulate space to position a short letter properly on the page? What are some shortcuts and efficient methods for editing, deleting, and moving text? How do you change the position of the date and closure information? How can you rework a document so that it fits on only one page instead of spilling a few lines over to a second page?

The answers to these and other formatting issues will be covered in this chapter. In addition, you'll also learn how to take advantage of a System 7.0 feature that allows Microsoft Word 5.0 to automatically update addressee information on the second page of your letter. Once you've learned these streamlined procedures, you'll be able to dramatically reduce the time it takes for you to produce your daily correspondence.

The Short Letter

Beginning Steps for Text Entry

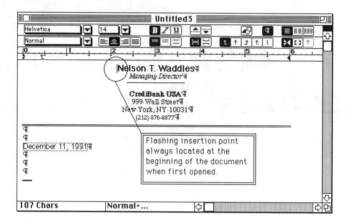

Figure 2.1

Use your Letterhead stationery document to open an Untitled document on your desktop. Notice that when you first open any document in Microsoft Word, the flashing insertion point is always located at the very top of the document (Figure 2.1). If you have not placed your letterhead information in a First Header, you'll need to reposition the flashing insertion point before you can start entering text in the area beneath the date.

NOTE: *To move letterhead information into a First Header, see Chapter 1, "Placing Letterhead Information in the First Header."*

Move the I-beam so that it is positioned next to the last paragraph mark in your document and click once (Figure 2.2). If you are more comfortable working with keyboard shortcuts, you can press the **Command** key and the number **3** on the numeric keypad. The flashing insertion point will jump to the end of the document so you can immediately enter your text.

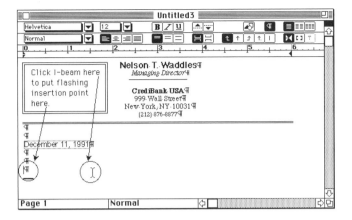

Figure 2.2

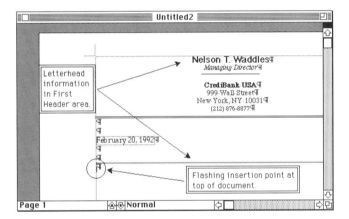

Figure 2.3

Having to reposition the flashing insertion point each time you begin a new letter may seem like a trivial matter; however, any techniques you can employ to save yourself a few extra keystrokes or mouse movements will serve to increase your overall productivity. The letterhead document in Figure 2.3 is displayed in Page Layout view so that you can see there is letterhead information in the First Header area. Notice that the flashing insertion point is positioned at the top of the document's text entry area, where you can begin entering text immediately.

Choosing Your Font

You may have chosen to set up your letterhead with elegant, more highly stylized fonts you wouldn't necessarily use for simple correspondence. For the body of your letters, you'd most likely want to work with an easy-to-read font that looks good both in print and on-screen and avoids unnecessary eyestrain. Some standard Apple fonts are better choices than others.

Palatino, New Century Schoolbook, and Bookman 12 point fonts are suitable for most correspondence. Although Helvetica is an easy font to read on-screen, 12 point prints out too large for professional letters. Downsizing the Helvetica font to 11 point to print satisfactorily does not align the font properly on a 72 dot per inch screen and causes irregular juxtaposition of letters. Where possible, avoid using Helvetica as a body text font. It is better suited for title and heading text.

Once you've settled on a standard font for your document production, you can have the font change updated for all your future correspondence. Choose **Default** from the **Font** menu.

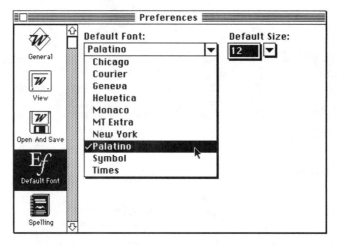

Figure 2.4

The Default Font option resides within the Preferences dialog box. Here you can choose the default font and size from two separate drop-down lists (Figure 2.4). Clicking in the Preferences **Close box** will set that font and size for the current and all subsequent new documents generated from your letterhead stationery.

NOTE: *If you change the Default font and then open previously saved documents, those documents will contain the old Default font settings. You will have to update the Default font for documents saved prior to the change.*

Writing the Letter

The inside address and salutation information is typically formatted as flush-left text, with a new paragraph for each new line of text. In what follows, you're going to explore some paragraph spacing options and learn how automatic word wrapping behaves within paragraphs.

Space Between Paragraphs

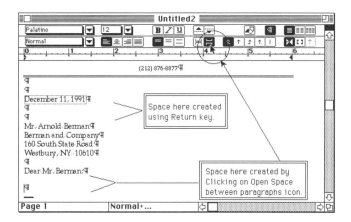

Figure 2.5

Once the preliminary address information is entered into a document, you can begin typing the body of your letter. Figure 2.5 illustrates how clicking on the **Open Space between paragraphs** icon places 12 points (one line) of space above the first paragraph of body text. This eliminates the need to press the **Return** key two times after each paragraph and also gives you some formatting advantages (which will be discussed later on in this chapter) when you need to squeeze a few extra lines onto a single page letter.

Word Wrapping

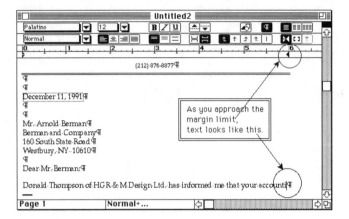

Figure 2.6

As you enter text, the flashing insertion point moves across the page. When it approaches the right indent or margin, as indicated by the ruler in Figure 2.6, Microsoft Word's automatic text-wrap feature is determining how many words will fit on the line.

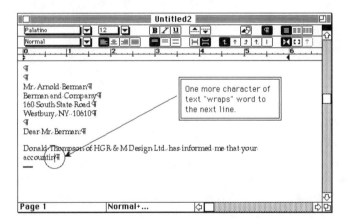

Figure 2.7

When the length of a word extends beyond the margin limit, it is automatically moved to the next line (Figure 2.7). The most common mistake you will make if you are new to word processing is pressing the Return key when you reach the end of each line, as you would normally do if you were using a typewriter. Only press the **Return** key when you have finished writing a full paragraph.

First-Line Indenting

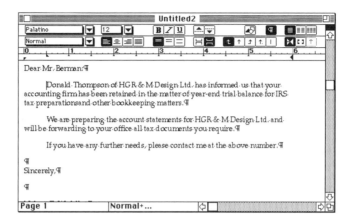

Figure 2.8

The rest of the example material in this chapter will be formatted with block left paragraph alignment. However, some users prefer to indent the first line of a paragraph (Figure 2.8). What follows are tips for the most efficient way to create an indented-first-line format with a word processor.

When using a typewriter, you could either press the spacebar (and count each space) or you could hit the **Tab** key to indent the first line. In Microsoft Word, you can quickly set the first-line indent so that each new paragraph you enter is automatically formatted for you.

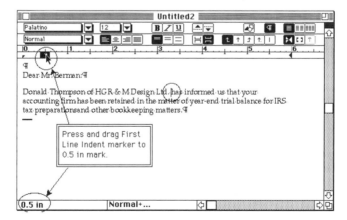

Figure 2.9

Make sure the flashing insertion point is either located in the first paragraph of body text in your letter or that all the appropriate text in your letter is selected. Move your pointer into the Ruler and position it over the top triangle of the Left Indent marker. This triangle is called the First Line Indent marker. Press and drag it to the 0.5 inch mark (Figure 2.9). When you release the mouse button, you will see your text is immediately indented.

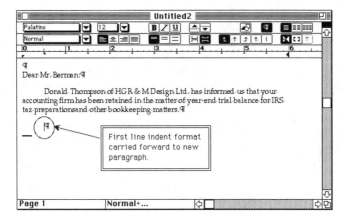

Figure 2.10

Once you have formatted the paragraph with a first-line indent, pressing the **Return** key at the end of the paragraph carries the format forward to the next new paragraph (Figure 2.10). In this way, you can continue to enter text in your letter by simply pressing the **Return** key to start each new paragraph with indented text.

However, when you use this indented first line formatting, you will need to change the indented first line before you enter text for your closure and signature.

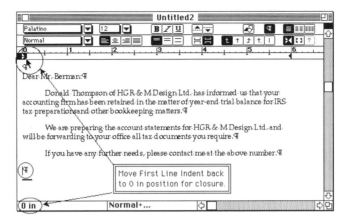

Figure 2.11

Press **Return** for the new paragraph that will begin your closure. Go to the Ruler and, using the pointer, press and drag the top triangle (First Line Indent marker) back to the 0 position on the Ruler. Closely examine the example in Figure 2.11 to make sure the First Line Indent marker is positioned exactly on top of the lower triangle of the Left Indent marker. You can also refer to the measurement displayed in the lower left status bar of your document window.

Formatting Space for a Closure

Once you've finished typing the body of your letter, you typically adjust the spacing for the closure of the letter and your signature. Therefore, your title, any enclosures, and other information such as the author and typist initials are often formatted as single paragraphs with no space between them, as shown in Figure 2.12.

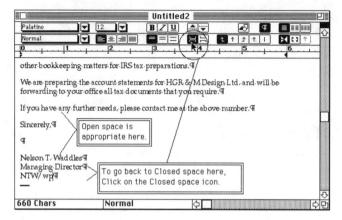

Figure 2.12

Changing the space above a paragraph is accomplished by a single click on the **Closed Space** icon in the Ruler.

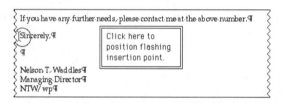

Figure 2.13

You might also want to adjust the amount of space that comes before the closure. The following examples demonstrate how to expand or condense the space above a paragraph using the Ruler icons. First, position the blinking insertion point in front of the paragraph of text you want to change (Figure 2.13).

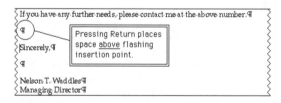

Figure 2.14

To add more space, press the **Return** key. This places another empty paragraph above the insertion point (Figure 2.14). If the closure paragraph has an Open Space format applied, the newly inserted paragraph will also contain the open space format.

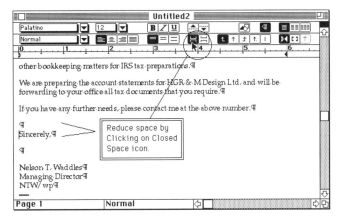

Figure 2.15

Two paragraphs with open space above them (a total of four lines of space) may be more than you want. In order to modify and reduce the space between the closure and the empty paragraph above it, you can click on the **Closed Space** icon in the ruler (Figure 2.15).

You might never choose to use the Open or Closed Space icons for expanding and condensing space above paragraphs. There are no steadfast rules that say you cannot use the Return key instead. However, the Open Space icon is an effective tool for quickly adjusting space within a document and can be easily applied to a single paragraph or a group of selected paragraphs with the click of a mouse.

Previewing Your Document

When executing documents on a word processor, you may lose your sense of where the page ends while working in **Normal** view. Choosing **Print Preview** from the **File** menu gives immediate feedback on how your entire letter will look when it prints out. Print Preview will also serve as a checkpoint to catch any last-minute formatting requirements, such as inserting empty white space in a short letter (Figure 2.16).

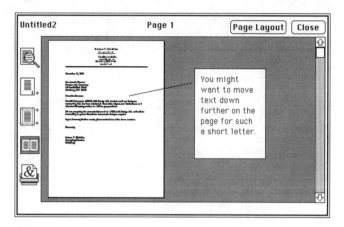

Figure 2.16

Repositioning a Short Letter on a Page

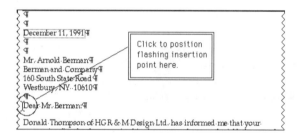

Figure 2.17

Typically, the "letting in and out" of empty space for a short letter is best executed from the space between the address and the salutation. You might also add space between the date and the address information or even before the date. The following example demonstrates the first option. Move the I-beam and click to position the blinking insertion point just before the salutation in your letter (Figure 2.17).

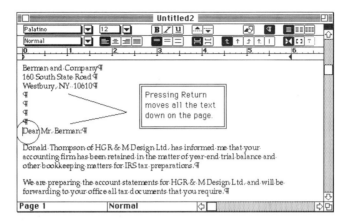

Figure 2.18

Pressing the **Return** key places a blank paragraph above the insertion point.
It also moves all the text beneath the insertion point further down on the
page (Figure 2.18).

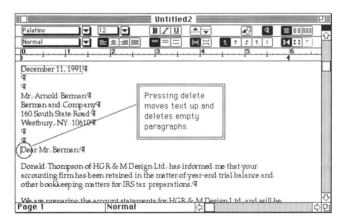

Figure 2.19

Unless you are working in Page Layout view with a full-page display monitor, there is no immediate visual reference to the bottom of the page. If you
are using the method described above to move body text with the Return
key, return to Print Preview and observe the results of your actions. If you
realize you have added more space than what you intended, go back to
Normal or Page Layout view. Press the **Delete** key to move the body text up
and delete some of the paragraphs you had inserted (Figure 2.19).

Editing and Moving Text

The most commonly used editing tool for users of word processing is the Delete key, which deletes text to the left of the blinking insertion point. Many users merely position the blinking insertion point after the offending error and tap away until the unwanted text is obliterated; however, using just the Delete key is not always the most expedient way for you to accomplish the goal. There are a few, simple techniques that will make a major timesaving difference when you are editing text.

Select and Delete

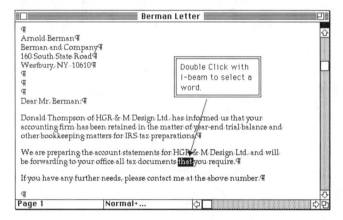

Figure 2.20

If you have to delete an entire word, select the word and the trailing space that comes after it by placing the I-beam anywhere over the top of the word and double-clicking (Figure 2.20). Now you only need to hit the **Delete** key once.

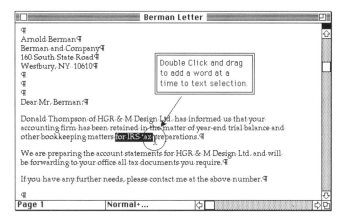

Figure 2.21

When you need to select several words, start by positioning the I-beam anywhere over the top of the first word in the group. Double-click, only keep holding the mouse button down after the second click, and drag the mouse over the rest of the text (Figure 2.21). This grabs text a word at a time, eliminating the need for more accurate mouse movements. Again, you'll only need to hit the **Delete** key once.

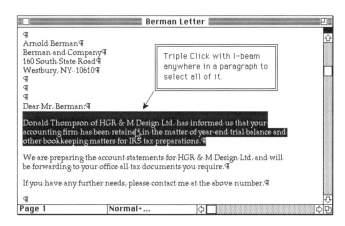

Figure 2.22

If it's an entire paragraph you need to delete, use the triple-click method to select your text before tapping the **Delete** key (Figure 2.22).

Select and Move

Figure 2.23

Moving text a short distance is easy with Word 5.0. Using any of the selection techniques described above, move the pointer into the highlighted text area. The I-beam will change into a left-pointing arrow. Simply press and drag the text to where you want it repositioned. A flashing, dotted gray line near the tip of the pointer will indicate where the text will be placed once you let go of the mouse button (Figure 2.23). This is called "drag-and-drop text editing" and is an option set through the Tools Preferences dialog box.

Moving larger bodies of text is accomplished more easily using the standard cut and paste techniques. However, here's a tip that makes for easier selection of large amounts of text.

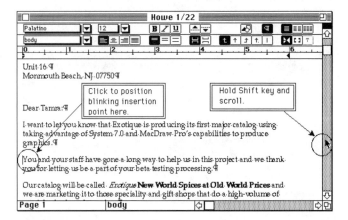

Figure 2.24

Position the I-beam at the beginning of the text and click once to position the blinking insertion point. Hold down the **Shift** key and scroll to the bottom of the text you want to include in your selection (Figure 2.24).

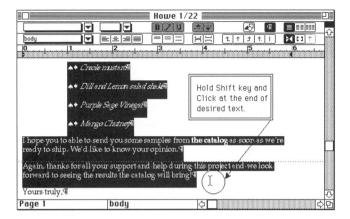

Figure 2.25

Keeping the Shift key depressed, move the I-beam to the end of the text you want selected and click once. All the text between the two "anchor" points (your first and second click with the I-beam) will be highlighted (Figure 2.25). You can then execute a cut, copy, or delete function.

Applying Bold, Italic, and Underline Formats

As you work with Microsoft Word, you will discover there are sometimes three or four ways to execute the same function. Some require memorizing a keyboard combination and others involve selecting a choice from a menu, a dialog box, or even clicking an icon in the Ribbon or Ruler. When you want to apply Bold, Italic, or Underline formats, you have all these choices. It is often a matter of which keyboard combination works best for you (Command B or Command Shift B for Bold), if you are viewing the Ribbon (click on the Bold icon) or if you feel more comfortable selecting the format from the Format menu or from within the Character dialog box.

You also have two opportunities for deciding when to apply these formats: 1) after you've already entered text, and 2) while you are keying in text in your document.

Once you've applied any of these formats, realize that the Ribbon provides an immediate visual reference for how text is formatted at the location of the insertion point or selected text. Knowing this, you can avoid a common problem illustrated by the following example.

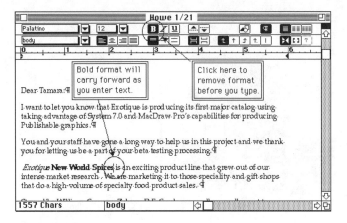

Figure 2.26

You decide to insert some text following a word that has bold format applied to it (Figure 2.26). As you start to type, you realize the format is still active as all the text you now enter has bold applied to it.

When you click to position the insertion point next to any text, all the text's character formats carry forward as you type. You will save time, confusion, and aggravation if you remove any unwanted formatting prior to entering the inserted text. An expedient way to accomplish this is to choose **Plain Text** from the **Format** menu. The Plain Text command will strip your text of all character formats except Size, Position (i.e., superscript), and Spacing (i.e., expanded).

Moving the Position of the Date and Closure

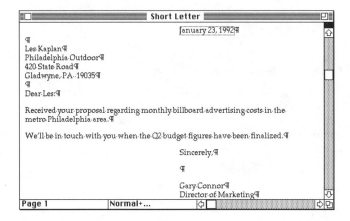

Figure 2.27

Not everyone belongs to the "flush-left, blocked" school of letter design. You might want to reposition the date and closure so that they both align somewhere to the right, just beyond the center of the page (Figure 2.27).

There are two techniques that accomplish this same task; however, one is better for a letter you've yet to write and the other is more expedient for the letter you've already written.

For an Existing Letter

For a letter you've already executed, you'll be working with the Left Indent marker in the Ruler. Open the document on the desktop. Select the **date** by positioning the right-pointing arrow in the Selection Bar and clicking once. Make sure the **Left Alignment** icon is highlighted. If it is not, then click on it once.

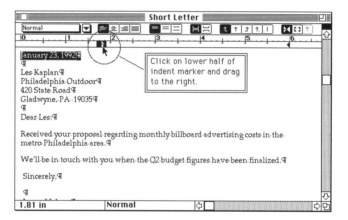

Figure 2.28

Next, place the pointer over the bottom half of the Left Indent marker. Press and drag the indent marker (Figure 2.28) to the place where you want the date positioned—probably somewhere around the 3.5- or 4-inch mark.

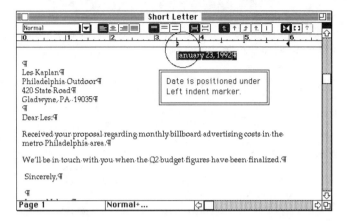

Figure 2.29

When you release the mouse button, your date will jump to where the indent marker is positioned (Figure 2.29).

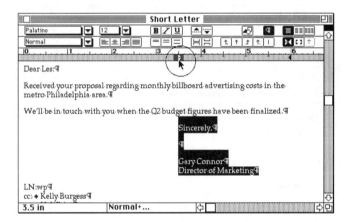

Figure 2.30

Scroll down to your closure information. Using the right-pointing arrow positioned in the Selection Bar, press and drag through each line of closure text to select it. As before, make sure the left-aligned icon is highlighted in the Ruler.

Don't be concerned if the Ruler becomes shaded. If you have some paragraphs that have the Open Space format applied and others that don't, the shading merely indicates that the selected paragraphs have inconsistent formatting. In this case, the left-aligned icon will not be highlighted, even if you try to click it.

Press and drag the lower half of the Left Indent marker over to the same 3.5- or 4-inch mark as you did for the date (Figure 2.30).

For a New Document

Rather than adjusting indent markers to move your text, you can place tabs in the Ruler and use the Tab key to position information.

Open your Letterhead stationery document (which opens as an Untitled document). Using the right-pointing arrow in the Selection Bar, select the **date** and any **blank paragraphs** that follow it. You're going to place a tab in the Ruler that will carry forward for the rest of your text entry.

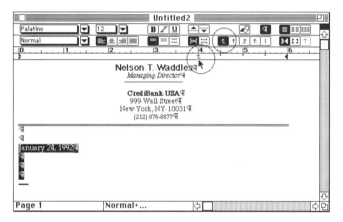

Figure 2.31

Make sure that the left-aligned tab mark is highlighted in the ruler (see Figure 2.31). If some other tab mark is highlighted, simply click on the left-most tab icon to select it. Position your pointer in the ruler and click once, just under the 3.5- or 4-inch mark. You can press and drag on the tab mark itself to reposition it if you initially click at the wrong spot.

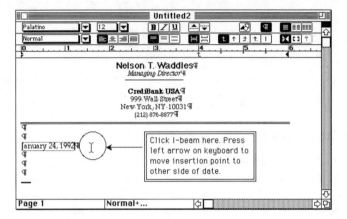

Figure 2.32

You're going to move the automatic date over to align with the tab mark in the Ruler. In order to do this, you will need to position the flashing insertion point to the left of the date. However, sometimes it's hard to click in front of text that is right next to the Selection Bar area.

Because the pointer changes rather rapidly from an I-beam to the right-pointing arrow in this area, here's a tip that will help you. Place the I-beam to the **right** of the automatic date and click once to position the flashing insertion point on the right side of the date. Use the left arrow key on your keyboard and press once to move the insertion point to the other side of the date (Figure 2.32).

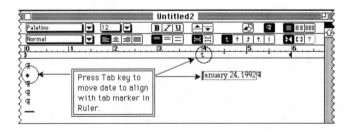

Figure 2.33

Press the **Tab** key on your keyboard once; this will move the left side of the date to align with the tab mark in the Ruler (Figure 2.33).

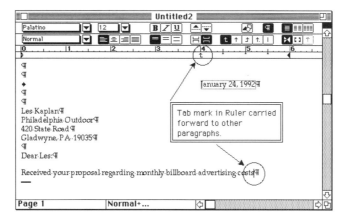

Figure 2.34

Reposition the I-beam in the last paragraph of the document. Type the address, salutation, and main body of your letter as you would normally. Notice that, as you press the **Return** key for each new paragraph of text, the tab you placed in the ruler is carried forward. In a sense, it is remaining "dormant" in your document for the moment when you will use it to align your closure information (Figure 2.34).

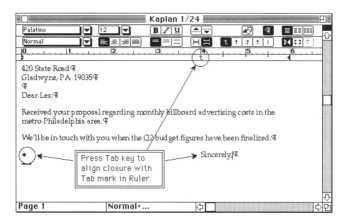

Figure 2.35

At the end of your letter, press the **Return** key as many times as necessary to give you the proper spacing before your closure. Press the **Tab** key once to align the flashing insertion point with the tab mark in the ruler and type the closure (Figure 2.35).

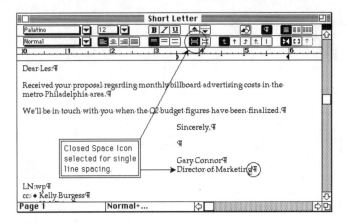

Figure 2.36

Press **Return** two times for signature spacing. Press the **Tab** key again to line up the signature. Enter your text and continue to press the **Return** and **Tab** keys to align the remainder of the closure information (Figure 2.36). You might also click on the Closed Space icon in the Ruler for your title information.

Typically, the author's and typist's initials and any enclosure or copy information are placed flush left in a document. Once you've clicked the Closed Space icon, you need only to enter the appropriate information and press the **Return** key for a new line.

Adjusting the Letterhead Template

If you decide that you want to use a tab mark to align the date and closure information at a point 3.5 to 4 inches from the left margin, you should adjust your letterhead template so that the formatting is always available to you.

Open the Letterhead document. Follow the steps above (Figures 2.31 to 2.33) to place a tab mark in the Ruler and position the date information. Save the document in the stationery format with the same file name and replace the original letterhead document.

The Long Letter

Though you may not be aware of it, there are specific formatting issues concerning letters that are longer than a single page. The section "Formatting Your Letterhead for Multi-Page Letters" in Chapter 1 addresses ways in which you can set up your document to handle a few of these issues—such as correct spacing at the top of the second and subsequent pages as well as pertinent information you might want to have appear in the area called a header (or footer) at the top (or bottom) of your document.

What will be addressed in this section are ways to control page breaks, efficient methods for replacing addressee information in the header or footer you might have created and, lastly, how to make adjustments for a few lines of text that flow over to a second page so that all the text fits on a single page.

Automatic Pagination

Most word processors, Word 5.0 included, have an automatic pagination feature that places a page break in your document as you enter text. Where Microsoft Word chooses to place the page break is determined by the margin settings you have chosen for the document. Obviously, if you have top and bottom margins of 2 inches, you will have more frequent page breaks in your text than if you have margins of 0.5 inch.

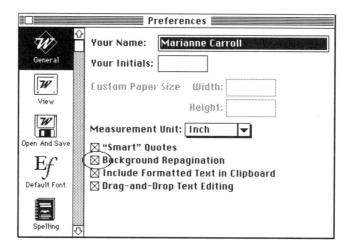

Figure 2.37

When working with Word 5.0, pagination can occur in the background while you are working by activating an option in the Preferences dialog box (Figure 2.37). To set this option, go to the **Tools** menu and choose **Preferences**.

From time to time as you work, you may notice that the page number status box in the lower left of your window turns gray. This means that the text you've entered may have altered the page breaks in your document and Word is waiting for you to stop entering text for a moment to update the pagination.

At any time you can force a repagination by choosing **Repaginate Now** from the **Tools** menu.

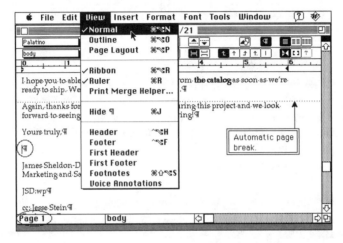

Figure 2.38

The pagination that Word determines for your document is called an Automatic page break, and is indicated in Normal view by a dotted line (Figure 2.38).

What Page Are You On?

One of the most confusing things to users of Word who write documents longer than one page is the issue of page number orientation. If you refer to Figure 2.38, the lower left status bar displays Page 1. However, if you look closely, the flashing insertion point is actually located on Page 2. Now, you might wonder why the page number in the status box is not displaying Page 2, since this is the location of the flashing insertion point.

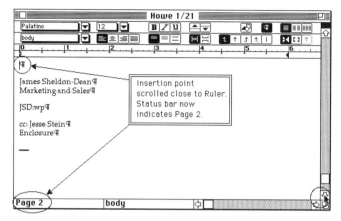

Figure 2.39

The lower left status bar reflects the page number of text that is closest to the Ruler and not the location of the flashing insertion point. Therefore, if you were to scroll your document up so that the flashing insertion point was just under the Ruler, you would notice that the status bar would now indicate that you were on Page 2 (Figure 2.39). Once you understand the nature of the information the status box is providing you with, you can determine which page your insertion point is located on and how many pages there are in your document.

Controlling Page Breaks

What if the location of the automatic page break separates text across a page at an inappropriate place? What if you want to make the page break come earlier in the text than Microsoft Word determines it should be? (For obvious reasons, you can't make the page break come later, unless you change the top and bottom margins for the entire document.) Here's where you can insert your own "forced" page break.

Forced page breaks are placed in your document by choosing **Page Break** from the **Insert** menu (or by holding the **Shift** key while pressing the **Enter** key). However, before you execute a page break, always make sure you have the blinking insertion point positioned in the correct place.

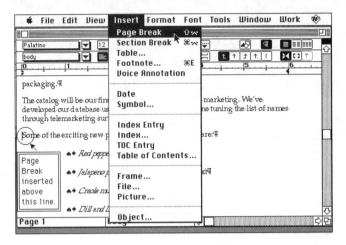

Figure 2.40

A forced page break will be inserted above the location of the flashing insertion point at the time you choose **Page Break** from the **Insert** menu (Figure 2.40).

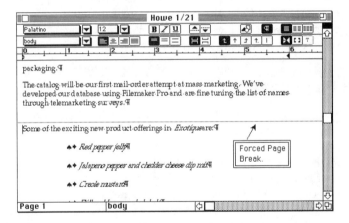

Figure 2.41

While in Normal view, a forced page break is displayed in your document as a closely dotted line (Figure 2.41). These dots are more tightly positioned than the ones displayed for an automatic page break.

Learn to distinguish between these two kinds of page breaks so that you can identify the probable source of any pagination problems. Automatic and forced page breaks are more clearly discernable from Normal view. In general, work with your document in Normal view. It can save you time scrolling through areas of blank space normally occupied by margins, headers, and footers that only appear in Page Layout view.

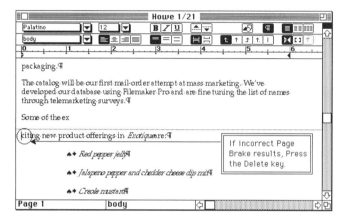

Figure 2.42

Be aware of the location of the insertion point before you decide to place a page break. If the insertion point is located in the middle of a word in a paragraph, choosing **Insert Page Break** will break the word and place the page break right between the text characters (Figure 2.42).

If you should accidentally place a page break where it wasn't intended, you have three recourses to that action:

1. If you have just completed the page break insertion, simply tap the **Delete** key once and the page break will be deleted; or

2. Go immediately to the **Edit** menu and choose **Undo Page Break**.

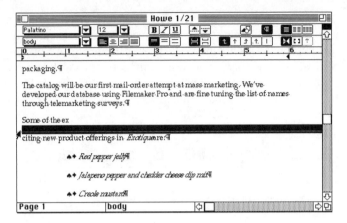

Figure 2.43

3. You may have gone on to work with other parts of your document and the flashing insertion point is no longer where it was when you first inserted the page break. Scroll to the area of the page break and move the pointer into the **Selection Bar**. Using the right-pointing arrow, click once to select the forced page break as shown in Figure 2.43 (you must be working in Normal view). Press the **Delete** key and the forced page break will disappear.

Adjusting Header Information for the Addressee

While executing the instructions in Chapter 1 for "Formatting Your Letter-head for Multi-Page Letters," you created a header with placeholder text for the addressee. If you are executing a long letter and text flows over to the second and subsequent pages, you will need to enter the addressee's name into the header.

There are several solutions for entering this information. They are dependent on your computer operating environment:

1. Solutions that are applicable to those who are working with Word 5.0 running either System 6.0.x or System 7.0; and

2. One solution which will only be available to those who are running under System 7.0.

System 6.0.x

The two methods described here require that you follow steps to replace text in a header for each and every new letter you execute that has more than one page. Regardless of whether you are working under System 6.0.x or

System 7.0, you have two ways to view information that is placed in a header—either in Normal or Page Layout view.

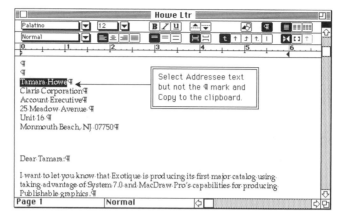

Figure 2.44

Before you proceed with either method, scroll to the top of your document and select the text for the person to whom you addressed the letter. Make sure you do not select the paragraph mark. Only select the text that comes before it (Figure 2.44). Choose **Copy** from the **Edit** menu.

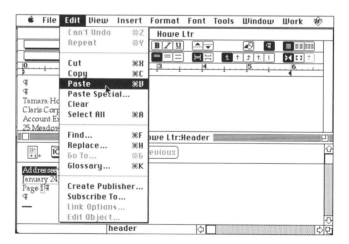

Figure 2.45

The first method applies if you are working in Normal view. (You will know if you are in Normal view as it will be checked in the View menu.) Go to the **View** menu and choose **Header**.

A separate window will appear containing your header text. Place the I-beam over the Addressee text and double-click to select it. With the text now highlighted, go to the **Edit** menu and choose **Paste** (Figure 2.45). The word "Addressee" will be replaced by the text in the Clipboard, which was copied from the first page of your letter. Click in the close box of the header when you are done.

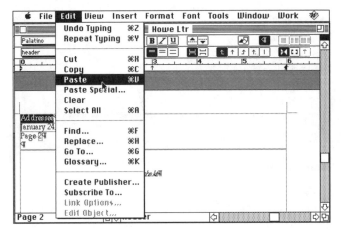

Figure 2.46

The second method can be executed from the Page Layout view. (Page Layout should be checked in the View menu.) Make sure you've first copied the addressee's name from the top of the letter. Scroll to page 2 and click in the header area.

> **NOTE:** *Once you have scrolled to page 2, you can also choose Header from the View menu, which will then place your insertion point at the top of the header.*

Place the I-beam over the addressee text and double-click to select it. With the text now highlighted, go to the **Edit** menu and choose **Paste** (Figure 2.46).

System 7.0

If you are working with System 7.0, you can take advantage of the new Linking features of Word 5.0 to make the updating of the header information automatic. You'll never even have to open the header for any letter in order to have the addressee's name placed there.

Since you'll want to have this process occur for each and every letter you write, you're going to add some information to an Untitled document and then save this document as your Letterhead stationery.

Locate your Letterhead stationery document and open it. An Untitled document should appear on your desktop. Go to the **View** menu and choose **Normal**.

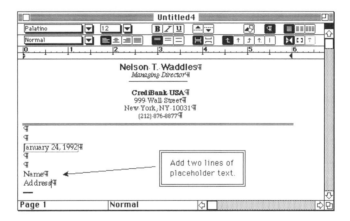

Figure 2.47

Click in the last line in the document, where you would normally enter the address information. (If you have placed your letterhead information in a First Header, you will then enter the following text at the top of the document.) Type the word **Name**, press **Return** for a new line, and then type the word **Address** (Figure 2.47).

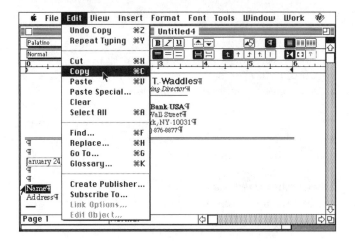

Figure 2.48

Place the pointer in the Selection Bar and click with the right-pointing arrow to select the line containing the word **Name**. Go to the **Edit** menu and choose **Copy** (Figure 2.48).

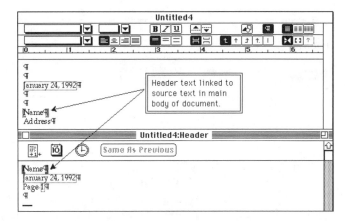

Figure 2.49

Choose **Header** from the **View** menu. Use the right-pointing arrow in the Selection Bar to select the addressee placeholder text. Hold down the **Shift** key on your keyboard while you go to the **Edit** menu and choose **Paste Link**. The highlighted text will be replaced with the word "Name" and two shaded brackets will appear around it (Figure 2.49). These brackets indicate that the text is linked to the source text on the first page of your document.

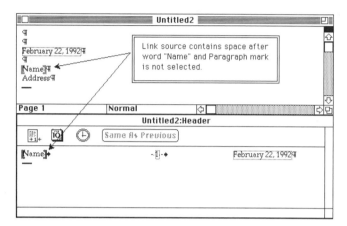

Figure 2.50

Using linked text for addressee information by the method described above requires the addressee information to be contained in a separate paragraph. You will not be able to successfully implement this solution for the single-line header described in Chapter 1 in Figure 1-53.

To create a link for a single-line header, type the word **Name** followed by a space. Then double-click to select the word **Name** and its trailing space. Do not select the paragraph mark that follows it. Copy the text into the Clipboard. Follow the steps above to Paste Link the text in your header, replacing only the word "Addressee" — not the entire paragraph—with the contents of the Clipboard (Figure 2.50).

As a final step, **save** your document in **stationery** format with the same file name and replace the original letterhead document.

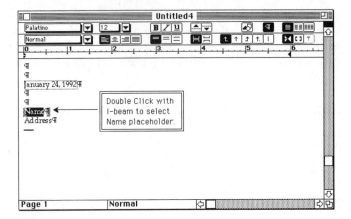

Figure 2.51

Now that you've created linked text for the addressee's name in the header, how do you utilize the link when you execute a letter? After opening the Letterhead document, position the I-beam over the word "Name" and double-click to select it (Figure 2.51).

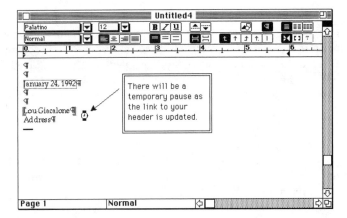

Figure 2.52

Type the name of the person you are writing the letter to. This text will replace the highlighted word "Name." When you have finished typing, there will be a temporary pause as Word updates the linked information in the header (Figure 2.52).

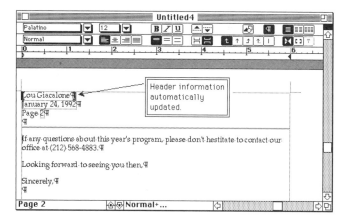

Figure 2.53

Next, move the I-beam down to the word "Address". Position the I-beam over "Address," double-click to select the text, and then type the appropriate address information to replace it. Continue to enter information as you would for a normal letter.

When the text of your letter extends beyond a single page, you can switch to Page Layout view. Because of the Linking features of Word 5.0 and System 7.0, you will see that the addressee's name will automatically appear in your header (Figure 2.53).

Resizing Tips to Fit a Letter on One Page

You've just written a letter that you thought would fit on a single page, but when you went to Print Preview, those few closing lines trail over onto a second, seemingly unnecessary, page. One of the most common, frustrating, and puzzling tasks in working with computer-generated letters is attempting to make the text fit on one page without rewriting the letter.

There are a number of techniques you can use to bring about the same one-page letter result. However, after trying some of the variations which follow, you may find that one method works better for you than another.

The following techniques will use an example document to clarify the methods. Once you are familiar with these techniques, you can experiment on your own documents and know there are several options to whichever method you implement.

Moving the Bottom Margin and Date

The variations that follow are all based on having first moved the bottom margin and the date. However, often either one or both of these techniques will do the job.

Moving the Bottom Margin

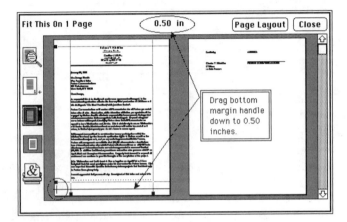

Figure 2.54

With the document open on your desktop, go to the **File** menu and choose **Print Preview**.

Position the pointer over the bottom margin handle. The pointer should turn into a cross hair. Press and drag the handle downwards, watching the numbers at the top of the Print Preview window until you reach 0.5 inch (Figure 2.54). If you move the handle any lower, your text might not print out because of certain margin restrictions on your printer.

If you pause for a few seconds, the display will update. If some text still remains on the second page, click on the **Close** button and return to Normal view to make further adjustments. Otherwise, you can click on the Printer icon and print your letter from within Print Preview.

Moving the Date

You can also retrieve some space in a document if you reposition the date so that it falls on the same line as the addressee. To make this alignment, you'd use a right-aligned tab mark.

> **NOTE:** *If you have used the linking features of Word 5.0 under System 7.0 to place the addressee's name in a second page header, select the entire addressee paragraph, including the paragraph mark, and delete. Reenter the addressee's name to break the link to the header on the second page (which you won't be needing!).*

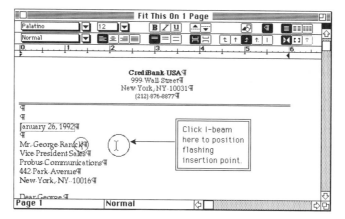

Figure 2.55

Move the I-beam to the white space beside the first line of your address (the addressee) and click once to reposition the blinking insertion point (Figure 2.55).

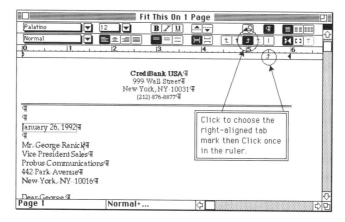

Figure 2.56

Go to the Ruler and click once on the right-aligned tab mark, as shown in Figure 2.56. Next, click in the Ruler at about the 5.5-inch mark to place the tab mark. Carefully position your pointer on top of the tab mark and press and drag it so that it lies over the top of the Right Indent marker.

Problems That Might Happen Along the Way

If your fingers should fumble and you are clicking in the Ruler several times without realizing it, you might end up placing several of these tabs on the Ruler by mistake. When this happens, use the pointer to press and drag the tab mark down below the Ruler and let go of the mouse button. The tab mark should disappear.

If the **Tabs** dialog box should also appear on your desktop, it's because you might have clicked on the tab mark two times in a row and not realized it. Double-clicking a tab mark automatically brings up the Tabs dialog box. Simply click on the **Cancel** button to close it.

Back on Track

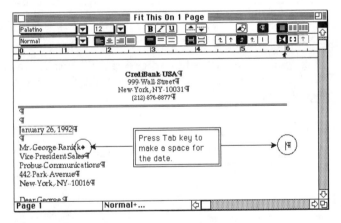

Figure 2.57

Your blinking insertion point should be flashing after the last letter in the addressee's name. Press the **Tab** key once to clear a space for the date (Figure 2.57). Select the date by pressing and dragging over it. Be sure you do not select the ¶ mark that follows it.

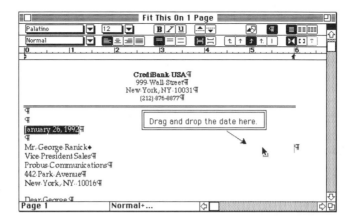

Figure 2.58

Place your pointer over the date. It should turn into a left-pointing arrow. Press and drag the date over to the other side of the tab mark in the line where the addressee's name appears (Figure 2.58) and let go of the mouse. The date should be moved.

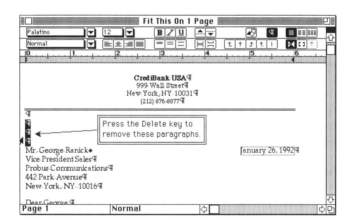

Figure 2.59

Use the right-pointing arrow in the Selection Bar to select two or three blank ¶ marks (Figure 2.59), then press the **Delete** key to remove them. Go to Print Preview to see the results of your changes.

NOTE: *If you have placed the date along with letterhead information in a First Header, you would need to cut the date and additional paragraph marks from the First Header. You could then insert a tab mark in the addressee line (as shown in Figures 2.55 to 2.57) and reinsert the date by choosing Date from the Insert menu.*

Adjusting the Left and Right Margins

While in `Print Preview`, you can also adjust the left and right margins so that your text takes up more space on the page. When the display refreshes itself, you can quickly judge the results.

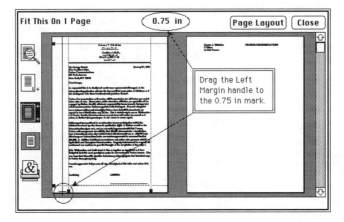

Figure 2.60

Place the pointer over the left margin handle. When it turns to a cross hair, move the handle to the left to readjust the margin (Figure 2.60). Move the right margin handle to the same position on the right. Often you might need to adjust the left and right margins to 1 inch, or even 0.75 inch to obtain the desired result.

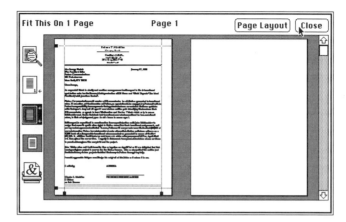

Figure 2.61

When the display refreshes itself, you might see that the text now fits on a single page (Figure 2.61). Click on the **Close** button to return to Normal view.

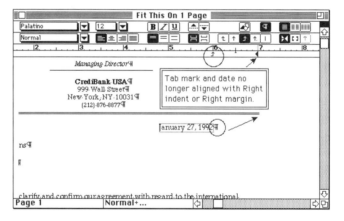

Figure 2.62

If you have adjusted the left and right margins, there is one last adjustment to make for the placement of the date. Depending on whether or not you chose to reposition the date on the other side of the addressee's name, you may or may not have to execute the following.

First, be sure the flashing insertion point is located in the paragraph that contains the date. Now that your page may be wider, depending on the size of your computer monitor, you may not be able to read all the text in the window. Click on the right arrow at the bottom of the window to scroll over to the right.

You might notice the tab mark you had placed over top of the Right Indent marker is now isolated on the Ruler (Figure 2.62). The Right Indent marker has moved to realign itself with the newly adjusted margins.

In order to have your date line up with the far right side of your page, carefully press and drag the tab mark over the top of the Right Indent marker, as you might have done before.

Changing the Size of the Font

This technique is for those who would like to maintain their letter margins at 1.25 inches and are using a 12 point font size for the text of their letter.

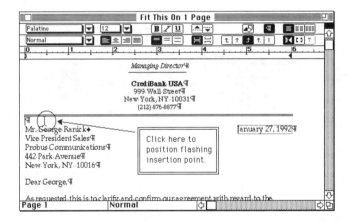

Figure 2.63

You'll want to leave the letterhead text intact so you should only select the entire contents of the actual letter. Place the I-beam beneath the letterhead border and click once to position the flashing insertion point (Figure 2.63).

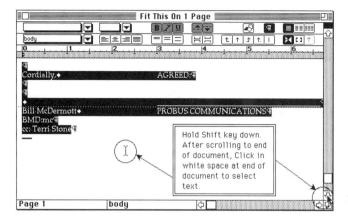

Figure 2.64

Hold down the **Shift** key and scroll to the bottom of the document. When you reach the end, keep holding the Shift key, move the I-beam within the white space at the end of the document, and click once. All your text should be highlighted (Figure 2.64).

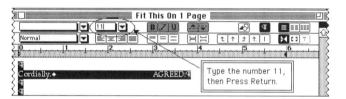

Figure 2.65

Go to the **Ribbon** and click inside the **font** size box. Type the number **11** (for 11 point) and then press the **Return** key (Figure 2.65).

Go to the **File** menu and choose **Print Preview**. The document should probably fit on a single page (Figure 2.66). You can often change a 12 point font to 11 points and still have a good readable font for the printed letter. However, working with 11 point fonts on-screen may cause some eyestrain. Though Word 5.0 supports True Type fonts when working with System 7.0, your particular computer and font setup may not take advantage of True-Type font scaling.

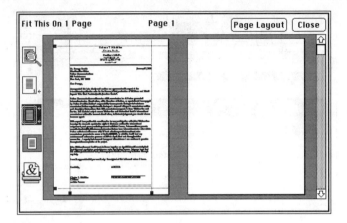

Figure 2.66

Changing the Space Between Paragraphs

This final variation is for those who want to maintain their font size at 12 points as well as the 1.25-inch margin settings. However, key to the success of this technique is to have applied the Open Space format by clicking its icon on the Ruler when entering body text.

If you had used the Return key with the Closed Space icon selected and pressed **Return** twice after each paragraph of text, you would need to make some adjustments to the body text before proceding with this solution. Remove the extra paragraph marks between each paragraph. Select the body text and apply the Open Space icon to put a line of space above each paragraph as shown in the example.

You're going to change the space between each paragraph in the main body of the letter. You'll be executing this change in one step so that you will need to highlight all the text it will apply to.

Begin by placing the I-beam in the first paragraph and triple-clicking, that is, clicking three times quickly in a row. This mouse technique selects the entire paragraph (Figure 2.67).

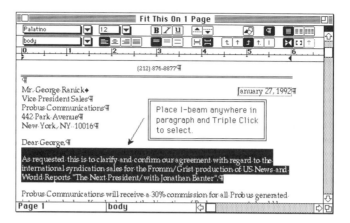

Figure 2.67

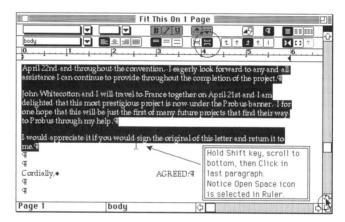

Figure 2.68

Hold down the **Shift** key and scroll to the last paragraph in the body of your letter. Keep the Shift key depressed and then click anywhere in that paragraph (Figure 2.68). All the text above it, up to the first paragraph, should be selected.

Notice that the Open Space between paragraphs icon is highlighted in the Ruler (Figure 2.68). This means that there is one line, or 12 points, of space before each paragraph. You're going to shave a few points off that space by using the Paragraph dialog box.

Go to the **Format** menu and choose **Paragraph**.

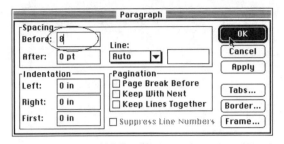

Figure 2.69

The **Before** edit bar is highlighted and should read 12 pt. Simply type the number **8** to replace it. You're going to narrow the space above each paragraph to 8 points of space rather than keep the 12 points of space it had previously. Click on the **OK** button (Figure 2.69).

> **NOTE:** *You would probably not want to place anything less than 6 points of space between paragraphs, and only if any of the other techniques did not yield successful results.*

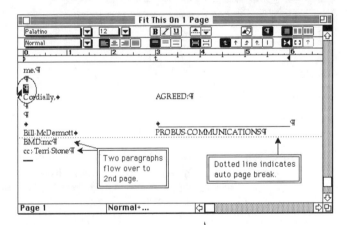

Figure 2.70

Scroll to the bottom of your document and see if there is an automatic page break, indicated by a row of dots beneath text (Figure 2.70). There might be a few lines of text you need to find room for. Often, just changing the space between paragraphs of body text is not the complete solution. Look before and after your closure as there might be empty paragraphs used to create space in the document. You can easily delete one of the blank paragraphs above or below the closure to compress the space. Using the right-pointing arrow, select any of the ¶ marks and press the **Delete** key.

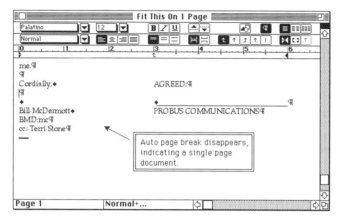

Figure 2.71

When your document repaginates itself, if you have eliminated enough space, the dotted lines indicating a page break should disappear altogether (Figure 2.71).

Conclusion

There are several methods one can use to force a letter to fit on a single page. You can employ various combinations of the methods described above to successfully achieve the results you need. However, in the long run, it all comes down to what works best for you and how you have initially entered text in your document. As you become more familiar with these techniques, you'll be able to make formatting decisions more easily, rapidly implement changes to your documents, and understand the implications of those changes to your work.

How to Format a Two-Page Letter for Preprinted Letterhead Stationery

You or your company has invested in printed letterhead stationery that you will want to use with your printer when generating correspondence. Typically, printed letterhead is used for the first page of the letter; a blank page of the same paper stock or one with a special second-page graphic is used for all subsequent pages.

In what follows, you'll execute a series of steps to set up a document which you can use to quickly and easily generate letters on your printed letterhead stationery.

Measuring for Margins

STEP ONE

The first order of business, however, is to locate a ruler so that you can measure where to set your margins from the edge of the page.

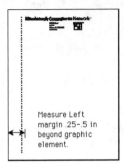

Figure 3.1

Begin by measuring the Left and Right margins. Some stationery may have a special graphic or list of names on the Left margin that you need to accommodate. You should allow 0.25–0.5 inch breathing space from the graphic before your text begins to print (Figure 3.1).

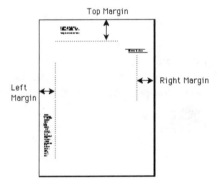

Figure 3.2

With other kinds of stationery, there might be a graphic on the right side that body text should not extend beyond (Figure 3.2). Remember, you are placing the 0 point of the ruler at the right edge of the paper and taking your measurement from there.

If you have no special graphics you need to account for, typical Left and Right margins for a letter can be either 1 inch or 1.25 inches, depending on how much space you want on the page. You should try not to make your margins less than 0.5 inch, as there are margin limitations set by some printers.

Figure 3.3

The Bottom margin is typically 1 inch from the lower edge of the page; however, your stationery might have printed text for an address, phone, and fax number, or other pertinent information (Figure 3.3). Just make sure you have included at least 0.25 inch of space above the printed text in your bottom margin measurement.

Figure 3.4

Finally, measure the distance from the top edge of your page, allowing approximately 0.5 inch of space underneath the printed text for where your letter will begin (Figure 3.4).

The top margin measurement is the most important one. Once you have this measurement, subtract 0.5 inch from it. You'll be adjusting the first page "header" using this number. (For the example in Figure 3.4, the measurement to remember would be 2.75 – 0.5 = 2.25 inches.)

Setting Up the Document Margins

STEP TWO

Go to the **Format** menu and choose **Document**. The Left margin edit bar
will be highlighted. Fill in the Left margin measurement you took. After the
number you can type **in** for inches; however, since the default settings in
Word 5.0 are for inches, this is not really necessary.

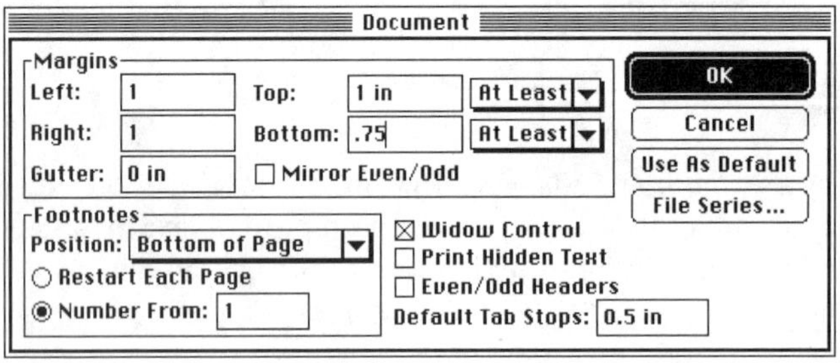

```
┌══════════════════════ Document ══════════════════════┐
│  ┌─Margins─────────────────────────────┐  ┌────────────┐ │
│  │ Left:  │1│    Top:    │1 in│  │At Least│▼│ │    OK      │ │
│  │ Right: │1│    Bottom: │.75│  │At Least│▼│ │   Cancel   │ │
│  │ Gutter:│0 in│  ☐ Mirror Even/Odd         │Use As Default│ │
│  └─────────────────────────────────────┘  │ File Series...│ │
│  ┌─Footnotes──────────────────┐  ⊠ Widow Control       │
│  │ Position: │Bottom of Page│▼│  ☐ Print Hidden Text   │
│  │ ○ Restart Each Page        │  ☐ Even/Odd Headers     │
│  │ ◉ Number From: │1│         │  Default Tab Stops: │0.5 in│ │
│  └────────────────────────────┘                        │
└═══════════════════════════════════════════════════════┘
```

Figure 3.5

Press the **Tab** key once to move into the Right margin edit bar. Enter the
correct measurement there. Press **Tab** once more. The Top margin should
have **1 in** entered. Do not change this, unless you have preprinted second-
page stationery with a graphic near the top edge of the page that you must
accommodate. If so, type in the measurement you have taken for the
second page top margin.

Press **Tab** again to move to the Bottom margin edit bar and enter the correct measurement there. Click on the **OK** button when you are through
(Figure 3.5).

Allowing Space for Preprinted Text Using a Header

STEP THREE

This next step involves setting up your document to alter the space on
the first page, allowing for the printed letterhead information. Go to the
Format menu and choose **Section**.

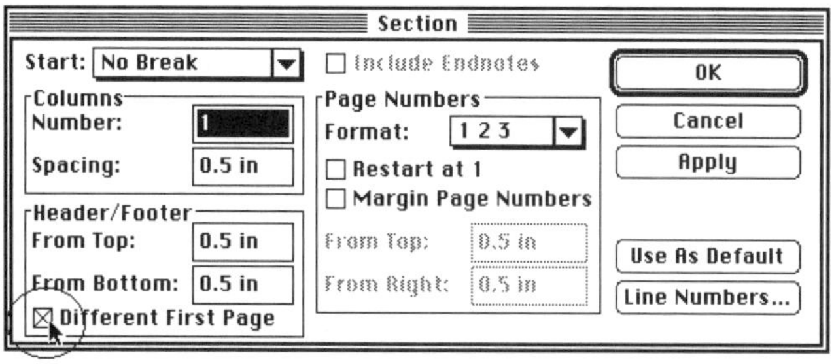

Figure 3.6

Simply click next to **Different First Page** (Figure 3.6) so that there is an X placed in the box. Also, note the information above this box. It indicates that the actual information contained in the header will be positioned 0.5 inch from the edge of the page.

In order to allow space for the preprinted letterhead information on the first page, the data in the first header itself will consist of blank space. Click the **OK** button when you are done.

Go to the **View** menu and choose **First Header**. During the preceding steps, you took a measurement for the top margin and subtracted 0.5 inch. Take whatever the resulting measurement was (in inches) and multiply it by 72. You are converting inches to points, as there are 72 points per inch. Here's a simple table that might help you.

Inches	Points
0.5	36
0.625 (5/8)	45
0.75	54
0.875 (7/8)	63
1	72
1.125 (1 1/8)	81
1.25	90
1.375 (1 3/8)	99
1.5	108
1.625 (1 5/8)	117

continues

Inches	Points
1.75	126
1.875 (1 7/8)	135
2	144
2.125 (2 1/8)	153
2.25	162

While keeping the first header window open, you make the space adjust-ment for the printed letterhead. Go to the **Format** menu and choose **Paragraph**.

When the Paragraph dialog box appears, press the **Tab** key twice so that the edit bar next to the word **Auto** is highlighted. Or, you can simply use the pointer to click next to the word Auto.

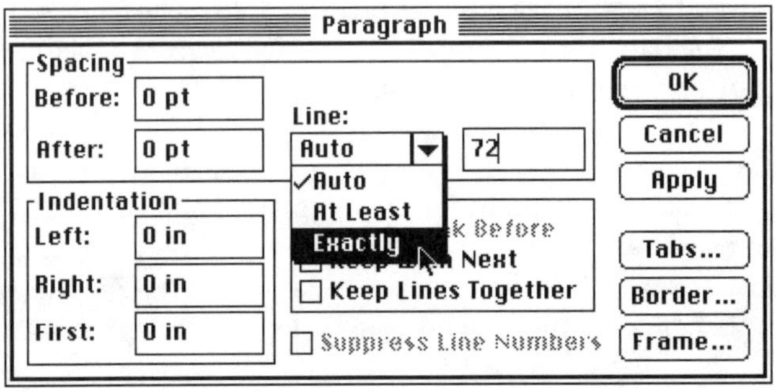

Figure 3.7

Enter the number of points of space that you calculated above. Then use the pointer to choose **Exactly** from the **Line** space drop-down list (Figure 3.7). Click the **OK** button.

Click the **Zoom** box for the header in the upper right hand corner so that you can see the results of the **paragraph** format you just applied.

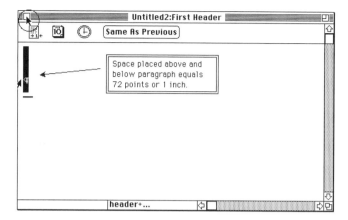

Figure 3.8

Using the right-pointing arrow, select the paragraph mark. As shown in Figure 3.8, there is space applied above and below the paragraph—space that allows for the printed information on your letterhead stationery. Click in the **Close** box on the upper left to return to your document.

Testing the Results

STEP FOUR

As a final test before you save this document as stationery, switch to **Page Layout** view by choosing **Page Layout** from the **View** menu .

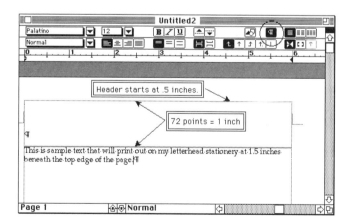

Figure 3.9

Make sure the flashing insertion point is in the area below the header and that the Show ¶ icon is selected in the Ribbon. Type a line or two of text as a sample to be printed out on a sheet of your printed letterhead stationery (Figure 3.9). Insert the paper in your printer. Go to the **File** menu, choose **Print**, and print your document.

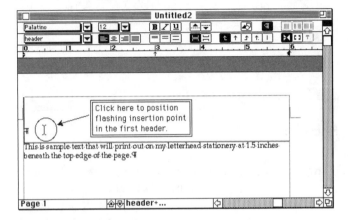

Figure 3.10

When you have examined the printed results and if the spacing is not satisfactory, place the I-beam in the header area of the document and click once to position the flashing insertion point (Figure 3.10).

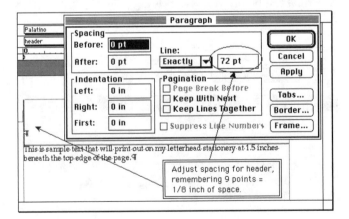

Figure 3.11

Go to the **Format** menu and choose **Paragraph**. Depending on whether the text is too high or too low, you will adjust the number for the **Line** edit bar to be larger or smaller (Figure 3.11). Remember, each 1/8 of an inch is equal to 9 points of space. This should help you fine-tune the spacing for the first page of your document. When you are satisfied, go to the **View** menu and choose **Normal**. Select your sample text and delete it.

Setting Up an Automatic Date

STEP FIVE

Microsoft Word has a function that will automatically insert the current date from your Macintosh control panel into your document. Not only does this save time, it takes the guess work out of determining what today's date actually is.

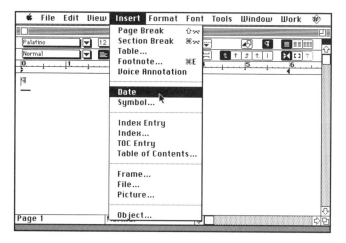

Figure 3.12

Place the date at the beginning of your document, right where the flashing insertion point should currently be located. Go to the **Insert** menu and choose **Date** (Figure 3.12).

Press the **Return** key a few times to give some space before you will actually enter the addressee information for a letter.

> **NOTE:** *The Insert Date function inserts the date for when you actually print out your letter. The use of the automatic date function may cause problems if you want to review the letter at some point in the future and refer to the date the letter was actually executed. Whenever a document containing the Insert Date entry is opened, the date will be updated to the current date set by the control panel of your computer. You may decide not to use the automatic date in your correspondence for this reason.*

Saving a Stationery Document

STEP SIX

Go to the **File** menu and choose **Save**.

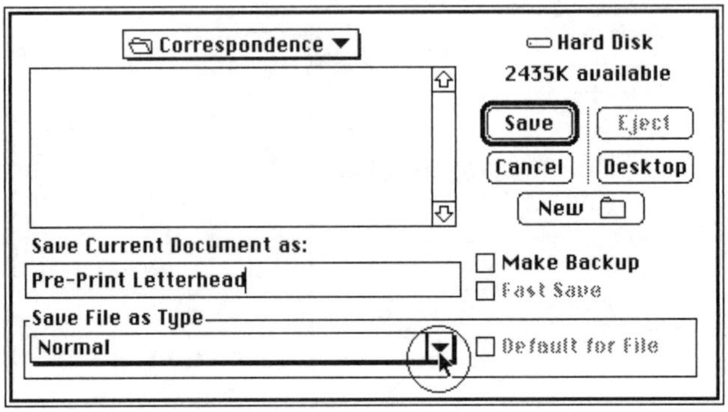

Figure 3.13

Name your document Preprint Letterhead (or whatever name you choose). Before you click on the Save button, there is one more step necessary. Position the mouse over the downward arrow as shown in Figure 3.13 and press.

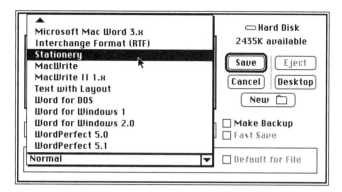

Figure 3.14

A list of file format types will pop up. Select the **Stationery** format (Figure 3.14) and release the mouse. Now you can click on the **Save** button. Don't be alarmed, however, that when you return to your document window the title bar still displays "Untitled." You never work with the original document when you are working with stationery documents.

Microsoft Word 5.0 has a special format called Stationery, which you just selected in the previous step. What exactly is a Stationery document? It's a type of document that serves as a template for the creation of other documents. When you save a document in a stationery format, it protects the original, master document. Each time you open a Stationery document, you are actually opening a copy of the stationery to work with. As you see, it's like having a fresh sheet of preformatted paper (letterhead stationery!) each time you want to write a letter.

You may be saying, "But what if I want to make changes to my Letterhead document?" You can and you will. In fact, you're going to make some more changes and save those changes once you've formatted the second page of the letterhead document.

Further Steps

As you may know, for letters printed out on more than a single page you'll use either plain stock paper or specially printed second-page stationery. See "Creating a Header" under the section titled "Formatting Your Letterhead for Multi-Page Letters" in Chapter 1.

You might also want to change the position where the date appears in your letterhead document. See Step 3 under the section, "Automating the Date of Your Correspondence" in Chapter 1 as well as the section "Moving the Position of the Date and Closure" in Chapter 2.

If you have not read Chapter 2 "How to Use Your Letterhead Document to Write a Letter," you will find it useful for working with the preprinted letterhead template. All the hints, solutions, and procedures for executing a letter are covered in depth within the chapter.

C H A P T E R

How to Make Lists of Items

When writing letters, memos, proposals, or even just a simple reminder, you might want to enter information in a list. You might also want to offset this list from the rest of the text in your document. In this chapter, you'll learn how to create different kinds of lists, alphabetize, sort, and/or number your lists as well as explore tips and shortcuts for easier listmaking in the future.

One-Line Item Lists

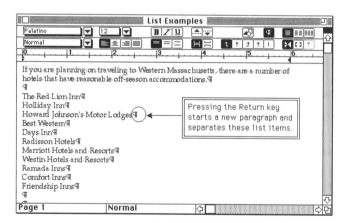

Figure 4.1

You've probably realized by now that in order to start a new line, you only need to press the **Return** key. A one-line item in a list, as shown in Figure 4.1, would be separated from the other items by a paragraph mark.

However, the next question might be, "How would you move this list over so it's not butting up against the left side of the page?" If you are used to a typewriter, you would invariably resort to the "spacebar method." Just tap 10 spaces (or 5, or whatever), and then enter your text. Press **Return**. Tap 10 spaces. Type. **Return**. Tap 10 spaces. . . .

This method not only tries your patience but also seems a waste of your ability to count. With word processing, there is a much easier way to accomplish this task, a way that gives you greater flexibility, takes very little time, and successfully lines up the text where you would expect it to print.

Whether you've tried it or not, the spacebar is notorious for not yielding reliable results when aligning proportionately spaced fonts on a computer. However, if you happen to have chosen Courier or Monaco (monospaced fonts) for your document production, then the spacebar method might have met your expectations.

In order to explore these techniques for working with lists, you can enter the text shown in the example (Figure 4.1) in a new document or open a document where you've already created your own list.

Using the right-pointing arrow in the **Selection Bar**, press and drag to select the list of items. Make sure the **Left-aligned icon** in the Ruler is highlighted (Figure 4.2). If it is not, click on it once.

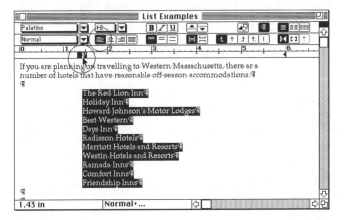

Figure 4.2

Move the pointer into the Ruler. You're going to move the left indent marker. Though the left indent marker is divided into two separate triangles, you need to focus on moving the lower triangle. Carefully place the very tip of the pointer over the lower triangle, then press and drag the indent marker to wherever it is that you want your list to be located—probably somewhere between the 1- and 2-inch mark (Figure 4.2). When you're satisfied with the placement, release the mouse button. If you'd like to make adjustments, keep your text selected (or if it's been deselected, reselect the list) and move the indent marker to where you want it.

Lists of More than One Item on a Line

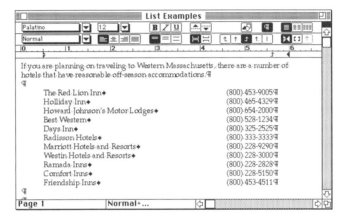

Figure 4.3

Aligning single items in a list has a fairly straightforward solution when using the indent marker as described above. However, what if you want to list another piece of information next to an item and align it as shown in Figure 4.3? The solution for this kind of a list involves the use of the Tab mark.

Creating a New List

If you're starting out fresh—before you've entered any data—you can set up formatting for your entire list that will carry forward as you press the **Return** key for a new line item.

STEP ONE

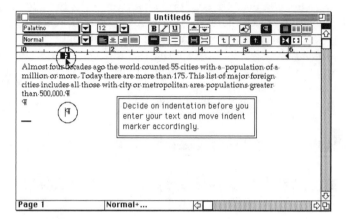

Figure 4.4

First, you should decide on whether or not you want the first item in the list to be indented from the rest of your text. If you do, move the left indent in the Ruler to the right and into position (Figure 4.4). You can always adjust the amount of indenting once you've finished.

STEP TWO

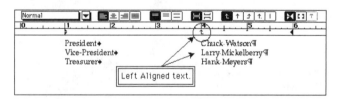

Figure 4.5

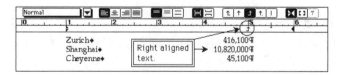

Figure 4.6

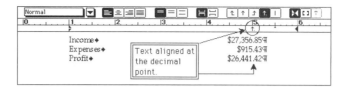

Figure 4.7

Next, you need to decide if you want the second item on each line of your list to align on the left side (Figure 4.5), or on the right (Figure 4.6), or at the decimal point (Figure 4.7). Each one of these decisions involves the use of a different kind of Tab mark.

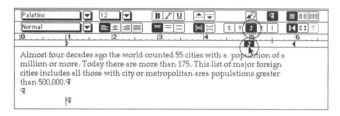

Figure 4.8

When you've decided which Tab mark best suits the kind of information you are listing, click on the correct tab icon in the Ruler. Next, click at the spot on the Ruler where you think your text will align correctly (Figure 4.8). You can always make adjustments later.

STEP THREE

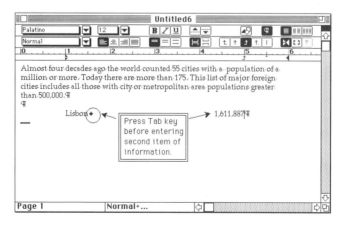

Figure 4.9

Enter the first item on your list. Press the **Tab** key and enter the second piece of information (Figure 4.9).

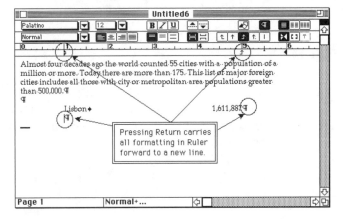

Figure 4.10

When you're finished with that item, press the **Return** key for a new line. The formatting carries over to the new line (Figure 4.10). Continue to enter your text, pressing the **Tab** and **Return** keys when appropriate.

Making Adjustments

Since you might want any adjustments you make to affect all the text in your list, first select the entire list using the right-pointing arrow in the Selection Bar.

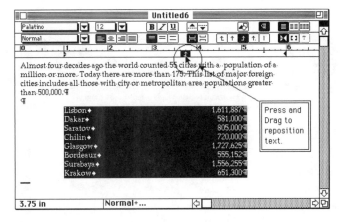

Figure 4.11

Once your text is selected, move the pointer into the Ruler and press and drag either the lower triangle of the left indent marker and/or the Tab mark to make your adjustments (Figure 4.11). When you release the mouse button, the text will reposition itself so that you can then examine the results of the readjustment.

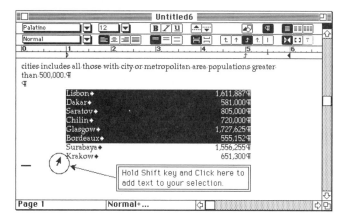

Figure 4.12

Just remember that the adjustments affect only the text that is selected. If, by mistake, you should leave some text out of the selection process, hold the **Shift** key down and click beside the line(s) you left out (Figure 4.12). They will then be added to your selection, and you can continue with your readjustment process.

Returning to the Nonlist Format

You've finished entering your list. As you press the **Return** key, you realize that you don't want the list formatting to carry forward. You want to get back to writing the main body of your text. You might be a little perplexed in how to return to your original text format. There are a couple of ways you can do so.

Method 1: Remove Formats

The most obvious method is to backtrack and remove the formats you applied to your list. For the list in the example, this involves two steps.

STEP ONE

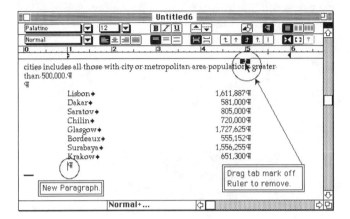

Figure 4.13

First, you need to remove the Tab mark from the Ruler. To do this, position the pointer in the Ruler and drag the Tab mark down beneath the Ruler (Figure 4.13). Once the tab is beneath the Ruler, let go of the mouse button. It's sort of like throwing the Tab mark into the Trash, only there's no trash can.

STEP TWO

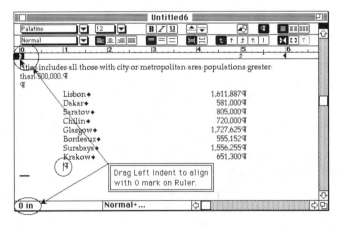

Figure 4.14

Next, position the pointer over the lower triangle of the left indent marker. Press and drag it to the left so that the back of the indent mark aligns with the 0 point on the Ruler. Look carefully at Figure 4.14 to see the correct positioning. The lower left status box in your window will also display 0 in.

You might want to press the **Return** key to give yourself some space between your list and the text you're about to enter, or you can simply click on the Open Space icon in the Ruler.

Method 2: Reapply Normal Format

Now, this method is going to prepare you for some of the more advanced techniques yet to come. You may have observed the word "Normal" displayed at the bottom of the document window, just to the right of the Page number status box. Although it doesn't seem to do much, you might also have noticed that, when you added a Tab mark to the Ruler or moved the indent mark, Normal had a +... appended to it.

"Normal" is a collection of paragraph settings, font, and character settings better known as a "Style." Whenever you move the indent marker or add a tab to the ruler, you add a few variations to the Normal style that are not part of its regular definition. Microsoft Word lets you know about these changes to the Normal format by subtly placing the +... at the bottom of the document window.

In order to return to Normal formatting (which is what you had in mind all along), you can execute the following two steps.

STEP ONE

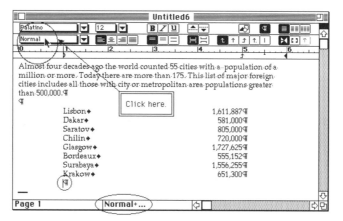

Figure 4.15

Move the pointer into the Ruler and click in the area known as the Style Selection box, in the upper left corner (Figure 4.15). The word Normal will become highlighted. Press the **Return** key.

STEP TWO

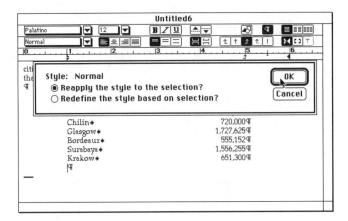

Figure 4.16

A dialog box will appear asking if you want to "Reapply the style to the selection." Indeed you do, so you can either click on the **OK** button, or press the **Return** key (Figure 4.16).

When you look at the Ruler, the Tab mark is gone, the left indent mark has returned to the 0 position, and the word Normal no longer has the +... following it.

This is a simple solution that you can use anytime you want to return to your "Normal" text entry mode after making adjustments to the Ruler for indents, tabs, or any other formatting. Simply reapply the Normal style.

Adding More Information to an Existing List

What if you have gone back to your regular (or Normal) text entry and decide you want to return to your list and enter more items? You'll need to insert a new paragraph, but depending on where you place the flashing insertion point, you will get different results.

Method 1: Insert New Paragraph Before Text

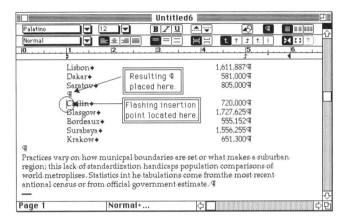

Figure 4.17

If the flashing insertion point is positioned at the beginning of a paragraph, pressing **Return** will place a new paragraph above the paragraph the insertion point is located in (Figure 4.17).

Before you can enter text into the new paragraph, you will need to reposition the flashing insertion point. Either click next to the blank paragraph or press the **Up arrow** on your keyboard and begin entering text.

Method 2: Insert New Paragraph After Text

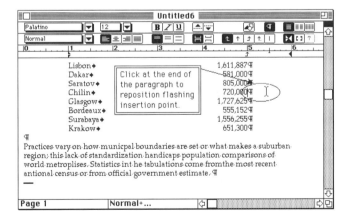

Figure 4.18

When the flashing insertion point is located at the end of a paragraph within the list (Figure 4.18), pressing **Return** will insert a new paragraph and carry the insertion point forward. You can then enter your text immediately.

Adding Another Column to an Existing List

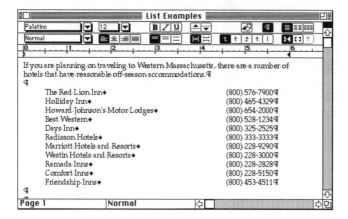

Figure 4.19

What if you've already created a list and you decide you want to add additional information for each item on the list (Figure 4.19)? This can be accomplished in a few short steps.

STEP ONE

Using the right-pointing arrow in the Selection Bar, press and drag to select all the text in your list.

STEP TWO

Decide which kind of Tab mark will best suit the information you are entering (see Figures 4.5 to 4.7) and click on the appropriate Tab mark icon in the Ruler to select it. Using the pointer, click in the Ruler to position the Tab mark (Figure 4.20). You can always reposition the Tab mark (remember to select all the text in your list first!) if you need to make any adjustments or fine tuning.

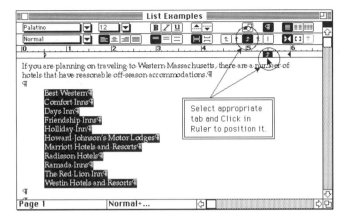

Figure 4.20

STEP THREE

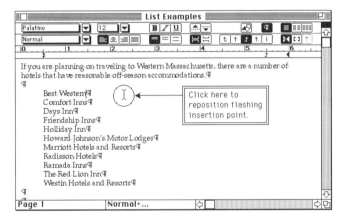

Figure 4.21

To begin entering text, click at the end of the first item in the list to posi-tion the flashing insertion point (Figure 4.21).

STEP FOUR

Press the **Tab** key and then enter your text (Figure 4.22). To continue adding text to each item on the list, you can press the **Down arrow** on your key-board to move the flashing insertion point directly to the end of the next line. Press the **Tab** key and enter text. Then press the **Down arrow**, press **Tab**, and repeat the text entry process.

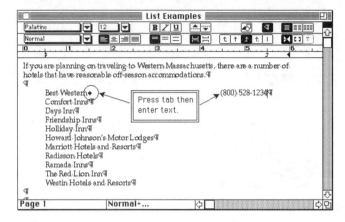

Figure 4.22

Connecting List Items with Guiding Dots

```
┌─────────────────────── List Examples ────────────────────┐
│ Palatino      ▼  12  ▼    B I U   ▲▼    ♫  ¶   ▤ ▤▤ ▤▤▤  │
│ Normal        ▼  ▤ ▤ ▤ ▤   ▤ ▤ ▤   ▤ ▤   ↑ ↑ ↑ ↑ I   ▶◀ ⬚ ↑ │
│ 0    1    2    3    4    5    ↑    6 │
│                                                           │
│  The Red Lion Inn...................................(800) 576-7900│
│  Holliday Inn.......................................(800) 465-4329│
│  Howard Johnson's Motor Lodges......................(800) 654-2000│
│  Best Western.......................................(800) 528-1234│
│  Days Inn...........................................(800) 325-2525│
│  Radisson Hotels....................................(800) 333-3333│
│  Marriott Hotels and Resorts........................(800) 228-9290│
│  Westin Hotels and Resorts..........................(800) 228-3000│
│  Ramada Inns........................................(800) 228-2828│
│  Comfort Inns.......................................(800) 228-5150│
│  Friendship Inns....................................(800) 453-4511│
│                                                           │
│  ──                                                       │
│ Page 1          Normal+...                                │
└───────────────────────────────────────────────────────────┘
```

Figure 4.23

Though "connecting list items with guiding dots" may not be a clear technical term for what is illustrated in Figure 4.23, hopefully the figure will help you to quickly understand the implied formatting you might want to apply to a list. The correct terminology in word processing for this feature is "leader tabs."

Once you've created a list using Tab markers placed in the Ruler, you can apply a special formatting that will place dots between the left and right line items within your list. Applying these dots is a simple three-step process.

STEP ONE

First, using the right-pointing arrow in the Selection Bar, press and drag to select all the text in your list.

STEP TWO

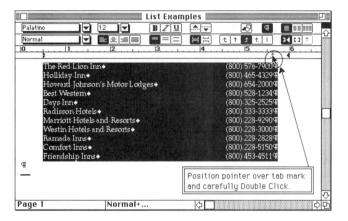

Figure 4.24

Once the text has been selected, place the tip of your pointer directly over the top of the Tab mark in the Ruler (Figure 4.24). Carefully click two times in a row (double-click), making sure you do not move the mouse slightly in any direction, as this might inadvertently reposition your Tab mark.

STEP THREE

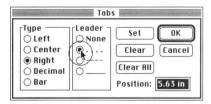

Figure 4.25

Double-clicking a Tab mark in the Ruler causes a Tabs dialog box to appear. In the section marker "Leader," click on the radio button next to the dotted format (Figure 4.25) or choose any of the other formats if they are more appealing. Click on the **OK** button.

Click anywhere in your document to deselect the highlighted text, or keep the text selected for the following alphabetizing procedure.

Alphabetizing or Sorting Lists

In order to reorder your list alphabetically or sort it numerically from highest to lowest or vice versa, you will use the Sort feature of Microsoft Word. If you are sorting lists with more than one column, you might prefer to sort the list according to the information contained in either one of the columns. This first method shows you how to sort a list based on the first item (or column) in the list; the second method shows you a technique for sorting on another column within a multi-column list.

Single-Column Lists or Items in First Column

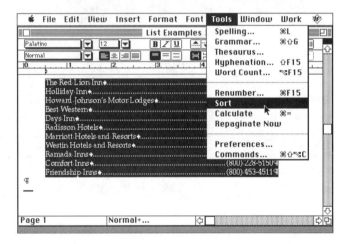

Figure 4.26

Using the right-pointing arrow in the Selection Bar, press and drag to select the text in your list. Go to the **Tools** menu and choose **Sort** (Figure 4.26). When you release the mouse button, your text will have been listed in ascending order—that is, from the lowest letter or number to the highest.

When alphabetizing text, Microsoft Word's Sort function looks at the first character of each paragraph (or line item in a list) and alphabetizes according to this first character. If you have several columns, using this method will always sort your text by the items listed in the first column on the left.

> **NOTE:** *To sort a list in descending order—that is, from the highest letter or number to the lowest—you must first press the Shift key on your keyboard before you move the pointer into the Tools menu. When you hold down the Shift key, the Tools menu will display the Sort Descending function.*
>
> *If Sort Descending does not appear in the Tools menu, you need to let go of the mouse and press the Shift key again before once more choosing from the Tools menu.*

Multi-Column Lists

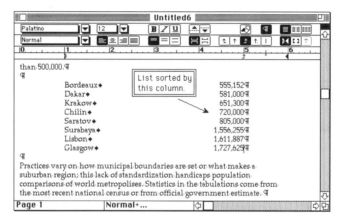

Figure 4.27

If you want to sort your list by the items listed in the first column, use the method described above. The following method is for sorting a list by any column other than the first column (Figure 4.27).

To select the specific items in the column you want sorted, you are going to use a "vertical text selection" technique. Hold down the **Option** key on your keyboard (it's located two keys to the left of the spacebar, next to the Command key). Place the I-beam to the left of the first item in the second (or third, etc.) column in your list. It is important that you start the selection of the column by placing the I-beam slightly to the left of the first item.

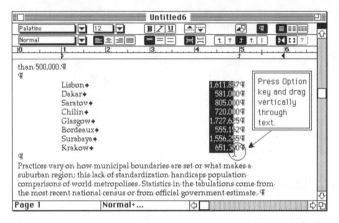

Figure 4.28

Keeping the Option key held down, press and drag down and to the right, highlighting the column (Figure 4.28). Release the Option key when you have finished selecting the column text.

Go to the **Tools** menu and choose **Sort**. If you want to sort the column in descending order, hold down the **Shift** key before choosing **Sort Descending** from the **Tools** menu.

Bulleted Paragraphs

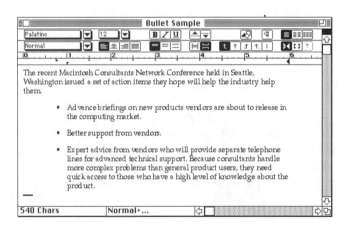

Figure 4.29

When you are listing a series of statements, you can use bullets to call attention to each item in the list. Bullets can also precede entire paragraphs of text that are offset, or indented, from normal body text (Figure 4.29).

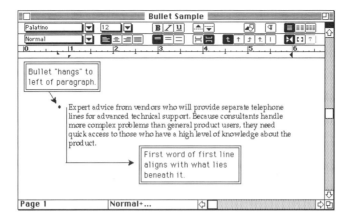

Figure 4.30

The most important concept you need to understand when formatting bullets is that bullets "hang" to the left of the paragraphs they are placed beside. The first word of text immediately following a bullet is vertically aligned to the paragraph indented text that appears beneath the first line (Figure 4.30).

When formatting a list of bulleted paragraphs, you will use the first line indent marker in conjunction with the left indent marker. Setting this format requires two steps.

Setting the Format

STEP ONE

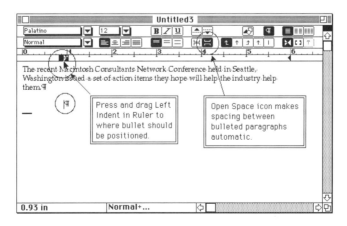

Figure 4.31

Place the pointer over the lower triangle of the left indent marker in the Ruler. Press and drag it to the location where you want the bullet to appear (Figure 4.31). You might also want to apply space before the paragraph by clicking on the Open Space icon in the Ruler.

STEP TWO

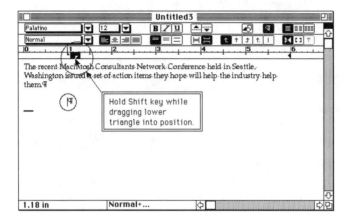

Figure 4.32

Press the **Shift** key on the keyboard and hold it down while you use the pointer to move the lower triangle further to the right (Figure 4.32). You are creating the "hanging" space for the bullet. Generally 0.25 inch of space, or slightly less, between the lower triangle (the left indent) and the upper triangle (the first-line indent) is sufficient for a bullet.

Producing the Bullet

To produce the bullet, press and hold the **Option** key with a finger on your left hand while typing the number **8** on your keyboard with your right hand (Figure 4.33). Let go of the Option key. Press the **Tab** key once.

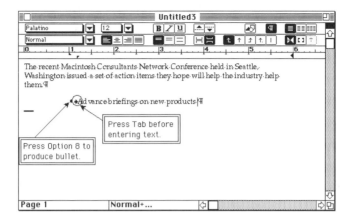

Figure 4.33

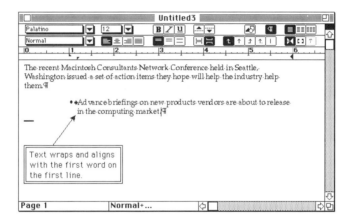

Figure 4.34

As you continue to enter your text, it will automatically wrap to the next line and align itself with the first word in the first line of your paragraph (Figure 4.34).

You might be confused as to why you would press the Tab key and why you would need to make these text alignments. The concept of the bullet and the "hanging indent"—as this formatting is properly named—are not easy to comprehend at first.

Even though there is no Tab mark in the Ruler, the lower triangle of the left indent acts as a Tab mark. This use of the left indent aligns the first word of your paragraph with the body of text that wraps and flows to second and subsequent lines of your paragraph.

Even if the text following the bullet is only a few words, be sure you press the **Tab** key before typing. If you use the spacebar to create the space between the bullet and text that follows it, text may not print out with the correct alignment.

Returning to Normal Text Entry

When you have finished creating your bullets, you will undoubtedly want to go back to entering text in the "normal" way. See the earlier section on "Returning to the Nonlist Format" for further instructions.

Numbering of Listed Items

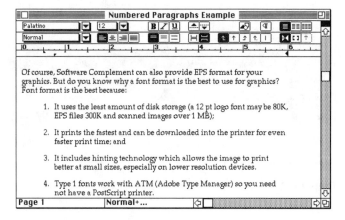

Figure 4.35

Rather than using bullets to make a series of statements, you might prefer, or need, to number your paragraphs (Figure 4.35). In this section, you'll learn there is an automatic numbering feature in Word that makes paragraph numbering a snap.

When numbering paragraphs, you will use the same formatting technique described in the section on bulleted paragraphs, which immediately precedes this section. In general, numbered paragraphs are formatted so the number "hangs" to the left of the paragraph text (Figure 4.35).

There are three different approaches for executing paragraph numbering:

1. **Post-Text-Entry:** Regular text paragraphs you have already typed that require numbering and formatting.

2. **Pre-Text-Entry:** Text you are about to enter into your document that needs to be numbered.

3. **Modified-Text-Entry:** Bulleted text you want changed to numbered paragraphs.

Post-Text-Entry

STEP ONE

Using the right-pointing arrow in the Selection Bar, press and drag to select the paragraphs in your list.

STEP TWO

Go to the **Tools** menu and choose **Renumber**.

STEP THREE

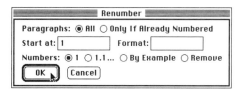

Figure 4.36

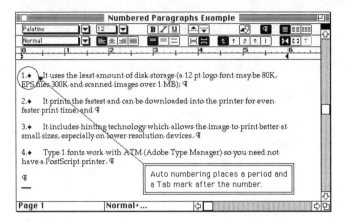

Figure 4.37

If you just click the **OK** button (Figure 4.36), your paragraphs will be auto-matically numbered as shown in Figure 4.37. However, if you want to use a parenthesis after the number—rather than a period—you need to execute one more step before clicking the **OK** button in the **Renumber** dialog box.

STEP FOUR

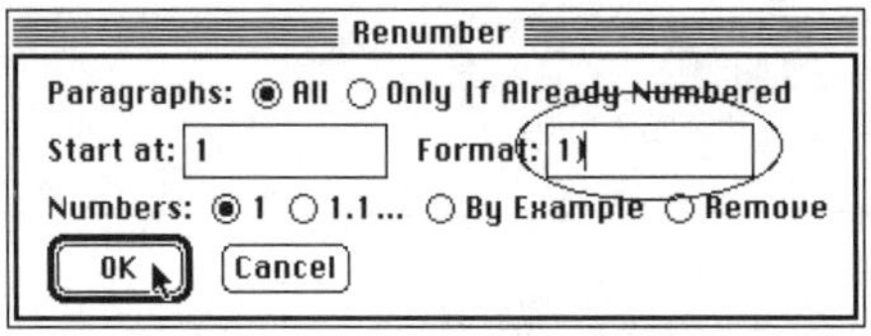

Figure 4.38

Click in the Format edit bar. Type the number **1**, followed by a right parenthesis (Figure 4.38). Click the **OK** button.

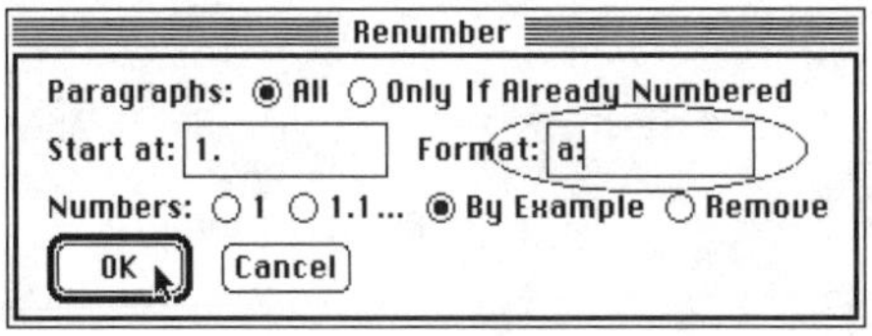

Figure 4.39

You can also letter your paragraphs by using the Format edit bar in the Renumber dialog box (Figure 4.39). Here are some of the formats you can try (you can also substitute the number 1 for the letter A):

A

A)

(A)

A:

a

a)

(a)

a:

Notice in Figure 4.37 that there is a Tab mark placed after the number and before the first word of your paragraph. Because Microsoft Word has default tab stops every 0.5 inch, the first word has been moved to the 0.5 inch position. From what you might have learned in the sections prior to this one, you might say the paragraph is demanding to be formatted with a hanging indent!

STEP FIVE

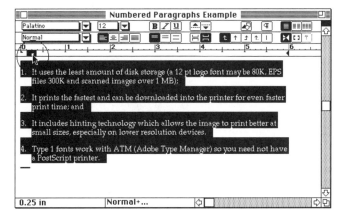

Figure 4.40

Make sure the numbered paragraphs are still selected, and if not, select them. Hold down the **Shift** key. Position the pointer over the lower triangle of the left indent and press and drag it to the 0.25-inch mark. When you release the mouse button, the text should realign itself. If the result does not look like the example in Figure 4.40, hold down the **Shift** key and reposition the lower triangle of the left indent a little further to the right.

You might want to indent all the paragraphs in your selection to offset them from the main body of your letter. Make sure the numbered paragraphs are still selected, and if not, select them. Position the pointer over the lower triangle of the left indent and press and drag them into the desired position. Do *not* hold the Shift key for this step. Note that the lower triangle and the upper triangle are "married" and therefore retain their relative positions for the hanging indent format when you move them in this manner.

Pre-Text-Entry

This method prepares you to insert your own numbering or lettering system as you enter your text. The automatic numbering feature described in the section preceding this (Post-Text-Entry) only applies to text that has *already* been entered.

This method is presented separately so that you can begin to acquire the habit of setting formats prior to text entry so as to avoid potential problems and frustrations.

First, decide whether or not you want the numbers (or letters) that precede the paragraph text in your list to be indented from the left margin of your letter. If you do, you will need to complete the second formatting step below, before you start to enter your text.

STEP ONE

To allow space for the number (or letter) and any characters that may follow it (a period or right parenthesis), you will need to reposition the lower triangle of the left indent marker accordingly. Hold down the **Shift** key and press and drag the lower triangle of the left indent marker to the 0.25- inch mark.

STEP TWO

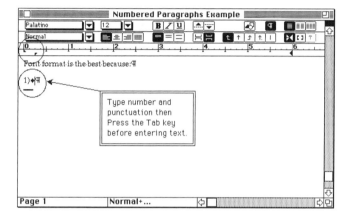

Figure 4.41

When you enter your list of items, type the number (or letter) followed by the punctuation mark of your choice (you might also wish to use no punctuation). Press the **Tab** key before entering the text of your paragraph (Figure 4.41).

STEP THREE

Press the **Return** key when you are ready to enter the next paragraph in your list. Remember to press the **Tab** key to offset or "hang" the number to the left of your list item.

STEP FOUR

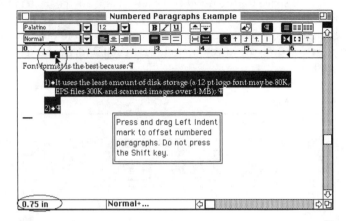

Figure 4.42

To indent your numbered paragraph items, first select the text you have entered. Position the pointer over the lower triangle of the left indent marker and press and drag it to the right into the desired position (Figure 4.42). Do *not* hold down the Shift key for this step.

Modified-Text-Entry

You may have a bulleted list you decide you would rather have numbered (or lettered). In the first step, you will remove the bullets; in the second, you will add numbering.

STEP ONE

You're going to use the vertical text selection technique to "grab" the bullets. Because vertical text selection is one of the handiest techniques you'll use in word processing, you'll want to remember this technique for other text editing circumstances.

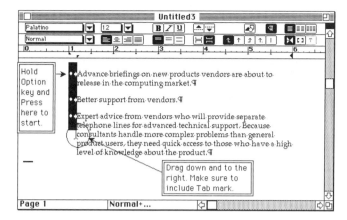

Figure 4.43

During these steps, make sure the **Show ¶** button is selected in the Ribbon. Hold down the **Option** key (located two keys to the left of the spacebar). Position the I-beam at the top of the list and to the left of the first bullet. Press and drag down and to the right, making sure that you include the Tab mark in your selection process (Figure 4.43).

STEP TWO

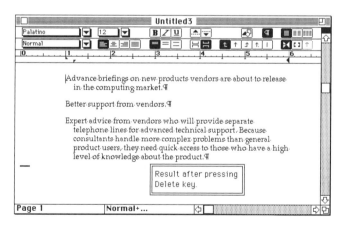

Figure 4.44

Press the **Delete** key to remove the bullets and Tab marks (Figure 4.44).

STEP THREE

Using the right-pointing arrow in the Selection Bar, press and drag to select the contents of your list. Go to the **Tools** menu and choose **Renumber**.

STEP FOUR

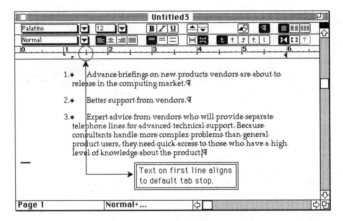

Figure 4.45

To number the list with a period following the number, simply click the **OK** button. If you want to format the list for lettering or some other punctuation mark, refer the section on numbering formats described earlier in the first method, "Post-Text-Entry."

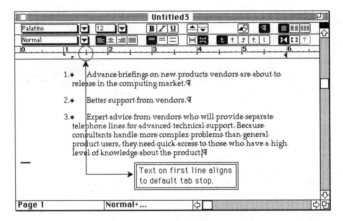

Figure 4.46

Because the amount of space required for a bullet is less than what's needed for a number and a period, the text you've selected for numbering may have shifted, as shown in Figure 4.46. The text in the first line jumped to the nearest default tab stop and chose this default as its point of alignment. You need to make a one-step adjustment to your hanging indent formatting.

STEP FIVE

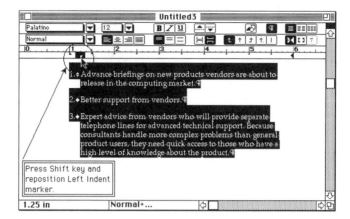

Figure 4.47

Keeping the text selected (if it became deselected, reselect it), hold down the **Shift** key. Move the pointer over the lower triangle of the left indent marker and move it further to the right. Because this may only be a slight 1/16-inch adjustment, move the left indent in small increments. When you release the mouse button, the text will move back into position (Figure 4.47).

Reordering Tips

There are methods other than cut and paste which you should be aware of that will make the reordering of your lists faster. A few tips for you to try out follow.

One-Line Items

For moving one-line items, first select the item by clicking with the right-pointing arrow in the Selection Bar.

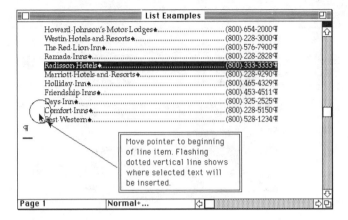

Figure 4.48

Move the pointer inside the highlighted text. The I-beam should turn into a left-pointing arrow. Press the mouse button down and drag the pointer so that it is at the beginning of the paragraph you want to appear beneath the text you have highlighted (Figure 4.48). Release the mouse button. Text is always inserted above and to the left of the flashing insertion point.

This technique uses the drag-and-drop text editing capabilities of Microsoft Word 5.0.

Bulleted Text

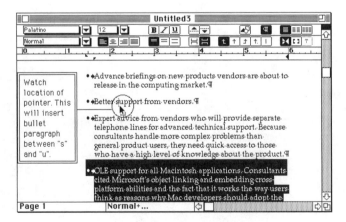

Figure 4.49

When moving bulleted text, select the entire paragraph or list item. Position the pointer inside the selected paragraph; then press and drag the pointer to where you want the paragraph to be repositioned. Be attentive to the location of the dotted vertical line, as the vertical line indicates where the paragraph will be placed. You might end up moving your text to a place you don't intend to (Figure 4.49).

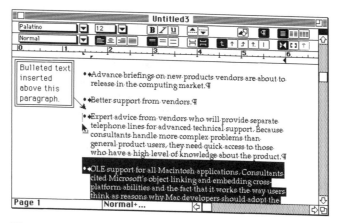

Figure 4.50

When positioning the flashing dotted vertical line, always place it to the left of the bullet. The selected paragraph will be inserted directly above and to the left of the dotted vertical line (Figure 4.50).

Numbered or Lettered Lists

When working with numbered or lettered list items, you can move the text as explained above, or you can change the numbering (or lettering) and resort (or realphabetize) the list.

Renumbering

If you have already moved numbered or lettered text and want to renumber your list to accurately reflect the new order, begin by selecting the text in your list. Then go to the **Tools** menu and choose **Renumber** (Figure 4.51).

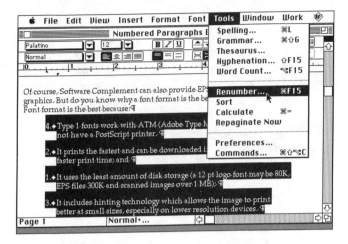

Figure 4.51

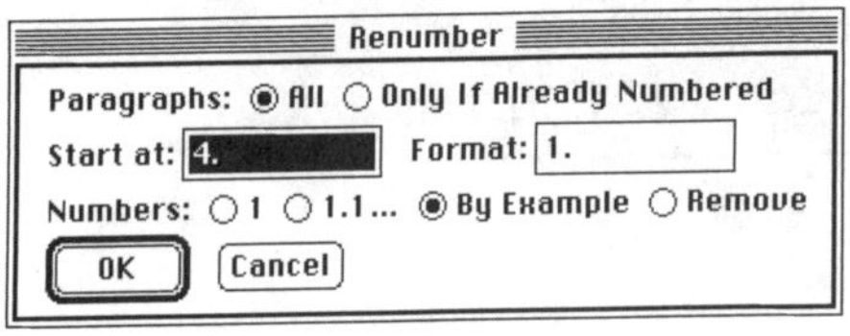

Figure 4.52

Depending on the number of the top item in your list selection, the Renumber dialog box may show a different starting point for your renumbering (Figure 4.52). The top item in the moved-list example (see Figure 4.51) was number 4.

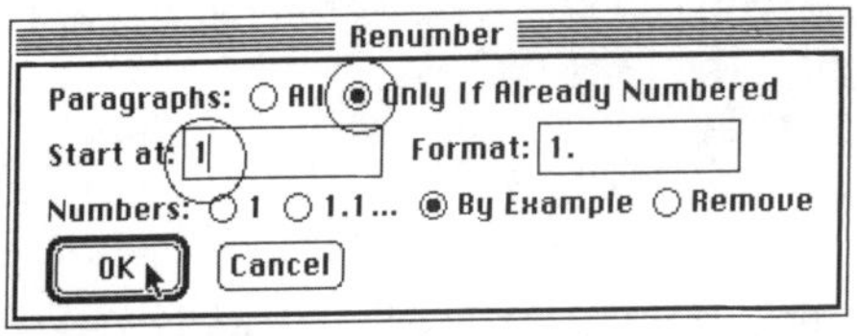

Figure 4.53

Change the starting number to 1. Click on the **Only If Already Numbered** button and click **OK** (Figure 4.53). The order will remain the same, but the numbers in front of your list items will have changed.

Resorting

If you don't want to move your text because the numbers in front of the paragraphs already indicate the order you want the items to be listed in, then you can use the Sort function to reorder the list.

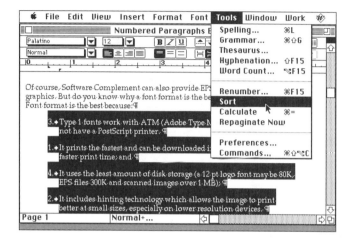

Figure 4.54

Select the list items you want to reorder. Go to the **Tools** menu and choose **Sort** (Figure 4.54). The list items will rearrange themselves according to the numbering (or lettering) you assigned.

Long Paragraphs

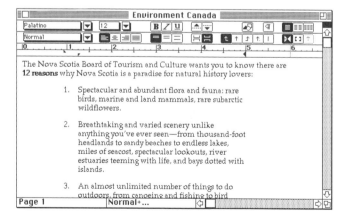

Figure 4.55

You may need to gain some sort of perspective on exactly how you can reorganize a long list of paragraphs that contain several lines of text each (Figure 4.55). In the steps that follow, you'll learn how to use the **Outline** view to easily view and restructure your document.

Go to the **View** menu and choose **Outline**.

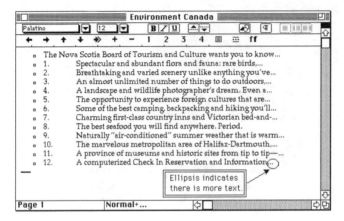

Figure 4.56

In Outline mode, you will view only the first line of each paragraph, making it easier to reorganize the list topics. Each line ends in an ellipsis, indicating more text exists, but it is not displayed (Figure 4.56).

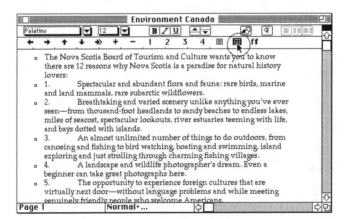

Figure 4.57

If, when you first arrive in Outline view, the entire contents of your list are displayed as shown in Figure 4.57, click on the **Ellipsis** button to contract the text.

To select the entire paragraph to reposition it, you need only to move the pointer into the Selection Bar area and click once. The first line of the paragraph with the ellipsis will be selected.

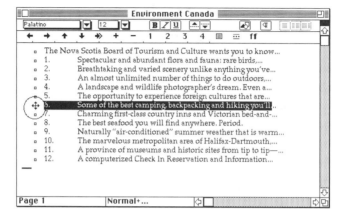

Figure 4.58

To move the paragraph, place the pointer over the small rectangle to the left of the paragraph. The pointer will change into a four-way arrow (Figure 4.58).

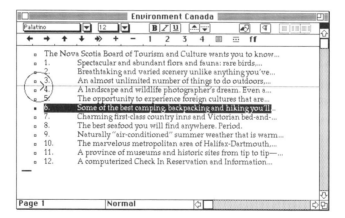

Figure 4.59

Press and drag to the new position. The guiding line and arrow indicate where the selected paragraph will be placed (Figure 4.59). Release the mouse button.

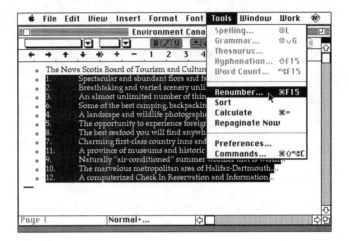

Figure 4.60

To renumber, select the list using the right-pointing arrow in the Selection
Bar. Go to the **Tools** menu and choose **Renumber** (Figure 4.60); then click **OK**.
To return to the Normal text entry view, go to the **View** menu and choose
Normal.

Quick Formatting Solutions

I f your daily work involves making bulleted or numbered lists, you would
probably appreciate a way to make all the adjustments to the Ruler
without having to go through a number of formatting steps each and every
time you create a list. And you'd probably like to return to the way you
normally enter text without always having to readjust the Ruler settings
back to the way they were before you started.

In the next several steps, you're going to learn some timesaving solutions
for having multiple format settings applied with a single mouse action.

You may not have noticed, but whenever you moved the left indent marker
to set up your bulleted or numbered lists, the word "Normal" —displayed at
the bottom of the window, just to the right of the Page number status box—
had a +... appended to it (Figure 4.61).

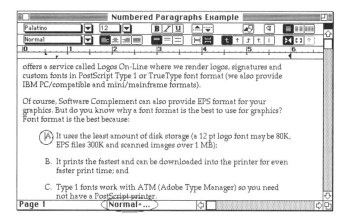

Figure 4.61

"Normal" is a collection of paragraph settings, font, and character settings better known as a "style." When you move the indent marker or click on the Open Space icon, you add a variation to the Normal style that isn't part of its regular definition. By subtly placing the +... at the bottom of the window, Microsoft Word lets you know this fact.

What you're going to do in the following steps is define some of your own "styles" that contain the formatting changes you made to the Normal style for your bulleted and numbered lists. Once defined, you'll be able to use these styles whenever you want to make a quick list in any document.

Defining a Style

The easiest way to define a style is to do it based on some formatting you've already decided works for you. Open a document that has a bulleted list that you've formatted using the steps outlined in this chapter.

STEP ONE

Position the I-beam anywhere inside one of the bulleted paragraphs and click once to position the flashing insertion point.

STEP TWO

If you glance down at the bottom of the window, you should see the +... after the word Normal. Move the pointer into the Ruler over the **Style Selection** box and click once to select the word **Normal**.

STEP THREE

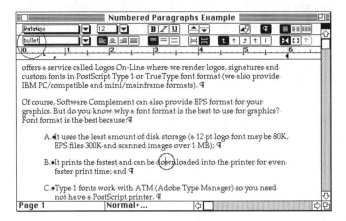

Figure 4.62

You're going to give your favorite bullet style a name. You could call it "bullet," "my bullet," "silver bullet," or whatever your heart desires. Just enter the name by typing from the keyboard and you'll see it appear in the Style Selection box as you type (Figure 4.62). You can even use the **Delete** key to modify the name if you change your mind in midprocess.

STEP FOUR

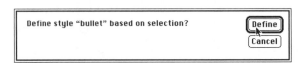

Figure 4.63

When you're satisfied with the name, press the **Return** key. A dialog box will come up and ask you if you want to "Define style '(your name here)' based on selection?" Click on the **Define** button (Figure 4.63).

You should now see the name of your newly defined style displayed in the bottom of the document window (where Normal used to be) in an area properly termed the "style name area."

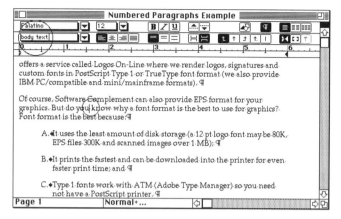

Figure 4.64

Using the same steps for defining a style as explained above, position the flashing insertion point in a paragraph of regular body text for your letter. Define this as a style with a name like "body" or "body text" or "text" (Figure 4.64).

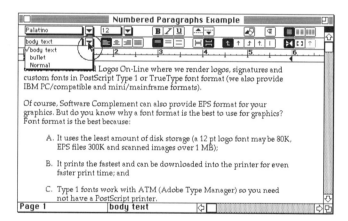

Figure 4.65

Now your document will have three kinds of styles (the names, other than Normal, will be your unique creation): Normal, bullet, and body text. To see a display of the style names, go to the **Style Selection** box in the Ruler and press and hold the **Down arrow**, as shown in Figure 4.65. When you save your document, the style names and definitions will be saved with it. Then go to the **File** menu and choose **Save**.

Defining a Default Style

Even though the styles defined above are only saved with the document you used as your example, the next steps show you how these styles can be made available to you in every new document you create.

STEP ONE

Go to the **Format** menu and choose **Style**.

STEP TWO

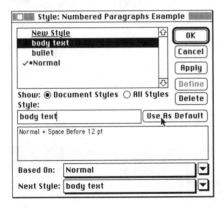

Figure 4.66

You should see the names of your styles in a list. Click on the body style name to select it. Then click on the **Use As Default** button (Figure 4.66).

STEP THREE

Figure 4.67

A dialog box will appear asking you if it's okay to record the style in the default style sheet. This may make absolutely no sense to you at the moment, but click the **Yes** button anyway (Figure 4.67).

STEP FOUR

Click on the "bullet" style name to select it; then click on the **Use As Default** button. As you did for the previous style, click on the **Yes** button when the default dialog box appears. Click on the **Close** button when you have finished.

The default style sheet mentioned above is a special "settings file" that resides in your System folder. The file is named Word Settings (5). It contains a lot of different information about preference settings, default styles, and other options you may have chosen for your overall word processing environment in Microsoft Word. When you quit from Microsoft Word, this file is updated with any changes you have made, such as setting the default styles.

Applying Styles

Go to the **File** menu and choose **New** to bring up a fresh, untitled document where you can test your new default styles.

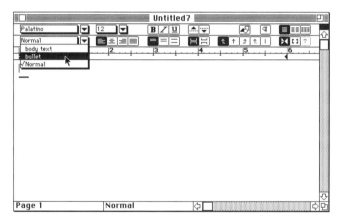

Figure 4.68

Start with a bullet format. Place your pointer on the **Down arrow** in the **Style Selection** box. Press and drag to select the bullet style, just as you would a regular menu item (Figure 4.68).

When you release the mouse button, you should notice that the flashing insertion point jumps, as well as a change in the Ruler settings. If you look at the style name area at the bottom of the window and in the style selection box itself, you should also see the name of your style displayed there (Figure 4.69).

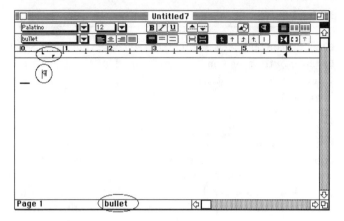

Figure 4.69

You're now set up so that you can enter a bullet (option 8), press the **Tab** key, and start typing a list item. Enter a few sample bulleted items.

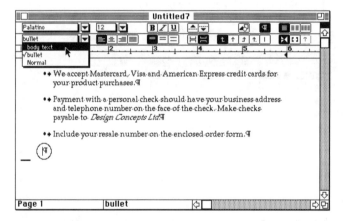

Figure 4.70

To switch to body text, first press **Return** for a new line. Place the pointer over the Down arrow for the Style Selection box in the Ruler. Press and drag to select your body text style (Figure 4.70).

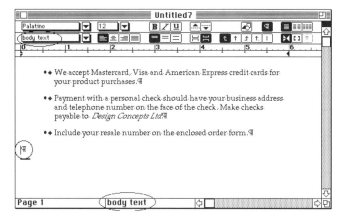

Figure 4.71

The flashing insertion point should jump again, and the body text style should be displayed in the Ruler and at the bottom of your window (Figure 4.71). Enter some more sample text.

Isn't this a lot easier to use than moving those indent markers around in the Ruler? You'll find that you might want to define several types of bullet styles, list styles, and/or body text styles as you become more comfortable with the convenience and ease that using styles brings to your word processing environment.

However, you might find that certain styles are more appropriate in some documents than they are in others. Microsoft Word gives you the flexibility to plan and use default styles where you think they might best suit your word processing needs.

Placing Styles in Your Letterhead Stationery Document

Now that you've defined text and bullet styles, you might want to use these styles whenever you write a letter using your Letterhead Stationery document. There are a few steps you'll need to take to make that possible.

STEP ONE

Go to the **File** menu and choose **Open**. If necessary, navigate to the folder where your Letterhead stationery document is stored. Don't open the Letterhead just yet. For the moment, you just need to make sure you're positioned in the same folder as the Letterhead document. Click on the **Cancel** button.

STEP TWO

Go to the **File** menu and choose **New**. Since this new document contains your newly defined default styles, you're going to save it and then use it as a model to bring its styles over into the Letterhead document.

STEP THREE

Go to the **File** menu and choose **Save**. Name this document **Style Sample** and make sure you are saving it in the same folder as your Letterhead Stationery document.

STEP FOUR

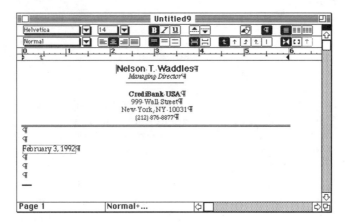

Figure 4.72

Go to the **File** menu and **Open** the Letterhead Stationery document. Remember, when you do this, you will see an untitled document on your desktop (Figure 4.72).

STEP FIVE

Go to the **Format** menu and choose **Style**.

STEP SIX

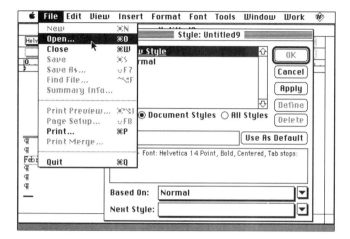

Figure 4.73

Keeping the Style Selection box open, go over to the **File** menu and choose **Open** (Figure 4.73).

STEP SEVEN

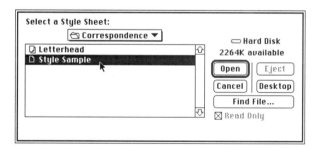

Figure 4.74

You should see the document you named "Style Sample" in the list of documents in the folder. Double-click on it to open it (Figure 4.74).

Figure 4.75

The Style dialog box should now list the names and definitions of the text and bullet styles you defined in the steps earlier in this section (Figure 4.75). What you have just done is officially called "merging a style sheet." It is probably one of the most powerful capabilities of Microsoft Word, and gives you the ability to merge styles you may have defined in other documents with any document you create. Click on the **Close** box in the upper left corner to return to the document window.

STEP EIGHT

Next, you need to save these changes to your Letterhead Stationery document. Go to the **File** menu and choose **Save**. Carefully enter the same name as your Letterhead Stationery document. You're going to replace it. But before you press the Save button, execute the following step.

STEP NINE

Press on the arrow next to **Save File as Type** and select **Stationery** from the list of formats.

STEP TEN

Click on the **Save** button. When a dialog box appears asking you if you want to replace your existing Letterhead document, click on the **Replace** button.

Removing Default Styles

Perhaps you will decide that you really don't want those bullet and body text styles in every new document you create. You're satisfied just having them for creating letters with your Letterhead Stationery document. Here are the steps you would take to remove the default styles from every new document you create.

STEP ONE

Go to the **File** menu and choose **New** to bring up an Untitled document.

STEP TWO

Go to the **Format** menu and choose **Style**.

STEP THREE

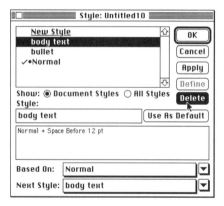

Figure 4.76

Click on the style name you wish to delete. Click on the **Delete** button (Figure 4.76).

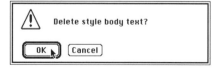

Figure 4.77

You'll be asked first, if it's okay to delete the style; then you'll be asked if you want to delete the style from the Default Style sheet. Click on the **OK** button for each question (Figure 4.77) and these styles will no longer appear in any new documents.

More Advanced List Techniques

There are a number of methods you can use to create lists within documents. The techniques described in the first part of this chapter explore simple methods that you can use when executing basic correspondence. More complex uses of lists and tables are covered in Chapters 7 and 8; however, a simple list can be generated by using a table format or by inserting sections into your document and using the column icons on the Ribbon.

Using Tables to Create Lists

Some of the drawbacks in using the tables function of Word 5.0 for simple list generation are:

- Tables do not allow for automatic numbering of list items using the Tools Renumber function.

- Tables are not a convenient solution for working with bulleted paragraphs or list items that require numbering or lettering to "hang" in an area to the left of regular text.

- Tables do not provide an easy method for creating and using "guiding dots" (or leader tabs) between list items.

However, if you want to create simple columns of text that don't require any of the above-mentioned formats, the use of a table will enable you to generate simple lists. The basic steps for working with lists in tables follow.

STEP ONE

Before you insert a table, check the Ruler to make sure there are no stray Tab marks in the Ruler, the left indent mark is at the 0 point, and any line spacing or text alignment icons are set to the way you would like your text to appear within the table (Figure 4.78).

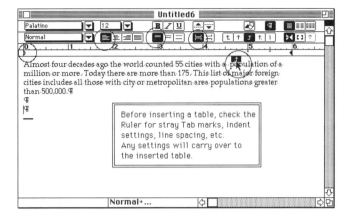

Figure 4.78

NOTE: *You might want to click on the Open Space between paragraphs icon to automatically add space between each item on the list.*

STEP TWO

Choose **Table** from the **Insert** menu.

STEP THREE

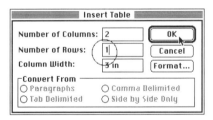

Figure 4.79

When the Insert Table dialog box appears, you can enter the number of columns you want for your list. The examples illustrated here will deal with only two-column lists; however, you can have up to 31 columns in a table. Press the **Tab** key once to highlight the Number of Rows edit bar. Type the number **1** (for a single row) and click the **OK** button (Figure 4.79).

STEP FOUR

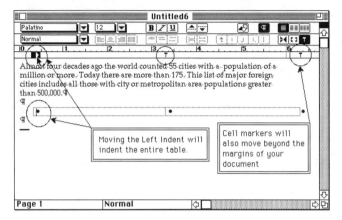

Figure 4.80

Make sure you are working with the Show ¶ icon selected so that you can see the table cells in your document. Whenever you insert a table, the Ruler will be automatically switched to the Cell Marker scale so that you can make adjustments to the column width.

If you want to indent your list of items, press and drag the left indent marker on the Ruler to the place where you want items in the left column to appear (Figure 4.80). All the column T-markers will move in conjunction with the left indent marker.

STEP FIVE

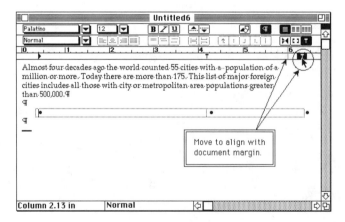

Figure 4.81

Press and drag on the T-markers in the Ruler to adjust the column width for each cell. If you have indented your table, you will need to realign the T-marker on the far right with the vertical dotted line indicating the margins for your document (Figure 4.81).

> **NOTE:** *Hold down the Shift key before you press on the T-marker and you will be able to move a single T-marker as if it were a regular Tab mark.*

STEP SIX

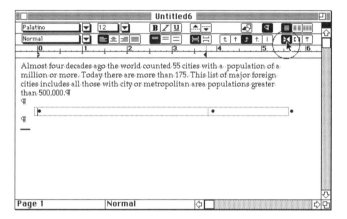

Figure 4.82

Once you have the column width set for each column in the table, click on the **Indent** scale in the Ruler (Figure 4.82).

STEP SEVEN

As you may recall from working with various kinds of tabs, different types of information may require different formatting options. Rather than working with tabs, you will find that paragraph alignment within table columns helps to quickly align text.

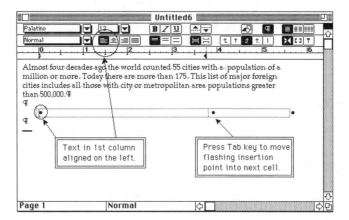

Figure 4.83

Typically, the column on the left will be formatted with left-aligned text. The column(s) on the right may use a variety of different formats. To move into another cell and adjust the formatting, press the **Tab** key (Figure 4.83).

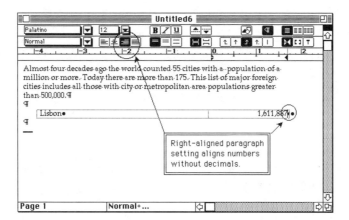

Figure 4.84

If you are working with numbers that have no decimals, the right-aligned paragraph format will align the numbers correctly (Figure 4.84).

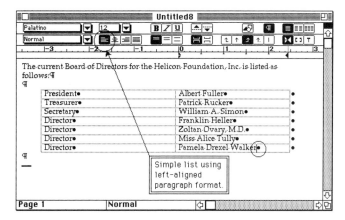

Figure 4.85

For regular text in a simple list, you can use left-aligned paragraph formatting (Figure 4.85).

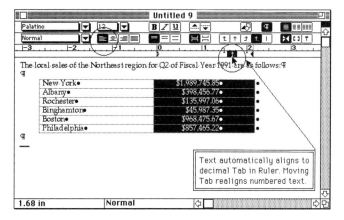

Figure 4.86

Place a decimal tab in the Ruler (left-aligned paragraph formatting must be set for this to function properly), and all numbers with decimals will align on the decimal point. In addition, you can adjust the positioning of the decimal by merely selecting the column of text and moving the decimal Tab mark in the Ruler (Figure 4.86).

STEP EIGHT

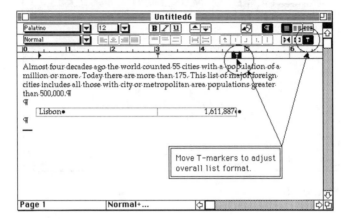

Figure 4.87

Make all the formatting adjustments to the first row of your table by entering sample text (the longest name and/or number on the list) to obtain the correct spacing allowance. You might want to readjust your column width to accommodate longer text by clicking on the **T-marker** scale icon in the Ruler. You also might want to narrow the column width for a cleaner presentation (Figure 4.87).

Once you have set your column formatting and entered text in the first row, you can enter the rest of the text in your table by pressing the **Tab** key. The Tab key will insert a new row beneath the last cell in a table and carry forward all the formatting of the first row in the table.

STEP NINE

Once you have finished entering text in your table, click in the paragraph beneath the table to continue with the rest of your document (Figure 4.88).

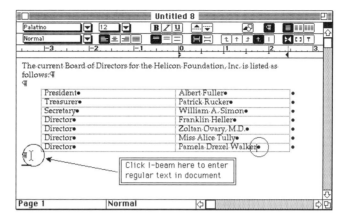

Figure 4.88

Alphabetizing Lists in "Snaked" Columns

You can create columns using several methods: tabs, tables, and the Ribbon or Section dialog box. By using the Ribbon or Section dialog, you would use what is often described as "newspaper style" columns, which "snake" from the top down and across your document.

You might have a long list of items that you would like to alphabetize and place in two (or more) columns in your document to save space. This can easily be achieved using the column icons on the Ribbon.

STEP ONE

First, locate and select the list of items that you would like alphabetized. Go to the **Tools** menu and choose **Sort** (Figure 4.89).

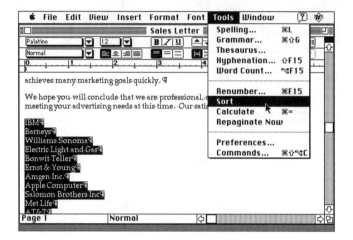

Figure 4.89

STEP TWO

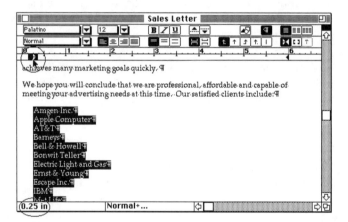

Figure 4.90

You might want to have the items slightly indented on the page to set them off from the rest of your text. With the list still selected, go to the Ruler, position the arrow on the lower left triangle of the left indent marker, and press and drag the left indent to somewhere around the 1/4- to 1/2-inch mark.

STEP THREE

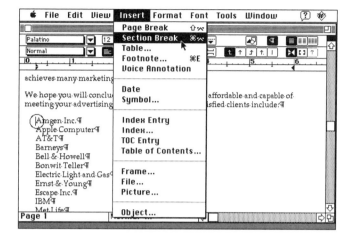

Figure 4.91

Position the flashing insertion point just before the first item in the list. Go to the **Insert** menu and choose **Section Break** (Figure 4.91).

STEP FOUR

Go to the **View** menu and choose **Page Layout**. Normal view will not display your columns as they will print.

STEP FIVE

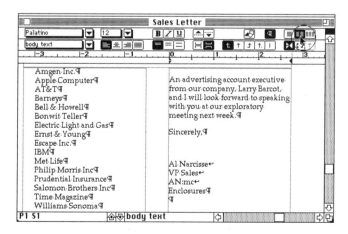

Figure 4.92

Click on the Two Column icon in the Ribbon (Figure 4.92).

STEP SIX

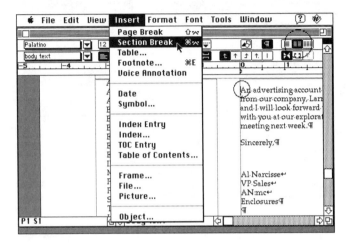

Figure 4.93

Click at the end of your list. Create a new paragraph if there is not one. Or, if there is existing text, click before the first character of the paragraph of text that should appear in one column and is not part of your list. Go to the **Insert** menu and choose **Section Break** (Figure 4.93).

STEP SEVEN

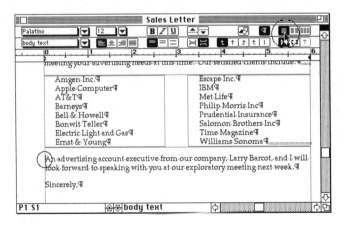

Figure 4.94

Click on the Single Column icon in the Ribbon (Figure 4.94).

Return to Normal view to work with your document and enter or edit text. If you add new entries to your alphabetized list and want to realphabetize it, select the list while in Normal view (it's easier) and choose **Sort** from the **Tools** menu.

STEP EIGHT

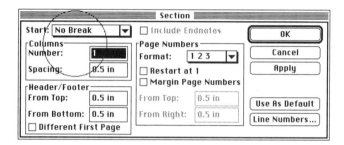

Figure 4.95

If you are working in Page Layout view and notice that, when you insert a section your document automatically scrolls to a new page, you may have the Section dialog box set to the "Start New Page" option. In order to "snake" alphabetized columns of text in the manner described above, you must have the Start option set to "No Break."

To adjust this setting, choose **Section** from the **Format** menu and select **No Break** from the drop-down list in the Start area of the dialog box (Figure 4.95).

Conclusion

There are a variety of techniques and methods you can employ when working with lists in documents. The most important step is for you to have a clear idea of what it is that you want to do with the list and then choose the technique that best suits the format your list requires.

How to Format Envelopes for Printing

Typically when you create a letter the logical next step in completing your correspondence is placing that letter in an envelope and dropping it in a mailbox. Though it might be faster to simply hand address the envelope, in certain situations a handwritten envelope may not present the professional image you would like.

Admittedly, addressing a single envelope with the use of a typewriter is probably faster than using a computer. However, once you have created a special document just to print an envelope, you will find the process of printing an envelope to be fast, efficient, and possibly more accurate than your faithful typewriter.

Which Printer Do You Have?

There are many different printers on the market to choose from, and your individual word processing environment may make use of any one of them. Each printer varies in the way an envelope is fed through it—from the right, in the middle, from the top, etc. Therefore, the starting point for where the text will actually print on your envelope similarly varies a great deal.

In order to execute the steps for setting up an envelope for printing, you'll need to know exactly what kind of printer is connected to your Macintosh. The best way to find out is by looking at the back of the printer itself. There should be some kind of metal identification tag with the printer name and model.

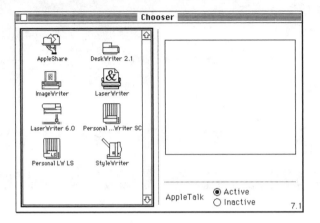

Figure 5.1

The Chooser, found under the Apple menu, may have a variety of printer drivers and driver versions (Figure 5.1). The correct printer driver for your system depends on which system software you are currently using and whether or not you have access to printers over a network. In order to create a document that will successfully print envelopes, you need to determine the specific printer and printer driver you are using.

Directions are given in this chapter for printing envelopes with the Hewlett-Packard DeskWriter and the following Apple printers:

LaserWriter, LaserWriter Plus

Personal LaserWriter LS and SC

Personal LaserWriter NT

LaserWriter IINT and IINTX

LaserWriter IISC

LaserWriter IIf and IIg

StyleWriter

ImageWriter II

If you are using a different model of laser printer, you'll have to determine which printer setup most closely approximates yours and use those settings.

The instructions that follow will be for printing on a standard U.S. business envelope (a #10 envelope, which measures 9.5 inches by 4.125 inches).

With a Return Address

Figure 5.2

Formatting a blank #10 envelope so that it will print with a return address is a little more involved than using an envelope that has the return address already printed on it. The return address should be located as close to the top left edge of your envelope as possible. You'll also need to allow for space between your address and the address of the person you're mailing to (Figure 5.2).

STEP ONE

Setting Up the Page

The critical first step is setting up the document page. For this, you'll be using the **Page Setup** dialog box from the **File** menu. Depending on which printer you have and which version of system software, this dialog box will have various kinds of options. After opening a **New** document, go the **File** menu and choose **Page Setup**.

Most Apple LaserWriters have the ability to print margins set to 0.25 inch, which is the setting the return address requires to print as closely as possible to the top left edge. However, some LaserWriters need to have an option set before they will allow the 0.25-inch margin setting to take effect. The easiest way to handle all the various printer options is to take this approach: If your **Page Setup** dialog box has an **Options** button—as shown in Figure 5.3— click on it now. Otherwise, skip to Figure 5.6.

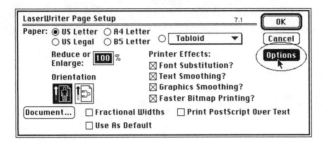

Figure 5.3

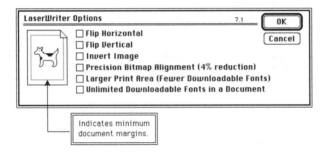

Figure 5.4

Clicking the **Options** button takes you to the famous Moof illustration. For the moment, observe the dotted margins set around the example page to the left. These represent a minimum margin setting of 0.5 inch (Figure 5.4).

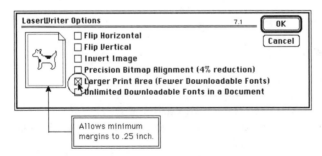

Figure 5.5

Click in the box next to the Larger Print Area option. You should see a much narrower margin between the edge of the page and the dotted lines (Figure 5.5). This is the setting you need for envelopes with a return address. Click the **OK** button.

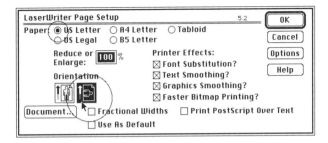

Figure 5.6

A number of printers and drivers have a separate paper setting for the #10 envelope. Format instructions for all Apple LaserWriters will use the U.S. Letter setting as this setting obtains better printing results. You'll also be using the Landscape Orientation. Click on the **Landscape** icon (shown in Figure 5.6) in the **Page Setup** dialog box if you have a LaserWriter printer of any type.

> **NOTE:** *See separate instructions for the DeskWriter, the StyleWriter, and the ImageWriter, which use different orientation and paper settings.*

You may decide you would like to experiment on your own with the envelope setting to see the difference in terms of printing performance. However, margin settings for the envelope paper setting will not be included in this chapter. Figure 5.7 illustrates the LaserWriter Driver for System 7.0—version 7.1—with options you can select for center- and edge-fed envelopes used by various LaserWriter printers.

STEP TWO

Setting the Margins

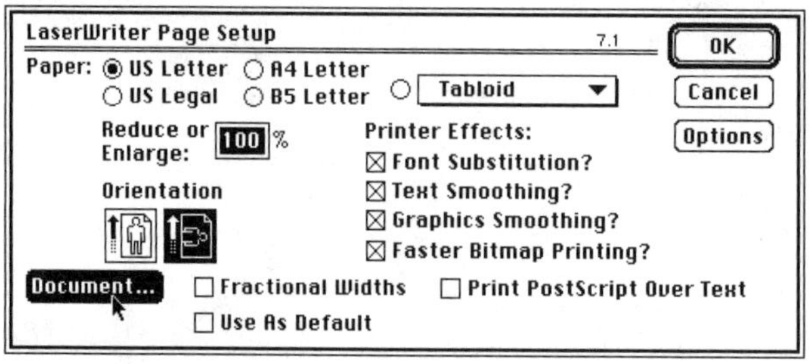

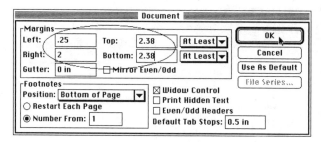

Figure 5.8

While in the **Page Setup** dialog box, there is a **Document** button which takes you directly to the **Document** dialog box where you can enter margin settings for your envelope. Click on the **Document** button (Figure 5.8).

Figure 5.9

To set margins for #10 envelopes with a return address, you'll need to refer to Table 5.1 and locate the specific settings (which are in inches) for your type of printer. Press the **Tab** key once you've entered the setting for the left margin, to move from edit bar to edit bar. Click on the **OK** button when you've finished (Figure 5.9).

Table 5.1 #10 Envelope Margin Settings (LaserWriter)

LaserWriter, LaserWriter Plus	Left	0.25	Top	0.25
	Right	2.0	Bottom	4.5
Personal LaserWriter LS and SC	Left	0.25	Top	4.63
	Right	0.25	Bottom	0.5

Personal LaserWriter NT	Left	0.25	Top	4.63
	Right	2.0	Bottom	0.5
LaserWriter IINT and IINTX	Left	0.25	Top	2.38
	Right	2.0	Bottom	2.38
LaserWriter IISC	Left	0.25	Top	2.38
	Right	2.0	Bottom	2.38
LaserWriter IIf and IIg	Left	0.25	Top	2.38
	Right	2.00	Bottom	2.38

In order to complete the page settings, click on the **OK** button in the **Page Setup** dialog box. To continue, move on to Step 3 called "Entering the Return Address," below.

Page Setup for the Apple StyleWriter

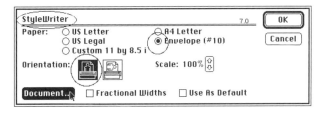

Figure 5.10

Envelopes are fed into the Apple StyleWriter differently from most printers. In order to accommodate this, you will need to set your document page setup accordingly.

Figure 5.10 shows the correct Page Setup options. Click on the **Envelope (#10)** setting, as well as the default Portrait orientation. Then click on the **Document** button to begin setting your margins (Figure 5.10).

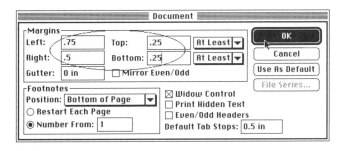

Figure 5.11

Enter the following margin settings, pressing the **Tab** key to move to the next edit bar.

Left   0.75   Top   0.25
Right 0.5   Bottom   0.25

Click on the **OK** button when you've finished (Figure 5.11). Click on the **OK** button for the **Page Setup** dialog box.

Page Setup for the Hewlett-Packard DeskWriter

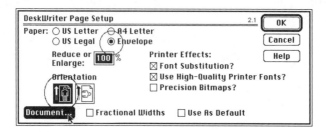

Figure 5.12

Because the DeskWriter from Hewlett-Packard requires the envelope to be fed from the top and center, you need to adjust your document page setup accordingly.

Figure 5.12 shows the correct Page Setup options. Click on the **Envelope** setting as well as the default Portrait orientation. Then click on the **Document** button to begin setting your margins (Figure 5.12).

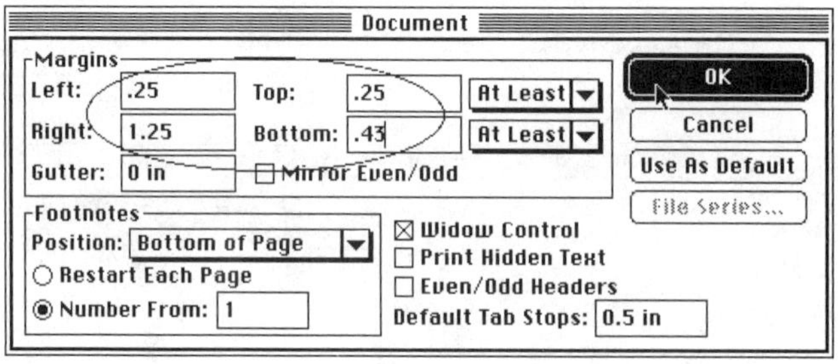

Figure 5.13

Enter the following margin settings, pressing the **Tab** key to move to the next edit bar.

Left   0.25   Top   0.25
Right 1.25   Bottom   0.43

Click on the **OK** button when you're done (Figure 5.13). Click on the **OK** button for the **Page Setup** dialog box. Move on to Step 3 called "Entering the Return Address" to continue.

Page Setup for the Apple ImageWriter II

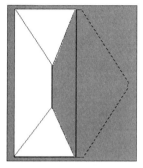

Figure 5.14

When printing envelopes on an Apple ImageWriter, you'll need to insert the envelope in a manner that initially seems quite foreign. Because the minimum margin for the ImageWriter is 0.5 inch, you'll have difficulty printing text near the top left edge of an envelope if you insert the envelope as though you were using a typewriter.

To overcome these difficulties, you'll need to feed the envelope as follows. Hold the envelope with the flap folded out to the right side (your right as you face the printer). The back of the envelope and the glue of the flap should be facing toward you, with the glue part under your right thumb. What you have is a tall, thin piece of paper entering the printer, rather than a short wide one (Figure 5.14). You'll need to align the envelope's bottom edge with the single-sheet icon you'll see on the back cover of the printer. With this envelope-feeding process in mind, you can now set up the page format.

Go to the **File** menu and choose **Page Setup**. Click on the **US Letter** paper setting as well as the Landscape orientation as shown in Figure 5.15. Also make sure the box next to No Gaps Between Pages does *not* have an X in it. Click on the **Document** button to begin setting your margins.

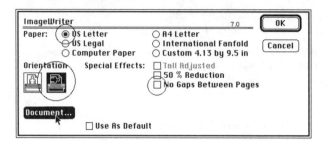

Figure 5.15

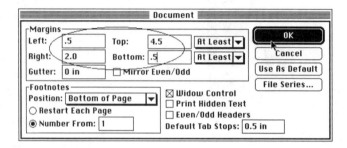

Figure 5.16

Enter the following margin settings, pressing the **Tab** key to move to the next edit bar.

Left	0.5	Top	4.5
Right	2.0	Bottom	0.5

Click on the **OK** button when you've finished (Figure 5.16). Click on the **OK** button for the **Page Setup** dialog box.

STEP THREE

Entering the Return Address

Now that your document has been set up for printing on the correct printer, you're going to format the information for your return address and the addressee information.

Enter your return address, pressing the **Return** key for each new line of the address. Make sure you have the Show ¶ icon selected in the Ribbon. When you've finished your address information, you'll need to add some space between your address and the addressee information. Press the **Return** key eight or nine times. Depending on the number of lines your address occupies, you will enter more or less space. The objective is to have a total of 10–12 lines before you start the addressee information (Figure 5.17).

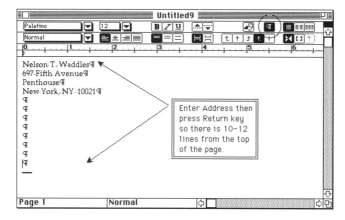

Figure 5.17

STEP FOUR

Formatting the Addressee Information

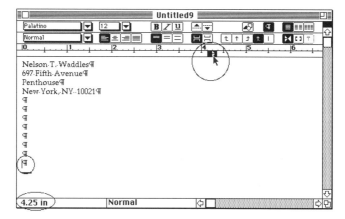

Figure 5.18

The flashing insertion point should be in the last paragraph. Move the pointer into the Ruler and position over the lower triangle of the left indent marker. Drag the left indent mark to the 4.25-inch mark in the Ruler (Figure 5.18).

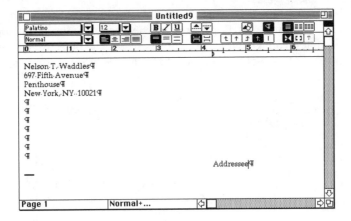

Figure 5.19

Insert the placeholder text **"Addressee"** (Figure 5.19).

STEP FIVE

Saving and Using the Envelope Template

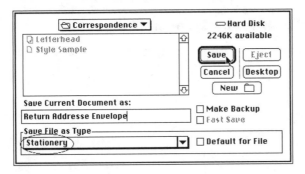

Figure 5.20

Save your document as a Stationery document in your Correspondence folder and name it "Return Address Envelope" (Figure 5.20).

As with all Stationery documents, you will return to an untitled window when you have saved and named the stationery document. To use the envelope template, simply place the I-beam over the word "Addressee" and double-click to select it (Figure 5.21).

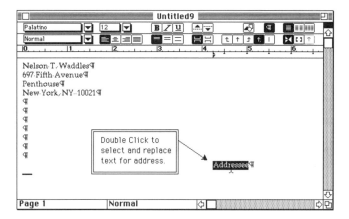

Figure 5.21

Type the name and address for the person you want to send a letter to, pressing the **Return** key for each new line. When you're done, insert your envelope correctly in the printer and go to the **File** menu and choose **Print**. Click the **OK** button to print your envelope.

STEP SIX

Making Adjustments

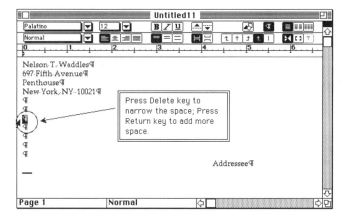

Figure 5.22

You might want to make a few adjustments to your template for spacing. Go to the **File** menu and **Open** the Return Address Envelope template so you're working with a new, untitled document.

If you'd like more space between the return address and the addressee information, click beside one of the blank paragraphs and press the **Return** key. To narrow the space, select one of the blank paragraphs and delete it (Figure 5.22).

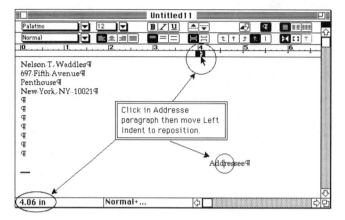

Figure 5.23

You might want to position the addressee information further to the left. Move the I-beam over the word "Addressee" and click once to place the flashing insertion point. Place the pointer over the lower triangle of the left indent mark in the Ruler and move the left indent mark further to the left and into a position that is to your preference (Figure 5.23).

When you've finished, save the document in **Stationery** format and rename it "Return Address Envelope."

On Preprinted Stationery

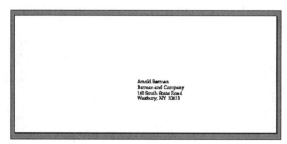

Figure 5.24

Preprinted envelopes eliminate the need to format a document for printing of a return address. This greatly simplifies the formatting process. However, there still are differences between printers and the specific page setups for those printers that need to be accounted for.

Your objective is to format an envelope template so that the addressee information will start printing at a location approximately 4.5 inches from the left edge of the envelope and 2.25 inches from the top (Figure 5.24).

STEP ONE

Page Setup

The page setup for preprinted envelopes will not differ from what was described in the preceding section for return address envelopes. Table 5.2 shows a simple listing of your page setup process.

Table 5.2 Printer Setup for Preprinted Envelopes

All Apple LaserWriters	Paper	US Letter
	Orientation	Landscape
	Larger print area	Not selected
Apple StyleWriter	Paper	envelope #10
	Orientation	Portrait
Hewlett-Packard DeskWriter	Paper	envelope
	Orientation	Portrait
Apple ImageWriter	Paper	US Letter
	Orientation	Landscape
	No gaps between pages	Not selected

Go to the **File** menu and choose **Page Setup**. Choose the appropriate settings for your particular printer. Click on the **Document** button to bring up the Document dialog box and continue with the next step.

STEP TWO

Margin Settings

In general, since you no longer have to accommodate the return address, you'll be adjusting the margin settings—given earlier for the return address envelope—by 2 inches from the top and 4.25 inches from the left.

Table 5.3 shows margin settings for each of the various printers.

Table 5.3 Appropriate Margin Settings for Representative Printers

LaserWriter, LaserWriter Plus	Left	4.5	Top	2.25
	Right	2.0	Bottom	4.5
Personal LaserWriter LS and SC	Left	4.5	Top	6.19
	Right	0.25	Bottom	0.5
Personal LaserWriter NT	Left	4.5	Top	6.19
	Right	2.0	Bottom	0.5
LaserWriter IINT and IINTX	Left	4.5	Top	4.5
	Right	2.0	Bottom	2.38
LaserWriter IISC	Left	4.5	Top	4.5
	Right	2.0	Bottom	2.38
LaserWriter IIf and IIg	Left	4.5	Top	4.5
	Right:	2.0	Bottom	2.38
StyleWriter	Left	5.0	Top	2.25
	Right	0.5	Bottom	0.25
ImageWriter	Left	4.5	Top:	6.5
	Right	2.0	Bottom	0.5
Hewlett-Packard DeskWriter	Left	4.5	Top	2.25
	Right	1.25	Bottom	0.43

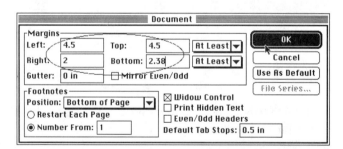

Figure 5.25

Enter the appropriate margin settings for your printer, pressing the **Tab** key to move to the next edit bar. Click on the **OK** button when you're done (Figure 5.25).

Click on the **OK** button for the **Page Setup** dialog box.

Save your document in the Stationery format and name it "Envelope."

STEP THREE

Using the Envelope Template

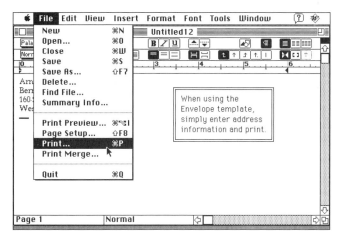

Figure 5.26

As with all stationery documents, you'll be working with an untitled document each time you open the Envelope template. To use the Envelope template for an envelope, simply enter the addressee information, place an envelope in your printer, and print (Figure 5.26).

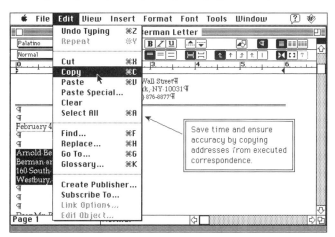

Figure 5.27

To save time and effort, you might want to copy the addressee information from a letter you've just created (Figure 5.27).

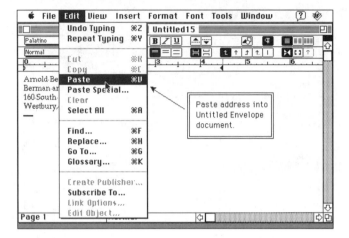

Figure 5.28

You can then switch to your envelope window and paste the addressee information into the untitled envelope document (Figure 5.28).

> **NOTE:** *You might not want to copy and paste addressee information from a letter into an envelope set up with the return address format. The addressee information in that template is formatted with a left indent. Copying and pasting addressee information will alter the indented style.*
>
> *If you choose to copy and paste, you will then need to select the addressee information and move the left indent mark to the 4.25-inch mark.*

For the most part, you'll have no reason to save an envelope document. Save the space on your hard disk by simply clicking in the **Close** box when you're through printing (Figure 5.29).

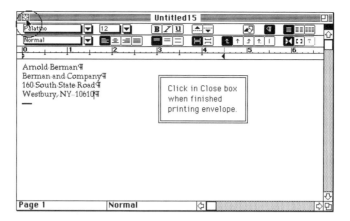

Figure 5.29

Conclusion

Once you've determined your printer setup and created a template for your envelope, you'll soon realize how easy it is to print a single envelope to accommodate your correspondence. See Chapter 10 to learn more tips on how you can have quick access to your Envelope template when you need it.

If you want to print out a group of envelopes or need to affix labels to envelopes for a mass mailing, see Chapter 6, "How to Mail Merge."

How to Mail Merge (You Need to Send Something to a Lot of People Right Away...)

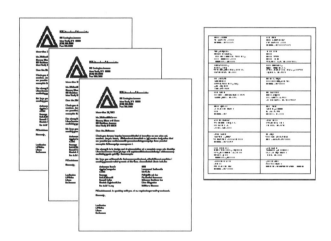

Figure 6.1

One of any word processor's most valued assets is its ability to produce "mass mailings." This is the function whereby special sales promotions, fund raising or job search letters, memos, or even invoices can be "personalized." Because mail merge is now so widespread, the once acceptable "Dear colleague and friend" no longer intimates the same level of familiarity as does "Dear Carole" or "Dear Mr. and Mrs. Makman."

The mail merge process usually begins with a document that you need to send to a number of people—probably under duress with some unattainable deadline looming over you. In the steps that follow, you'll learn how you can quickly create and manage special documents that contain lists of information (or data) about the people you are mailing to. You'll learn how easy it is to personalize letters that may have exceptions or variations on certain criteria. You'll also learn how to merge your list for printing on labels, or envelopes or to the back of a folded one-page flyer.

How to Create DATA Documents (Who Are You Sending This To?)

When executing a "print merge" (what the mail merge process is called in Microsoft Word) you merge two documents:

1. a document containing a list of all the names you want to send the letter (or memo, or flyer, etc.) to; and

2. a document that is the actual letter.

In this section you'll concentrate on learning how to create and manage the "list" or DATA document.

Creating a Database (You don't have the list anywhere on the computer, yet)

You may have been collecting names on small pieces of paper thrown in an unmarked folder or names may have been ticked off with a variety of color-coded check marks in your rolodex and/or datebook, but so far, there is no organized list of information entered in your computer for this (or any) particular mailing.

Therefore, by virtue of circumstance, you're going to start from scratch and create your own base of information (data) called a "database." Don't let the word "database" throw you. Databases have many different forms and, for print merge purposes, they are essentially organized lists of information. Microsoft Word has a very simple tool to help you get started in keeping track of simple data. It's called the "Data Document Builder."

Using the Data Document Builder

The Data Document Builder is accessed through the Print Merge Helper on the View menu. The Print Merge Helper has been designed to assist you during the actual mail merge process; therefore, if you have already created the document you want to send to your list of people, have it open as you begin the following steps. Otherwise, go to the **File** menu and open a **New** document.

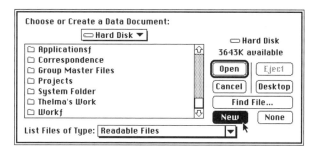

Figure 6.2

STEP ONE

Go to the **View** menu and choose **Print Merge Helper**. A dialog box will appear asking you either to choose an existing Data document or to create a new one. You'll be visiting this dialog box again—once you've actually created your database. However, to activate the Data Document Builder and start building your database, click on the **New** button (Figure 6.2).

STEP TWO

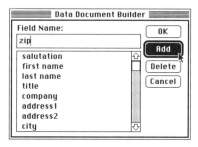

Figure 6.3

The Data Document Builder is a simple dialog box that assists you in setting up your database "field" names—the categories your information will be organized by. A typical mail list contains several fields of information. Simply type the field name and click on the **Add** button or press the **Return** key. Field names you'll probably want to enter (though you might have other category names you'd prefer to use—feel free to be creative!) are:

Salutation

First Name

Last Name

Title

Company

Address1

Address2

City

State

Zip

Country

Add each field name you think you'll need for your list using the Data Document Builder dialog box. If you want to delete any of the fields, click on the field name and then click the **Delete** button. When you're through creating your list, click the **OK** button (Figure 6.3).

STEP THREE

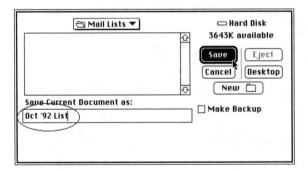

Figure 6.4

You'll be brought to a Save dialog box where you can name and save your document (Figure 6.4). Call the list by some name that you will easily recognize as a list.

STEP FOUR

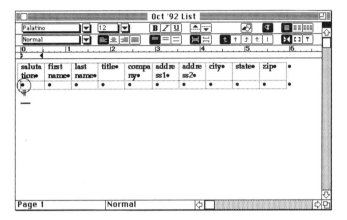

Figure 6.5

A document like the one shown in Figure 6.5 will flash briefly on your screen and then you'll be returned to the document from where you first activated the Print Merge Helper.

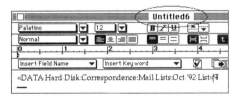

Figure 6.6

Wherever the flashing insertion point was located, a "Data statement" will have been inserted into your document (Figure 6.6). A Data statement is surrounded by print merge characters (known as chevrons) and contains the word DATA followed by the pathname of the hard disk and folders which locates the data document and then the data document name itself.

What this DATA statement does is notify Microsoft Word during the final merge process of the location of the data file and signals Word that there is information to be merged. However, if you were working with a blank,

Untitled document, you can either save it to create your letter (or flyer, etc.) later on or just close it with no changes. If you had opened the actual document you want to perform a mail merge with, then save your document.

Reformatting the DATA Document

Go to the **Window** menu and select your newly created Data document. Make sure Show ¶ is turned on. You'll see that the field names you entered with the Data Document Builder have each been placed in a cell within a table and the flashing insertion point is located in the blank cell directly beneath the first field name (Figure 6.5).

You're going to be using this table to enter all the information for your mailing list. However, the next few steps will help you to reformat the table so you can see the information more clearly as you enter it.

STEP ONE

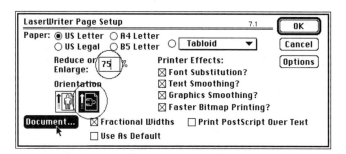

Figure 6.7

Go to the **File** menu and choose **Page Setup**. Click on the Landscape orientation icon. If you have a LaserWriter, type 75 in the Reduce or Enlarge edit bar (Figure 6.7). Click on the **Document** button to reset the margins.

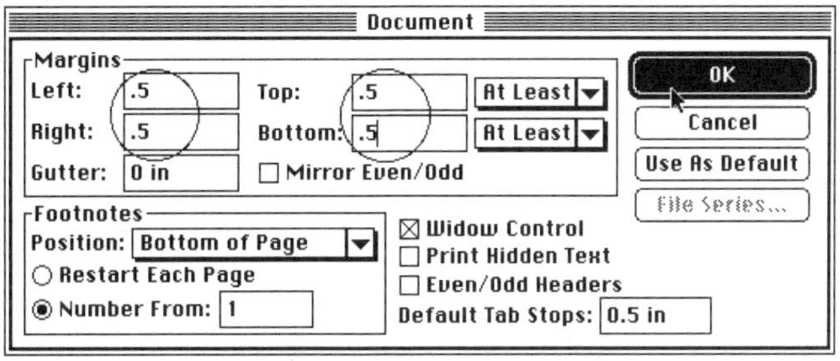

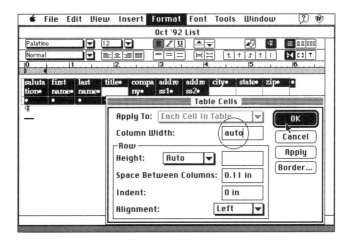

Figure 6.8

Type 0.5 in each of the margin edit bars, pressing the Tab key to move from edit bar to edit bar. Click on the **OK** button and then click on the **Page Setup OK** button.

The combination of these page setup and margin settings will give your document a much more luxurious space within which to work with your information.

STEP TWO

Hold down the **Option** key (two keys to the left of the spacebar) and double-click to select the entire table. You're going to adjust the length of each cell so that the table spreads out to the new dimensions you just set for your document. Go to the **Format** menu and choose **Table Cells**.

Figure 6.9

The Column Width edit bar will be highlighted. Just type the word "auto" as shown in Figure 6.9 and click the **OK** button. The cells in your table will expand to automatically fit the margins of your document.

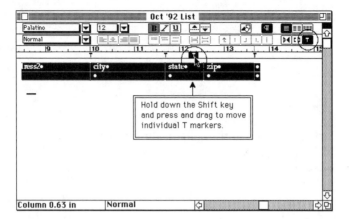

Figure 6.10

You might want to scroll to the right and make some adjustments to the width of certain cells, such as narrowing the state and zip cells and widening the address1 and address2 cells. Whenever you adjust cell width, first make sure that the entire table is selected, before moving the T markers in the ruler.

If the T markers are not showing, click on the Cell marker scale icon in the Ruler. To move individual T markers without disrupting the cell position of adjacent cells, hold down the **Shift** key before pressing and dragging the T marker (Figure 6.10).

Easier Text Entry Tips

If you are working with a small monitor, you might not be able to see the entire width of the data document table. As you start to enter information, you will end up scrolling from side to side as you move from cell to cell. As you enter more names in the list, you will scroll further away from the column headings and might not recall which column of information you are using to enter text. A few tips follow that you can try to make the text entry process less painful.

STEP ONE

Turn off the **Ruler** and **Ribbon** to give yourself more vertical space.

STEP TWO

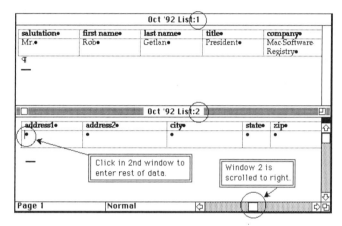

Figure 6.11

Go to the **Window** menu and choose **New Window**. Another window for the same document will appear. The Title bar will reflect this by placing a colon and the number 2 after the Title. Turn off the **Ribbon** and **Ruler** for the new window as well. Resize the windows so they are each one half the height they are normally and position them as shown in Figure 6.11.

You can move Window:2 by positioning the pointer anywhere within the vertical lines that lie on either side of the document Title and pressing and dragging. Scroll Window:2 to the right so that the cell following the last visible cell in Window:1 is the first visible cell in Window:2.

Click in the first cell and enter text. Press the **Tab** key to move to the next cell and enter more text. Continue to press the **Tab** key to advance to the next cell and enter text; however, once you've entered the data for the company name (or the last visible cell in the top window), don't press the Tab key to move to the next cell. Instead, use your mouse pointer and click in the first visible cell in the bottom window (Figure 6.11).

Enter data and press the **Tab** key as before to move to the next cell. When you reach the last cell (possibly the Zip code cell), enter text but don't press the **Tab** key to move on.

STEP THREE

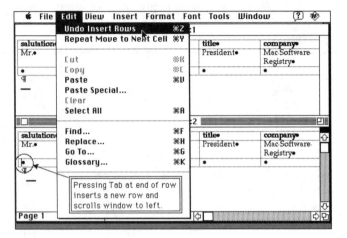

Figure 6.12

When working with a table, pressing the **Tab** key at the end of a row will insert a new row *beneath* the last row and carry forward the insertion point. It will also scroll your bottom window to the far left to display the beginning of the new row. Since you don't want this to happen, you are going to use another shortcut. However, if by accident you do press the **Tab** key and insert a new row, choose **Undo Insert Rows** from the **Edit** menu (Figure 6.12). The row will be removed and you will have to readjust the window by scrolling slightly to the left.

STEP FOUR

Once you've entered the Zip code information, press the following keyboard combination: **Command** (the key next to the spacebar) **Control V**. This will insert a new row above the current row the flashing insertion point was located in (Figure 6.13).

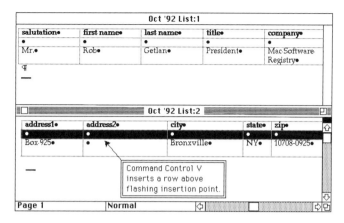

Figure 6.13

Click in the top window in the first cell and continue entering text for another person as before, moving to the bottom window to enter the second half of your information. Again, when you reach the last cell, press **Command Control V** to insert a new row for the next person's address information.

This technique of always inserting a new row above the last row keeps the top row (which defines your field names) always in view. This top row is called the "header record." Each row in your Data table is properly called a "record" in the print merge process. Each cell is called a "field."

Sorting and Alphabetizing

As you enter your information in the table, you can enter names in any or no particular order. Once you are done entering information, you can alphabetize your list by last name, sort by zip code or state or even company name. However, in order to make sure the header record containing the field names always remains at the top of your table, you'll need to make an adjustment to your field names before you begin the sorting process.

STEP ONE

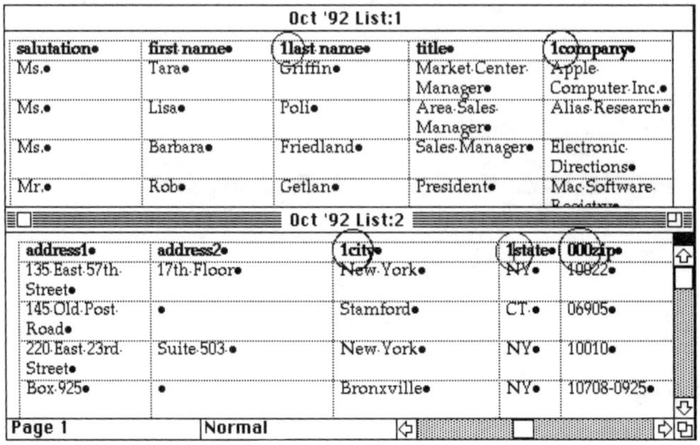

Oct '92 List:1
salutation• | first name• | 1last name• | title• | 1company•
Ms.• | Tara• | Griffin• | Market Center Manager• | Apple Computer Inc.•
Ms.• | Lisa• | Poli• | Area Sales Manager• | Alias Research•
Ms.• | Barbara• | Friedland• | Sales Manager• | Electronic Directions•
Mr.• | Rob• | Getlan• | President• | Mac Software
Oct '92 List:2
address1• | address2• | 1city• | 1state• | 000zip•
135 East 57th Street• | 17th Floor• | New York• | NY• | 10022•
145 Old Post Road• | • | Stamford• | CT • | 06905•
220 East 23rd Street• | Suite 503 • | New York• | NY• | 10010•
Box 925• | • | Bronxville• | NY• | 10708-0925•
Page 1
Normal

Figure 6.14

Place the flashing insertion point just before the first letter of the "header field" you want to sort your list by. Enter the number 1. If it is the zip code field, enter three 0s—you want to ensure that the zip code field will be at the top after sorting (Figure 6.14).

STEP TWO

File Edit View Insert Format Font Tools Window
Oct '92 List:1
Spelling... ⌘L
Grammar... ⌘⇧G
Thesaurus...
Hyphenation... ⇧F15
Word Count... ⌥F15
Renumber... ⌘F15
Sort
Calculate ⌘=
Repaginate Now
Preferences...
Commands... ⌘⇧⌥C
salutation• | first name• | 1last name•
Ms.• | Tara• | Griffin•
Ms.• | Lisa• | Poli•
Ms.• | Barbara• | Friedland•
Mr.• | Rob• | Getlan•
Page 1
Normal
address1• | address2• | 1city•
135 East 57th Street• | 17th Floor• | New York
145 Old Post Road• | • | Stamford• | CT • | 06905•
220 East 23rd Street• | Suite 503 • | New York• | NY• | 10010•
Box 925• | • | Bronxville• | NY• | 10708-0925•

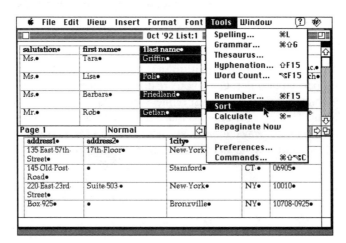

Figure 6.15

To select the column for sorting, hold down the **Option** key and Click anywhere within the column. Go to the **Tools** menu and choose **Sort** (Figure 6.15).

Quick-List Method

If you want to have the flexibility for sorting your mail lists a number of different ways (by zip code, last name, state, city, etc.), you should enter your data using the field names described above. However, what if you want to generate a simple list and you're not concerned about sorting under a variety of criteria?

What follows is a quick list method that might make it easier for you to enter text in a table. It also allows for "variable field length," meaning that you can have as many lines for your address as you want, without leaving blank spaces for the title or second address line.

STEP ONE

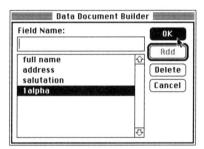

Figure 6.16

Begin by executing the same steps as you would for Figure 6.2. When creating the new data file with the Data Document Builder, define four fields as shown in Figure 6.16.

STEP TWO

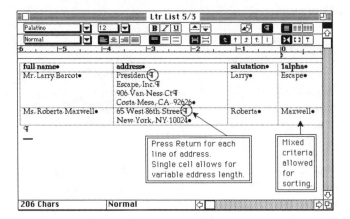

Figure 6.17

Before entering data in your list, you might want to adjust your table cell width and page orientation as described earlier (Figures 6.7 and 6.8). When you enter information into the Address column, you'll enter all the information for title, company name, and address as you would for an envelope, pressing the **Return** key for each new line (Figure 6.17). Doing this groups your information and displays it in a manner that is easy to read on-screen.

You can decide on the criteria for alphabetizing your list and enter that information in the 1alpha column. This will allow for mixed criteria— sometimes you might want to have either a last name or a company name entered in the column. Just remember, this will be the only column you'll be using for the sorting process.

Managing an Existing DATA File (The names in this file come from your database)

More common to word processing mail merge execution is using a letter you've written in Microsoft Word and merging it with information that has been selected and exported from a database program.

For the most part, you will manage the data used for your mail merge within the existing database program. However, what about the circumstance where you are using someone else's list and want to "massage" the data and edit the information?

This section will show you some variations on how data is exported and give you some tips on how to work with the information contained in these lists.

What Does the Data Look Like?

Figure 6.18

Most databases export text in a "tab delimited" format, meaning that between each field is a Tab mark and at the end of each record is a paragraph mark (Figure 6.18). Most databases have the option for the field names to be exported with the text, creating the necessary "header record" required for the mail merge process.

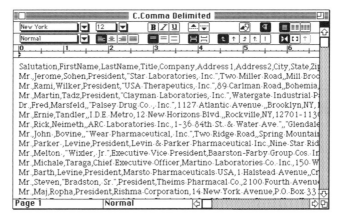

Figure 6.19

Other database programs might export data in a "comma delimited" format as shown in Figure 6.19. Here each field is separated by a comma and each record ends with a paragraph mark. Claris Corporation's Filemaker Pro uses this format.

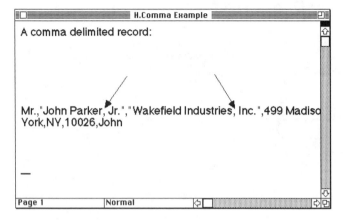

Figure 6.20

It is possible to create your own lists in Microsoft Word using the comma delimited format (rather than the table format). However, it is a tedious process involving strict attention to the placement of commas and quotes around any field data that might contain a comma within it (Figure 6.20).

When working with comma delimited text, it is difficult to track the insertion of the same number of fields for each record. You need to insert a comma for any blank fields (such as a second address line or unknown title). When working with tables, a blank cell is easy to identify and tab through if you don't have information to place in it. As you probably surmise, using comma deleted text format to create lists in Microsoft Word is not highly recommended.

Converting Data to a Word Table

Lists exported from a database typically are saved in text or ASCII (American Standard Code for Information Interchange) format. If you want to convert this information so that you can work with it as a Microsoft Word document, you'll be prompted to use a text converter for the process.

What follows are steps for taking a tab-delimited text file and converting it into a table so that you can begin to edit and refine the information within Microsoft Word.

STEP ONE

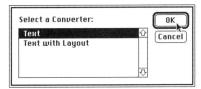

Figure 6.21

Go to the **File** menu and choose **Open**. Make sure the "Readable Files" option is selected from the **List Files of Type** menu so you can locate your exported data document (it should have been saved as a text file).

When you first open a text file, a dialog box will appear asking you to "select a converter." Select the **Text** format. ("Text with Layout" may place unwanted extra spaces in your document and takes considerably longer to convert your file into an Untitled document.)

STEP TWO

Go to the **File** menu and choose **Page Setup**. Enter **50** percent (or higher if you have fewer than 10 fields) in the reduction edit bar and choose **Landscape** orientation.

STEP THREE

Click on the **Document** button and set all your margins for **.5** inches. Click the **OK** button for both the **Document** dialog box and the **Page Setup** dialog box. These settings should give your document a generous amount of room to work with the list information.

STEP FOUR

Select the entire document by choosing **Select All** from the **Edit** menu. Go to the **Insert** menu and choose **Text to Table**.

STEP FIVE

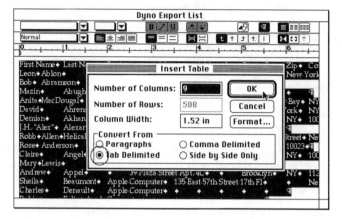

Figure 6.22

Microsoft Word automatically determines the number of columns your
information will require for a table (the example in Figure 6.22 shows nine
columns). The area of this dialog box called "Convert From" shows the
various kinds of formats that can be converted into a table. Tab delimited
should automatically be selected. Click the **OK** button.

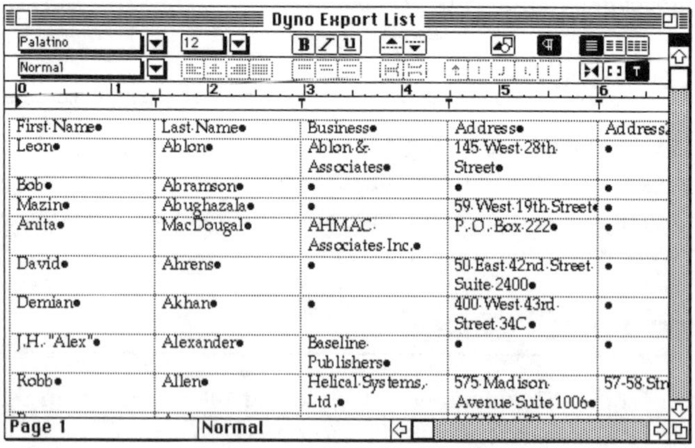

Figure 6.23

The conversion process may take a few minutes, depending on the amount
of data you have for your table. Once completed, the table structure will
allow you to quickly spot errors, add more entries, and edit information.

You might want to use the "new window" method described in Figure 6.11 to add new records or simplify editing.

Formatting and Executing the Print Merge (What Are You Sending?)

You've made your list, checked it twice, and now you're ready to send off a letter or notice to all the people on it. In this section, you'll be working with the "main document" you want to send for your mailing. In order to execute the print merge process, your main document needs to be formatted with instructions that tell Microsoft Word what to do.

Here is where the Print Merge Helper really goes to work. It's like a guardian angel guiding you through the process and simplifying its correct execution. You'll learn how to personalize each letter, how to accommodate letters that have some variation or restriction, as well as what some of the various print merge instructions mean.

Formatting Personalized Letters

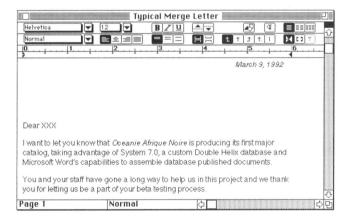

Figure 6.24

The typical merge letter will require the of use the address and salutation information from your data file to personalize each letter (Figure 6.24). This could be the extent of what you may need to do with most of your mail merge projects. However, once in a while you might need to insert some special information for certain circumstances that could save you a lot of time with little effort. In what follows, you'll learn how to prepare the main document to accommodate either situation.

Formatting Letters with No Variations

The first example below demonstrates a merge letter using a data document that was created using the "quick list method." This kind of data document format allows for what is called "variable field length," meaning that no adjustments need to be made for those records that may not have certain information, such as a title or second address line.

The second example will show you how you can accommodate blank lines that might be inserted into your merged letter if the record contains a blank field—such as no title or second address line.

Document with Variable Field Lengths

STEP ONE

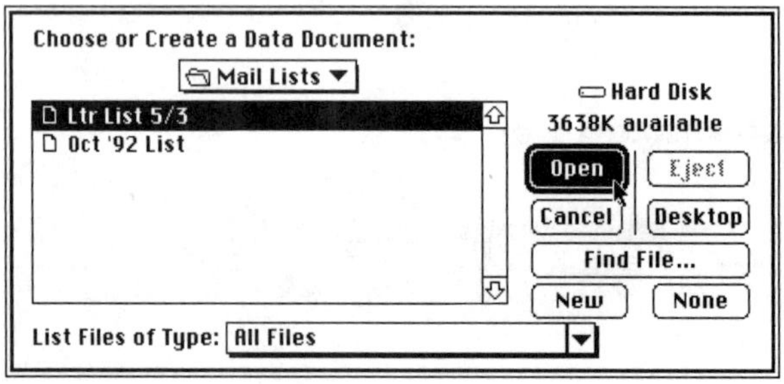

Figure 6.25

To begin formatting your document, open the letter you want to send. Go to the **View** menu and choose **Print Merge Helper**. Since you have already formatted and created a Data file, you're going to choose the list you want merged with the letter. Navigate to the folder that contains the list, select the list, and click on the **Open** button (Figure 6.25).

STEP TWO

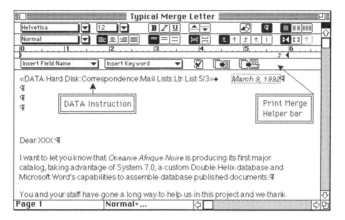

Figure 6.26

A "Data statement" will be inserted at the top of your document. This is the instruction that informs Microsoft Word of the file to use for the merge process and its location on your hard disk. You should also notice the Print Merge Helper bar positioned just above the data instruction (Figure 6.26).

STEP THREE

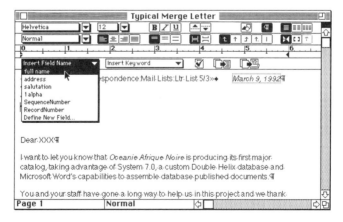

Figure 6.27

You're going to use the Print Merge Helper bar to insert instructions into the document so that Microsoft Word knows where to place the address and salutation information when you print the letter. Inserting these field names is like selecting items from a drop down menu.

Position the flashing insertion point at the beginning of the line where you would like the address information to appear. Move the pointer into the Insert Field Name list box and press and drag to select the Name field. When you let go of the mouse, the field name will be inserted into your document surrounded by the print merge characters. The example in Figure 6.27 shows the Insert Field Name choices for a list created using the "quick list" method described earlier in this chapter.

STEP FOUR

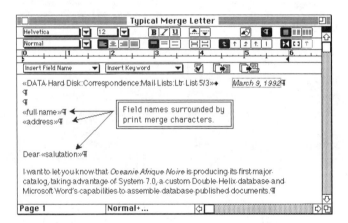

Figure 6.28

Press the **Return** key for a new line and then insert the remaining fields into your document using the **Insert Field Name** menu (Figure 6.28). If you had entered any place holder text, you can delete it by inserting a field in its place.

STEP FIVE

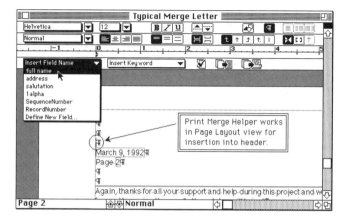

Figure 6.29

If you have a two-page letter, you'll probably want to place the person's name on the second page header so that the two pages don't become separated during the mailing process. To insert the name field in the header, you'll need to switch to Page Layout view and scroll to the second page header. Click to position the flashing insertion point where you want the name field inserted and choose the field from the **Insert Field Name** list (Figure 6.29).

> **NOTE:** *To place a field name within a header in Normal view, you'd have to use standard Copy and Paste techniques and copy existing field names already inserted in your document.*

Document with Unnecessary Blank Lines

Execute the same steps as you would for the document in Example 1 to insert the Data statement and view the Print Merge Helper. The following steps show you how to create print merge instructions for fields that might not contain information in the title, company or second address line. These instructions ensure that blank lines won't be inserted in the address area when the final document is printed.

STEP ONE

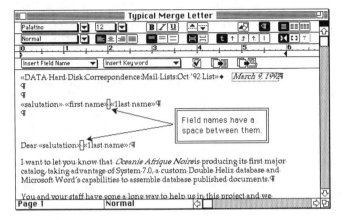

Figure 6.30

Using a mail list that has separate fields for the salutation, first and last names requires that you "build" the first line of information to accommodate the full name. Insert the **Salutation** field name from the **Insert Field Name** list then type a space on your keyboard. Insert the **First Name** field then type a space before you insert the **Last Name** field (Figure 6.30).

STEP TWO

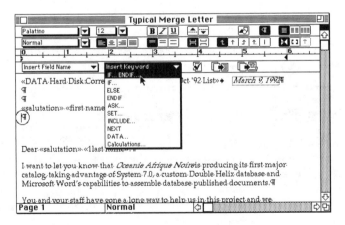

Figure 6.31

On a new line, go to the **Insert Keyword** list on the Print Merge Helper bar and choose **IF...ENDIF** (Figure 6.31).

STEP THREE

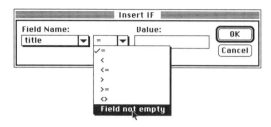

Figure 6.32

What you are setting up is a "conditional" statement. "IF the following meets some kind of condition, do this." Choose the field Title from the Field Name list in the **Insert IF** dialog box. Next choose the "Field not empty" condition from the list of operators (Figure 6.32). Click the **OK** button.

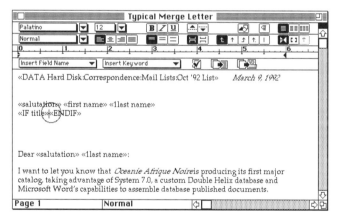

Figure 6.33

When you click the **OK** button, the first part of your conditional statement will be inserted into the document. The flashing insertion point will be positioned just before the ENDIF statement (Figure 6.33).

STEP FOUR

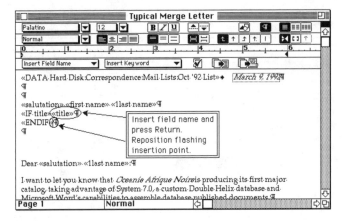

Figure 6.34

Go to the **Insert Field Name** list in the Print Merge Helper bar and choose the **Title** field. Once this is inserted into your document, press the **Return** key for a new line.

Your conditional statement is now complete. In plain English, what this statement is saying is "IF the Title field in the data document for this record is not empty, then place the title information here and press the **Return** key for a new line. End of request (ENDIF)."

In order to continue with constructing the rest of the merge instructions, you need to reposition the flashing insertion point on the other side of the ENDIF merge instruction (Figure 6.34). Place another field next to the ENDIF statement using the **Insert Field Name** menu.

STEP FIVE

Continue inserting the appropriate field names into your document, placing IF...ENDIF... conditional statements for those fields you think might have blank entries in your data document. The ones shown in Figure 6.35 are the typical fields where blank information might be located. However, if you are uncertain, you can examine the data document or just insert more conditional statements to cover for your uncertainties.

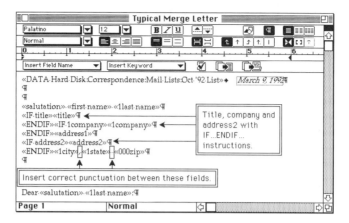

Figure 6.35

When placing the city, state, and zip code fields, make sure you enter the correct punctuation between each field—a comma and space after the city and two spaces after the state.

STEP SIX

If the main document is a two-page letter, be sure to place the Salutation, First Name and Last Name in the header on the second page (do this from Page Layout view).

Executing the Print Merge

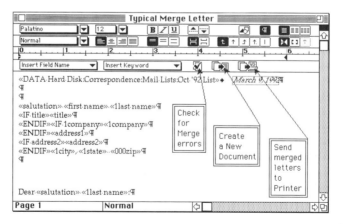

Figure 6.36

When you are finished inserting fields and prior to executing the final print merge, you can check your document for any print merge language syntax errors you might have made. Click on the **Error Checking** button located in the Print Merge Helper bar (Figure 6.36).

Print merge errors that might occur are flagged in a Merge document with a series of asterisks on either side of the message. Generally the message appears close to the offending field. However, using the Print Merge Helper will help to eliminate many errors such as missing print merge characters or ENDIF statements.

If no errors exist, you can then generate a new document or print your mail merge documents by clicking on the appropriate icon in the Print Merge Helper bar as illustrated in Figure 6.36.

When you click on the **New Document** button for your print merge, a single Merge document window will appear. This document will display a copy of each letter with the address information inserted from your data document. A "section break" will be placed between each letter created. What you will see is one, long continuous document containing multiple letters. You can scroll through this document to examine each letter and then choose **Print** from the **File** menu to print as you would for a normal document

Clicking on the **Print** button in the Helper bar will initiate the print merge and bring up the **Print** dialog box. Make sure your paper tray is loaded with the correct paper and click the **OK** button.

Formatting Letters with Some Variations

Just as you saw that you can set up a conditional statement for whether or not your data document has blank cells (for fields such as the title, company, or second address lines), you can also "program" your document with other conditional print-merge statements.

If a certain condition is met, based on the criteria in your database, it can trigger the insertion of text or even another document. What follows are some examples of ways you can execute documents to handle a variety of needs, making your merging process more efficient.

Inserting Conditional Text within a Letter

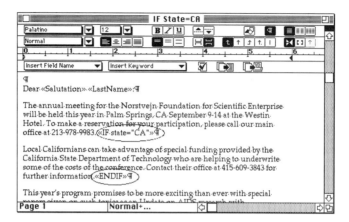

Figure 6.37

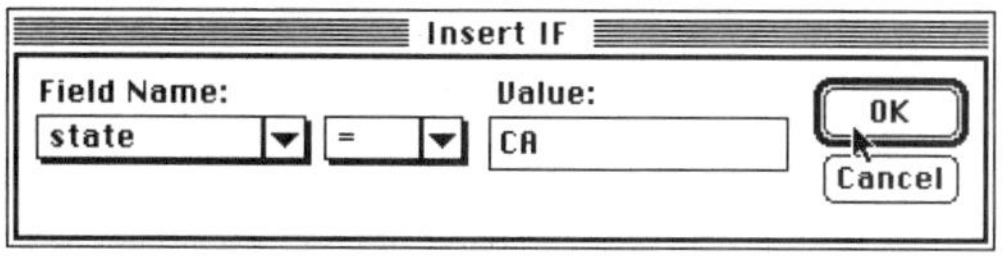

Figure 6.38

Using the Print Merge Helper you can insert the **IF…ENDIF** keywords prior to pressing the Return key for a new paragraph. Once the keywords are inserted, you can enter text in a paragraph that may only pertain to certain people listed in your database.

For the example shown in Figure 6.37, after choosing **IF…ENDIF…** from the **Insert Keyword** menu in the Print Merge Helper bar, you would then choose the **state** field name, use the = operator, and enter **CA** in the **Value** edit bar for the **Insert IF** dialog box (Figure 6.38). Once the statement is placed in the document, press the **Return** key and enter your text.

Including Other Documents

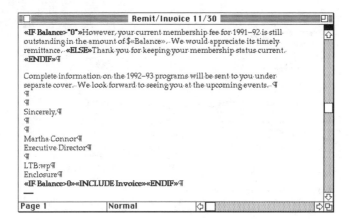

Figure 6.39

Depending on what kind of information you keep in your database (or enter into your DATA document lists), different criteria can be used during the merge process to execute invoices or renewal notices along with regular letters. Data can be exported from your database to include balance due information along with standard address information.

The bold text shown in the example in Figure 6.39 illustrates how balance due information on membership dues can be placed within the main text of the letter. The example uses the IF keyword to create the conditional statement, "IF balance >0" as well as an ELSE keyword to allow for those circumstances where a balance is not due. Text entered after the ELSE statement will be placed in those letters where no balance is due.

After every IF statement, there must be an ENDIF keyword. You can insert the IF, ELSE, and ENDIF keywords separately by choosing them from the Insert Keyword list in the Print Merge Helper bar.

The conditional IF statement at the bottom of the example in Figure 6.39 takes one more step in creating a variation for your print merge mailing. It will include the text of another document during the merge process. In this case, if the balance is greater than 0, a document called "Invoice" will be inserted after the main merge document and before the next document to be printed in the list.

When using the INCLUDE keyword, remember to ask yourself if you want a document to be included with every letter you are merging. If you only want this document under certain conditions, use the IF keyword to set up the criteria. As the example shows, the INCLUDE statement falls in between the IF statement and the final ENDIF keyword.

To place an INCLUDE statement within your main document, simply choose INCLUDE from the Insert Keyword list in the Print Merge Helper bar. A dialog box will ask you to select the document you want included.

If you want the document to be inserted at the end of the current document, make sure the flashing insertion point is located at the *end* of your document before choosing the INCLUDE keyword. Otherwise, the IN-CLUDE statement will appear wherever your flashing insertion point is located and the contents of the included document will appear at that point in every document created during the merge process.

Formatting a Memo or Notice

If you need to print out a number of memos, you may find that the print merge process will help you to execute this task more quickly—especially if you have the same memo you need to "individualize" for a list of people.

Many Individualized Memos

You may have a standard memo form you always use to generate notices. **Open** that document and choose **Print Merge Helper** from the **View** menu. You probably don't have a data document set up for distribution lists, but you might start doing this, once you see how easy it is to execute.

STEP ONE

Click on the **New** button while in the **Choose or Create Data Document** dialog box. Use the Data Document Builder and create one field called "Name." **Save** the document. You might want to give it a name by a distribution category such as "Sales Distrib."

STEP TWO

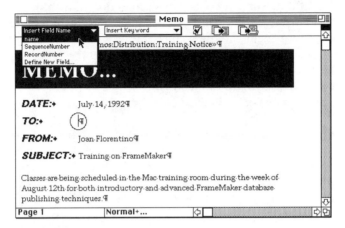

Figure 6.40

While in your memo document, Click in the area where you would normally type the TO: information and insert the Field "Name" using the Print
Merge Helper bar (Figure 6.40). Fill in the rest of your memo.

STEP THREE

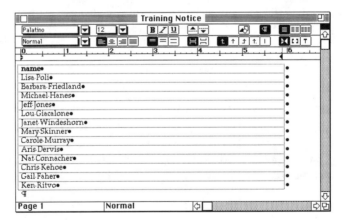

Figure 6.41

Go to the **Window** menu and select your data distribution document. Enter
each person's name, press the **Tab** key for each entry, and save your document (Figure 6.41).

STEP FOUR

Go to the **Window** menu and select the original memo. Click on the **Print Merge** button in the Print Merge Helper bar (or the **New Document** button if you want to preview your memos first). One memo will be generated for each name on the list.

You can build distribution lists that you use often, which might help you save you time and effort on a daily basis.

Single Memo, Many People

Many times you might want others to see the distribution list of a memo or notice, rather than send individualized memos. You can use the print merge process and place all the names in your distribution list into a single document using the **NEXT** Keyword.

STEP ONE

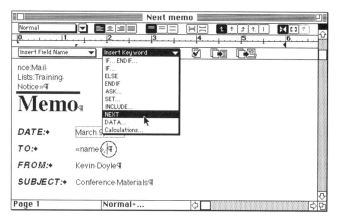

Figure 6.42

Follow the same steps as you would for the individual memos described above. The only difference here is that you'll be adding more information beside the **Name** field. Place the insertion point to the right of the name field and type a comma followed by a space. Go to the **Insert Keyword** list and choose the **NEXT** instruction (Figure 6.42).

STEP TWO

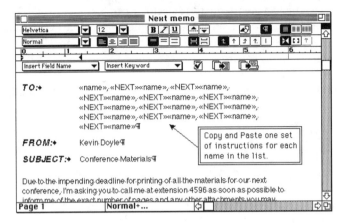

Figure 6.43

Select the field "name" and the NEXT instruction and **Copy** them to the clipboard. **Paste** one set of these instructions for each person in the distribution list. (If there are 14 people on the list, you need to paste the instructions 13 more times.) The last name should NOT have a NEXT Keyword beside it, as there are no more names left on the list to follow it (Figure 6.43).

STEP THREE

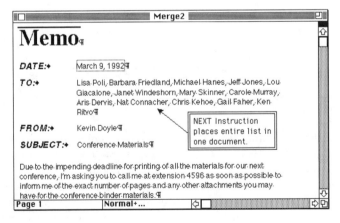

Figure 6.44

Click on either of the print merge buttons in the Print Merge Helper bar to generate a new document or print (Figure 6.44).

STEP FOUR

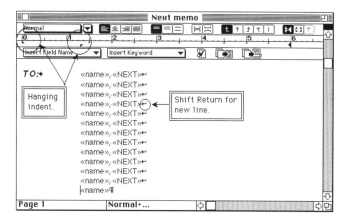

Figure 6.45

If you'd prefer to format the distribution list so that each name is on a single line, create a hanging indent for the TO information and insert a new line by pressing **Shift Return** after each NEXT instruction (Figure 6.45).

How Are You Sending the Letters?

Mass mailings require the generation not only of a letter, notice, or invoice but also the envelope or mail label for sending your mailing off to its destiny. In this section, you'll learn how to use your Data document and merge it for individually printed envelopes, mail labels and a folded one-page flyer.

Formatting Individually Printed Envelopes

Some laser printers have a special tray that will feed approximately 50 envelopes at a time through your printer. Otherwise, you might have to stand by your printer and hand-feed each envelope. You would print individual envelopes for those mailings that require the aura of your "personal" touch for which the use of a mailing label is no substitute.

You'll be using an envelope template—either one with a return address or one formatted for a preprinted envelope—to create the merge document. Go to the **File** menu and **Open** the template.

> **NOTE:** *For instructions on how to create an envelope, see Chapter 5, "How to Print Envelopes."*

STEP ONE

Choose **Print Merge Helper** from the **View** menu. Locate and **Open** the Data file you will be using for your mailing.

STEP TWO

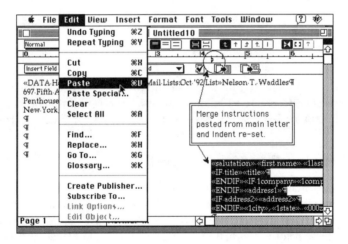

Figure 6.46

If you have already inserted merge instructions within the main document you are sending, simply **Copy** and **Paste** the merge instructions from that document into your envelope document (Figure 6.46). Otherwise, insert the field names into the envelope document following the directions given in the earlier section, called "Executing the Print Merge."

When working with a return address template, make sure you select the addressee print merge instructions and reposition the left indent marker (Figure 6.46).

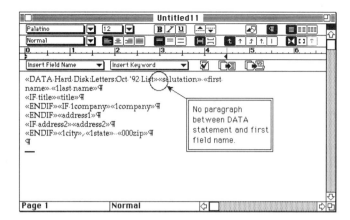

Figure 6.47

Make sure that you do not place any spaces between the DATA statement and the first line of your merge fields (Figure 6.47). Any spaces or paragraph returns that might appear there would also be carried over to each and every envelope when it prints out.

STEP THREE

Click on the **New Document** button or the **Print Merge** button in the Print Merge Helper bar to create your individual envelopes.

For Return-Address Envelopes Using "Quick-List" Data Documents

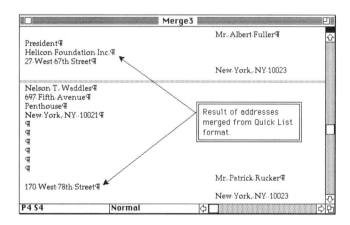

Figure 6.48

The quick-list format uses a Return key for each new address line within a single cell to give you a "variable address length." Using the quick-list fields with a return-address envelope requires some "extra" formatting steps to accommodate the indented Addressee information. If you do not execute these steps, you may be surprised to find that the second and middle lines of your addressee information will be placed next to the far left margin of the envelope (Figure 6.48).

To remedy this situation, after you have executed Steps 1 and 2 above, go to the **File** menu and **Open** your data document that was constructed using the "quick-list" method described earlier. Execute the following steps.

STEP ONE

Select the first two cells containing the header records for "name" and "address" and remove the **Bold** formatting by clicking on the Bold icon in the **Ribbon**.

STEP TWO

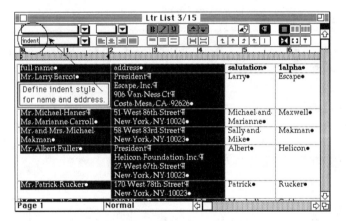

Figure 6.49

Hold down the **Option** key and press and drag to select both the name and the address columns. Click inside the Style Selection bar in the Ruler and type the word "indent." Press the **Return** key. Click on the **OK** button when you are asked if you want to define a style named "indent." This will both define the style and apply it to the columns you selected.

If you wish, you can re-apply the bold format to the header record fields ("name" and "address"). **Save** your data document.

STEP THREE

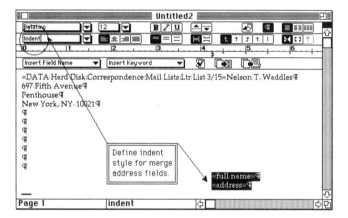

Figure 6.50

Go to the **Window** menu and choose your return envelope document. Select the name and address fields. Go to the Style Selection box in the Ruler and click once. Type the word "indent" and then press the **Return** key (Figure 6.50). Click on the **OK** button to define the style named "indent."

STEP FOUR

Click on the **New Document** button or the **Print Merge** button in the Helper bar to create your individual envelopes. Because both documents contain the "indent" style (and your address and name fields in the data document are formatted with the indent style), the addresses will be properly indented in your final merged document.

Formatting a Folded One-Page Flyer

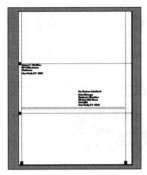

Figure 6.51

To save on envelopes and/or mailing labels, you can take a one-page flyer and run it through your printer to place the address on the reverse side (Figure 6.51). You could then fold it, tape one side, affix postage, and mail it. These next steps explain how you can modify the Return-Address Envelope template for this purpose.

> **NOTE:** *For instructions on how to create a Return Address Envelope, see Chapter 5.*

STEP ONE

Go to the **File** menu and **Open** a Return Address document. If you had created a stationery document template, an Untitled document should appear on your desktop.

STEP TWO

Go to the **File** menu and choose **Page Setup**. Choose the **US Letter** paper option. Click on the **Portrait** orientation icon then click on the **Document** button.

STEP THREE

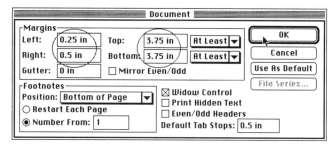

Figure 6.52

Set the document margins as shown in Figure 6.52. Click the **OK** button for both the **Document** dialog box and the **Page Setup** dialog box.

STEP FOUR

Choose **Print Merge Helper** from the **View** menu. Select the correct Data document for your flyer mailing and click on the **Open** button.

STEP FIVE

Double-click to select the Addressee place holder text. Using the Insert Field Name and Insert Keyword list menus in the Print Merge Helper bar, replace the Addressee text with the correct merge fields, and use merge instructions for the kind of list you are merging.

> **NOTE:** *If you are merging a data file that used the "quick-list" method, execute the formatting steps above relating to Figures 6.49 and 6.50. These steps create an indent style for the addressee information and ensure correct printing.*

STEP SIX

Place a stack of your flyers in your printer so that they will print on the blank side of the paper. Click on the **Print Merge** button in the Print Merge Helper bar to execute the printing process.

Formatting Labels

Figure 6.53

There are a variety of label shapes and sizes for both laser and dot-matrix printers. A set of label templates for a number of label sizes and printers ships with the Microsoft Word 5.0 application. However, this section explains the basic techniques and principles you can use for creating your own label template for any size label you might discover in your supply room or stationery store.

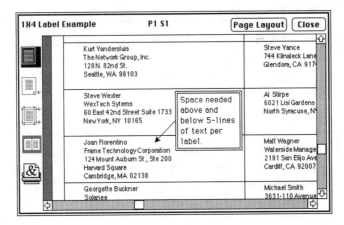

Figure 6.54

Critical to the successful printing of mail labels is allowing for space above and below your MAXIMUM address length (generally five lines, possibly six lines for foreign mail). Your first important step is evaluating your mail list information. Determine the exact number of lines your longest record may require and begin planning from there. Also look at the longest name, title, or company name in your list. These two factors will help you decide which label size best accommodates your mailing list requirements.

Some mail labels come with a 1/4 inch blank strip (or more) on the top and bottom of the actual labels. This strip takes up the "slack" for the even distribution of as many labels as possible per 8.5" × 11" sheet. Most mailing labels are either 1 inch, 1 1/3, inches, or 2 inches high.

The factor that determines the difference in label width is the number of columns of labels on the sheet and whether or not you are using the new "clear" address labels or the standard white labels. Most white labels have a 3/16" space "cut out" between the columns, whereas the clear labels have no space between them.

When you figure that the sheet width is the standard 8.5 inches, two columns would equal 4.25 inches for each column. However, if there is a 0.25 inch blank "strip" on either side of the label, the width would be reduced to 4 inches. Three columns per page would result in a label width of 2 5/6 inches for no "strip" and 2 5/8 inches for labels with a blank strip that lies between each label and on the left and right edges of the sheet.

All this may seem to make for very complicated math when trying to figure out how to print labels evenly on a page. However, Microsoft Word's table function reduces most of the "figuring" process to a few steps. To demonstrate, what follows are directions for setting up a table to print two columns of 1-inch labels that have a 0.5 inch blank strip on the top and bottom of the page and a 0.25 inch strip on the left and right margins (Avery label #5161). The individual label sizes will be 1 inch by 4 inches.

Setting Up the Document

STEP ONE

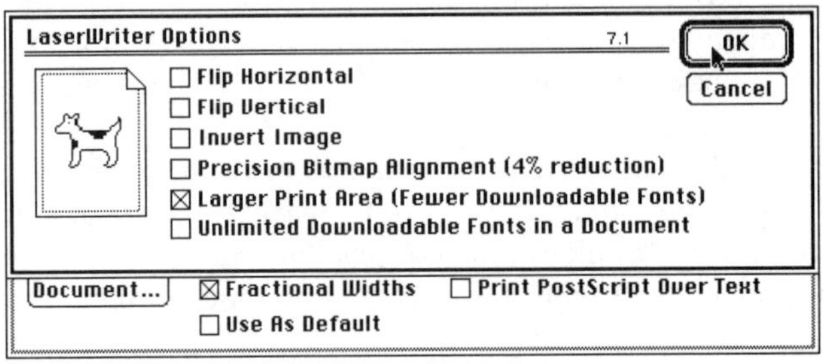

Figure 6.55

In a new document, choose **Page Setup** from the **File** menu. Make sure the **Fractional Widths** option is chosen. Click on the **Options** button and choose **Larger Print Area** to accommodate 0.25 inch margins (Figure 6.55).

STEP TWO

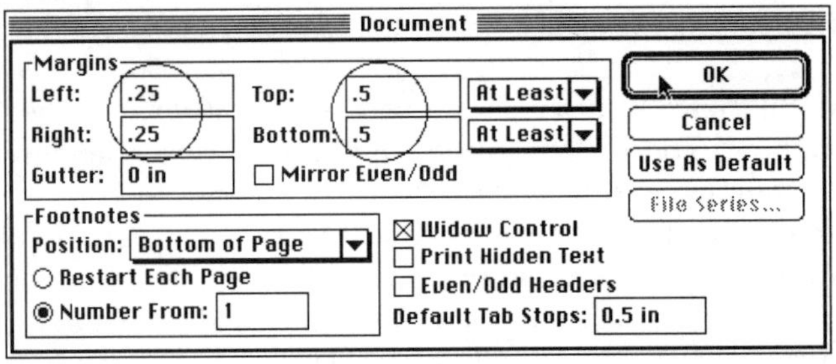

Figure 6.56

Click on the **Document** button and set the margins to **.25** inches Left and Right and **.5** inches Top and Bottom (Figure 6.56). Click on the **OK** button for the **Document** and **Page Setup** dialog boxes.

The document margins will not only accommodate the 0.5 inch strip on the top and bottom of the label sheet, but also the 0.25 inch strip on the left and right.

> **NOTE:** *When using these instructions for creating a template for other label configurations, make sure you take precise measurements of the blank strips that may surround the actual labels and set your margins accordingly.*

STEP THREE

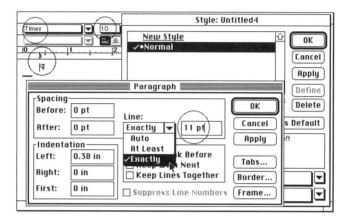

Figure 6.57

Setting the correct font, size, and line spacing for your labels is important when determining how many lines will actually print per label. You will also need to allow for some breathing space on the left edge of the label—you don't want important information cut off during the printing process. The easiest way to accomplish this is to change the Normal style for your document.

Go to the **Format** menu and choose **Style**. Click on the word **Normal**. Choose **Times** and **10 pt** from the **Ribbon** or **Font** menu. Move the Left Indent in the Ruler to the **3/8** inch position. Choose **Paragraph** from the **Format** menu. Select **Exactly** from the **Line list** menu and type **11 pt** in the Line edit bar. Click the **OK** button and then click on the **Define** button (Figure 6.57).

> **NOTE:** *Different font sizes will require different line spacing. Setting an Exact line space through the Paragraph dialog box fixes the maximum number of lines you can expect per label. Generally allow 1 to 2 points more than the actual font size.*

STEP FOUR

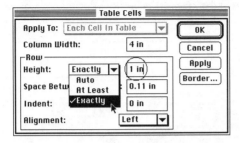

Figure 6.58

The document is now ready for you to insert a table that will act as a "grid" for the spacing of your labels. Choose **Table** from the **Insert** menu. Keep the default settings set for two columns and click on the **Format** button. In the row **Height** area, choose **Exactly** from the list menu and type **1 in** within the edit bar (Figure 6.58). Note that there is an automatic 0.11 inches of space between each column so that the text for the labels won't print dangerously close to the edge of the label paper. Click on the **OK** button.

> **NOTE:** *When setting up a table for 3 columns, you'd enter 3 in the number of Columns edit bar in the Insert Table dialog box. You would then format the row height for either Exactly 1 inch or Exactly 1.333 inches.*

Formatting the Merge Instructions

You now have the basic "grid" for producing the label template. Next you'll need to enter print merge instructions in each cell to set it up for the merging process with your data document. When creating the mail label template, you need to decide which set of field names you will be using most often with the template. If you have a variety of field name structures (one structure uses Full Name and Address and another structure uses Salutation, First Name, Last Name, Title, etc.), you should probably create a separate template document for each different set of field names.

STEP ONE

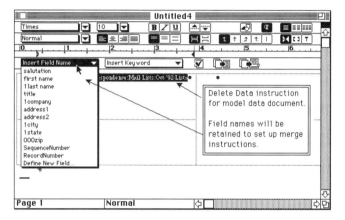

Figure 6.59

Make sure you have Show ¶ turned on and position the flashing insertion point in the first cell of the table. Go to the **View** menu and choose **Print Merge Helper**. Choose the Data document that contains the field name structure you use most often and click on the **Open** button. When the DATA instruction is inserted in your document, select the instruction and delete it (Figure 6.59). You will "hook up" the data document again, once you've formatted all the print merge instructions for each cell and are about to initiate the actual print merge process.

STEP TWO

Insert the Field names using the Print Merge Helper bar. Be sure you include IF...ENDIF... statements to accommodate any blank fields in your data document. (You might want to copy a set of merge instructions from another merge document you've already created and saved.)

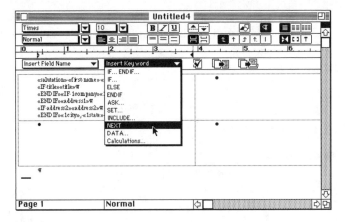

Figure 6.60

When you're finished, make sure the flashing insertion point is located to the right of the last field (possibly the zip code). You're going to insert one more instruction within the cell. Go to the **Insert Keyword** list in the Print Merge Helper bar and choose NEXT (Figure 6.60). This instructs Microsoft Word to insert the "next" address record in your data document on the same page (instead of placing a section break and starting a new page).

STEP THREE

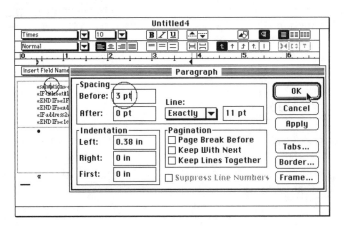

Figure 6.61

Click in the first line of text in the cell. Choose **Paragraph** from the **Format** menu. Type **3 pt** in the Before edit bar (Figure 6.61). This will place some breathing space between the first printed line and the edge of the label. Click on the **OK** button.

STEP FOUR

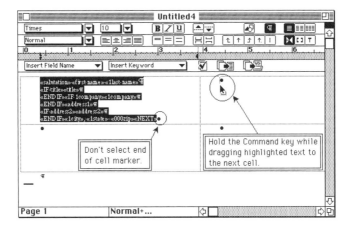

Figure 6.62

Make sure that you have Show ¶ turned on so that you can see the paragraph marks for each line of text. Select the text in the first cell, being careful not to select the end of cell marker indicated by a black dot. Place the pointer over the text and hold down the **Command** key. Press and drag the pointer over to the next cell and release the mouse button (Figure 6.62). You have just made a copy of the text using the drag-and-drop text editing process. (If this did not work for you, make sure you have the Drag-and-Drop Text Editing option turned on in the Preferences dialog box.) Hold down the **Command** key and press and drag a copy of the same merge instructions into each of the two empty cells below the first row.

STEP FIVE

Press the **Option** key and double-click within the table to select all the cells. Choose **Copy** from the **Edit** menu. Click in the empty paragraph beneath and outside the table grid. Go to the **Edit** menu and choose **Paste**. Do this same step **4** times, so that you have a total of 10 rows containing print merge instructions.

STEP SIX

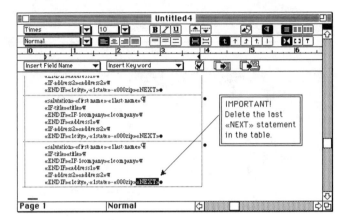

Figure 6.63

Scroll to the bottom of your document. Click in the last cell and delete the NEXT instruction (Figure 6.63). This step instructs Microsoft Word that it's okay during the print merge process to create a new page (replicating this one) for the remaining address labels. Be careful not to delete the right merge character from the "Zip" (or some other) field.

STEP SEVEN

Save your document as a Stationery document and name it. You might want to code the document name to the actual Avery label it uses and/or to the dimensions of the label (i.e., Avery 5161 1×4). You might also make separate folders for label templates you create for the various field structures you use (i.e., a folder each for Quick List Labels and Full List Labels).

Executing the Print Merge

N ow that your template is completed, you can execute a print merge for your mailing list. But first, you need to "hook up" the template to the correct data document.

STEP ONE

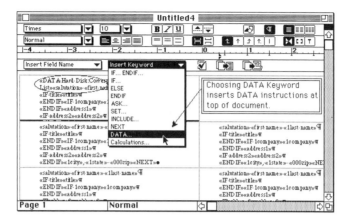

Figure 6.64

If the Print Merge Helper bar is still showing, you can use the Insert Keyword menu to insert the DATA instruction at the top of the document (Figure 6.64). Otherwise, choose **Print Merge Helper** from the **View** menu and choose the appropriate data document.

STEP TWO

Click on the appropriate print merge button in the Print Merge Helper bar to either Create a new document or Print your labels.

Recovering From the Paper Jam Error

Y ou've successfully created your main document, inserted all the correct merge fields, and begun the process of printing all the merged addresses for your mass mailing. But somewhere in the middle of the printing process, the printer jams and you have to abort the print merge. How can you quickly get back on track without reprinting all the letters (or envelopes) from the beginning and still make that impossible deadline?

The most important step (after calming down) is to look at the last letter (or envelope or sheet of labels) that printed correctly. You're going to use the name on that document to locate where you were in the print merge process and continue forward from there.

There are two options for arriving at the correct restarting point. One option requires you to determine what "record number" belongs to the name of that last printed document. The other requires you to count the actual *number* of letters (or labels or envelopes) that printed correctly so that you can move forward from where that document fell in the sequence of what was being printed. You'll learn what steps you can take to execute either solution in what follows.

Automatic Record Numbering of Your DATA File

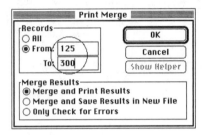

Figure 6.65

Go to the **File** menu and **Open** the Data document you used for the mail merge. Typically, data files do *not* contain "record numbers" that tell you where in the order of the list each name falls. The reason for knowing the actual record number for each record is tied to using the **Print Merge** dialog box to execute the print merge process.

In the **Print Merge** dialog box (which is accessed from the **File** menu), there is an option to restrict the mail merge to a range of record numbers (Figure 6.65). You can single out a specific record and print just one letter or you can print your letters in batches for a range of records.

You can either number each record in your data file and then find the record number that corresponds to the name on the last printed document or you can manually count the number of different names on the documents that printed successfully and use the next highest number to execute the print merge (see Step 5 below).

Counting each name printed may be an immediate, simple solution if you were near the beginning of the mail merge when the jam occurred. However, if you were further along in the process, there is a lot of room for inaccuracy. Though numbering each record in the data document can be a time-consuming process (unless you use some of the built-in features of Microsoft Word), it will yield more accurate and controllable results.

One method for record numbering is the "quick-fix method"—you're in a time crunch and you need to make this happen NOW. It will only work for tables that have a field for each part of the address (i.e. Name, Title, Company, Address1, Address2, etc.). The other method requires you to insert a number for each record (and should be used for lists that use the "quick list" format). However, this second method (though slightly more time-consuming) will automatically renumber your records if you ever re-sort the data document or enter more records.

Tools Renumber

If your data document is formatted as a table, the Renumber function in Microsoft Word cannot number cells in a particular column or row. It will number each and every cell in your document. Therefore, if your data document is set up as a table, you will need to convert the table into tab delimited text which you can then easily renumber. If your data is already tab delimited, you can proceed directly to Step 2.

STEP ONE

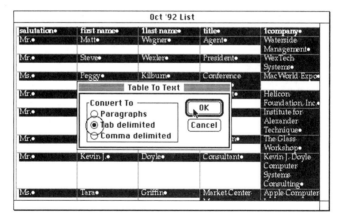

Figure 6.66

Press the Option key and double-click to select the entire table. Go to the **Insert** menu and choose **Table to Text**. Click on the conversion option for Tab delimited text (Figure 6.66).

STEP TWO

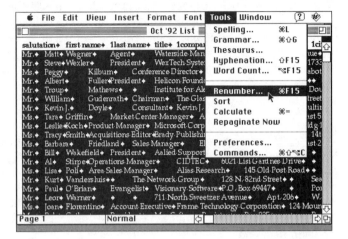

Figure 6.67

Select all the text in your document EXCEPT the field names in the header record. Go to the **Tools** menu and choose **Renumber** (Figure 6.67). Click on the **OK** button.

STEP THREE

Figure 6.68

The renumbering process places a number followed by a period and a tab mark at the beginning of each paragraph (or record). This now becomes a record number "field." Therefore, you need to enter another field name to the header record. Click at the top of the document. Type the number sign (#), then press the **Tab** key (Figure 6.68).

STEP FOUR

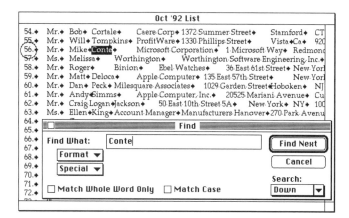

Figure 6.69

Go to the **Edit** menu and choose **Find**. Enter the name that appeared on the last successfully printed document in the Find What edit bar. Click on the **Find Next** button. Make a note of the record number (Figure 6.69). Scroll to the end of your data document and note the last record number there.

STEP FIVE

Go to the **File** menu and **Open** the main document you were using for the print merge process (or choose it from the **Window** menu if it's already open). Go to the **File** menu and choose **Print Merge**. In the **From** edit bar, enter a record number that is one number higher than the one you found in Step 4. Press the **Tab** key. In the **To** edit bar enter the last record number in the data document. Click on the **Merge and Print results** option then click the **OK** button (see Figure 6.65).

STEP SIX

You can go back to the data document, choose **Select All** from the **Edit** menu and return the tab delimited text to the table format by choosing **Table** from the **Insert** menu. Once the print merge is successfully completed, you might want to select the Record # column and choose **Clear** from the **Edit** menu. You could then enter a footnote (see Step 2 below) to create an automatic numbering system and speed future sorting and record entry processes.

Inserting Footnote Numbers

You can use this method for both tables or tab-delimited text, but it will take a few more minutes to execute than Method One above. However, it is the only successful numbering solution for tables where you don't need to convert the table to text format in order to execute the process.

STEP ONE

Click inside the first table cell in your data document. Choose **Table Layout** from the **Format** menu. Click on the **Column** option then click the **Insert** button.

STEP TWO

In the first cell of this new column, enter a header record name for the column (you can use "#" or "Record #"). Press the **Down arrow** on your keyboard to move the flashing insertion point to the cell below.

STEP THREE

Go to the **Insert** menu and choose **Footnote**. Click on the **OK** button (Figure 6.70). The document window will "split" to reveal a footnote area at the bottom of the window. Don't enter any text. Place the I-beam in the next empty cell in the main window and insert another Footnote.

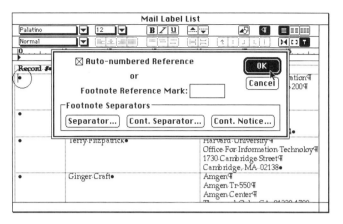

Figure 6.70

NOTE: *To speed the entry process, you can use the keyboard shortcut Command E to insert a footnote and press the Return key to activate the OK button. Press the 0 key on the numeric keypad to return to the table window. (If this does not work, Delete the 0 that may have been inserted as a footnote then press the Clear button on your numeric keypad to take off the "num lock" function.) Press the down arrow on your keyboard to move into the next cell.*

STEP FOUR

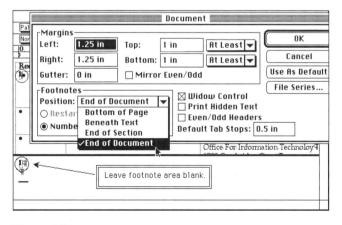

Figure 6.71

Go to the **Format** menu and choose **Document**. Choose the **End of Document** option for the position of the Footnotes and click the **OK** button (Figure 6.71). Save your document.

NOTE: *To make the Footnotes window disappear when you are done, choose* **Footnotes** *from the* **View** *menu.*

STEP FIVE

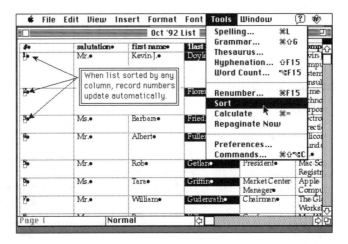

Figure 6.72

Using Footnotes to number your records has an added benefit. If ever you sort your mail list by different header record criteria (Zip Code, Last Name, State, etc.), the record numbers will automatically update themselves so that the first record in the list is always number 1 (Figure 6.72).

Conclusion

N ow that you understand the basics of what mail merge can do for your document production efficiency, you might feel more confident in exploring ways you can further automate documents you use every day. Begin to assess your documents to see if there is repetitive text or "boiler plate" language you can set up as a separate document and then include in other documents by using the INCLUDE print merge statement. You can also program a complex level of IF...ELSE...ENDIF statements within a merge document that can accommodate a variety of criteria.

You might start to analyze how you've set up your data documents and determine the most efficient way to structure those documents for sorting and record numbering so that you can restrict your mail merge to a single name and address for quickly creating a letter. You would simply type the same record number in the From and To edit bars within the Print Merge dialog box—much as you would in the Print dialog box when you only want to print a single page in the middle of a long document.

The more you explore the capabilities of the Print Merge language, the sooner you will realize it is a simple, logical, and powerful tool that offers a rich opportunity for consistent document production. Some other ways to use this language for generating forms and creating report formats will be discussed in Part II of this book.

More Timesaving Solutions

Forms Generation

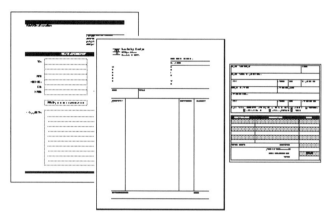

Figure 7.1

When you finally decide that you need to sit down and create a form, it's usually either when the original form has been so over-photocopied you can't use it any more or when you've decided there might be a better way to organize your information on paper.

Creating forms takes some time and patience. You have to be willing and able to move lines and boxes around easily, to see what looks (and fits) best on the page, and to just plain "fiddle" with the form until it looks right. You might also like to give the document a bit of pizzazz—even if you're not a graphic artist, you'd probably like to know how to achieve some pleasing effects that get people's attention.

The first part of this chapter will be dealing with two kinds of forms: the ones you simply print one copy of and photocopy because everyone fills them in by hand (such as the fax transmission sheet sitting next to the fax machine), and the ones you need to fill in on the computer and send to someone (such as a memo, purchase order, or invoice). Step-by-step instructions will be given for creating several kinds of memos, faxes, and invoices so that you can learn and practice some of the techniques used in creating forms. By executing these steps, you will become familiar with the fastest way to create many similar kinds of documents.

Because no two forms are alike, in the last part of the chapter you'll see some special techniques and ideas for creating form "parts." There are a variety of methods you can combine to achieve similar results but, depending on how the overall document is structured, one solution may prove better than the other.

Before you get started, here are some important points you need to be aware of:

- Set your document margins *before* you start to work with tables, boxes, and grids. Readjustments for margin settings that you change while you are in the middle of formatting your document are annoying and time-consuming.

- Make sure the "fractional widths" option is selected in the File Page Setup dialog box *before* you start working with your document. Spacing for line "leader tabs" and other kinds of formats used for forms will print strangely if fractional widths are not on. Turning on fractional widths while you are in the process of formatting your document will cause a difference in the way the text lines up on the page and will waste your time making the necessary readjustments.

- Do yourself a favor and don't try to "fix" a document you might have been working with—especially if it contains a lot of unnecessary tab marks, spaces made with the spacebar, and blank paragraph marks. You will save yourself time, effort, frustration, and confusion by learning the techniques described in this chapter and applying them from a fresh vantage point in a new document.

- Try to sketch out your form to get a clear idea of what you want where before you start. If you want boxes, underline, and shading, be aware of the limitations of certain formats before you get too involved and work yourself into a corner you can't get out of easily.

- Give yourself plenty of time. Creating forms is "nitpicking" work and you should not feel the pressure of the clock. Because you will want to explore, try things, and get a little creative, plan this kind of activity for an easy day when no deadlines are hounding you.

Memos

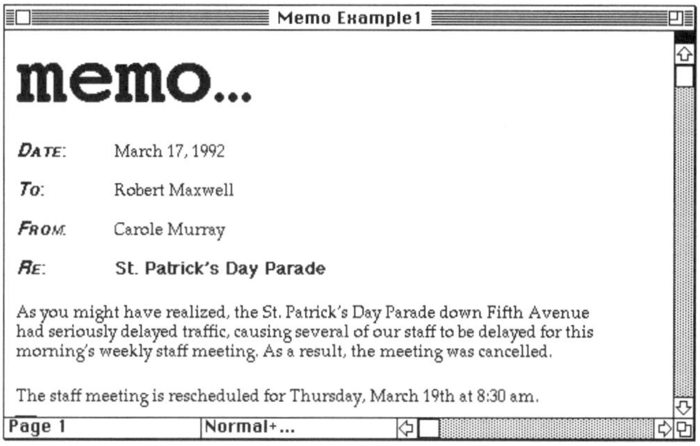

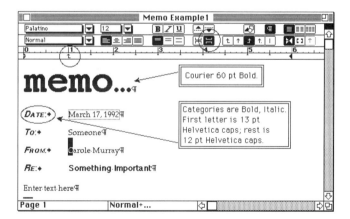

Figure 7.2

Memos are probably one of the easiest forms to set up because the information they contain is relatively straight forward. A memo form is generally entered on the computer, printed and distributed. In the three examples that follow you'll learn some techniques that illustrate the use of tabs, graphics and tables.

Figure 7.3

You can set up a memo using tabs and a variety of font characteristics. To achieve the results of the memo illustrated in Figure 7.3, you would need to apply fonts, font sizes, paragraph spacing, bolding, and italic from the Ribbon and Ruler. Execute the following steps to create this memo.

1. Choose **Courier 60 pt Bold** from the **Ribbon** and type the word "memo." Hold the **Option** key and type a semicolon (**;**) to obtain the "ellipsis." Press **Return** for a new line.

2. Press **Command Shift P** to apply the Normal style. Click on the **Open Space** between paragraphs icon in the Ruler. Choose a **Left Aligned tab** mark and click once at the **1 inch** mark.

3. Select **Helvetica** font, **13 pt**, **Bold** and **Italic** from the Ribbon. Type the first letter of the category. Select **12 pt** from the Ribbon and type the rest of the word. Press the **Tab** key. Choose **Palatino** font from the Ribbon and remove Bold and Italic formats. Go to the **Insert** menu and choose **Date**. Press **Return**.

4. Repeat step 3 for the other category lines and enter place holder text for each category. For the final Subject line, apply **Helvetica 12 pt Bold**.

5. Press **Return** for a new line for the memo text. Press **Command Shift P** to return to Normal. Select the **Palatino** font and click on the **Open Space** between paragraphs icon in the Ruler.

6. To execute the memo, you could save it in a **stationery** format and simply double-click to select the place-holder text and type over the highlighted text.

> *To send the memo to a list of people, see Chapter 6, the section on "Formatting a Memo or Notice."*

This example combines a graphic with the "memo" text and illustrates a different kind of alignment for the memo categories. Some people prefer to have category titles align at the colon mark (Figure 7.4). The steps to achieve this follow.

1. Click on the **Graphics** icon in the Ribbon, pick a line thickness, and use the line tool to create the "page." Use the text tool and select **Courier** from the **Font** menu. Choose the largest size on the menu (probably 24 pt). Type **memo**, followed by the ellipsis. Select all your text. In order to increase the font size, you will need to press **Command]**. Pick up the text and place it inside your graphic (Figure 7.5). If you need to adjust the text size, select the text and use the keyboard shortcut until it is the appropriate size. Press **Command A** to select all your graphic elements and move them to the upper left corner of the Edit Picture window. This will reduce the amount of white border space around your graphic. Click in the Edit Picture **close box**.

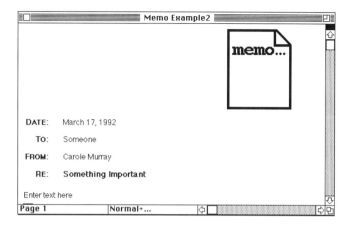

Figure 7.4

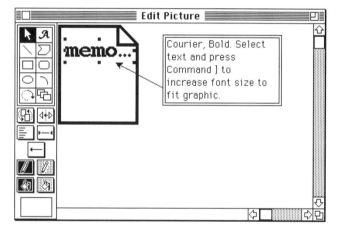

Figure 7.5

2. Click on the **Right Aligned paragraph** icon in the **Ruler** to move the graphic to the far right of the document. Press **Return**.

3. Click on the **Left Aligned paragraph** icon in the Ruler. Click on the **Right Aligned Tab** icon in the Ruler and insert a **Right Aligned Tab** mark as illustrated in Figure 7.6. Click on a **Left Aligned Tab** icon in the Ruler and click to insert a **Left Aligned Tab** in the Ruler, just to the right of the first tab mark. Click on the **Open Space between paragraphs** icon in the Ruler.

4. Press the **Tab** key and follow the character and text formatting steps as you did in the first example, above. Save your document.

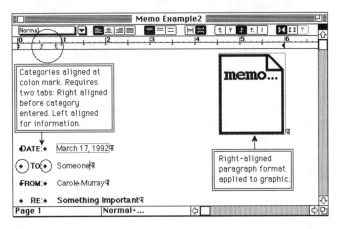

Figure 7.6

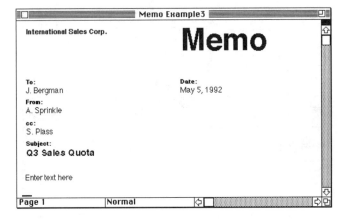

Figure 7.7

The memo example in Figure 7.7 uses table cells and fixed spacing to achieve a different kind of memo design. To execute this kind of formatting, you'll need to apply different font sizes and/or bolding to the Helvetica font.

1. Go to the **Insert** menu and choose **Table**. Click the **OK** button to accept the default settings. Select the entire table and adjust the cell width that you find appropriate using the T markers in the Ruler.

2. Select the second row. Go to the **Format** menu and choose **Table Cells**. Select **Exactly** from the **Height** list menu and enter **32 pt** in the Height edit bar (Figure 7.8).

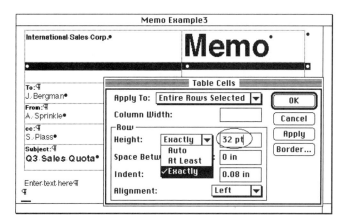

Figure 7.8

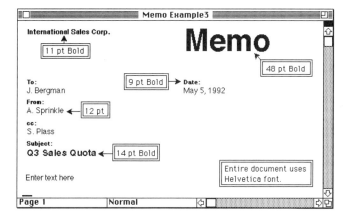

Figure 7.9

3. Click in the various cells and select the proper font sizes as shown in Figure 7.9. Press the **Return** key for a new line within a cell (where appropriate) and apply the correct font. Press the **Tab** key to move to a new cell and to create a new row. Apply the correct font sizes and enter your text.

4. When you enter the body of your memo text, be sure you click outside the table before typing. You might want to apply **Open Space between paragraphs** format.

Fax Transmission Sheets

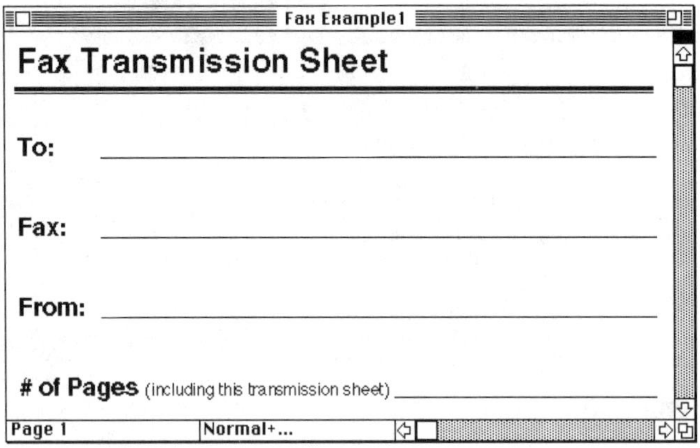

```
┌─────────────────────────────────────────────┐
│ ▤☐▤▤▤▤▤▤▤▤▤▤▤ Fax Example1 ▤▤▤▤▤▤▤▤▤▤▤ ▤☐▤ │
│                                             ⇧ │
│ Fax Transmission Sheet                        │
│ ───────────────────────────────────────────  │
│                                               │
│  To:      _____ │
│                                               │
│  Fax:     _____ │
│                                               │
│  From:    _____ │
│                                               │
│  # of Pages (including this transmission sheet) _____ │
│                                             ⇩ │
│ Page 1          Normal+...    ⇦☐▨▨▨▨▨▨   ⇦⇩ │
└─────────────────────────────────────────────┘
```

Figure 7.10

Typically, faxes are sent in a hurry. If it wasn't important for the information to get there quickly, you'd put the material in the mail. When it comes time to send a fax, you often reach for a photocopy of a fax cover sheet, dash off a quick note and place it in the fax machine.

Time notwithstanding, there might be the circumstance where your hand writing is just not sufficiently legible or you might want to keep a record of the fax transmission sheet as a kind of "fax memo." In those cases, you'd want to "fill out" the fax transmission sheet on the computer, print it, and/or save it.

In the examples that follow, you'll learn how to use tabs and tables to create two different kinds of fax transmission cover sheets.

There are any number of ways to design a fax cover sheet. This example will help you understand some of the formatting processes that create a form—space between lines of text, special border effects, creating evenly spaced lines, etc.

The first part of the example demonstrates how to create a fax that will be photocopied and filled out by hand. The second part will show you how to alter the fax sheet so that text can be entered in it on your computer.

Creating a Blank Fax Form

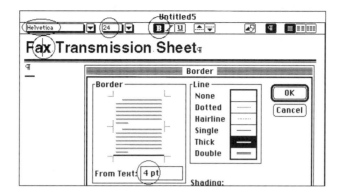

Figure 7.11

1. Enter and format the title text as **Helvetica 24 pt Bold**. Go to **Format** menu and choose **Border**. Press the **Tab** key and enter **4** in the **From Text** edit bar. Apply a **Thick** border to the **bottom** of the diagram and click **OK** (Figure 7.11).

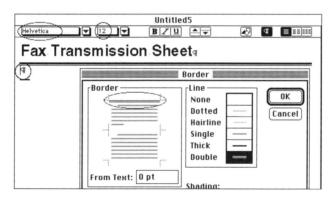

Figure 7.12

2. Press the **Return** key for a new line. Press **Command Shift P** to apply Normal style. Choose **Border** from the **Format** menu and apply a **Double** border to the **top** of the diagram (Figure 7.12).

3. Press the **Return** key for a new line. Press **Command Shift P** to apply Normal style. Apply **Helvetica 18 pt Bold** formatting and enter the **To:** text. Choose **Paragraph** from the **Format** menu and enter **18 pt** in the **Before** edit bar (Figure 7.13). Click the **OK** button.

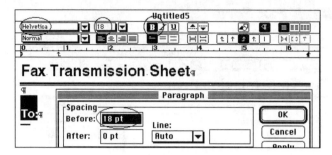

Figure 7.13

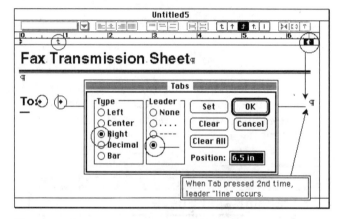

Figure 7.14

4. Place a **Left Aligned Tab** mark in the Ruler at the **7/8** inch mark. Select the **Right Aligned Tab** icon in the Ruler and click near the **Right Indent** in the Ruler to place a **Right Aligned Tab** mark there. Press and drag the tab mark into position over the top of the **Right Indent** mark. Double-click on the **Right Aligned Tab** mark to display the **Tabs** dialog box. Click on the **Leader line** option; then click the **OK** button. Press the **Tab** key twice—once to advance to the first Tab mark, the second time to activate the line leader tab (Figure 7.14).

5. Press the **Return** key for a new line. Go to the **Format** menu and choose **Paragraph**. Enter **36 pt** in the **Before** edit bar. Click the **OK** button (Figure 7.15). Enter the text for **Fax:** and press the **Tab** key **twice**. Press the **Return** key and enter the text and press the **Tab** key for the **From:** information as you did for the Fax information above it.

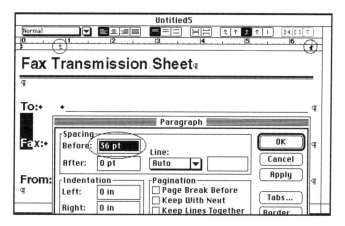

Figure 7.15

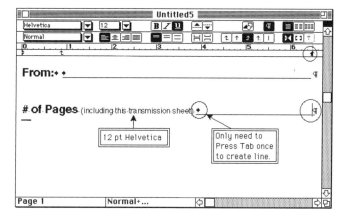

Figure 7.16

6. Press the **Return** key and enter **# of Pages**. Choose **12 pt** and remove the **Bold** formatting. Enter the text in parenthesis and press the **Tab** key only *once* to obtain the underline (Figure 7.16).

7. Press **Return** for a new line. Choose **Border** from the **Format** menu. Apply a **Double** line border to the **bottom** of the box. Do not enter any From Text spacing (Figure 7.17).

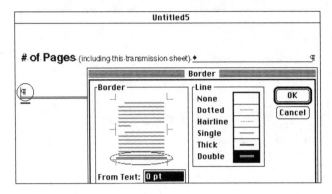

Figure 7.17

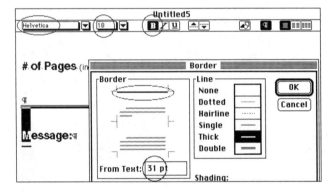

Figure 7.18

8. Press **Return**. Enter the **Message:** text. Choose **Border** from the **Format** menu. Press the **Tab** key and enter **31 pt** (maximum allowed) in the **From Text** edit bar. Choose the **Thick** border and apply it to the **top** of the diagram (Figure 7.18). Click the **OK** button.

9. Press **Return**. Choose **Paragraph** from the **Format** menu. Enter **24 pt** in the **Before** edit bar. Click on the **Border** button. Click on the **None** box to clear the border. The From Text edit bar should display 0 pt (Figure 7.19). Click the **OK** button for both the Border and Paragraph dialog boxes. Enter place holder text for a message, or leave the message space blank.

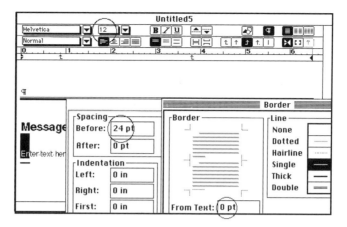

Figure 7.19

Modifying a Fax Form for Text Entry

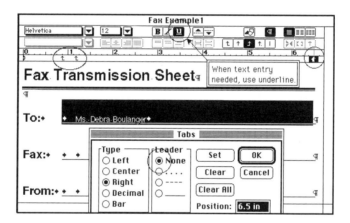

Figure 7.20

1. Click on the **Left Aligned Tab** icon in the Ruler. Click to the right of the first tab mark (about 1/4 inch) and place another tab mark in the Ruler. Double-click on the tab mark that is positioned over top of the Right Indent marker to display the **Tabs** dialog box. Click on the **Leader None** option and click the **OK** button. Highlight the two tab marks in the text and apply **Underline** by clicking on the Underline icon in the Ribbon (Figure 7.20). Repeat this step for each of the categories where text will be entered.

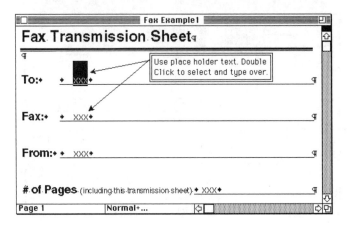

Figure 7.21

2. Click after the last tab mark in each category. Apply **Helvetica 12 pt** and remove the **Bold** format. Enter some XXXs as place holder text. Press the **Tab** key to produce a line to the end of the paragraph. **Save** the document as a template or in stationery format. When working with the document, double-click to select the place holder text and type over it (Figure 7.21). The line to the end of the paragraph will be preserved no matter what the length of your information is.

If you did not follow these procedures to alter the tab marks so that they are now **underline** tabs rather than leader tabs, there will be no consistency in terms of maintaining the underline text effect when you enter text in the fax form. The leader tab would place a line from the end of your entered text to the end of the right indent. If you are wanting to enter text "on a line," use underline tab marks to achieve this effect.

Figure 7.22

This example uses a table to create entry "boxes" for more categories of fax cover sheet information. It also has reverse type with black borders and shaded boxes to dress up the document (Figure 7.22).

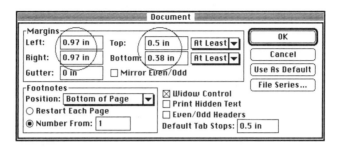

Figure 7.23

1. Choose **Document** from the **Format** menu and set the margins to what is shown in Figure 7.23. Click on the **OK** button. Choose **Style** from the **Format** menu, select **Normal,** and choose **Helvetica 12 pt** from the **Ribbon**. Click on **Define** and **Close** the style window.

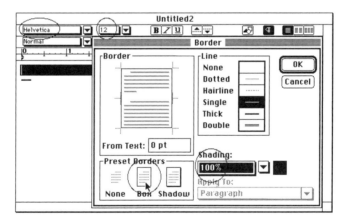

Figure 7.24

2. Go to the **Format** menu and choose **Border**. Apply **100%** shading, choose a **Single** line, and click on the **Box** border (Figure 7.24). Click on the **OK** button.

3. Press the **Return** key for a new paragraph. Press **Command Shift P** to apply Normal style. Choose **14 pt, Bold**, and **Italic** from the **Ribbon**. Choose **Format Paragraph** and **Tab** once to the **After** edit bar and enter **30 pt**. Click **OK** (Figure 7.25). Enter your company name.

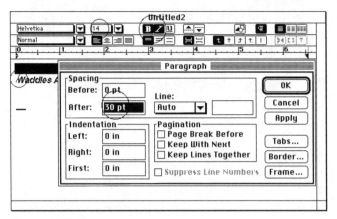

Figure 7.25

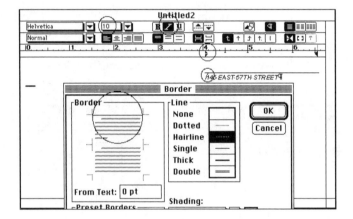

Figure 7.26

4. Press the **Return** key for a new paragraph. Press **Command Shift P** to apply Normal style. Remove the **Bold** formatting from the **Ribbon** and apply **10 pt**. Move the **Left Indent** mark to near the **4 inch** mark (less if your company has a long address). Choose **Format Border** and apply a **Hairline** border to the **top** of the Paragraph (Figure 7.26). Click **OK**. Press **Return** and enter each line of your address.

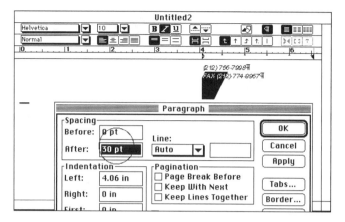

Figure 7.27

5. For the last line of your address (or fax telephone), choose **Format Paragraph**. **Tab** once into the **After** edit bar and enter **30 pt** (Figure 7.27). Click **OK**.

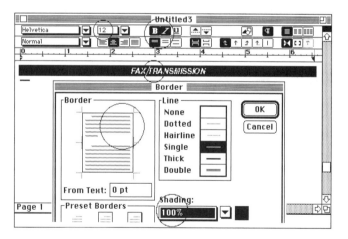

Figure 7.28

6. Press the **Return** key for a new paragraph. Press **Command Shift P** to apply Normal style. Click on the **Centered** paragraph icon in the Ruler and apply **Italic Bold** format. Enter text for Fax Transmission (or whatever you like). Choose **Format Border**, select **100%** shading, and apply a **box** border (Figure 7.28).

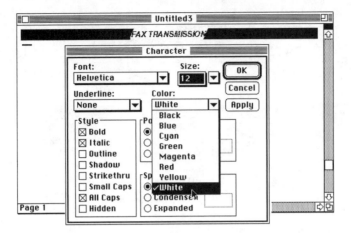

Figure 7.29

7. Select the fax title text and choose **Format Character**. You can apply All Caps if you like. More importantly, choose **White** from the **Color** list menu (Figure 7.29). If you don't execute this step with reverse type text, your text will be black against a black background (and not visible). Click **OK**.

NOTE: *When working with Show¶ turned on, Black text in a black border box will appear as White. With Show¶ turned off, the box will appear as solid black and your text will not be visible.*

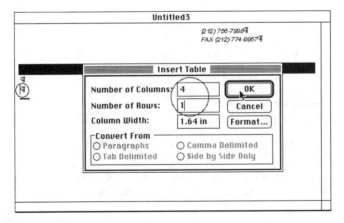

Figure 7.30

8. Press the **Return** key for a new paragraph. Press **Command Shift P** to apply Normal style. Press the **Return** key a second time. Go to the **Insert** menu and choose **Table**. Enter **4** columns, press the **Tab** key, and enter **1** row. Click the **OK** button (Figure 7.30).

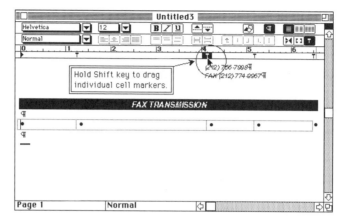

Figure 7.31

9. Hold down the **Shift** key and move the individual **T markers** in the Ruler to adjust the cell width to something similar to what is shown in Figure 7.31. (If the T markers are not showing, click to highlight the Cell Marker scale icon on the far right in the Ruler.)

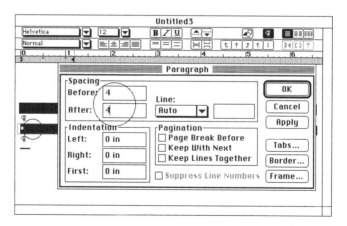

Figure 7.32

10. Using the right pointing arrow inside the table, double-click to select the entire row. Choose **Paragraph** from the **Format** menu. Enter **4** in the **Before** edit bar, press the **Tab** key, and enter **4** in the **After**

edit bar (Figure 7.32). This will allow for some breathing space around your text. Click **OK**.

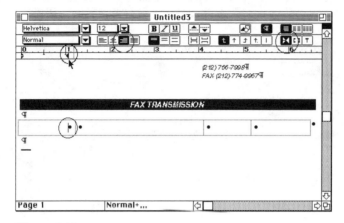

Figure 7.33

11. Click on the **Indent** scale in the Ruler. Click to place the flashing insertion point in the first cell. Click on the **Right Aligned** paragraph icon in the Ruler. Move the **Right Indent** to the left as shown in Figure 7.33.

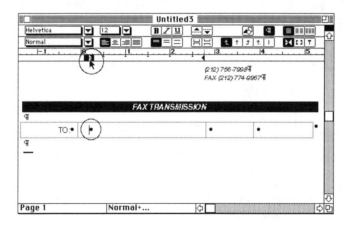

Figure 7.34

12. Enter the word **TO:** then press the **Tab** key to move to the next cell. Move the **Left Indent** in slightly, as shown in Figure 7.34. This will put some space between the cell (which will have a border) and the text that might be entered later. Press the **Tab** key to move to the next cell.

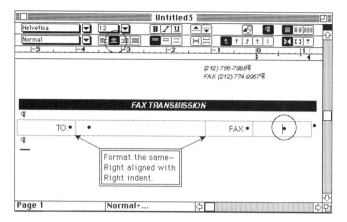

Figure 7.35

13. Format the cell the same way as you did in Step 11 (Figure 7.33) and enter the word **FAX:**. Press the **Tab** key and move to the last cell in the row. Click on the **Centered** paragraph icon in the Ruler (Figure 7.35).

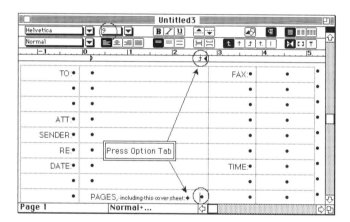

Figure 7.36

14. Press the **Tab** key to create a new Row. To enter more rows, press **Command Option V** and a new row will be inserted above the current one. You can enter text and blank rows (for space) as shown in Figure 7.36. For the row containing the Page information, text after the comma is entered in **9 pt Helvetica**. Place a **Right Aligned Tab** mark in the Ruler. Press the **Option Tab** key to prepare a space for the page number entry.

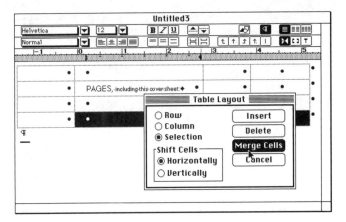

Figure 7.37

15. Press the **Tab** key to move to the adjacent cells and then create a new row. Insert another blank row so that there are two blank rows after the Page information. In the bottom blank row, click in the widest cell (where page information was entered) and remove the **Tab** mark from the Ruler. Click on the **Left Aligned paragraph** icon in the Ruler. Press and drag to select the three right cells. Go to the **Format** menu and choose **Table Layout**. Click on the **Merge Cells** button (Figure 7.37).

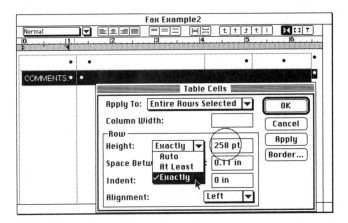

Figure 7.38

16. Double click to select the bottom blank row. Go to the **Format** menu and choose **Table Cells**. Select **Exactly** from the **Height** list menu and enter **258 pt** in the Height edit bar. Click **OK**.

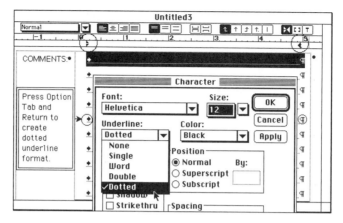

Figure 7.39

17. If you want to enter text in the larger cell, you can format the cell with dotted underline tabs (they will also act as a "rule" for filling the form out by hand). Move the **Left Indent** mark in the Ruler as circled in Figure 7.39. Also move the **Right Indent** mark to the left (for some breathing space before the cell border line). Place a **Tab** mark over top of the Right Indent mark in the Ruler. Press the **Option Tab** key and select the Tab mark within the cell. Choose **Character** from the **Format** menu and apply **Dotted Underline** format (Figure 7.39). Click **OK**. Press the **Return** key and **Option Tab** key in succession to create lines to fill the entire cell (it will take **10 lines**).

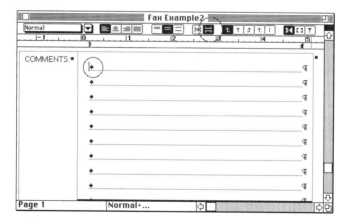

Figure 7.40

18. Click in the first line of the Comments box. Click in the **Open Space** between paragraphs icon in the Ruler (Figure 7.40). This will apply

12 points of space before the first line (rather than 4 pts) and give the you a little more space for the first line of text. It also looks better on the page.

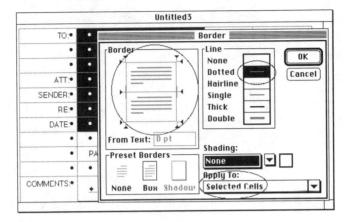

Figure 7.41

19. For the final steps, you'll be applying a dotted border format to certain cells in the fax form to make them stand out. Select the group of cells highlighted in Figure 7.41. Go to the **Format** menu and choose **Border**. Click on the **Dotted Line** option. Click on every line in the border display area. You want borders on every side of the selected cells. Click **OK**.

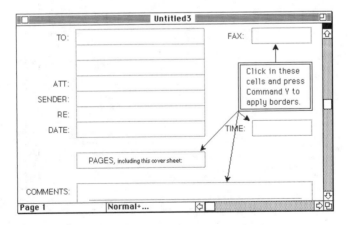

Figure 7.42

20. To apply the same border format to the rest of the cells in the fax form, you can repeat the same border formatting by using the Repeat

function. Click in the cells indicated in Figure 7.42 (you can turn off Show ¶ if you want to see them more clearly) and press **Command Y**. Make sure this is your next action or the repeat format process won't work. (You can also choose **Repeat Border** from the **Edit** menu or **Undo Border** if you apply it to the wrong cell.)

21. You might want to copy the border from the top of your fax document and paste it at the bottom for another decorative border. Press the **Return** key a couple times after the table to give the table some space before pasting the border.

Hopefully you've been saving your fax document as you've followed these steps to create it. When you're finished, you can either print the document and make photocopies for your fax bin or save the document in **Stationery** format and use it as a template to enter actual fax "memos." Just click in the appropriate cell and enter your text.

Invoices and Purchase Orders

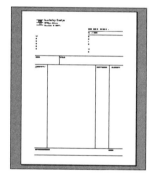

Figure 7.43

Though invoices and purchase orders are generally tracked more effectively through database programs, you might need a form that you can fill in by hand so that the invoice or purchase order can then be generated or entered into the computer database. You might also be in the design phases of creating your database and simply need to use your word processor to get the bills out so that you can have some much needed product and cash flow.

There are any number of ways you can set up an invoice or a purchase order—from using a simple letter format to a more complexly automated document. The first example in this section will demonstrate the use of tables to format a purchase order. Generally purchase orders and invoices are similar in design, so that you can substitute "invoice number" and "invoice date" where appropriate. In this step-by-step description, you will see the integration of many word processing techniques that give you fast, great-looking results. You'll be building the document row by row—merging and splitting cells, applying borders, readjusting cell width and height—so that you can learn an overall approach to working with tables when creating forms.

The second example will give you some ideas of ways you can use the print merge language to automatically generate a batch of invoices that use address information from a data document.

Creating a Blank Purchase Order Form

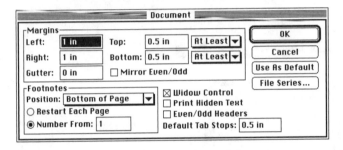

Figure 7.44

1. Choose **Document** from the **Format** menu and set the margins to what is shown in Figure 7.44. Click on the **OK** button. Choose **Format Style**, select **Normal,** and choose **Helvetica 12 pt** from the **Ribbon**. Click on **Define** and **Close** the style window. Copy or create your company address (and/or telephone) information. You might use the Edit Picture graphics capability to create your own logo.

2 In a new paragraph, choose **Table** from the **Insert** menu and insert 2 rows and 2 columns by clicking on the **OK** button (Figure 7.45).

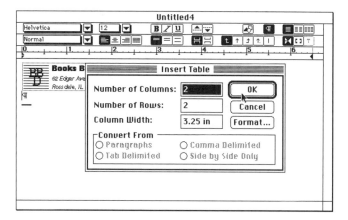

Figure 7.45

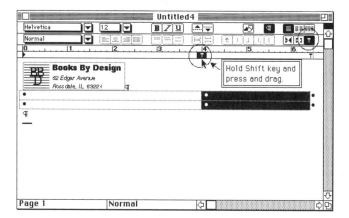

Figure 7.46

3. Hold the **Option** key and click once on the right column cells to select them. Click on the **T marker Scale** icon in the Ruler. Press the **Shift** key and press and drag to reposition the **T marker** to the **4 inch** mark (Figure 7.46).

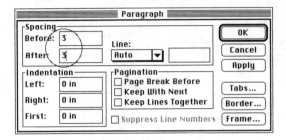

Figure 7.47

4. Keep both cells selected and go to the **Format** menu and choose **Paragraph**. Enter **3 pt** in the **Before** and **After** edit bars (Figure 7.47). Click **OK**.

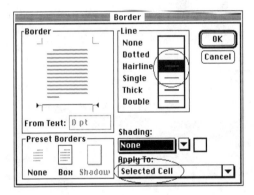

Figure 7.48

5. Click in the top right cell and go to the **Format** menu and choose **Border**. Select the **Hairline** width and apply it to the bottom of the cell (Figure 7.48). Click **OK**. Click in the cell beneath and press **Command Y** to repeat the border format.

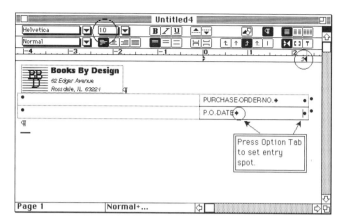

Figure 7.49

6. Select both cells in the right column and apply **10 pt Helvetica**. Click on the **Indent Scale** icon in the Ruler. Click on the **Right Aligned Tab** icon then click in the Ruler at the position shown in Figure 7.49 to place a **Right Aligned Tab**. Enter text in the first cell for the purchase order number and then move to the cell beneath for the date information. Press **Option Tab** to make a text entry space for each cell.

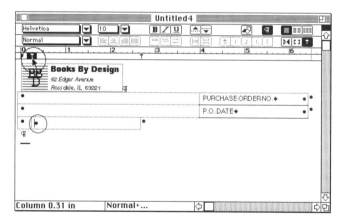

Figure 7.50

7. Press **Tab** to create a new row. Click in the last cell. Drag the **Tab** mark off the Ruler to remove it. Go to the **Format** menu and choose **Border**. Click on the **None** box to remove the hairline border. Click **OK**. Click the **Cell Marker Scale** in the Ruler. Press and drag the **T marker** at the **4 inch** mark (don't press the Shift key this time!) over to the left to the **1/4 inch** mark (Figure 7.50).

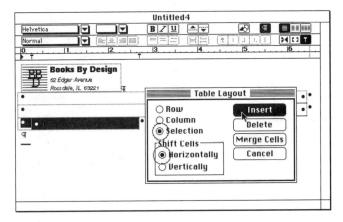

Figure 7.51

8. Select both cells. Go to the **Format** menu and choose **Table Layout**. Click on the **Selection** button, and the **Horizontally** button; then click the **Insert** button (Figure 7.51).

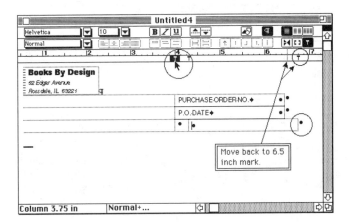

Figure 7.52

9. Press and drag the second **T marker** from the left and move the two new cells to the right. Position the **T marker** you are dragging at the **4 inch** mark. Press and drag the right **T marker** so that it is in line with the **6.5 inch** margin (Figure 7.52).

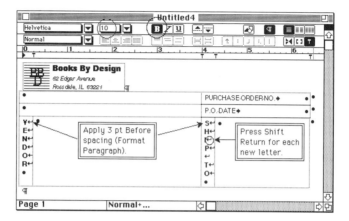

Figure 7.53

10. In each of the narrow columns, apply **Helvetica 10 pt Bold**. Choose **Paragraph** from the **Format** menu and apply **3 pt Before** format (to allow some space beneath the border for the P.O. Date). Press the **Caps Lock** key and enter the Vendor text, pressing **Shift Return** before each new letter. Do the same for the column containing the Ship To information (Figure 7.53).

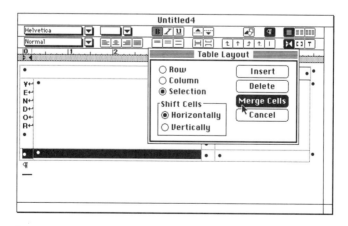

Figure 7.54

11. Press the **Tab** key to move to the next cell and again to enter a new Row. Select the two left cells, as shown in Figure 7.54, go to the **Format** menu, and choose **Table Layout**. Click on the **Merge Cells** button. Select the two right cells and press **Command Y** (Repeat Merge Cells). Click on the **Cell Marker Scale icon**, hold the **Shift** key, and move the cell marker that is positioned at the **4 inch** mark over to the **1 3/4 inch** mark.

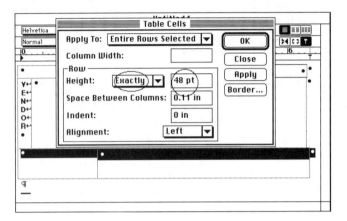

Figure 7.55

12. Double-click with the right-pointing arrow to select the row. Go to the **Format** menu and choose **Table Cells**. Select **Exactly** from the **Height** list menu and enter **48 pt** in the Height edit bar (Figure 7.55). Click **OK**. Keep the row selected and apply **10 pt Bold** format from the Ribbon. Choose **Paragraph** from the **Format** menu and enter **3 pt** in the **Before** edit bar. Click **OK**.

13. This particular invoice is for a book store and uses **ISBN** and **TITLE** information in these cells. You could enter shipping terms, payment terms, or FOB, etc., in these cells just as easily. Format each cell's borders separately. The ISBN cell has a **Hairline Border** on the **Top**, **Bottom**, and **Right**. The TITLE cell has a **Hairline Border** on the **Top**, **Bottom**, and **Left**. Press the **Tab** key for a new row.

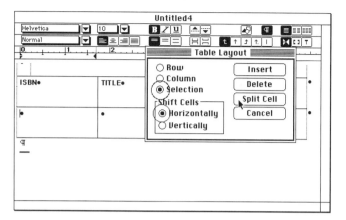

Figure 7.56

14. You need to format four cells for Quantity, Description, Unit Price, and Amount. Rather than insert cells, you can split the two cells (they had been previously merged) back into four cells. Click in the first cell. Go to the **Format** menu and choose **Table Layout**. If the **Selection** and **Horizontally** options are not selected, click on them and then click on the **Split Cells** button (Figure 7.56). Click in the second cell in your document and press **Command Y** to repeat the Split Cell function.

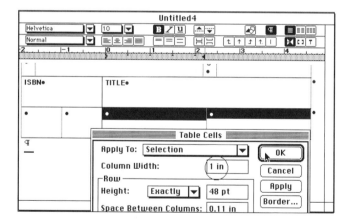

Figure 7.57

15. In this step, you are going to format three of the cells so that they are of equal width. Select the two cells on the far right, as shown in Figure 7.57. Go to the **Format** menu and choose **Table Cells**. In the cell

width edit bar, enter **1 in** and click **OK**. Click in the cell on the far left and press **Command Y** to format that cell's width to 1 inch.

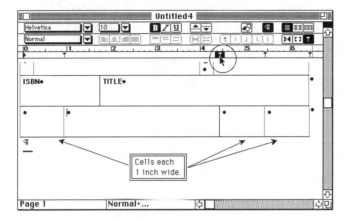

Figure 7.58

16. If the Cell Marker scale icon is not highlighted, click on it to select it. Move the second **T marker** on the Ruler as shown in Figure 7.58 to the right. Align the far right **T marker** with the same right border (near the right margin) as the row above.

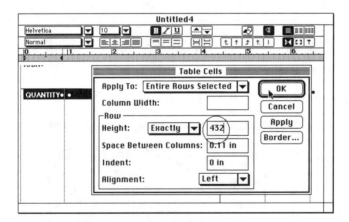

Figure 7.59

17. Select the row, click on the Indent scale icon in the Ruler, and then click on the **Centered** paragraph icon. Press the **Caps Lock** key and enter the text for each column header—Quantity, Description

(optional), Unit Price, and Amount. Double-click to select the entire row. Go to the **Format** menu and choose **Table Cells**. Enter **432** in the **Height** edit bar and click **OK** (Figure 7.59).

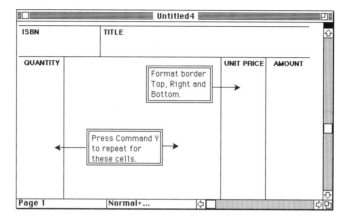

Figure 7.60

18. To apply borders, click in the cell for Unit Price. Choose **Border** from the **Format** menu and apply **Hairline** borders to the **Top**, **Right**, and **Bottom**. Click **OK**. Click in the cell to the left of Unit Price. Press **Command Y** to apply the same borders. Click in the Quantity cell and press **Command Y** again (Figure 7.60).

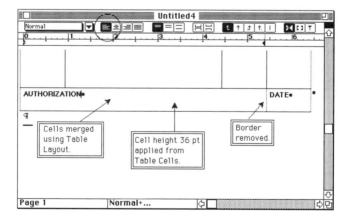

Figure 7.61

19. Press the **Tab** key until you insert a new row. This final row should be formatted with a **Table Cells** row **Height** of **Exactly 36 pt**. Select the three cells on the left and **merge** them into one cell using the **Format Table Layout** dialog box. Select the row and click **Left Aligned paragraph** icon in the Ruler. Click in the left cell and use **Format Border** to remove the right hairline border. (Click on the **None** line weight and then click the right border.) Enter text for Authorization in one cell and Date in the other (Figure 7.61).

This form can be saved and printed so that it can be filled out by hand. However, if you want to use the form for text entry on the computer, you'll need to execute the steps in the following section.

Modifying a Purchase Order Form for Text Entry

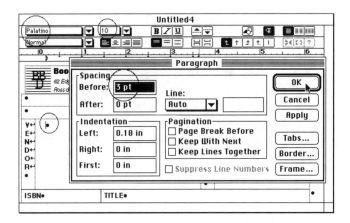

Figure 7.62

1. Click in the cell next to the vendor information. Apply **Palatino 10 pt** from the Ribbon. Move the **Left Indent** to the **3/16 inch** mark in the Ruler. Choose **Paragraph** from the **Format** menu and apply **3 pt Before** spacing (Figure 7.62).

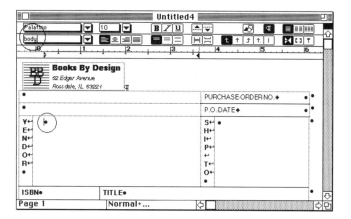

Figure 7.63

2. Define this set of formats as a body style. Click in the **Style Selection** box in the Ruler, type the word **body,** and press the **Return** key (Figure 7.63). When a dialog box appears asking you if you want to define the body style, click the **OK** button.

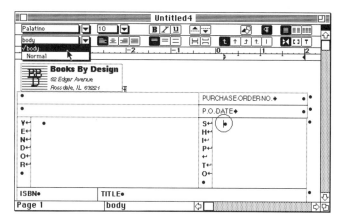

Figure 7.64

3. Click next to the Ship To cell and apply the body style by selecting it from the **Style Selection box** in the Ruler (Figure 7.64).

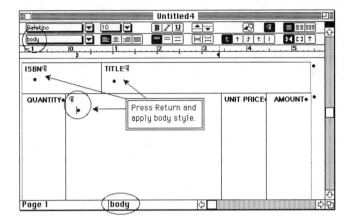

Figure 7.65

4. Click at the end of the text in the cells shown in Figure 7.65. Press the **Return** key and apply the body style from the Ruler as you did in step 3.

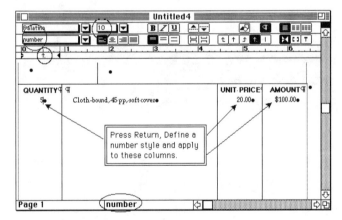

Figure 7.66

5. For the columns containing numbered information, press the Return key for a new line. Create a new style with **Palatino 10 pt**, **not bold**, **3 pt Before** format. To make sure the numbers align correctly, click on the **Left Aligned** paragraph icon in the Ruler. Select the **Decimal Tab** icon from the Ruler and click in the Ruler to position it—somewhere to the right of the middle of the cell (Figure 7.66). Click in the **Style selection box** in the Ruler and define the **number** style (follow the directions in step 2). Apply the number style to the other numbered columns.

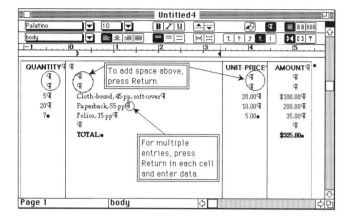

Figure 7.67

6. The row containing the quantity, description, etc., information is formatted so that it maintains an exact height of 432 points (6 inches). This allows you to print out a blank form that has the necessary space for your information. However, when entering information in this row using the computer and the "number" style defined above, you will need to use the **Return** key to space each line of information in each cell (Figure 7.67). This is not the most expedient way to use tables and to align your information. Most likely, you would want one row for each line of information you enter. Techniques for building this kind of a form are illustrated in the last part of this chapter under "Forms Formatting Tips" (Figure 7.102).

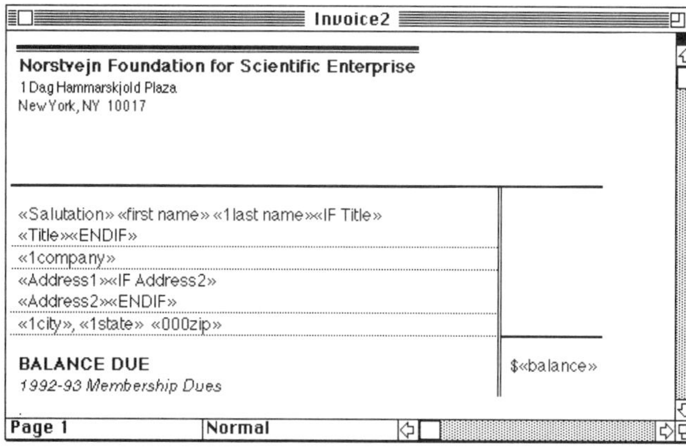

Figure 7.68

This invoice example works on the premise that you are required to send out invoices to names that are stored in a data document you normally use for mail merge purposes. Using the information from that data document, the address specifics will be automatically entered when you perform the mail merge. Here, you'll learn how you can set up the document to "prompt" you for the actual invoice amount.

Using this format you can process a single invoice at a time—based on the person's "record number" in the data document—or you can process a group of records that fall sequentially within the data document itself.

> *To learn how to number data documents, see Chapter 6; the section called "Automatic Record Numbering of Your DATA File."*

Before you start learning how to format the example invoice for print merge automation, you may want to review and execute the document-formatting techniques already described in this chapter (which this invoice utilizes) as follows.

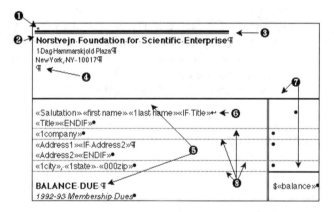

Figure 7.69

❶ A single paragraph with **Helvetica 4 pt** format applied. Border is a **Thick** line applied **below** the paragraph. The **Right Indent** is placed near the **4 inch** mark in the ruler (to achieve a short line).

❷ Company name formatted in **12 pt Helvetica bold**. Border is a **Double** line applied **above** the paragraph.

❸ Both paragraphs have the **Right Indent** mark placed near the **4 inch** mark in the ruler.

❹ Paragraphs beneath company name have borders removed. Last blank paragraph has **Paragraph** format with **36 points** of space applied **After**.

❺ 2-column table inserted. Columns widths 5 inches and 1 inch. Cells indicated have paragraph text formatted with **12 points** of space **Before** (Open Space between paragraphs icon was selected in Ruler). All other cells have no spacing above the paragraph.

❻ New line within same cell achieved by pressing **Shift Return**.

❼ **Thick** border applied **above** these table cells. **Double** border applied **between** columns.

❽ **Dotted** border applied **beneath** these cells. (See Figure 7.68 for blank cell border formats.)

Formatting an Invoice for Print Merge Automation

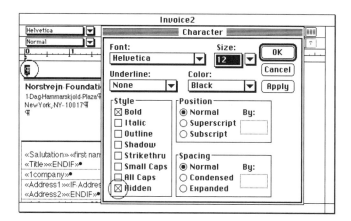

Figure 7.70

1. If you are beginning with a blank document, you should start out by invoking the Print Merge Helper so that you can use the field names from your data document to build the invoice. However, if you have already formatted a document with the decorative paragraph borders described in the section above (Figure 7.69), the first paragraph of the document may be formatted with 4 pt text. In order to view the text of the data statements and create new merge prompts, you'll need to insert a **new paragraph** and format it as **12 point Helvetica**. If you don't want to view this text every time you use the Invoice template,

format it as **Hidden** text using the **Character** dialog box (Figure 7.70). (Make sure you have **Show Hidden Text** turned **on** in the Tools Preferences dialog box.)

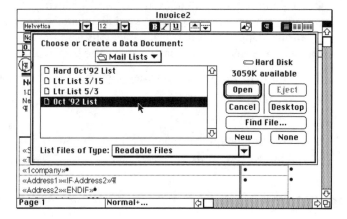

Figure 7.71

2. Place the insertion point at the top of the document. Go to the **View** menu and choose **Print Merge Helper**. Navigate to the folder that contains your data document and select it (Figure 7.71).

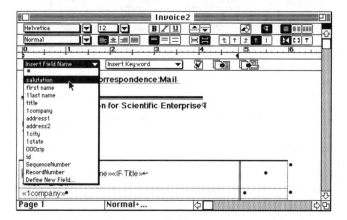

Figure 7.72

3. Create your document using the formats described in Figure 7.69. Use the **Insert Field Name** list in the Print Merge Helper bar to place the fields within the table. Make sure you put correct punctuation between city, state, and zip fields as well as salutation, first names and last names.

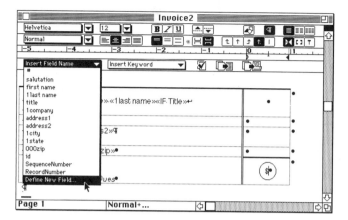

Figure 7.73

4. Click in the cell where you want your invoice balance amount to be entered and type a **$**. Go to the **Insert Field Name** list in the Print Merge Helper bar and choose **Define New Field** (Figure 7.73).

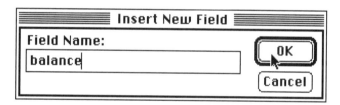

Figure 7.74

5. Name the field **balance** and click the **OK** button (Figure 7.74).

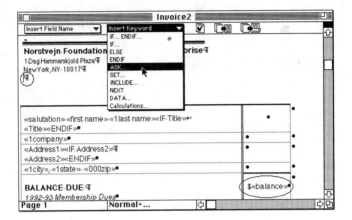

Figure 7.75

6. Click in the blank paragraph above the table. You're going to insert a "prompt" print merge instruction. Choose **ASK** from the **Insert Keyword** list in the Helper bar (Figure 7.75).

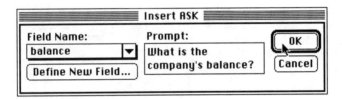

Figure 7.76

7. The "balance" field name should appear on the left in the Insert ASK dialog box. Click in the **Prompt** edit bar and enter the text which poses the question, "What is the company's balance?" and click **OK** (Figure 7.76).

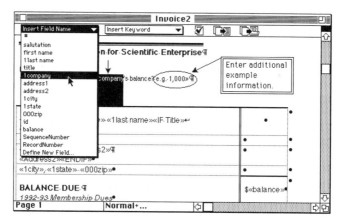

Figure 7.77

8. The ASK prompt instruction will be inserted in your document. Click on the inside of the right print merge instruction and add an example of how you want the information to be entered. Select the word "company" (don't select the 's) and choose the **company** field name from the **Insert Field Name** list in the Helper bar (Figure 7.77). Insertion of this field within a merge prompt makes "company" a "nested" field. The nested field displays and verifies the specific company name you are referring to during the actual merge process (which will create the final invoice). (See Figure 7.81.)

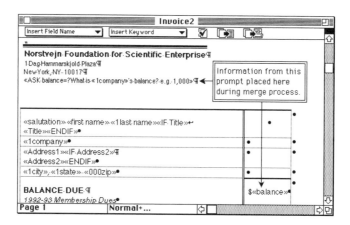

Figure 7.78

9. Figure 7.78 illustrates how the ASK merge statement relates to the balance field you created to insert the information in your invoice during print merge.

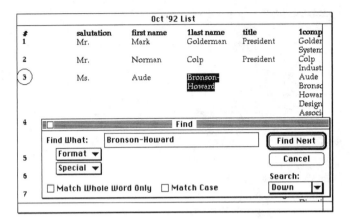

Figure 7.79

10. To generate a single invoice, you need to ascertain the record number for the invoice you want to generate. **Open** the data document you are merging with. Choose **Find** from the **Edit** menu and enter the last name of the person (or company name) you are sending the invoice to. Click on the **Find Next** button. You can then determine what the record number is for the specific name you are using for the print merge (Figure 7.79).

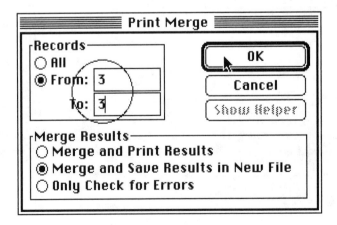

Figure 7.80

11. Select the Invoice from the **Window** menu. With the document open, go to the **File** menu and choose **Print Merge**. Enter the same record number in the **From** and **To** edit bars to restrict the merge process to the specific name you want and click **OK** (Figure 7.80).

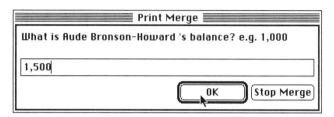

Figure 7.81

12. A prompt dialog box will appear asking you to enter the amount of the invoice for the specific company name. Enter the information in the edit bar and click **OK**.

```
▤◻▭▭▭▭▭▭▭▭ Merge2 ▭▭▭▭▭▭▭▭◻▤
┌──────────────────────────────────────────────────┐ ⇧
│ Norstvejn Foundation for Scientific Enterprise     │
│ 1 Dag Hammarskjold Plaza                           │
│ New York, NY 10017                                 │
│                                                    │
│                                                    │
│ Ms. Aude Bronson-Howard                            │
│ President                                          │
│ Aude Bronson-Howard Research                       │
│ 1 West 67th Street                                 │
│ New York, NY 10023                                 │
│                                                    │
│ BALANCE DUE                              $1,500    │
│ 1992-93 Membership Dues                            │
│                                                    │
│ ─                                                  │ ⇩
├────────────┬────────────┬─────────┬───────────────┤
│ Page 1     │ Normal     │⇦◻▨▨▨▨▨▨▨▨⇨▣
```

Figure 7.82

13. Figure 7.82 shows you the merge result. A new document will be created with the address information, as well as the balance, inserted. You can then print the invoice as you would a regular document.

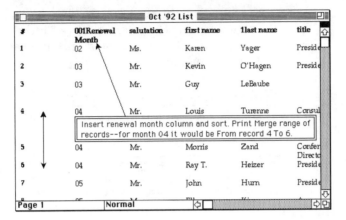

Figure 7.83

14. If you plan to use a specific data document to generate invoices on a regular basis, you might want to insert a column that organizes your information so that you can process the invoices in batches. The example in Figure 7.83 sorts the list on a **Renewal Month**. You could then select **Print Merge** from the **File** menu and enter a "range" of record numbers in the **From** and **To** edit bars in the Print Merge dialog box. Each record would have its own prompt for you to enter balance information during the merge process. The invoices could either be sent directly to the printer, or a new document could be created containing all the invoices, with a section break separating each one.

You can also execute a print merge for the entire list of names in your data document by clicking on the All button in the Print Merge dialog box and selecting the correct Merge Result option.

Special Techniques

Forms Formatting Tips

This section will provide examples of methods you might use to create different kinds of grids, lines, boxes, shading, and check boxes when preparing forms. There are a variety of ways to achieve different kinds of results, each with its own ease of implementation or format shortcomings. The following will make you aware of the strengths and benefits of a number of solutions.

Lines and Grids

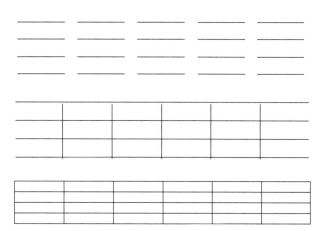

Figure 7.84

There are a number of ways to achieve lines, grids, and boxes. The first question you need to ask yourself is whether or not you will need to enter information into the "box." If you are simply creating a form that needs to be printed, with no computer text entry involved, an easy way to accomplish this is with tabs. In particular, if you need lines with "spaces" between them, tabs are your tool for the job. This first section will deal with usage of tabs. Once you understand what tabs can do for you, you'll move on to tables.

Using Tabs

When using "leader tabs" (you learned how to apply these when setting up a Fax transmission sheet in Figure 7.14), you should realize there is a beginning and an end to where the line will be applied. You can control these with the use of more tabs in the ruler. To create the line, you will only need to press the **Tab** key once for each tab mark you have placed in the Ruler.

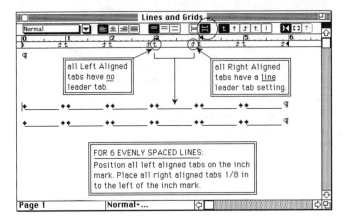

Figure 7.85

Whereas any tab (left, right, center, or decimal) can have a leader tab line applied to it, save yourself some confusion and always use right-aligned tabs when you format your leader tabs. Left-aligned tabs can be used to create space within the paragraph line.

To figure out how to have evenly spaced lines, use a document with **1.25 inch** left and right margins—giving you 6 inches of document "space" to work with. For 6 lines in a paragraph, place a **Left Aligned Tab** on all the "inch" markings. Place a **Right Aligned Tab** 1/8 inch to the left of each left-aligned tab (Figure 7.85). Double-click on any one of the **Tab** icons in the Ruler to display the **Tabs** dialog box. Click on each **Right Aligned Tab** and assign it a **line leader tab** format.

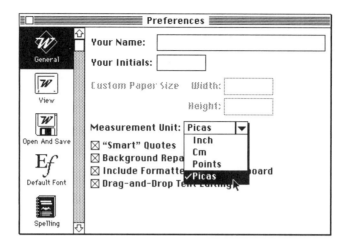

Figure 7.86

Sometimes the Ruler settings in inches don't help you to easily determine an even placement for tabs. Go to the **Tools** menu and choose **Preferences**. You can choose a different unit of measurement for the Ruler that may make it easier to place your tabs (Figure 7.86).

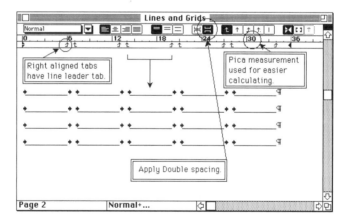

Figure 7.87

In Figure 7.87, you can see how a **pica** measurement ruler lets you easily figure 5 lines per paragraph at a length of 6 picas each. You can also control the vertical space between your lines using the **double space** icon in the ruler (or apply wider line spacing through the **Paragraph** dialog box).

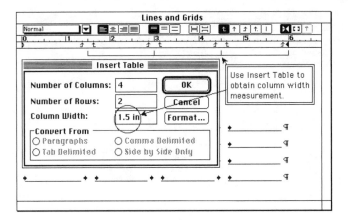

Figure 7.88

If your math is a little shaky, you can use the **Insert Table** function, enter the number of "columns" you want, and have the function calculate how you might divide up the space. Click on the **Cancel** button once you have the measurement. In Figure 7.88, knowing that there are 4 columns of 1.5 inches possible within a 6-inch document text space, you can place your tabs 1/8 inch on either side of measuring factors of 1.5.

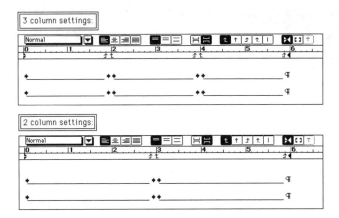

Figure 7.89

Keeping with the idea of 1/8 inch blank space between each line, Figure 7.89 illustrates the tab settings you would create for three and two columns per paragraph.

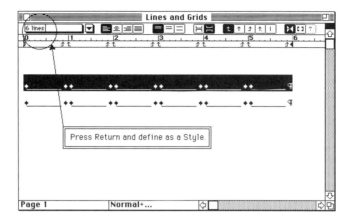

Figure 7.90

Once you've gone to the trouble of figuring out a number of line and grid variations, you can define them as a "style." All the tab formatting will be applied to your paragraph by simply choosing the style name from the **Style Selection box** in the Ruler. All you'd have to do then is press the **Tab** key to make the lines "appear" in your document.

Create and save a special document that has all the various lines, grids and form ideas illustrated in this chapter. You can then copy a particular paragraph's line formatting into the specific document you need it for. If a line format has a style defined for it, that style definition will also be copied over into the document you are working on. You can then quickly apply the style anywhere in the document where it is needed.

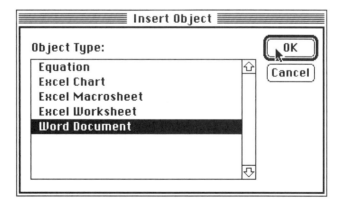

Figure 7.91

If you are working with Microsoft Word 5.0 and using System 7.0, you have another unique advantage when working with lines and grids. You can create tabbed grid settings in a "object" window and then resize them to fit your document as if they were graphics! Here's how you would accomplish this. Go to the **Insert** menu and choose **Object**. Click on the **Word Document** option and click **OK** (Figure 7.91).

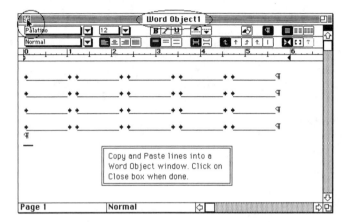

Figure 7.92

A "Word Object" window will appear. You have total access to every function you normally use with Word. Create your grid format (you can paste items in this document window, just like any other document). When you're done, click on the **Close box** in the upper left corner.

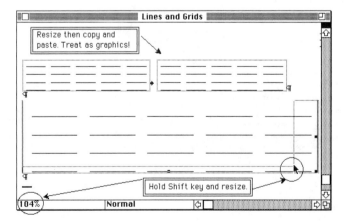

Figure 7.93

Your grid is now a "graphic" which you can resize, copy, paste, etc. Hold down the **Shift** key and press and drag on the lower right handle to change its size proportionately (Figure 7.93). In this way, you can shape your grid to fit in any document with margin settings other than the 1.25 inch setting you might have started out with.

If you need to make the lines in the graphic align to the left margin (there might be some space on the left side of the lines), move the **Left Indent** mark of the particular paragraph the graphic is located in, so that it is negatively indented (i.e., to the *left* of the **0** point in the ruler).

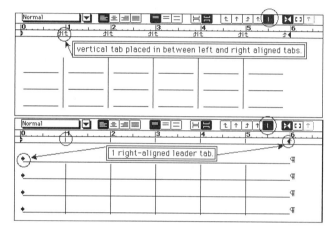

Figure 7.94

You can also make use of the **Vertical Line Tab** mark to place vertical lines in your document. If you have leader tabs set up, the vertical line tab can be placed in between them. Be careful! When tabs are very close together, you can easily misalign them. Start by selecting the vertical line tab icon in the Ruler. Click in the Ruler where there is a "clear" space, then press and drag the tab mark into position. Vertical line marks appear in your document *without* pressing the tab key.

The examples in Figure 7.94 show how you can achieve a grid with vertical line tabs. The bottom example uses one right-aligned leader tab and places vertical line tabs in the ruler. Observe that the vertical line marks don't "meet" the top of the leader line in the first paragraph and that they extend slightly below the last paragraph. Also, when a grid like this—created with tabs—prints out, the leader tab lines are a thinner line weight than the vertical tab lines. (For this reason, you might want to use tables, where you have more control over line weight choices.)

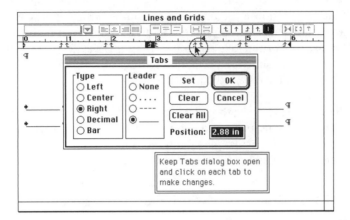

Figure 7.95

As you work with tabs and are assigning leader tab formats, work with the **Tabs** dialog box open. You can click on each **Tab** mark to choose it for formatting as a leader tab or change it from left to right alignment (Figure 7.95). The **Tabs** dialog box is also an easy way to clear all the tabs on the Ruler (click on the **Clear** or **Clear All** buttons).

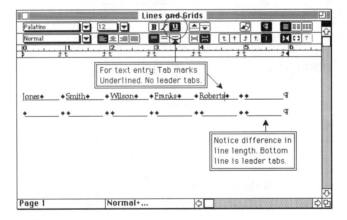

Figure 7.96

When using tabs for a document you need to enter text into, you will need to reformat the tab marks as "underlined" and remove the leader tab lines. To underline the tab marks, simply select the **Tab** mark in your document text using the **I-beam** and click on the **Underline** icon in the **Ribbon**. Figure 7.96 illustrates the difference between using underline tabs and leader tab lines. Underline tabs make for longer line length.

Using Tables

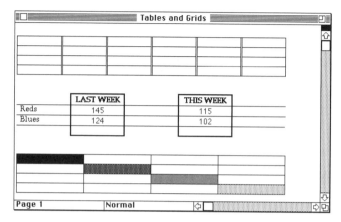

Figure 7.97

Tables offer a rich environment for shading, border line weight, and text entry. However, they can take longer to set up and require frequent trips to the Border, Table Cells, and Table Layout dialog boxes.

> **NOTE:** *If you work with tables extensively, consider setting up keyboard shortcuts for specific border settings, inserting, and deleting columns and merging cells. See Chapter 10 for ways to customize your keyboard.*

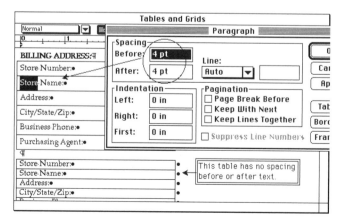

Figure 7.98

When working with text in a table that has "grids," you might want to consider adding space above and below the text so there is vertical breathing room before the border lines. Figure 7.98 illustrates the difference between a table with and without paragraph spacing.

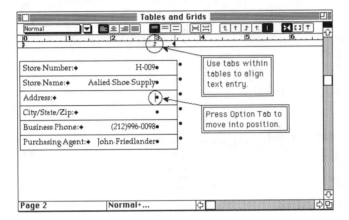

Figure 7.99

You can also place tab marks within table cells. Figure 7.99 shows a **right aligned** tab mark within a single-column table. With the placement of a tab in a cell, you need to press **Option Tab** to move the flashing insertion point to the position of the tab mark for text entry.

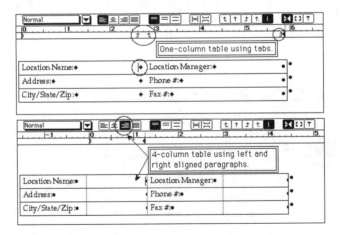

Figure 7.100

You can choose between using either right-aligned **tabs** within a single cell or create more columns and use left- and right-aligned **paragraphs** to align your text (Figure 7.100). When entering text into a form, it is easier to press the **Tab** key and enter text into a blank cell than it is to position the I-beam in regular text and click next to a blank tab mark.

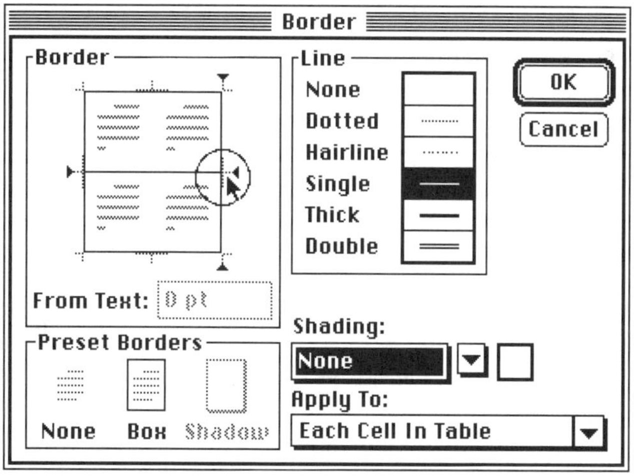

Figure 7.101

Applying borders to tables can be tricky. Here's a simple timesaving tip. When formatting the borders for the four-column table in the example in Figure 7.100, select the entire table. Choose **Border** from the **Format** menu and choose your line weight. Click on the **Box** icon in the **Preset Borders** area, then click precisely at the point indicated in Figure 7.101.

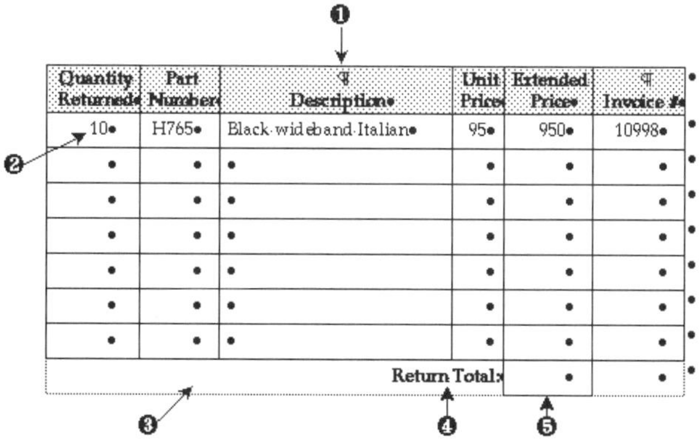

Figure 7.102

The table illustrated in Figure 1-102 is similar to the one created for the purchase order example in the early part of this chapter; however, it uses a separate row for each "line" entry. What follows is a description for each numbered "part" of the table illustration.

❶ The column headers are shaded cells. To place column titles that are only one line in length, press the **Return** key for a new line.

❷ Columns with numbers have a **decimal tab** placed in the ruler. Numbers automatically line up to a decimal tab as if it were a right aligned tab mark, only you don't ever need to press the **Option Tab** key to have them align correctly. The cell also must have **Left Aligned paragraph** format applied for this to work correctly. All text within the unshaded cells has a **Paragraph** format of **4 pt Before** and **After** spacing applied.

❸ The bottom cell was created by merging four cells (use the **Table Layout** dialog box to do this after selecting the cells to be merged).

❹ **Right Aligned paragraph** format was applied to this cell.

❺ To make this cell total stand out, it is the only cell in the row that has box border format applied.

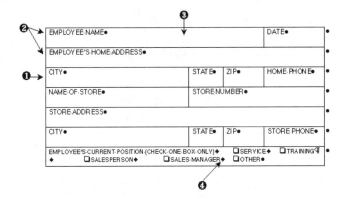

Figure 7.103

The table in Figure 7.103 illustrates how you can work with one "model" row of cells as a pattern for the rest of the table.

❶ This four-column row was formatted first with a cell **Height** of **exactly 36 points**. The font is **Helvetica 10 pt Caps** with no spacing before or after.

❷ Once the cell widths were adjusted in the row indicated as "1" in Figure 7.103, the two rows indicated here were inserted above the model row by pressing **Command Control V**. They both have the same formatting for cell height and font characteristics. Rows were added *beneath* the model row by pressing the **Tab** key when the flashing insertion point was located in the last cell.

❸ Cells were selected and merged using the **Table Layout** dialog box—one row merged three cells, the other row merged all four cells.

❹ This last row uses a **9 point** font size. Tabs were placed in the ruler and **Option Tab** pressed to align the check box information. The **Zapf Dingbat** font was used to create the box (press the *letter* "o").

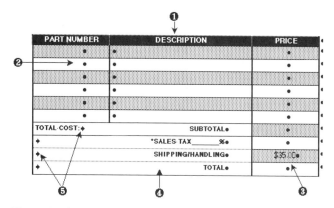

Figure 7.104

The table in Figure 7.104 uses alternate shading "ribbons" for an attractive form that is easy to read.

❶ Table cell borders are shaded as 100 percent. Text is **10 point Helvetica Bold White** (reverse type) and has a **centered** paragraph alignment.

❷ These text entry cells are formatted with **Palatino 12 point** font and have **2 points** of space **Before** and **After**. Both the Part Number and Price columns have a **decimal tab** placed in the ruler to align numbers automatically. Paragraph alignment is **Left Aligned**.

❸ A number that is a constant (such as a shipping and handling fee) is entered into the form. The cell has been formatted with a **decimal tab** in the Ruler to align numbered text.

❹ The four bottom rows have merged two cells and use **9 point Helvetica Bold** font. The last three cells were selected as a group and a **single box border** placed around them.

❺ To align the text in these cells, a **Right Aligned** tab mark was placed in the ruler. The **Option Tab** was pressed before entering the text that appears on the right side of the cell.

Fill-in-the-Blanks

Figure 7.105

The following series of examples demonstrate techniques you can use when creating forms that require someone to fill in blanks—generally by hand on a printed document. The rule of thumb for creating blank lines is—if you don't need to use the computer to do it—format a **line leader tab** mark in the ruler using the **Tabs** dialog box. If you need to enter information by computer in the underline area and still preserve the line length, apply an **Underline** format from the **Ribbon** to regular left- and right-aligned tab marks.

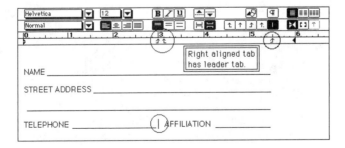

Figure 7.106

Use **Left Aligned Tab** marks for regular text alignment and format—**Right Aligned Tabs** with **leader tabs**. In the example illustrated in Figure 7.106, the right-aligned tab controls where the line will end. The left-aligned tab controls the amount of space between the line and where the text begins.

Place right-aligned leader tabs at the same position at the end of each paragraph so that, when you press the final **Tab** key for each paragraph, all the lines will print to the same position. Remember, also, to make sure you have **Fractional Widths** turned on (choose **Page Setup** from the **File** menu) when you print—otherwise, with some fonts, the lines might print as dashes.

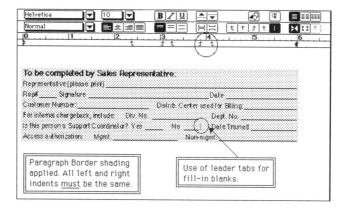

Figure 7.107

Figure 7.107 is another example using right- and left-aligned tabs with leader tab format. However, you can also shade a selected group of paragraphs using the **Border** dialog box shading options to add emphasis for certain parts of a form. If, for some reason, you've altered the left or right indent marks for the group of paragraphs you want to shade, you'll immediately see that there is an inconsistency between the indents, as there will be breaks in the shading pattern.

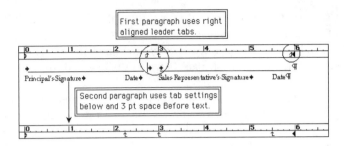

Figure 7.108

Creating signature lines, not only in forms but in regular contracts or letters of agreement, can sometimes be confusing to format. Signature lines require two differently formatted paragraphs. You can try using a **Border** above a single paragraph, but it will place a single line for both signatures. The objective is to have two different lines, one for each signature.

The first paragraph shown in Figure 7.108 uses three tabs settings in the Ruler—two of which are formatted with `line leader tabs`. Once you've formatted the tabs in the Ruler, you simply press the `Tab` key to create the lines.

The second paragraph uses only left-aligned tab marks with no line leader tab formats. To create space between the text and the line above it, format the paragraph with **3 pts** (or more) of space **Before** the paragraph.

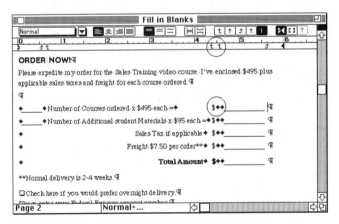

Figure 7.109

Isolating dollar signs in forms or even regular financial tables requires an "extra" left-aligned tab mark as shown in Figure 7.109.

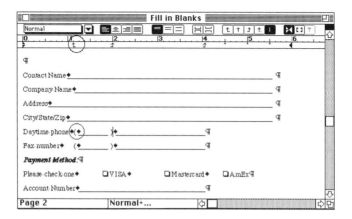

Figure 7.110

When you want to place parentheses for an area code in a form, place a **Left Aligned Tab** mark in the ruler and enter the open-parenthesis symbol. Place two **Right Aligned Tab** marks with a **Line Leader Tab** format in the ruler as indicated in Figure 7.110. Press the **Tab** key, enter the close-parenthesis symbol, then press the final Tab key to create the rest of the line for the phone number.

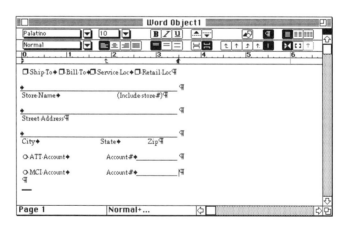

Figure 7.111

The following requires you to be running Word 5.0 under System 7.0. (The Insert Object function does not appear if you are using System 6.0.x.) If ever you need to repeat a form "part," choose **Object** from the **Insert** menu and create the form as a **Word Document** in the Object window.

The example in Figure 7.111 places the **Right Indent** mark at the **3.5 inch** mark to shorten the length of the paragraph lines. It also alters lines formatted with a single leader line tab mark with regular text spaced using left-aligned tabs—much like a series of the "signature lines" that were described above in Figure 7.108. When you have finished creating the form in the Object window, click in the upper left **Close box** to return to your main document.

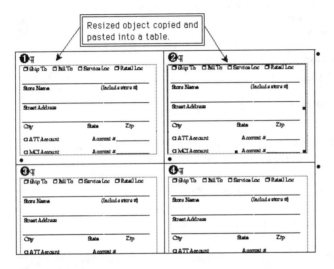

Figure 7.112

The object appears as a graphic in the main document. You can then resize the object, copy and paste it several times into a table as shown in Figure 7.112. The timesaving beauty of using Word Objects to create form parts is that you can easily (and almost magically) resize the graphic to fit on any size page!

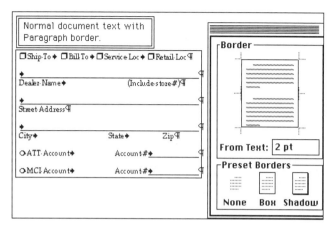

Figure 7.113

Don't forget that you can place a border around a series of paragraphs using the **Format Border** function. You might want to place some more space between the actual border and your text. Just remember that all the left and right indent markers need to be positioned identically.

Checkmarks and Boxes

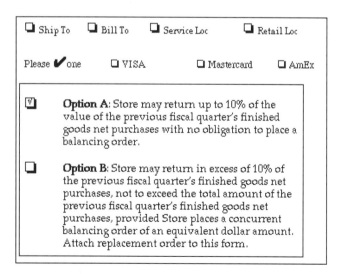

Figure 7.114

Most forms have a box somewhere that needs to be checked or "X"ed. Whether this will be filled out by hand or on the computer, you'd probably like to know how to make some of those boxes you see on forms you get in the mail.

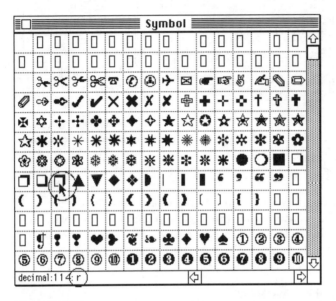

Figure 7.115

There is a postscript font called Zapf Dingbat that has an entire assortment of boxes, checkmarks, and other symbols you can explore. To examine these symbols, choose **Symbol** from the **Insert** menu; then select the **Zapf Dingbat** font from the **Font** menu. You might want to choose a larger font size from the Font menu while you are at it. When you click on the symbol, it will be inserted into your document at the position of the flashing insertion point. You will also see what keys on your keyboard you would press to obtain the particular symbol you just clicked on (Figure 7.115).

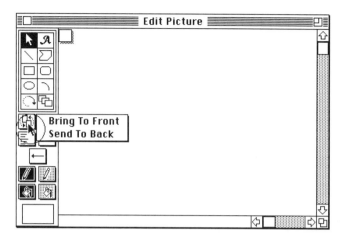

Figure 7.116

However, what if you don't have the Zapf Dingbat font installed on your computer? How can you create boxes that you can use in your forms? Word 5.0 has a graphics tool box that will let you create a wide variety of shapes for boxes. Simply click on the **graphics icon** in the **Ribbon** (the one that has a circle, triangle, and a box).

When in the **Edit Picture** window, create boxes. You can create a "drop shadow" effect by filling a regular rectangle with white paint, then duplicating it and filling it with a shaded paint pattern as well as a shaded line pattern. When you position the white filled box on top of the shaded box, you might also need to use the **Bring to Front** tool to create the effect you want (Figure 7.116).

To make sure the box is inserted into your document with as little white space around it as possible, select all the parts and move them as far to the top and left of the Edit Picture window as possible. Click in the **Close box** of the Edit Picture window when you are done.

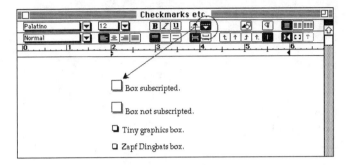

Figure 7.117

When aligning your graphics-created box with text on the page, you might need to apply subscripting format to the box using the **subscript icon** in the **Ribbon** (Figure 7.117).

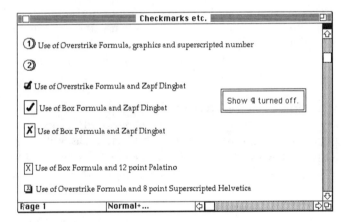

Figure 7.118

One of the final challenges in forms generation is creating a box or a graphic and placing a check mark or an X inside it. This last technique is a bit tricky and requires the use of **Formulas**. Formula results (similar to what you see in Figure 7.118) are obtained when the Show¶ function is turned off. To create the formula and assemble its "parts," you need to work with Show¶ turned on (located in the **Edit** menu or by clicking on the ¶ icon in the **Ribbon**).

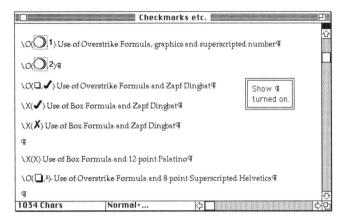

Figure 7.119

To begin with, you will need to press the following key combination to signal Microsoft Word that you are creating a formula: `Command Option \` (backslash). Next, you enter an **0** for Overstrike. Then, enter the left (open) parenthesis, and place the graphic or enter the Zapf Dingbat you want to use. Type a **comma** (,) and enter the number or letter you want to appear inside the box or graphic and press the right closing parenthesis.

You might also need to select the number, checkmark, or letter within the parentheses and superscript it using the `superscript` icon in the `Ribbon`. Open the `Character` dialog box if you need to superscript more than 3 points. Remember, this character needs to go inside your graphic and needs to clear the bottom line or circle position (Figure 7.119).

You can also use the Box formula. Press `Command Option \` and type an **X**. Then place the character you want to appear in a box inside parentheses. This might prove to be a lot easier than the overstrike formula.

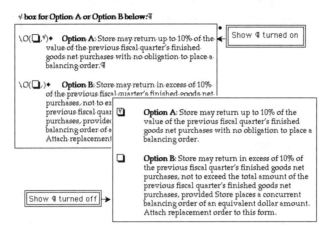

Figure 7.120

When using the overstrike formula, you can place it in a form you need to check mark using the computer (Figure 7.120). You would simply click inside the parentheses and enter the checkmark where it is appropriate (option "v" in most normal fonts creates the check mark shown).

Conclusion

Creating forms requires the integration of a variety of word processing techniques from tables and tabs to graphics and formulas. Your "repertoire" of formatting solutions can be saved in a "master forms library" document so that, when you don't have much time to play with the various formatting options, you can quickly adapt a known solution to meet your immediate needs.

Handy techniques for quickly gaining access to your formatting solutions when you need them (rather than opening your "master forms library" document) are covered in Chapter 10 in the sections on Glossaries and Keyboard Shortcuts.

8

CHAPTER

Expense Reports and Financial Tables

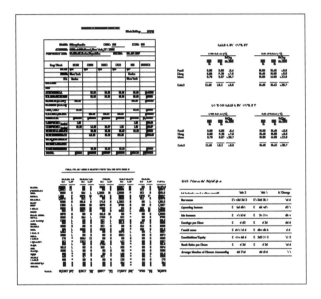

Figure 8.1

Formatting numbers and text for financial tables or expense reports requires you to plan and shape your information so that it is easy to read. Just as you saw in the preceding chapter on forms generation, financial tables take time and effort to prepare.

What you'll learn in this chapter are some efficient approaches to working with numbers in tables, how to choose the right kind of format for the type of information you are entering, and ways you can present financial information so that it looks more interesting on the page. You'll also learn how you can place "links" to financial tables you've created in Excel 3.0 or even other Word documents plus some timesaving techniques for resizing tables using System 7.0.

There are numerous techniques for formatting tables and you'll be exposed to a good sampling of possibilities. You might want to review the "preformat" suggestions made at the beginning of the forms generation chapter as they most definitely apply to the examples you'll be seeing in this chapter. You might also want to replicate some of the figure examples so that you get a feel for the way you can work with the various kinds of tables you might encounter in your daily document production tasks.

Financial Table Formatting Basics

EISA Consortium Shipments (Worldwide, All Units)						
(Units 000)	**1987**	**1988**	**1990**	**CAGR** **87/90**	**1993**	**CAGR** **90/93**
MicroTan	285	320	432	15%	790	22%
Cambisol	397	499	711	22%	1,301	22%
Progistra	625	746	975	26%	1,833	19%
Xaranex	517	522	623	6%	929	14%
Nebusil	350	414	555	17%	960	20%
Other	530	753	1,532	42%	3,761	35%
Consortium	2,693	3,255	4,826	21%	9,374	25%
% of Mkt	16%	16%	18%		22%	
Erbitron	2,082	2,297	2,762	10%	4,085	14%
% of Mkt	13%	12%	11%		10%	
Robitun	1,380	1,566	2,063	14%	3,745	22%
% of Mkt	8%	8%	8%		9%	

Figure 8.2

Most basic financial tables consist of column headings, rows of numerical information, and a table title. To become acquainted with some straightforward spacing and alignment concepts, you can execute the following steps to recreate the table shown in Figure 8.2.

Right-Aligned Columns

STEP ONE

In setting up a table, begin with counting the number of columns you'll be needing and choose **Table** from the **Insert** menu. However, before you insert the table, you should clear the paragraph of any formatting you have applied to the title text of the table—such as bold, centering, reduced font size, or space after a paragraph.

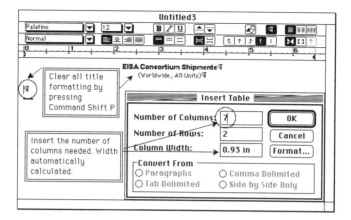

Figure 8.3

Remember that all paragraph and text formats carry forward to a new paragraph when you press the Return key. These same formats will also carry over into the table when you insert it, if you don't go through the clearing process first. Therefore, you should press `Command Shift P` to reapply the Normal style (Figure 8.3). Enter the number of columns you'll be needing for your table in the Insert Table dialog box. The column width is automatically calculated. Click `OK`.

STEP TWO

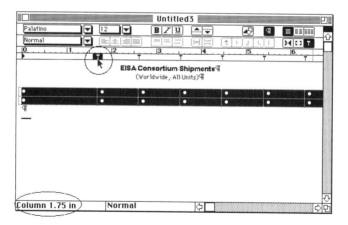

Figure 8.4

When a table is inserted, all the table cells are of equal width. However, most tables have category text entered in the left column—text that requires more space than numbers require. Your next step is to widen the category column. Press the **Option** key and double click to select the entire two rows of the table.

Press and drag on the first T-marker in the ruler and move it to the **1.75** inch mark (also indicated in the lower left status bar of the document window). As you move the T-marker, all the other cell markers move to the right in unison (Figure 8.4).

STEP THREE

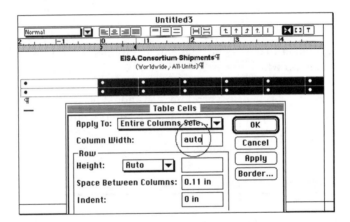

Figure 8.5

You'll need to readjust the cell width of the columns to the right of the category column so that they are all of equal width and they fit within the document margins. There's no need to guess what that width might be. Microsoft Word can automatically calculate that for you.

Press and drag to select the columns to the right of the category column, as indicated in Figure 8.5. Go to the **Format** menu and choose **Table Cells**. Type the word "**auto**" in the **Column Width** edit bar and click the **OK** button.

STEP FOUR

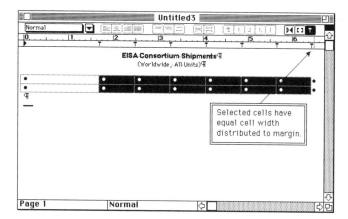

Figure 8.6

As illustrated in Figure 8.6, the cell width of the selected cells is adjusted so that they are all equal and fall within the margins of your document. Keep the columns selected for the next step.

STEP FIVE

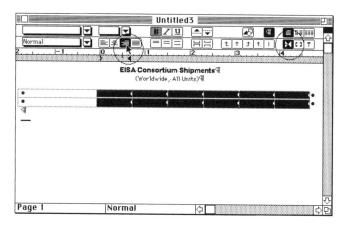

Figure 8.7

Click on the **Indent** scale icon in the Ruler; then click on the **Right Aligned** paragraph icon (Figure 8.7).

STEP SIX

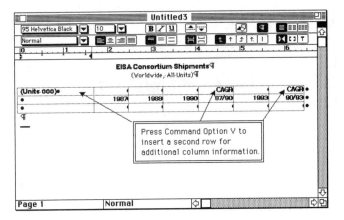

Figure 8.8

Select the cells in the first row and format them with the font, size, and/or bolding of your choice. Typically, the column headers will indicate years or some period of time. Enter the text. Sometimes, there are column headings that require two lines of space. Generally, this additional information should be placed above the series of numbers that make up the column headings. Press **Command Option V** to insert a row above the text you just formatted and entered. This new row will have the same formatting as the row beneath it. Enter text in the appropriate columns (Figure 8.8).

STEP SEVEN

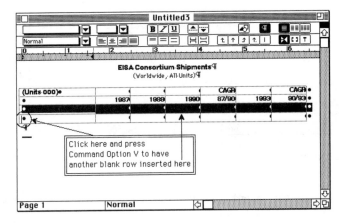

Figure 8.9

Click in the blank row beneath the columns headings. It's always a good idea to put some space between the column headings and the text that will follow it. There are a number of ways to achieve this, but the simplest method is to insert another row. Press **Command Option V** and another blank row will be inserted above the flashing insertion point (Figure 8.9).

STEP EIGHT

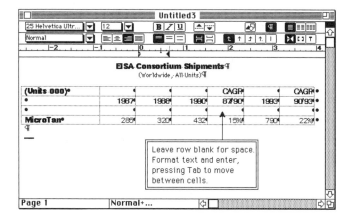

Figure 8.10

Click in the bottom row and format the text for the category heading and for the numbered text you will enter. As you enter the numbered text, you will see that the right aligned paragraph format aligns both the regular numbers and the percentages contained within this table (Figure 8.10). Right aligned paragraph format is the correct format for aligning both numbers, percentages and/or other kinds of characters. Press the **Tab** key for a new row and continue to enter text.

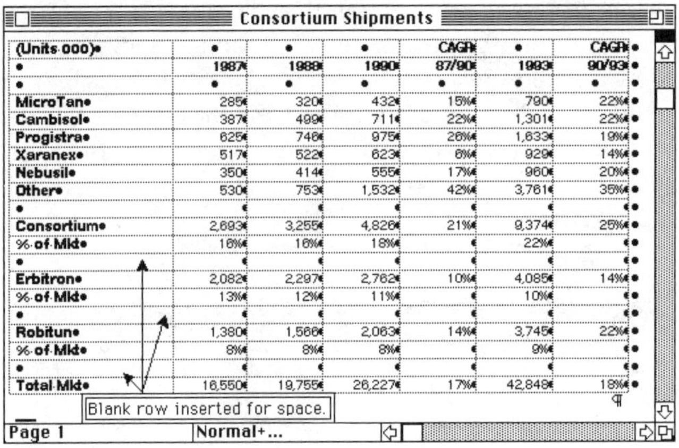

(Units 000)•	•	•	•	CAGR•	•	CAGR•
	1987•	1988•	1990•	87/90•	1993•	90/93•
•	•	•	•		•	•
MicroTan•	285•	320•	432•	15%•	790•	22%•
Cambisol•	387•	499•	711•	22%•	1,301•	22%•
Progistra•	625•	746•	975•	26%•	1,633•	19%•
Xaranex•	517•	522•	623•	6%•	929•	14%•
Nebusil•	350•	414•	555•	17%•	960•	20%•
Other•	530•	753•	1,532•	42%•	3,761•	35%•
•	•	•	•	•	•	••
Consortium•	2,693•	3,255•	4,826•	21%•	9,374•	25%••
% of Mkt•	16%•	16%•	18%•	•	22%•	••
•	•	•	•	•	•	••
Erbitron•	2,082•	2,297•	2,762•	10%•	4,085•	14%•
% of Mkt•	13%•	12%•	11%•	•	10%•	••
•	•	•	•	•	•	••
Robitun•	1,380•	1,566•	2,063•	14%•	3,745•	22%•
% of Mkt•	8%•	8%•	8%•	•	9%•	••
•	•	•	•	•	•	••
Total Mkt•	16,550•	19,755•	26,227•	17%•	42,848•	18%••

Blank row inserted for space.

Figure 8.11

The simplest way to create space between sections of your table is to leave a blank row, as shown in Figure 8.11.

Indented and Centered Columns

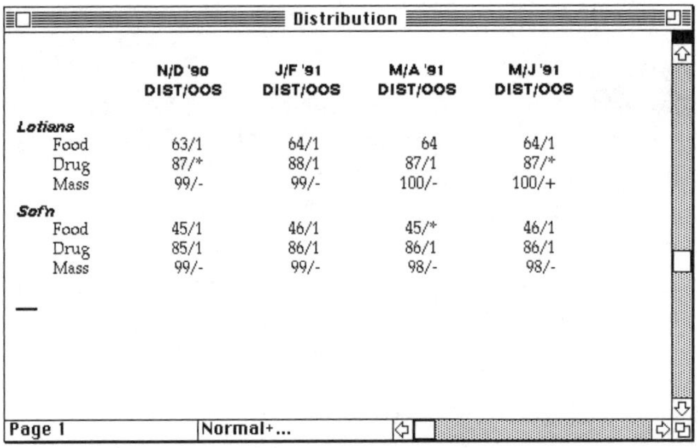

	N/D '90 DIST/OOS	J/F '91 DIST/OOS	M/A '91 DIST/OOS	M/J '91 DIST/OOS
Lotiana				
Food	63/1	64/1	64	64/1
Drug	87/*	88/1	87/1	87/*
Mass	99/-	99/-	100/-	100/+
Sof'n				
Food	45/1	46/1	45/*	46/1
Drug	85/1	86/1	86/1	86/1
Mass	99/-	99/-	98/-	98/-

Figure 8.12

When deciding which format works best for your information, you might want to try working with indented columns and centered text within columns. To properly align the type of number information displayed in Figure 8.12 requires a right-aligned paragraph format. However, to have the numbers form a column beneath the *center* of the column headers involves the use of an indented paragraph format.

What follows is a clarification of each formatted part of the table.

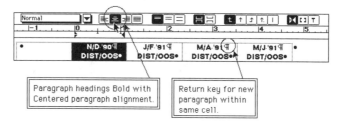

Figure 8.13

Here is another example of a way to format two lines of column title text. Since each title requires two lines, simply press the **Return** key for a new line within the cell. Clicking the **Centered** paragraph alignment icon in the Ruler easily centers the text within each cell (Figure 8.13).

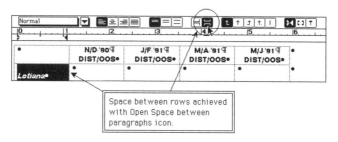

Figure 8.14

Rather than inserting a blank row, an alternate way to place space between the first row of information and the column titles is to format text with 12 points of space before the paragraph. Click on the **Open Space between paragraphs** icon in the Ruler (Figure 8.14). The entire row accommodates the cell with the tallest spacing so there is no need to format the other cells.

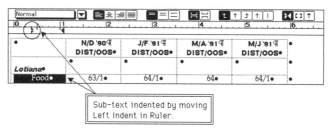

Figure 8.15

To indicate subtext within each category, you can move the **Left Indent** mark in the Ruler over to the right (Figure 8.15).

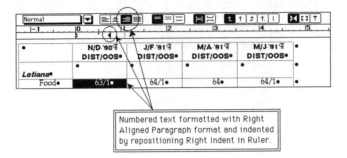

Numbered text formatted with Right Aligned Paragraph format and indented by repositioning Right Indent in Ruler.

Figure 8.16

Because the numbered text has an average length of about four characters, just using right-aligned paragraph format to align the numbers properly leaves too much "open" space to the left of the text. Move the **Right Indent** mark on the Ruler to the left so that the text falls somewhere near the middle of the column. This format gives numbered text the appearance of being centered on the column title information.

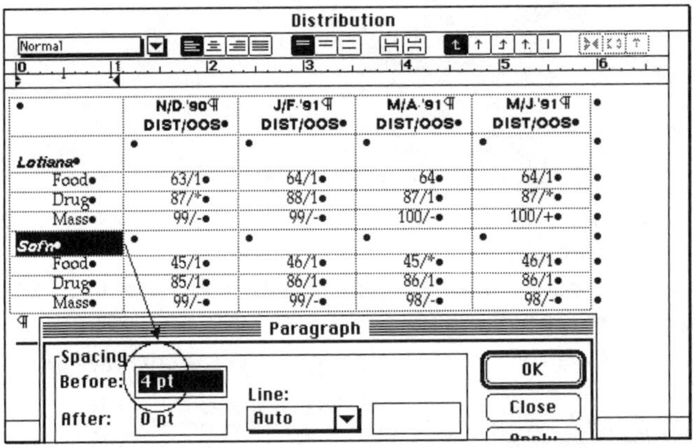

Figure 8.17

To place a little space between the category title information, select **Paragraph** from the **Format** menu. Enter **4 pt** in the **Before** edit bar and click **OK** (Figure 8.17).

Underlining Column Title Text

Costs & Expenses (per month)	1990	1991	1992
	1990	1991	1992
	<u>1990</u>	<u>1991</u>	<u>1992</u>
Rent	1,990.50	1,296.22	1891.11
Utilities	53.50	43.75	36.25
Telephone	159.45	122.70	98.45
Total:	<u>2,203.45</u>	<u>1,462.67</u>	2025.81

Figure 8.18

You should be aware of the different kinds of effects you can achieve for underlining title text in a column. The three techniques (Figure 8.18) you can choose from follow.

Using Cell Borders

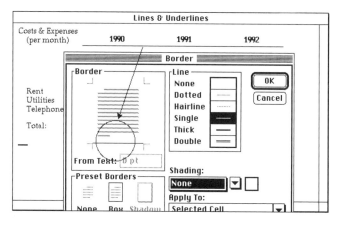

Figure 8.19

Applying a Cell Border (go to the **Format** menu and choose **Border**) creates a line along the table grid and extends the line the entire length of the cell. In Figure 8.19, the three columns with cell borders applied are "joined" as if they had a single line beneath them. If you want to control the distance between the bottom of the text in the cell and the border itself, you will need to apply space **After** the paragraph text using the **Paragraph** dialog box. When you use cell borders, you have a variety of border line weights to choose from.

Using Paragraph Borders

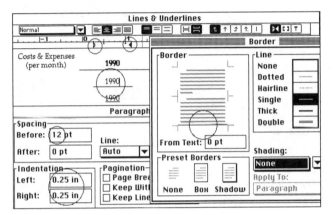

Figure 8.20

If you want to control the amount of horizontal space between the lines in your column title text, you would need to apply borders through the Paragraph dialog box (choose **Paragraph** from the **Format** menu and click on the **Border** button). To alter the border line length, you can move the **Left** and **Right** indent markers on the ruler or use the Indentation edit bars in the Paragraph dialog box. Note that, with centered text, you would need to indent the paragraph equally on the left and the right (Figure 8.20). You also have the flexibility in the Border dialog box of choosing how much space will appear between the line and your text, as well as the kind of line width.

Underlining Text

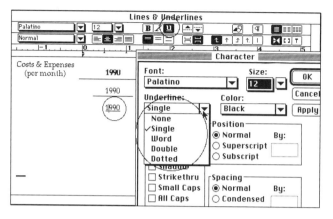

Figure 8.21

The final underlining choice is applied through the Character dialog box (go to the **Format** menu and choose **Character**). This requires you to select the text of your column title and then choose the appropriate line format (Figure 8.21). You can also apply a **Single** underline format by clicking on the **Underline** icon in the **Ribbon**. With Character underlining, you have no flexibility in terms of how much space appears between the actual text and the line. You also cannot easily extend the length of the line to the left or right of the title text—unless you enter blank spaces (press **Command spacebar** for fixed spacing) on either side of the title, select the spaces, and apply Underline format to them as well.

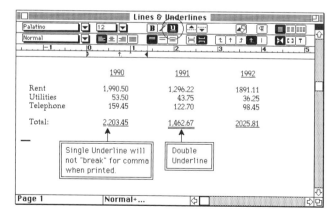

Figure 8.22

When applying Underline format to numbers with commas, though the screen will display a "break" in the underline for the comma, the actual text will print with one continuous underline (Figure 8.22).

Aligning Column Numbers with Decimal Tabs

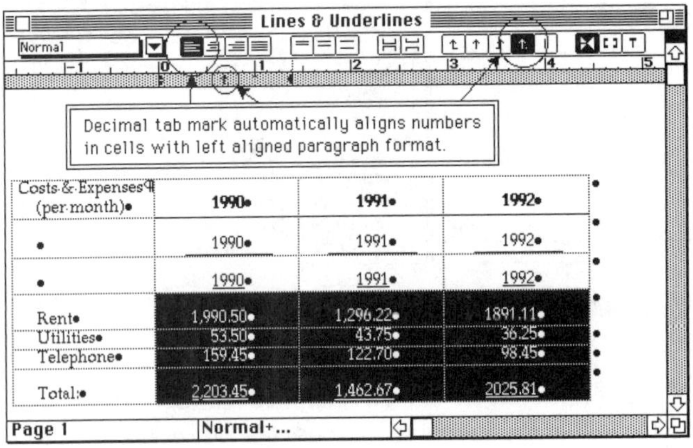

Figure 8.23

So far, you've seen columns of numbered text aligned using the **Right Aligned** paragraph format. This format is best used for numbers that have additional text such as percent signs and other characters (e.g., 64/1, 45/*, 95/+, etc.). You can easily alter the position of the numbers by moving the **Right Indent** mark in the Ruler (see Figure 8.16).

When working with straight numbered text that may or may not have decimals, you can easily align the numbers using the **Decimal tab** mark. When using decimal tabs, cells must be formatted with the **Left Aligned** paragraph format. The selected cells in Figure 8.23 were immediately aligned when a decimal tab was placed in the Ruler. You then have the flexibility to press and drag the tab mark in the Ruler and fine-tune the results of the text alignment. There is no need to press the Option Tab key to align numbers when you use a decimal tab mark in a cell.

Calculating Column Totals

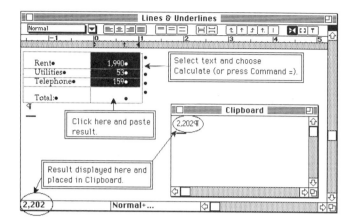

Figure 8.24

You can use Microsoft Word's calculation function to add columns of numbers within cells. Any negatively formatted numbers—such as -29 or (29)—will be subtracted from the calculation. If there are / (slash) or * (asterisk) marks combined with the numbered text, these will serve as math operators and either divide or multiply as part of the overall calculation.

To quickly add a subtotal, select the numbers in the cells and choose **Calculate** from the **Tools** menu (or press **Command** =). The result of the calculation will be displayed in the lower left status box of your window. It will also be pasted into the Clipboard so that you can position the flashing insertion point in the subtotal or total cell and then choose **Paste** from the **Edit** menu or press **Command V** (Figure 8.24).

The calculation results are sensitive to the format of your numbers. If your numbers contain any commas, then the result will display a comma. Likewise, if there are any decimals in the number format, the results will have decimals as well (Figure 8.25). Unfortunately, if you have dollar signs ($) before your text, these will not be placed in the result and you will have to enter them yourself.

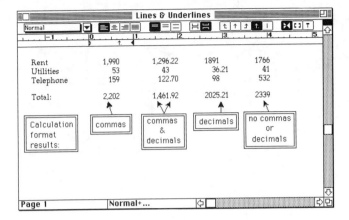

Figure 8.25

Lines for Total and Subtotal Columns

	1990	1991	1992
Rent/month	1,990.50	1,296.22	1,891.11
Utilities	53.50	43.75	36.25
Telephone	159.45	122.70	98.45
Sub-total:	2,203.45	1,462.67	2,025.81
Insurance	215.00	235.00	245.00
Total	2,418.45	1,697.67	2,270.81

Figure 8.26

Probably one of the most confusing and frustrating tasks in working with financial tables is figuring out how to achieve the kind of line you want prior to your total or subtotal information. In this section, you'll look at the various ways you can format these lines and what some of the advantages and drawbacks are for each method.

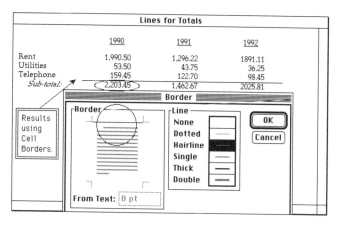

Figure 8.27

For many people, one of the easiest formats to apply is the cell border. Select the cells in the Total or Subtotal row. Go to the **Format** menu and choose **Border**. Click on the line weight of your choice and then click on the top of the diagram to apply a border to the top of the cell (Figure 8.27).

However, there are formatting limitations. As you might remember from Figure 8.19, cell borders extend the entire length of the cell. Standard financial information rarely makes use of this kind of line format for subtotal or total information.

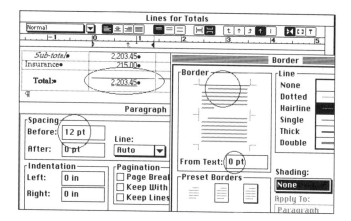

Figure 8.28

Using paragraph borders rather than cell borders gives you the flexibility you need to size the line to the length you need it. However, there are spacing considerations you should know about. For example, the Total row in Figure 8.28 has 12 points of space before it (applied through the Paragraph dialog box). This space provides some breathing room from the numbered text above it. The border in the example was obtained by choosing **Paragraph** from the **Format** menu and clicking on the **Border** button. The line was applied to the top of the diagram. Notice how close the border is to the actual text. Space Before a paragraph does not affect the placement of the border.

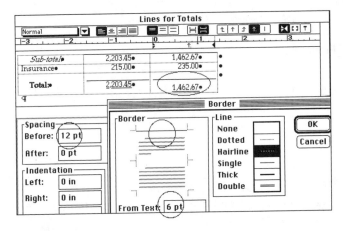

Figure 8.29

In this example (Figure 8.29), space was applied from within the **Border** dialog box by an entry in the **From Text** edit bar. (You must enter the amount of space in the **From Text** edit bar **before** you click to apply the line.) Whereas this gives some breathing room between the text and the line above it, you should also notice that the text is now positioned lower than the text to the left of it. Obviously, this is not the solution that will meet your needs.

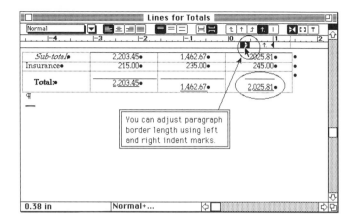

Figure 8.30

Although the example in Figure 8.30 still does not resolve the spacing problem, it does display how you can adjust the length of the line above the text in the cell by moving the **Left** and **Right indent** marks in the **Ruler**. Notice also that, if you align numbered text using a **Decimal tab** (and **Left aligned** paragraph format), you can move the left and right indent marks without affecting the alignment of the numbers themselves.

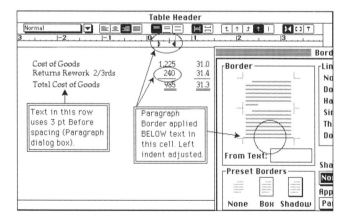

Figure 8.31

The secret to the line formatting solution lies in applying a paragraph border format below the row that comes *before* the total or subtotal information. You can control the line length using the **Left** and **Right indent** marks and the line does not fall too closely beneath the text. You also have the flexibility to place more space above the Total or Subtotal row by using the **Before** edit bar in the **Paragraph** dialog box.

Now that you are familiar with most of the formatting concerns you need to address when working with financial information in tables, you can apply some of these techniques and try your hand at formatting a weekly expense report.

Creating a Weekly Expense Report

WEEKLY EXPENSE REPORT

Week Ending: _____

NAME: _____   DEPT: _____   DIV#: _____
ADDRESS: _____
PURPOSE OF TRIP: _____   PHONE: _____

Day/Week	MON	TUES	WED	THU	FRI	TOTALS
DATE:						
FROM:						
TO:						
MILEAGE						
GAS						
AUTO RENTAL						

Figure 8.32

There are any number of ways you can report expense information and your organization might have a standard format that is used corporatewide. Because the goal of an expense report is to detail daily expenses by categories and then total the results, more often expense reports are executed in a spreadsheet application where you can make use of automatic calculations or "formulas." Microsoft Word does not have the full-bodied calculating features of a spreadsheet. Therefore, if you are familiar with spreadsheets and use Microsoft Excel to create expense reports, you should continue to do so.

However, if you want to place information from a spreadsheet expense report into a Microsoft Word document, you can dynamically "link" this information so that your Word document receives all the updates and changes to the master Excel worksheet document. Ways to link information between the Excel 3.0 and Word 5.0 applications are discussed later in this chapter.

Perhaps you do not own or use a spreadsheet application for tracking weekly expense information. This section will guide you through a step-by-step process for setting up a Word table to help you accomplish this task.

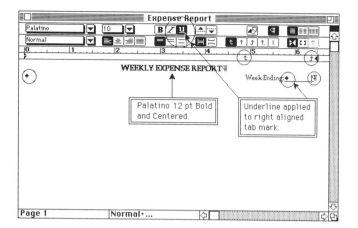

Figure 8.33

1. In a new document formatted with **left** and **right** margins of **1 inch**, **Center** your text, and enter a **Bold**, **Caps** document title (such as, Weekly Expense Report). Press **Return** for a new line. **Press Command Shift P** to apply Normal style. Place a **left aligned** and a **right aligned** tab mark in the ruler as indicated in Figure 8.33. Press the **Tab** key once. Format your text as **10 point** and enter **Week Ending:** text. Click on the **Underline** button in the **Ribbon**. Press the **Tab** key once. Go to the **Format** menu and choose **Paragraph**. Press the **Tab** key to move into the **After** edit bar and enter **24 pt**. Click **OK**.

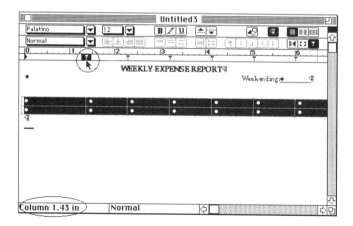

Figure 8.34

2. Press the **Return** key for a new paragraph. Press **Command Shift P** to apply Normal style. Choose **Table** from the **Insert** menu. Enter **7** in the **Number of Columns** edit bar and click **OK**. Press the **Option** key and double-click to select the entire table. Move the **Left T marker** to the **1 3/8 inch** mark (Figure 8.34).

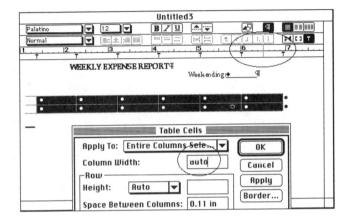

Figure 8.35

3. Select all the columns except the left column and choose **Table Cells** from the **Format** menu. Type the word **Auto** in the **Cell Width** edit bar and click **OK** (Figure 8.35). Your cells will now be of equal width and fit within the margins of your document.

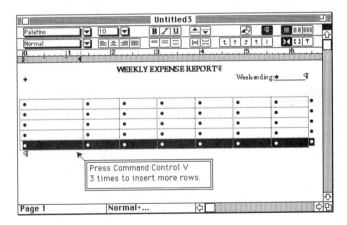

Figure 8.36

4. Click in one of the rows within the table. Press **Command Control V** three times to insert more rows into your table (Figure 8.36).

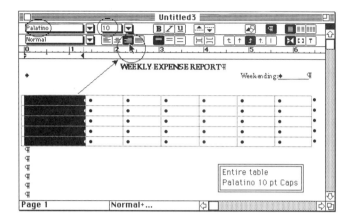

Figure 8.37

5. Press the **Option** key and click to select the left column. Click on the **Right Aligned** paragraph icon in the **Ruler**. Press the **Option** key and double-click to select the entire table. Format the text as **Palatino 10 pt Caps** by choosing **Character** from the **Format** menu.

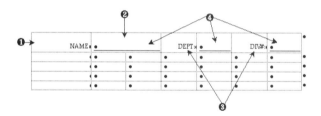

Figure 8.38

6. The illustration in Figure 8.38 details a combination of the following formatting steps:

   ❶ Double-click to select the row. Choose **Paragraph** from the **Format** menu and apply **18 pt Before** and **2 pt After** spacing.

   ❷ Select the two cells represented by this space. Choose **Table Layout** from the **Format** menu and click on **Merge Cells**.

❸ Click in each of these cells. Enter text and click on the **Right Aligned** paragraph icon in the **Ruler**.

❹ Click in the widest cell first. Choose **Paragraph** from the **Format** menu and click on the **Border** button. Choose a **Hairline** line weight and click on the bottom of the diagram to apply the line. Click the **OK** button for both dialog boxes. Click in each of the other cells, in turn, and press **Command Y** (Repeat Paragraph).

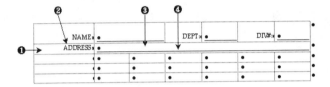

Figure 8.39

7. The combination of formatting steps displayed in Figure 8.39 are as follows:

❶ Double-click to select the row. Choose **Paragraph** from the **Format** menu and apply **2 pt Before** and **2 pt After** spacing.

❷ Click in this cell and enter the "Address:" text.

❸ Select the six cells represented by this space. Choose **Table Layout** from the **Format** menu and click on **Merge Cells**.

❹ Choose **Paragraph** from the **Format** menu and click on the **Border** button. Choose a **Hairline** line weight and click on the bottom of the diagram to apply the line. Click the **OK** button for both dialog boxes.

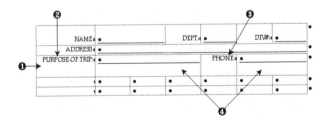

Figure 8.40

8. Figure 8.40 represents yet another combination of formatting steps, listed below.

➊ Double-click to select the row. Choose **Paragraph** from the **Format** menu and apply **2 pt Before** and **2 pt After** spacing. Keep the row selected and go to the **Format** menu and choose **Table Cells**. Select **Exactly** from the **Row Height** list menu and type **36 pt** in the Height edit bar.

➋ Enter the text "Purpose of Trip:" in this cell.

➌ Click in this cell. Enter the "Phone:" text. Click on the **Right Aligned** paragraph icon in the **Ruler**.

➍ Select the appropriate number of cells (3 on the left and 2 on the right), choose **Table Layout** from the **Format** menu and click on **Merge Cells**. Position the cursor in one of these cells. Choose **Paragraph** from the **Format** menu and click on the **Border** button. Choose a **Hairline** line weight and click on the bottom of the diagram to apply the line. Click the **OK** button for both dialog boxes. Click in the other cell and press **Command Y** (Repeat Paragraph).

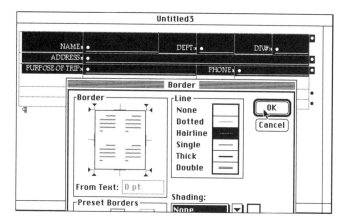

Figure 8.41

9. Select all the rows illustrated in Figure 8.41. Choose **Border** from the **Paragraph** menu and select the **Hairline** border. Click on the **Box** preformatted border and click **OK**.

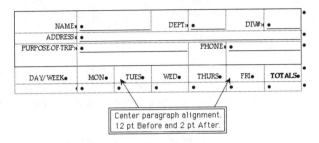

Figure 8.42

10. Double-click to select this row. Choose **Paragraph** from the **Format** menu and apply **12 point Before** and **2 point After** spacing. Click on the **Centered** paragraph alignment icon in the Ruler and click **OK**. Enter the text for the days of the week and totals. Select the **Totals** cell and the cell beneath it. Apply **Bold** format from the **Ribbon.**

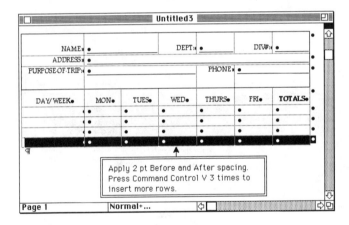

Figure 8.43

11. Double-click to select the last blank row. Choose **Paragraph** from the **Format** menu and apply **2 pt Before** and **After** spacing. Click **OK**. Press **Command Control V** 3 times to insert more rows.

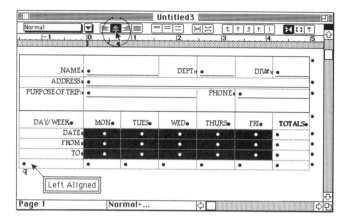

Figure 8.44

12. Enter text for Date, From, and To as illustrated in Figure 8.44. Click in the bottom left cell and apply **Left Aligned** paragraph format from the **Ruler**. Select the cells indicated in Figure 8.44 and click on the **Center Aligned** paragraph icon in the Ruler.

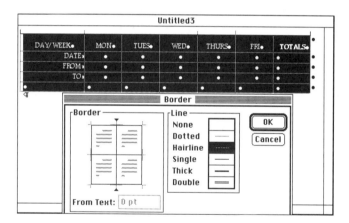

Figure 8.45

13. Select the cells indicated in Figure 8.45 and choose **Border** from the **Format** menu. Choose the **Hairline** line weight and click on every possible line in the diagram, so that every cell has a border.

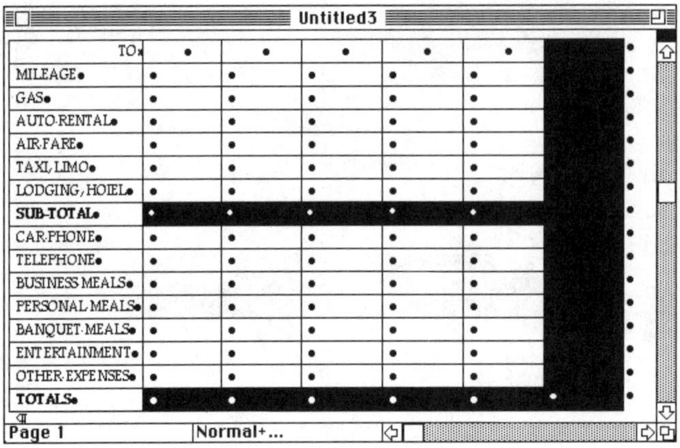
Untitled3
TO
MILEAGE
GAS
AUTO RENTAL
AIR FARE
TAXI, LIMO
LODGING, HOTEL
SUB-TOTAL
CAR PHONE
TELEPHONE
BUSINESS MEALS
PERSONAL MEALS
BANQUET MEALS
ENTERTAINMENT
OTHER EXPENSES
TOTALS
Page 1
Normal+...

Figure 8.46

14. Click in the bottom row. Press **Command Control V** 14 times to insert all the rows shown. Enter the various expense categories. Choose the cells in the rows and columns indicated in Figure 8.46 and apply **Bold** format. You will have to select three different sets of cells in order to apply the Bold format—the illustration in Figure 8.46 merely indicates the cells you should highlight to apply this formatting.

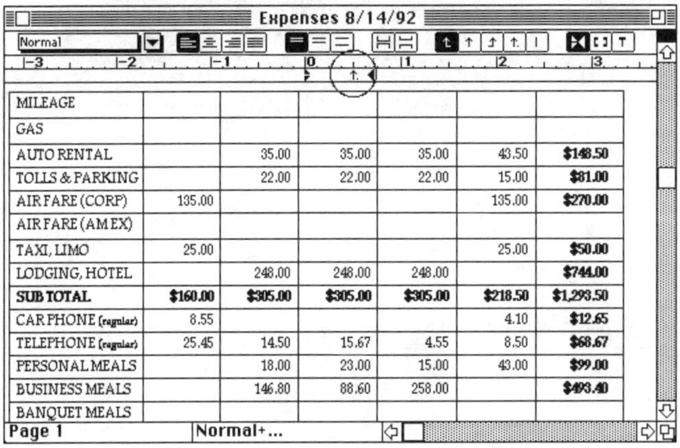
Expenses 8/14/92
Normal
MILEAGE
GAS
AUTO RENTAL 35.00 35.00 35.00 43.50 $148.50
TOLLS & PARKING 22.00 22.00 22.00 15.00 $81.00
AIR FARE (CORP) 135.00 135.00 $270.00
AIR FARE (AMEX)
TAXI, LIMO 25.00 25.00 $50.00
LODGING, HOTEL 248.00 248.00 248.00 $744.00
SUB TOTAL $160.00 $305.00 $305.00 $305.00 $218.50 $1,293.50
CAR PHONE (regular) 8.55 4.10 $12.65
TELEPHONE (regular) 25.45 14.50 15.67 4.55 8.50 $68.67
PERSONAL MEALS 18.00 23.00 15.00 43.00 $99.00
BUSINESS MEALS 146.80 88.60 258.00 $493.40
BANQUET MEALS
Page 1
Normal+...

Figure 8.47

15. Select all the cells that will contain numbered text. Click on the **Decimal** tab icon in the **Ruler**. Click in the Ruler at the **1/2 inch** mark (Figure 8.47).

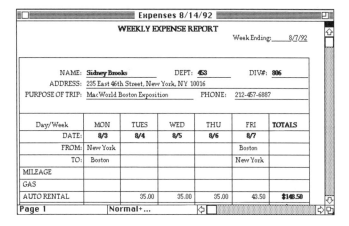

Figure 8.48

16. Save your document as a **Stationery** document. You might choose to apply **Bold** format to some of the name and ID cells shown in the sample completed expense report in Figure 8.48.

When using the Expense Report to fill in the information for expense amounts, remember that you can select a group of cells and press **Command** = to calculate a total. You'd then click in the appropriate Total cell and Paste in the results.

More Table Formatting Variations

This section will illustrate an array of table formatting possibilities and point out the significant techniques that were relevant to the solution. By becoming aware of some of the variations possible for displaying financial information, you can successfully apply these formats to your own work.

1990 AUDITS & SURVEYS¶

DATA TABLES¶

❶

		(INDEX VS.	(INDEX VS.		
	1990•	......1988)•	...TOP 20)•	1988•	1986•
Total•	73•	(118)•	(77)•	62•	77•
Kids 6-11•	40•	(105)•	(62)•	38•	61•
Teens 12-17•	69•	(103)•	(70)•	67•	85•
Adults 18-34•	86•	(212)•	(88)•	71•	85•
Adults 35+•	76•	(121)•	(82)•	63•	74•

Milk Total Awareness¶ ❷ ❸ ❹ ❺

Figure 8.49

This example uses a combination of Bold Helvetica and Palatino fonts.

❶ Thick border with **2 pt** of spacing **From Text** applied above this paragraph. All text is centered. Using the **Paragraph** dialog box, **56 points** of space were applied **After** the paragraph.

❷ Because this heading format was applied to a series of other similarly formatted tables beneath it, the table title has **24 points Before** and **6 points After** spacing applied through the **Paragraph** dialog box. The **Left** and **Right indents** have been moved so that the **Border** applied beneath it (with **2 pt** of **From Text** spacing) spans the columns under it. (A similar format could have been applied if the heading had been made part of the table using merged cells.)

❸ A blank paragraph spaces the column titles so that they align with the titles in the columns to the left. Text is **Centered**. The underline for the titles is achieved by using a **Paragraph Border** with **2 pt From Text** spacing applied at the bottom of the paragraph. **Left** and **Right indents** are of equal length (**.25 inches**).

❹ Spacing achieved in this row by applying **12 point** of space **Before** and **After** using the **Paragraph** dialog box.

❺ All numbered text in the columns is aligned using a **decimal tab** placed in the Ruler at the **5/8 inch** mark. Notice that the all negative numbers surrounded by parenthesis are in their own columns. When you have a mixture of negative numbers in parenthesis and regular positive numbers, you will need to align the text using a different technique, explained later in Figure 8.63.

SALES BY OUTLET

	Unit Sales (%)				Dollar Sales (%)		
	1990 %	1991 %	% Chg vs. YAG		1990 %	1991 %	% Chg vs. YAG
Food	5.86	5.66	-3.4		24.95	25.45	+2.0
Drug	6.86	7.18	+7.5		29.45	32.33	+9.8
Mass	4.76	5.27	+10.7		15.09	16.82	+11.5
Total	17.48	18.1	+3.6		69.49	74.61	+15.7

Figure 8.50

Often, financial information needs to be formatted with blank space to help clarify the data that is being presented (Figure 8.50). You can use blank columns or space before and after paragraphs to adjust the amount of space you need. The figure below diagrams the kinds of formatting you would apply to achieve various spacing results.

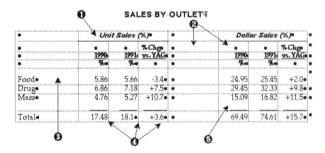

Figure 8.51

❶ The title for this group of cells was created by merging three cells and centering **Bold Italic** text with the **Center** paragraph icon in the Ruler. The **Hairline Border** is a **Cell border** applied through the **Format Border** dialog box.

❷ An entire column was left blank to separate the comparison information for Unit versus Dollar sales. This row has **4 points** of **space Before** applied through the **Paragraph** dialog box so that the title text in the % Chg cell has some space beneath the cell border. Each line of the title is in a separate row. Text for the year and percent has a **Right aligned** paragraph format and the year has **Underline** format applied through the **Ribbon**.

❸ This row has **12 pt** of space applied by clicking on the **Open Space between paragraphs** icon in the Ruler.

❹ All the numbered text in these columns (and the similar ones in the columns on the right) is formatted using a **Decimal** tab mark in the **Ruler** at the **3/8 inch** mark.

❺ The line for each column total was produced by choosing **Paragraph** from the **Format** menu and clicking on the **Border** button. In the **From Text** edit bar **12 pt** was entered and a hairline border applied at the bottom of the diagram. The line length was adjusted by moving the **Left indent** mark to the right **.18 inches**.

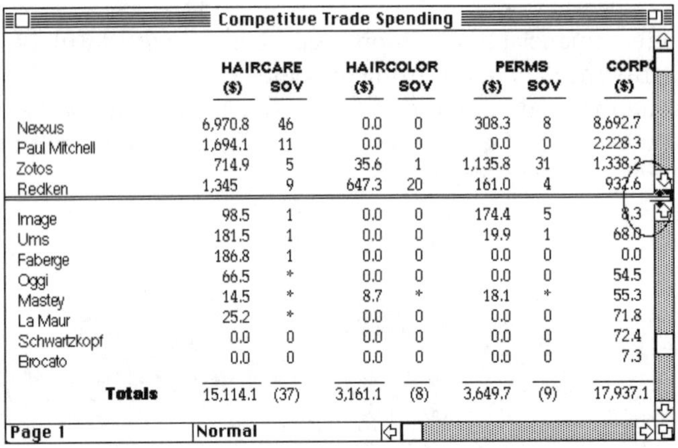

Competitve Trade Spending	HAIRCARE ($)	SOV	HAIRCOLOR ($)	SOV	PERMS ($)	SOV	CORP ($)
Nexxus	6,970.8	46	0.0	0	308.3	8	8,692.7
Paul Mitchell	1,694.1	11	0.0	0	0.0	0	2,228.3
Zotos	714.9	5	35.6	1	1,135.8	31	1,338.2
Redken	1,345	9	647.3	20	161.0	4	932.6
Image	98.5	1	0.0	0	174.4	5	8.3
Ums	181.5	1	0.0	0	19.9	1	68.0
Faberge	186.8	1	0.0	0	0.0	0	0.0
Oggi	66.5	*	0.0	0	0.0	0	54.5
Mastey	14.5	*	8.7	*	18.1	*	55.3
La Maur	25.2	*	0.0	0	0.0	0	71.8
Schwartzkopf	0.0	0	0.0	0	0.0	0	72.4
Brocato	0.0	0	0.0	0	0.0	0	7.3
Totals	15,114.1	(37)	3,161.1	(8)	3,649.7	(9)	17,937.1

Page 1 — Normal

Figure 8.52

Tables that are longer that your screen are sometimes difficult to enter text into because the column headings are at the top of the document. You can "split" the screen and view your headings by moving the pointer into the solid black rectangle above the scroll arrow on the upper right of your document window. Pressing and dragging with the split window pointer creates two views for your table information (Figure 8.52). You can click between windows to enter text.

> **NOTE:** *To remove the split window, double-click on the black rectangle in the vertical scroll bar area.*

Sometimes information in tables needs to be presented in column "pairs" as shown in Figure 8.52. Solutions for this kind of formatting are detailed in the diagram that follows.

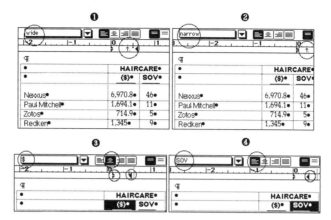

Figure 8.53

❶ Each of the columns containing numbers within the table are of equal cell width. However, you can position the text in the columns so they group themselves closer together (creating the pairs) by using a different **decimal tab mark** placement in the **Ruler**. The left column of the pair has a decimal tab at the **3/8 inch** mark. Because there are a number of columns using this format, the easiest way to apply the same format is to define it as a style. (To define the style, click in the **Style Selection box** in the ruler, type the name for your style (e.g., **wide**) and press the **Return** key two times.)

❷ The **decimal tab** mark placement for this column is at the **2/8 inch** mark on the Ruler. A style (narrow) has also been defined for this column.

❸ The column headings are formatted differently so they "appear" to be centered over the columns of text. The ($) heading has a **left** and **right indent** adjustment as shown in the diagram and has **Centered** paragraph alignment applied. There is also a **Paragraph Border** applied with **2** points of space **From Text**. This heading is defined as a style as well.

❹ The other column heading has **Left aligned** paragraph format and a **Right indent** setting so that the Paragraph border line (with **2 points** of space **From Text**) is the same length as the text. The row above these column headings has the larger "group" heading (e.g. Haircare), which was created by merging two cells in the row.

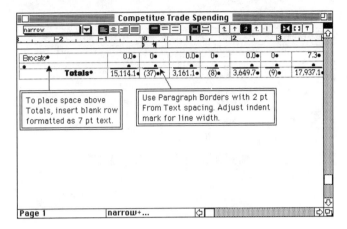

Figure 8.54

Another way to approach spacing before column totals is to insert a blank row before the Total information. Format this row with **7 pt** text. In the Total row, format the number totals with a **Paragraph Border** above the paragraph with a **2 pt From Text** spacing. You can then use the indent marks in the Ruler to adjust the line length above the numbers for each column.

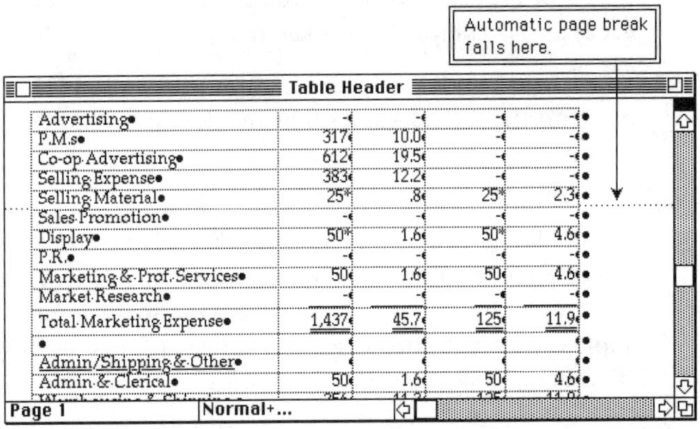

Figure 8.55

When working with tables, often the financial information spills over onto a second page, splitting your information (Figure 8.55).

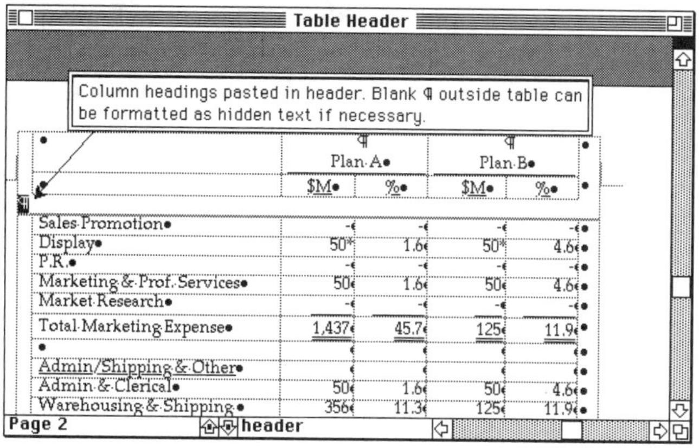

Figure 8.56

You can copy and paste column heading information into the header. However, if the header information is in a table format, there is always a blank paragraph mark placed under the table (Figure 8.56). If the space provided by the blank paragraph is not bothersome, you can ignore the blank paragraph. However, if you want your table header information to "sit" directly on top of the rest of your table information, select the paragraph mark and format it as **Hidden** text using the **Character** dialog box. You might also select the paragraph mark and format it as **4 pt** text.

If you are working in a long document and the table falls between pages 4 and 5, you would need to insert a new section mark, so that the table header information is not placed throughout your document. For more information on working with various headers and long document formatting, see Chapter 9, *"Long Document Structuring and Management."*

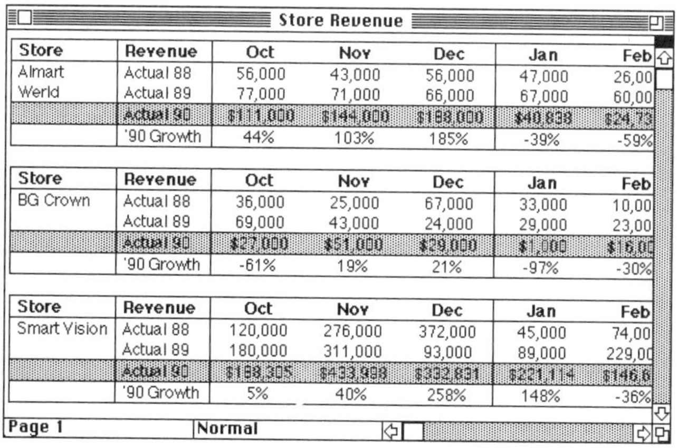

Store	Revenue	Oct	Nov	Dec	Jan	Feb
Almart	Actual 88	56,000	43,000	56,000	47,000	26,00
World	Actual 89	77,000	71,000	66,000	67,000	60,00
	Actual 90	$111,000	$144,000	$188,000	$40,838	$24,73
	'90 Growth	44%	103%	185%	-39%	-59%
Store	**Revenue**	**Oct**	**Nov**	**Dec**	**Jan**	**Feb**
BG Crown	Actual 88	36,000	25,000	67,000	33,000	10,00
	Actual 89	69,000	43,000	24,000	29,000	23,00
	Actual 90	$27,000	$51,000	$29,000	$1,000	$16,00
	'90 Growth	-61%	19%	21%	-97%	-30%
Store	**Revenue**	**Oct**	**Nov**	**Dec**	**Jan**	**Feb**
Smart Vision	Actual 88	120,000	276,000	372,000	45,000	74,00
	Actual 89	180,000	311,000	93,000	89,000	229,00
	Actual 90	$188,305	$433,998	$333,831	$221,114	$146,6
	'90 Growth	5%	40%	258%	148%	-36%

Figure 8.57

You can use borders and shading of table cells to highlight important information within a table. A table header can be repeated within a document to create sections or strips of information that are easy to follow (Figure 8.57).

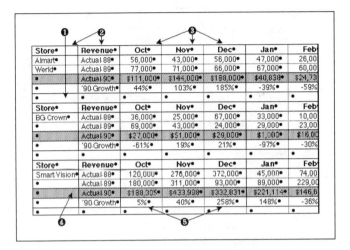

Figure 8.58

Significant points about the formatting for this table follow:

❶ A blank row is inserted between each "strip" of information to create space. The row is not formatted with any borders.

❷ Vertical column "headings" have **Left aligned** paragraph format applied.

❸ All the other columns use a **Centered** paragraph alignment.

❹ An entire row uses **Cell Border** shading of **25%**. Anything above this percentage of shading will cause difficulty when reading black text.

❺ Cells are selected in groups of three and a **Box Border** applied through choosing **Border** on the **Format** menu.

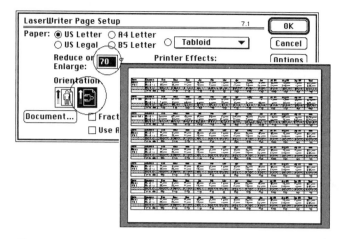

Figure 8.59

If you have difficulty fitting wider tables on a single page and want to work with the table text in a font size that is readable on screen, consider reducing the table by using the **Page Setup** dialog box (Figure 8.59). Reducing a table widens the available margins for the table while retaining the same screen font size.

Long-Term Debt

Long-term debt consisted of the following at December 31:

(in thousands)	1991	1990
Convertible Subordinated Debentures, 8-1/2%, due 2012	$103,500	$103,500
Unsecured Notes, 8-3/4% to 9-5/8%, due 1991 to 1998	18,500	20,500
Bank Note, floating rate (10.8%)	17,525	—
Industrial Development Bonds, 13-1/2% and floating rates, due 1991 to 2011	14,870	14,940
Revolving Credit facility	—	79,000
Bank Borrowings, 8.88%	—	30,167
Unsecured Note, 12.85%	—	25,000
Other	2,900	4,943
	157,295	278,050
Less current portion	(4,088)	(18,756)
Total	$153,207	$259,294

Figure 8.60

Financial information can be presented in a table format that uses cell borders that are applied to the entire width of the table rather than fussing with individual cell or paragraph border formatting (Figure 8.60).

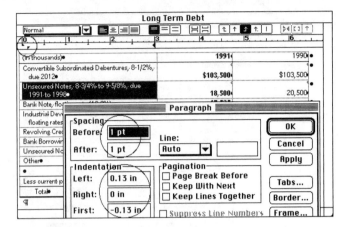

Figure 8.61

Consider formatting text with 1 pt of space before and after each paragraph within the table, as well as using "hanging indent" paragraph format for lengthy descriptions (Figure 8.61).

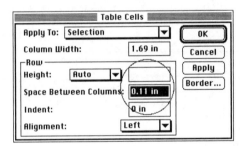

Figure 8.62

Whenever you insert a table, the default setting for space between columns is .11 inches. This space is applied equally between the left and right side of the cell. You can "use" this space allotment when formatting cells for negative numbers expressed in parentheses.

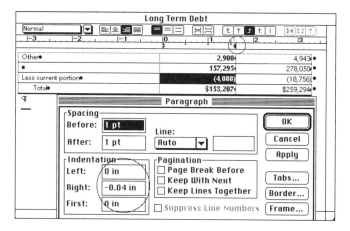

Figure 8.63

The **Right Indent** marker can be moved into this narrow space between columns through the **Paragraph** dialog box. Click in the **Right Indentation** edit bar and enter **-0.04 inches**. (If you enter a higher number, the parenthesis will not print.) This formatting only works when you are aligning columns using the **Right Aligned** paragraph format. When using **decimal tabs** and **Left Aligned** paragraph format, you would need to position the decimal tab for the particular cell containing the negative number .04 inches further to the right.

1991 Financial Highlights			
(In Thousands, except per share amounts)	1992	1991	% Change
Revenues	$1,436,262	$1,305,397	10.0
Operating Income	$ 98,591	$ 60,461	63.1
Net Income	$ 41,976	$ 24,774	69.4
Earnings per Share	$ 0.63	$ 0.38	65.8
Total Assets	$ 841,750	$ 894,699	-6.0
Stockholders' Equity	$ 414,588	$ 353,772	17.2
Book Value per Share	$ 6.26	$ 5.36	16.8

Figure 8.64

Formatting table text with dollar signs that need to be uniformly positioned from your figures often pose a formatting challenge and/or headache. Some examples of formatting solutions you might want to try appear below.

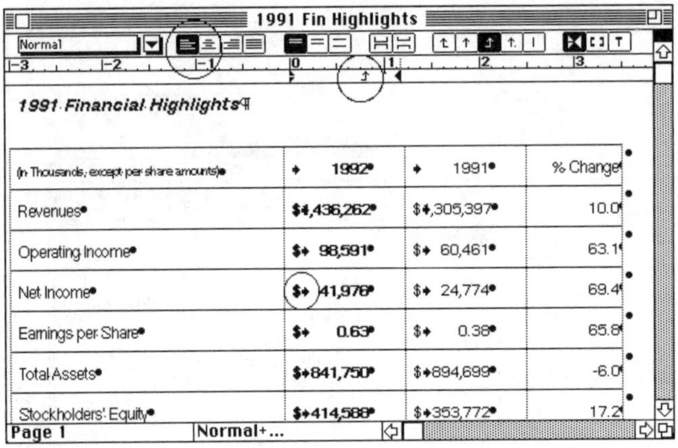

Figure 8.65

Place a **Right Aligned** tab mark within a cell that is formatted with **Left Aligned** paragraph format (Figure 8.65). To determine the correct positioning of the right-aligned tab, enter the largest number in your table data series. Click to place the tab mark on the ruler at some arbitrary position. Enter a dollar sign before the number and then hold the **Option** key and press the **Tab** key. Reposition the Tab mark in the Ruler until the number is a close as possible to the dollar sign. Format the other cells in your number columns using this same tab placement. The major drawback is that you will have to press **Option Tab** after entering the dollar sign for each number and this action might slow your text entry speed.

		(In thousands)
	1990	1989	1988
Income of foreign subsidiaries not taxable	$ 145,900	$ 94,649	$ 78,023
Warranty, bad debt, and other expenses	(11,719)	(17,165)	(4,089)
Depreciation	(20,919)	(9,643)	3,175
Inventory valuation	(2,315)	(1,734)	(7,666)
State income taxes	2,972	(436)	(9,688)
Income reported on installment method	—	—	(21,362)
Other individually immaterial items	16,647	1,287	10,497
Total deferred taxes	$ 130,566	$ 66,958	$ 48,890

Figure 8.66

This example aligns only the first and last dollar signs within a column. It also has negative numbers within parentheses.

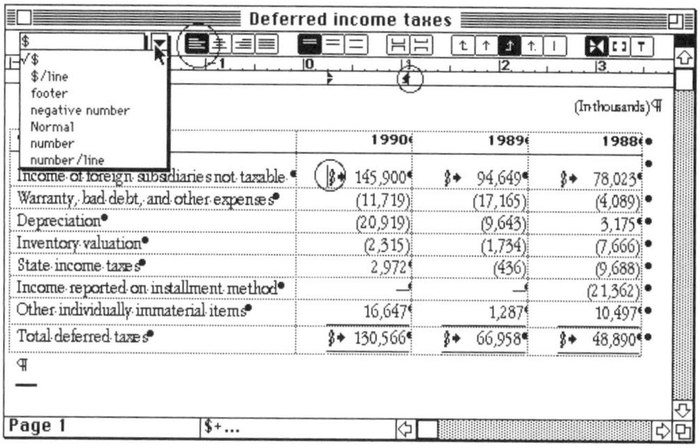

Figure 8.67

Because there are several different formatting requirements for the kind of numbers entered (with a dollar sign, regular numbers, negative numbers, numbers before the total, and totals with a dollar sign and a border line), you should define styles for each of the various formats. The numbers with dollars will use `Left aligned` paragraph format and the `Right aligned` tab mark. Negative numbers will require right-aligned paragraph format with a `-.04 right indent`. You can then copy or merge these style definitions in other financial tables you might need to prepare.

Consolidated Statements of Income

For the years ended
December 31, 1991, 1990 and 1989
(in thousands)

	1991	1990	1989
Net Sales	**$227,502**	$187,536	$169,255
Cost of sales	**142,897**	116,709	111,517
Gross Profit	**84,605**	70,827	57,738
Selling and admin expense	**56,689**	50,000	47,801
Corporate, general and other	**4,614**	4,242	3,005
Interest (income), net	**(8,662)**	(7,334)	(5,563)
Income before Income Taxes	**31,964**	23,919	12,495
Provision for income taxes	**12,698**	10,623	5,767
Income from Continuing Operations	**19,266**	13,296	6,728
Income from spun off operation, net of income taxes	*6,199*	*14,953*	*15,802*
Net Income	*$ 25,465*	*$ 28,249*	*$ 22,530*

Figure 8.68

This final example illustrates some rather attractive formatting that you might want to consider adopting for your financial documents. The diagram in Figure 8.69 details how to achieve these results.

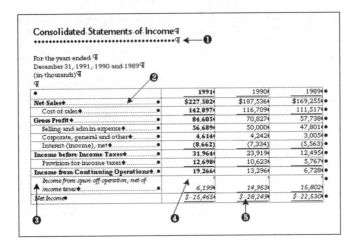

Figure 8.69

❶ This border was created by using a `Right Indent` to shorten the length of the paragraph and pressing the `Option 8` keys to create a series of "bullets."

❷ Place a `Right Aligned` tab in the `Ruler` that is formatted with a `dotted leader` tab. When you are entering **Bold** text, **remove** the **Bold** formatting before you press `Option Tab` to create the dotted line. Otherwise, the dots created by the leader tab will be darker than the dots created by the cells that use regular text. (To learn how to apply leader tabs, see Figure 4.25 in Chapter 4.)

❸ Move the `Left Indent` for text in subordinate cells.

❹ Any cells that have text that wraps to two lines will require you to press the `Return` key to properly align the numbered text you will enter in other cells.

❺ You might want to try pressing the spacebar to align dollar signs. Since this text is formatted as Italic, the precision factor in the dollar sign alignment is not as noticeable as with regular text.

Linking Excel 3.0 Documents with Word 5.0

So far you've been learning formatting tips and suggestions for working with tables and numerical information from within Microsoft Word. You might also have experimented with the calculation function for adding columns of numbers. But what if you have more complex mathematical formulas that you would like to incorporate into your financial data that goes beyond the limitations of Microsoft Word?

Fortunately, Microsoft has a compatible spreadsheet application (Excel 3.0) that allows you to freely exchange information between the two programs. If you are working with Microsoft Word and System 6.0.x, you can take advantage of the Linking features of these two programs. Computers configured with System 7.0 allow you a greater level of flexibility, with a different range of options. This section will explore some of the ways you can gain more productive results for creating and working with documents that contain financial information.

Linking with System 6.0.x

The initial steps for executing a "link" to information you have within an Excel spreadsheet are the same, no matter what version of system software you are running. In the example that follows, you'll learn how to set up a link to an Excel document and what the limitations are when working with System 6.0.x. In the next section, you'll see the advantages you will have access to when working under System 7.0, and how it can increase your productivity on several levels when working with financial data.

Creating a Link to an Excel Worksheet

STEP ONE

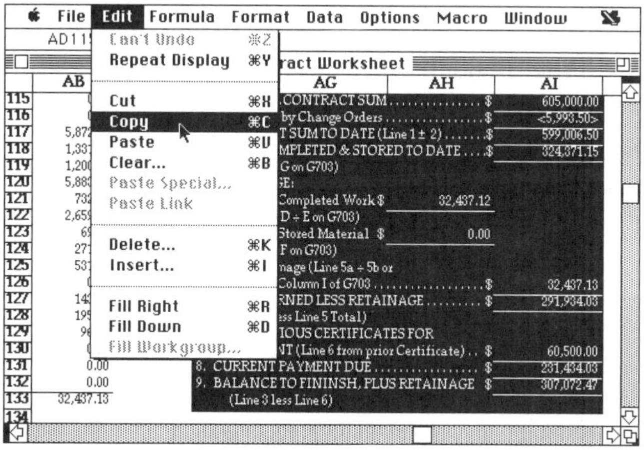

Figure 8.70

In order to work with the linking features of Word and Excel, you need to have both applications launched and running at the same time. If you are working with System 6.0.x, this means you have to be running in

MultiFinder mode. Within the **Excel** application, **open** the document that contains the financial information you want to link to your Word document and **select** the desired information. Go to the **File** menu and choose **Copy** (Figure 8.70).

STEP TWO

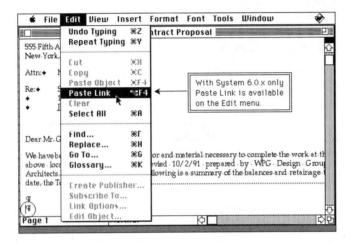

Figure 8.71

Switch over to Microsoft Word. Position the flashing insertion point at the appropriate position in your document and go to the **File** menu and choose **Paste Link** (Figure 8.71).

NOTE: *If you were working in System 7.0, the Paste Special function would also be available.*

STEP THREE

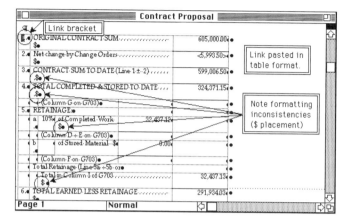

Figure 8.72

The information will be pasted into your Word document in a table format. You should notice that at the beginning and the end of the table there are large gray brackets that signify that the information is "linked" information.

Though most information from an Excel worksheet is not as highly formatted as the example in Figure 8.72, you should know that sometimes the information will not be as clearly displayed in Word as it is in Excel. There may be displacement of $ signs, odd column format adjustments, and—if you have any shading or borders in your Excel document—the formats may not come over as cleanly (if at all). This is because System 6.0.x only has the ability to link information in the RTF (Rich Text Format) mode. The other formatting options will be explained in the section, *"Linking with System 7.0."*

Updating Linked Information

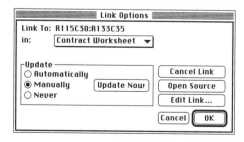

Figure 8.73

You can make formatting changes to the linked information—such as font changes or cell width changes. However, any format changes you make will *disappear* once the Excel link is updated. You should make all changes in the format of your information within the original (or **source**) Excel document. For lack of a better metaphor, your Word document is merely "borrowing" the information and its formats from the Excel document. The Word document where the information is "lent" is called the **destination** document.

To execute an update of your Excel information and control some of the updating frequency procedures, click anywhere within the linked table information in your Word document, go to the **Edit** menu and choose **Link Options**. The dialog box shown in Figure 8.73 shows that you can set updates for linked information to be automatic or manual. You can also break the link to the Excel document and use the table independently of the source document by clicking on the **Cancel Link** button.

> **NOTE:** *You cannot reset or reestablish a link once you've canceled it.*

You can also Click on the **Open Source** button to make changes to the "source" Excel document. Once the changes are made, depending on whether or not you have the Automatic or Manual update options chosen, your Word document will be modified to contain the latest Excel information.

Linking with System 7.0

Linking Information as a Picture

STEP ONE

The initial steps you would take to link Excel worksheet information into a Word document would be identical to those you would take using System 6.0.x. That is, **Open** your Excel worksheet document, select, and **Copy** the information then switch to your Word document.

STEP TWO

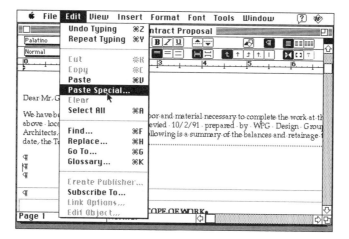

Figure 8.74

In addition to the Paste function on the Edit menu, you have **Paste Special** when using System 7.0 (Figure 8.74). Selecting Paste Special gives you a variety of formatting options from which to choose.

STEP THREE

Figure 8.75

Here, you can see the option for Formatted Text (RTF) which System 6.0.x uses. However, you'll find that you have better format results and more flexibility if you choose the **Picture** option when linking Excel information (Figure 8.75).

STEP FOUR

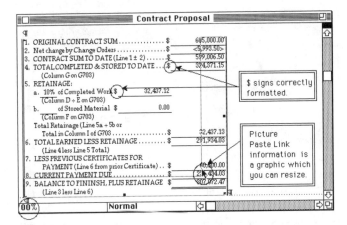

Figure 8.76

As you can see from the example in Figure 8.76, the $ signs that were problematic with System 6.0.x (and if you had chosen the RTF option) are now correctly formatted. Additionally, since the information is pasted as a graphic, you can hold down the **Shift** key and press and drag on the lower right graphics handle to resize the picture to whatever size fits best in your document.

STEP FIVE

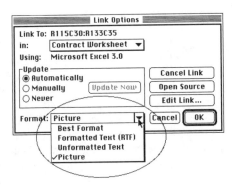

Figure 8.77

If you choose **Link Options** from the **Edit** menu while your link is selected, you can see a few more options than those shown for System 6.0.x (see comparison Figure 8.73). If you want to "convert" your link to any other format, you can easily execute that change through the **Link Options** dialog box (Figure 8.77).

Linking Information as Unformatted Text

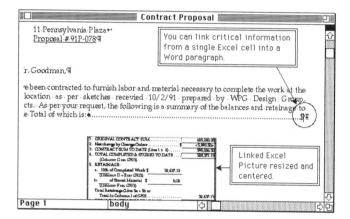

Figure 8.78

There are situations where you might need to include only a single piece of information contained in an Excel worksheet that is relevant to the particular document you are preparing. You don't require the entire worksheet and would like the data to be placed within a paragraph that contains regular text as well (Figure 8.78). In order to place information from a single Excel worksheet cell, you'll need to Paste Link the information in as unformatted text.

STEP ONE

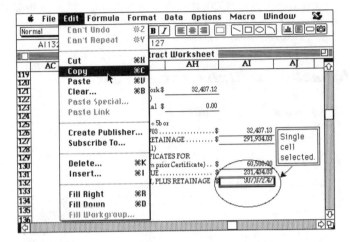

Figure 8.79

Click on the cell in the Excel "source" worksheet and choose **Copy** from the
Edit menu (Figure 8.79).

STEP TWO

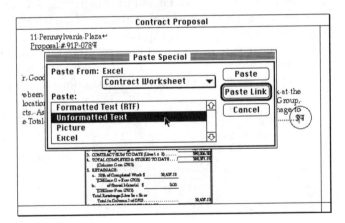

Figure 8.80

Switch to Microsoft Word and position the flashing insertion point in the "destination" paragraph. Choose **Paste Special** from the **Edit** menu. Select the **Unformatted Text** option from the **Paste Special** dialog box and click **Paste Link**.

STEP THREE

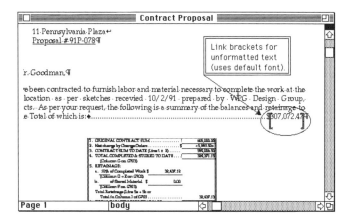

Figure 8.81

The information will be pasted into your document and will be surrounded by link brackets (Figure 8.81). These brackets will not print and will disappear when you turn off Show ¶. The unformatted text uses the default font for Microsoft Word so that if the destination document is formatted with a different font, you will have to change the default font (or reapply the document font to the linked text) to resolve any font formatting differences.

Updating Linked Information

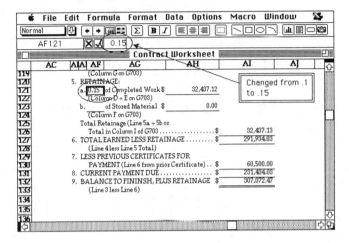

Figure 8.82

You must alter or edit the linked information from within the "source" application (in this case, Microsoft Excel). In the example (Figure 8.82), the retainage percentage has been changed from 10 percent to 15 percent, which will alter quite a few numbers that appear in the summary information cells.

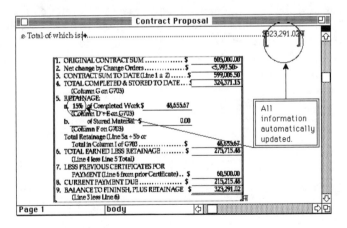

Figure 8.83

Once you've entered that information in the Excel document and switch back to Microsoft Word, you'll see that all the information in your Word document has been automatically updated, unless you set the Link Options to Manual updating (Figure 8.83).

Linking Information Between Word Documents

It is also possible to link information between Word documents without using Excel. For example, you can take the Weekly totals from your Word expense report and link them to a Monthly Expense report.

STEP ONE

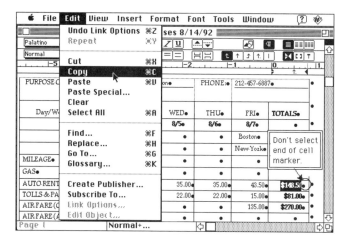

Figure 8.84

Select a single cell within your Weekly expense report total—be careful not to select the end of cell marker—and Copy the information (Figure 8.84).

STEP TWO

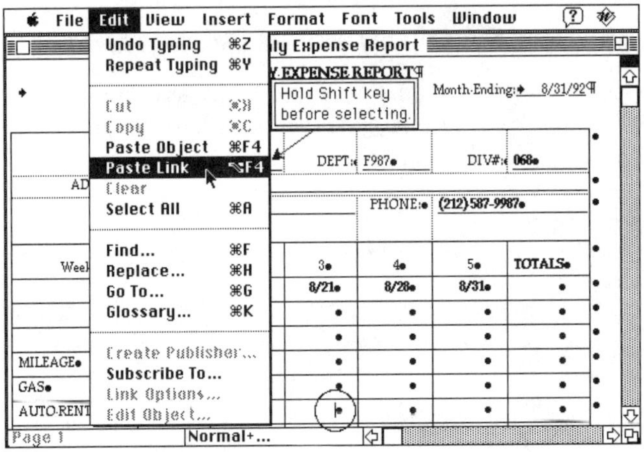

Figure 8.85

Open the Monthly expense report and click in the appropriate cell. Rather than choosing Paste Special, you can use a keyboard shortcut to paste the information in as RTF format. Hold down the **Shift** key and then go to the **Edit** menu. Paste Special will now say Paste Link. Choose **Paste Link** (Figure 8.85).

STEP THREE

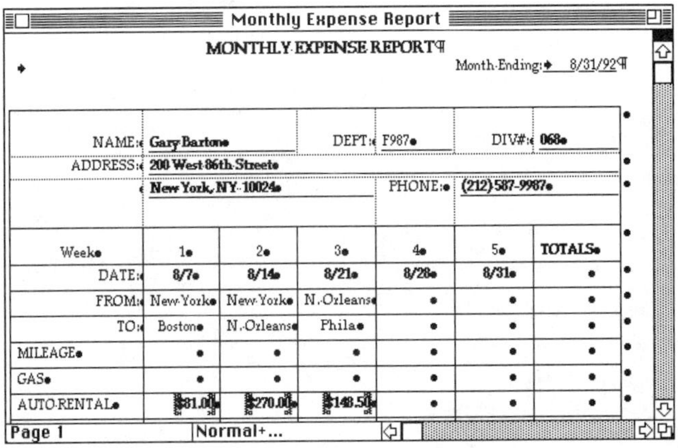

Figure 8.86

The link will be pasted, alongside links from other weekly reports (Figure 8.86). You can still select the information, use the Calculate function to get the total sum of the expenses and Paste it in the Total column as you would with a Weekly expense report form.

Embedding Financial Information

When working with System 7.0, you have another option for placing financial information in your documents. You might not need to link information from an existing Excel worksheet but perhaps you'd like to create a financial table that needs to contain some calculated information. You can make use of the Excel application to create this kind of a table. The Excel table would then become an "object" within your Word document.

Unlike linking—where you have a "source" document and a "destination" document (two different documents)—embedded objects are only saved within your Word document. You simply "borrow" the Excel application to create the object. The following example will help to clarify how this process can be a tremendous benefit to your financial document production.

Embedding Excel Objects

STEP ONE

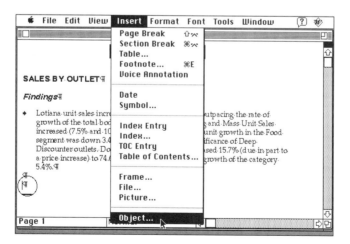

Figure 8.87

To create an Excel table you'll be using the Insert Object function within Word. Open the document that you want to place this table in (or practice with a blank document). Go to the **Insert** menu and choose **Object** (Figure 8.87).

STEP TWO

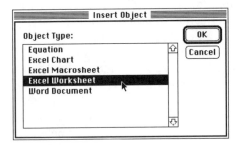

Figure 8.88

If you have already opened the Excel application while you were in a Word session, you should see the choices listed within the **Object** dialog box as shown in Figure 8.88. Otherwise, you should click on the **Cancel** button, launch Excel, and then repeat Step 1. Select the **Excel Worksheet** option and click **OK**.

STEP THREE

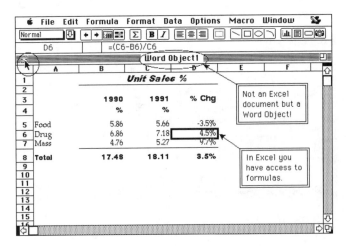

Figure 8.89

You'll be taken to the Excel application where you have complete access to all Excel tools, as if you were creating a typical Excel document. Notice, however, that the title in the window says "Word Object1." This is a Word Object window and not an Excel document window. You are merely "borrowing" the Excel application to create some information you want to have placed—or embedded— in your Word document.

Enter and format your table using the Excel tools and calculation formulae. When you are done, go to the **Options** menu and choose **Display**. Turn off the **Gridlines** option (or the gridlines will appear in your Word document). Click in the **Close box** in the upper left corner of the Word Object window (Figure 8.89).

STEP FOUR

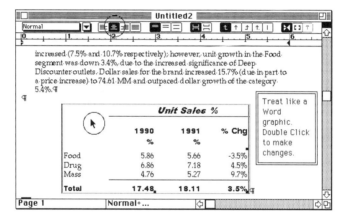

Figure 8.90

You'll be returned to your Word document and the table will be inserted. You might want to click on the **Centered** paragraph alignment icon in the Ruler to center the information. You can also hold down the **Shift** key and press and drag on the graphic handle in the lower right corner to resize. If you want to make changes to the information in the table, move your pointer into the graphic and double-click (Figure 8.90).

STEP FIVE

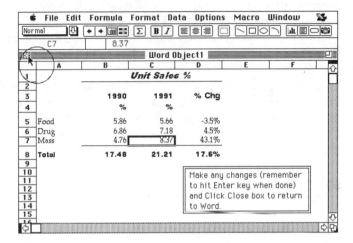

Figure 8.91

You'll be taken into the Excel application where you can make any revisions you want. Click on the Close box when you are done (Figure 8.91).

Embedding Word Objects

You can also use Word's Object Embedding functions to help you out of potential table formatting "snags." How often have you spent hours creating a table and formatting it only to realize you need to enter another column of information? Inserting a new column can wreak havoc with trying to fit all the information within the margins of your document. Here's an invaluable tip that will save you a lot of time and effort if you are running System 7.0.

STEP ONE

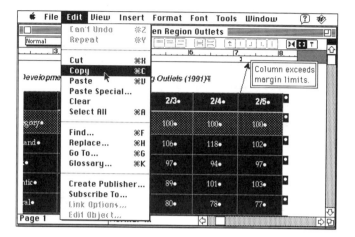

Figure 8.92

Open the document that contains the table you need to add more information to. Hold down the **Option** key and Double-Click to select the entire table. Go to the **Edit** menu and choose **Copy** (Figure 8.92). Go to the **Format** menu and choose **Table Layout**. Click on the **Delete** button.

NOTE: *When you delete a table using Table Layout, the contents of the table do not go into the Clipboard as with the normal Cut function. This is why you should first Copy a table to the Clipboard, if you plan to place it elsewhere once the original is deleted.*

STEP TWO

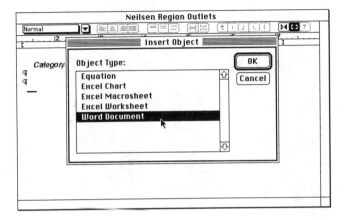

Figure 8.93

Go to the **Insert** menu and choose **Object**. Click on the **Word Document** option (Figure 8.93).

STEP THREE

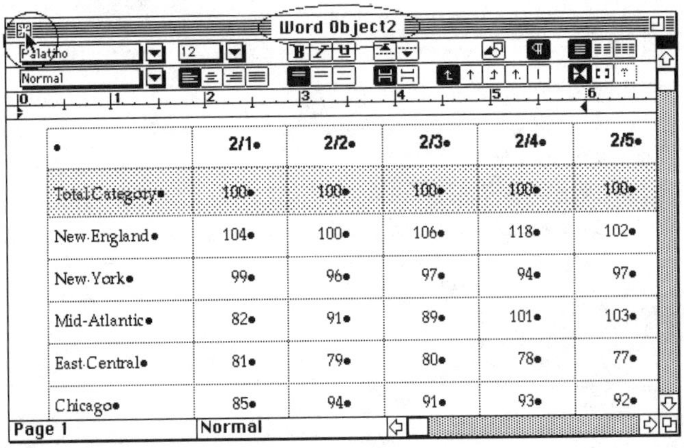

•	2/1•	2/2•	2/3•	2/4•	2/5•
Total Category•	100•	100•	100•	100•	100•
New England•	104•	100•	106•	118•	102•
New York•	99•	96•	97•	94•	97•
Mid-Atlantic•	82•	91•	89•	101•	103•
East Central•	81•	79•	80•	78•	77•
Chicago•	85•	94•	91•	93•	92•

Figure 8.94

Go to the **Edit** menu and choose **Paste Cells**. Your table will be pasted into a **Word Object** window. Now, insert the necessary column and enter your information, paying no attention to the fact that the table may exceed the margins of your document. When you're done, click in the window **Close Box** (Figure 8.94).

STEP FOUR

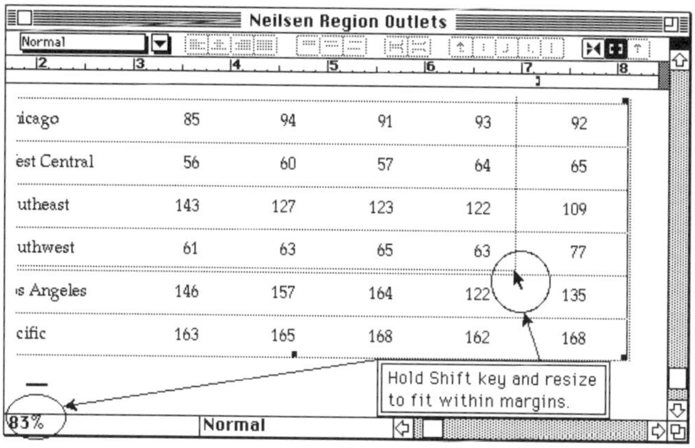

Figure 8.95

Hold down the **Shift** key and click on the lower right graphics handle. Press and drag to resize the table so that it fits within your document's margin settings (Figure 8.95). If ever you need to make changes and adjustments to the table, you simply Double-Click within the object and you'll be taken to the **Word Object** window where you can make your changes. Always remember that the way to get back to your Word document is to click in the window **Close Box** when you are done.

Conclusion

Formatting and working with financial information in tables can be fairly complex. However, knowing what your options are when setting out to create a table will help you to save time and become more efficient with this process. The Object Linking and Embedding (OLE) technologies of Word 5.0 and System 7.0 provide you with more accurate information updates and greater flexibility when making necessary formatting changes.

9

C H A P T E R

Long Document Structuring and Management

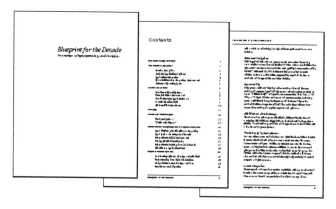

Figure 9.1

Long documents such as proposals, business plans, and reports require special kinds of formatting that enable you to produce a title page, a table of contents, section headings, and consistent page numbering. And some of these reports can also include financial tables, figures, and graphics. Long documents are usually the most complex documents you will need to create with a word processor. However, Microsoft Word has some powerful features that, once you are familiar with them, enable you to quickly structure, organize, and manage your information so that it is consistent, easy to modify, and attractive.

In this chapter, you'll learn more advanced capabilities of styles, as well as how styles can be used to rapidly generate a table of contents, quickly enter preformatted information in your document, and provide you with a structured view for the overall contents of your document. You'll learn how to create within long documents sections with various headings and page numbering schemes. You'll also learn a quick technique for formatting a title page and how to incorporate all these techniques into a standard report format you'll want to use again and again.

Formatting Proposals and Reports

Often long documents "evolve" as part of a long-term project. You may not even work on an entire document from beginning to end in the order that it will eventually be presented. More typically, you work on "pieces" of a long document as it is being written and assembled. Certain sections are probably missing and will be "filled in" as the information becomes available. In what follows, you'll examine the various formatting techniques you can employ as you are setting up and building your document that will save you hours of time when the final deadline draws near.

Using Styles for Section Headings and Body Text

The most valuable tool you can use in working with fragments of long documents is **styles**. As you look through the examples presented in this section, you'll quickly realize how much flexibility styles give you when both formatting your document and assembling the various pieces it might contain.

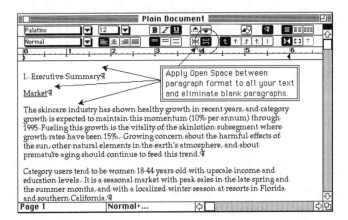

Figure 9.2

When you first start entering your text, instead of using blank paragraph marks for spacing between paragraphs, use the **Open Space** between paragraphs setting in the **Ruler** (Figure 9.2). As you create style definitions for the various parts of the text in your document, you can easily adjust the amount of space you want wherever you want it, rather than searching out and deleting or adding paragraph marks for more or less space. With style definitions you have a powerful set of "controls" you can manage for your document's formatting requirements.

Applying, Altering, and Redefining Default Styles

STEP ONE

Microsoft Word has a set of "default" styles that tie into other functions within Microsoft Word, such as outlining and generating tables of contents. You're going to apply these default styles and then modify them for your particular document. Either enter the text shown in the sample document (Figure 9.2) or open an existing document (making sure all blank paragraph marks are removed and **Open Space** formatting applied).

STEP TWO

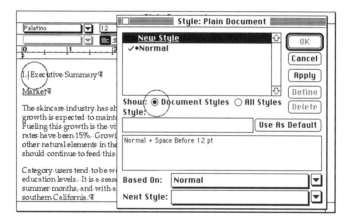

Figure 9.3

Position the flashing insertion point within the first main heading of your document. Go to the **Format** menu and choose **Style**. Click on the button that says **Document Styles** (Figure 9.3). Most likely the only style name displayed will be Normal (unless you defined some default styles following the steps in Chapter 4, Figure 4.66).

STEP THREE

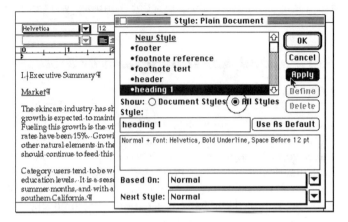

Figure 9.4

Click on the **All Styles** button to see a listing of all the default styles that are part of the Microsoft Word application. You will recognize default styles because they have a bullet before the style name. Scroll through the list and click on **heading 1** to select it. Click on the **Apply** button (Figure 9.4).

STEP FOUR

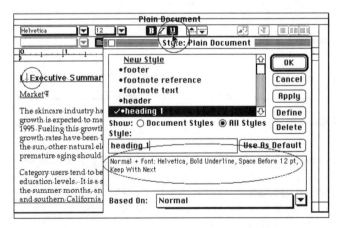

Figure 9.5

You will see the text where your flashing insertion point is located take on the characteristics of the **heading 1** style. Move the **Style** dialog box by pressing and dragging on the **Title** bar if you cannot see the text in your document. In the area within the **Style** dialog box circled in Figure 9.5, you will see a definition of what the heading 1 style formatting consists of. You can alter these formatting characteristics—changing indents, tabs, bolding, italics, etc.—and redefine the style while you have the **Style** dialog box open. Go to the **Ribbon** and click on the **Underline** icon to remove the underline format (Figure 9.5).

STEP FIVE

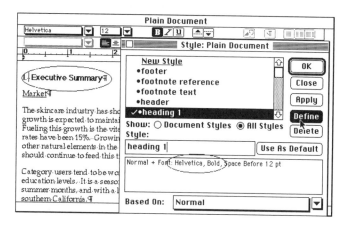

Figure 9.6

Notice that the removal of the underline format is reflected in the description box for the style. Click on the **Define** button to "redefine" the heading 1 style so that it no longer has underline format (Figure 9.6).

STEP SIX

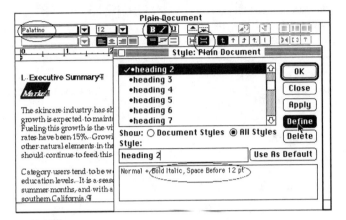

Figure 9.7

Locate a second level heading you would like to format as a style. Click within the paragraph. Go to the **Format** menu and choose **Style**. Select **heading 2** from the styles list and click on the **Apply** button. You can modify how you want the style to be formatted by choosing formats from the **Ribbon** and **Ruler**, or even selecting the **Character** and **Paragraph** dialog boxes from the **Format** menu. In the example in Figure 9.7, **Palatino** font, **Bold**, *Italic*, and the **Open Space** icon (for 12 points of space before) were applied. Click on the **Define** button to redefine the style. When you are through, click on the **Close** button.

STEP SEVEN

As you scroll through an existing document or enter text in a new document, you can apply the heading 2 style to the text in the specific paragraph by selecting **heading 2** from the **Style Selection** box in the **Ruler** (Figure 9.8). You can either highlight the entire text within the heading or simply click anywhere within the paragraph to position the flashing insertion point. The heading 2 style will be applied to the entire paragraph.

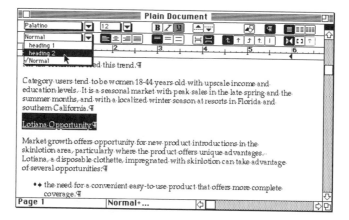

Figure 9.8

Creating Document Styles

STEP ONE

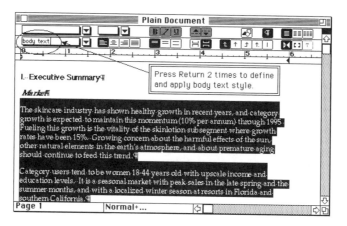

Figure 9.9

You should also define a body text style for the text within your document. Typically, this text might have an Open Space between paragraphs format. Since the body text style is not a "default" style, you can define this style by using the Style Selection box in the Ruler. Select the body text paragraphs, click inside the **Style Selection** box in the **Ruler**, and type the name "body text" (or whatever you want to name it). Press the **Return** key twice—once to bring up the **Define Style based on selection** dialog box and the second time to activate the **OK** button (Figure 9.9). Once defined, the style will be applied to the highlighted text.

STEP TWO

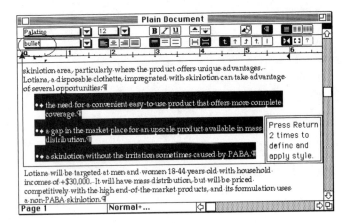

Figure 9.10

Similarly, you might want to scroll through your document and locate any bullet text you might have included and define a "bullet" style. This can easily be done by using the **Style Selection** box as you did in Step 2 (Figure 9.10).

Using Styles to Adjust and Create Page Breaks

Once in a while, you may come across a situation where your title heading ends up at the bottom of a page while the body text that follows it appears on the next page. You can control this "severing" of heading text from body text by applying a **Paragraph** format called **Keep With Next**.

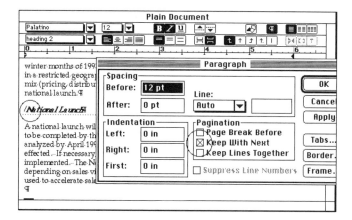

Figure 9.11

Click in the heading text paragraph and choose **Paragraph** from the **Format** menu. Click on the **Keep With Next** option (Figure 9.11). Click **OK**.

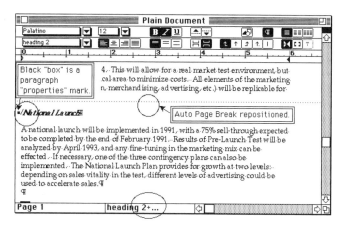

Figure 9.12

If you have **Background Repagination** turned on (through the **Preferences** dialog box), you will quickly see the automatic page break altered so that the heading text is moved to the top of the next page (Figure 9.12). If you have **Show** ¶ turned on, you will notice a tiny black box next to the beginning of the line. This is called a "paragraph properties mark" and indicates that one of the **Pagination** options in the **Paragraph** dialog box has been applied. It will disappear when you turn **Show** ¶ off and will not be printed.

It's a good idea to make "Keep With Next" paragraph formatting a part of your style definition so that you don't ever have to worry about "severed" headings. If you look at the bottom window in Figure 9.12, you'll see that the heading 2 style in the style indicator box has a "+..." appended to it. This means that the heading 2 style has had its format altered in some way and is a clue that you should incorporate this change into your overall style definition.

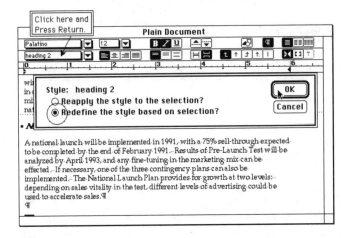

Figure 9.13

You can "redefine" your heading 2 style without opening the Format Style dialog box. Simply click inside the **Style Selection** box in the **Ruler** (make sure the flashing insertion point is located in the heading 2 style paragraph, first) and press the **Return** key. A dialog box will appear asking you if you want to Reapply or Redefine the style. Click on the **Redefine style** option and click **OK** (Figure 9.13). All the other paragraphs in your document that are formatted with the heading 2 style will now have the paragraph properties mark appear next to them, indicating the Keep With Next format has been applied.

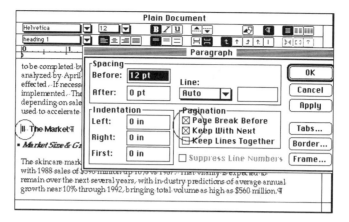

Figure 9.14

You might be working with a formatting requirement that necessitates the placement of anything with a heading 1 style appear on a new page, regardless of the automatic pagination of your document. You can easily accomplish this by applying the **Page Break Before** paragraph formatting (Figure 9.14) to your heading 1 text.

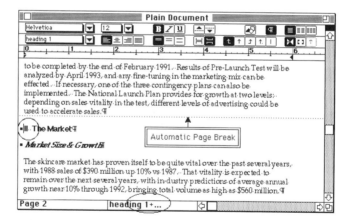

Figure 9.15

Page Break Before formatting causes an automatic page break to occur just before the heading (Figure 9.15).

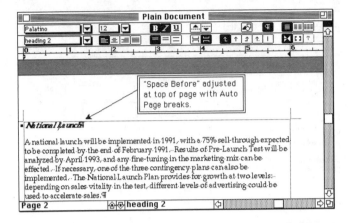

Figure 9.16

When you view your document in **Page Layout View**, you will see that—if your heading 1 style had Open Space between paragraphs formatting applied (so that 12 points of space come before the text)—the text will align itself to the top margin of your document (Figure 9.16). The **Open Space** formatting will be ignored, which you probably would want, so that text begins at the same place at the top of each page, for a heading or for regular body text.

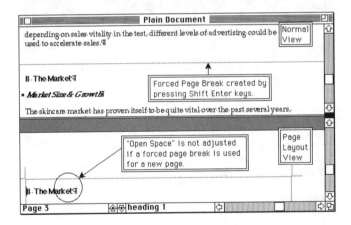

Figure 9.17

The example in Figure 9.17 uses a Split Window for the same document to illustrate how a Forced Page Break (applied by choosing **Page Break** from the **Insert** menu) alters the way text formatted with **Open Space** between paragraphs appears in your document. Using a forced page break to place your heading 1 text at the top of a page maintains the 12 points of space before the heading. Therefore, it's recommended that you use the **Page Break Before** paragraph formatting for your headings if you have applied a 12 point **Open Space** format to your heading style.

NOTE: *You can choose to apply Page Break Before paragraph format only to those specific headings within your document for which it is appropriate. Therefore, you can also choose* **not** *to incorporate the Page Break Before format into your overall style definition.*

Indented Body Text Styles and "Based On" Formatting

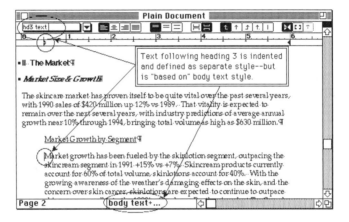

Figure 9.18

Perhaps you have defined a level of a default heading style that requires some indenting. The body text that falls beneath that heading may also require indentation. When you define a new style for text that has been originally formatted with another style (such as body text), you are basing the new style definition on characteristics of the original style (Figure 9.18). Typically the original style is **Normal**.

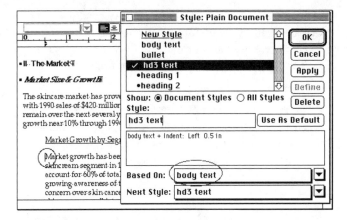

Figure 9.19

You won't become aware of this "based-on" capability for styles unless you bring up the **Style** dialog box by choosing it from the **Format** menu. In Figure 9.19, you'll see the **hd3 text** style has been chosen and that **body text** is displayed in the **Based On** list menu. Whether or not you realized it, all the default styles you might have been working with are all based on the **Normal** style.

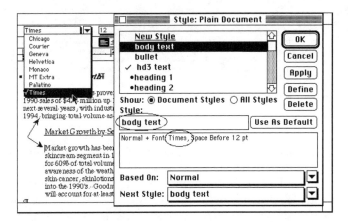

Figure 9.20

You might be saying, "Well, fine. But so what? What does this mean to me and my document production needs?" It means that changes you make to the based-on style may effect overall style definitions. Figure 9.20 illustrates that a change was made to the **body text** style. The **Times** font was applied. Without your doing anything, the **hd3 text** style would also now be formatted with the **Times** font (Figure 9.20).

Understanding the capability for altering styles and document formats by simply changing one "central" style (the one that other styles are based on) can explain why some unexpected things might happen to your documents or help you plan the speedy implementation of document formatting changes.

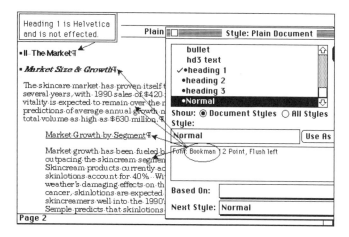

Figure 9.21

For example, let's say you decide to change the **Normal** style **font** to **Bookman**. Every style that is based on Normal will now have the Bookman font as part of their format, except those style definitions that specified another font (such as heading 1 in Figure 9.21, which uses Helvetica).

Speeding Text Formatting with Next Style

When you are entering text and you apply the default heading 1, heading 2, etc., styles, and you press the Return key for a new line of text, you will automatically be taken back to the Normal style. You then probably move your pointer to the **Style Selection** box in the Ruler and apply the body text style. There's a simple way to eliminate this unnecessary trip to the Ruler for each paragraph of text you enter and it involves redefining your default styles.

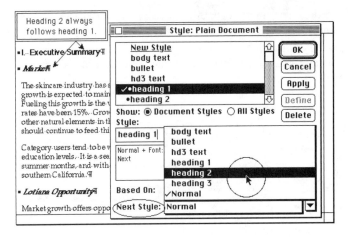

Figure 9.22

Go to the **Format** menu and choose **Style**. Select the **heading 1** style from the list. In the area beneath called **Next Style**, there is a list box. Press and drag to select the **heading 2** style. What this does is set your style so that, when you enter text in the heading 1 style and press the Return key, you will immediately begin working in the heading 2 style (Figure 9.22). Click on the **Define** button.

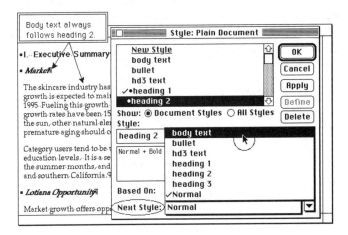

Figure 9.23

Once you enter heading 2 style, you typically might want to enter body text. Choose the **heading 2** style from the style list and then choose **body text** from the **Next Style** list menu (Figure 9.23). Click on **Define**.

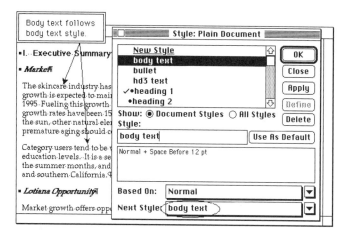

Figure 9.24

If you choose the body text style, you'll see that when you press the **Return** key, you can continue to enter text in the body text style. That is because the **Next Style** is set to the **body text** style. For this reason you would leave the Next Style setting as is (Figure 9.24).

NOTE: *You might also want to redefine a heading 3 style so that a hd3 text style is the Next Style.*

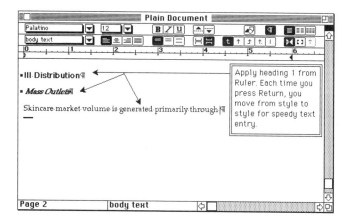

Figure 9.25

Once you've redefined your styles to apply different Next Styles, test the efficiency of this style formatting technique by entering some text in your document. Begin by selecting **heading 1** from the **Style Selection** box. Press the **Return** key and enter the next line and then another line of text (Figure 9.25). You'll notice that at the end of each paragraph return, you don't need to pause from your work to make a trip to the Ruler for the style you need. Just enter your text and Press **Return**.

> **NOTE:** *You might want to apply default styles (such as heading 1 or heading 2) using the Ruler in a new document where you have not yet altered or redefined the default style. Hold down the Shift key before you Click on the Style Selection box arrow and all the default document styles will appear on the Style Selection box list menu.*

Alternate Style Formats

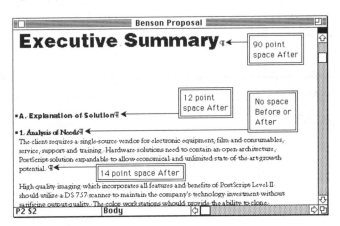

Figure 9.26

When creating the overall design format for your business plans, reports and other long documents, you might find that using space After paragraph headings and body text better accommodates your document design. By entering **Space After** settings from within the **Paragraph** dialog box, you can create a heading format that sits closely to the body text—as illustrated in Figure 9.26. Space After also eliminates any concerns for spacing variances if you happen to want to place a forced page break within your document.

Applying Styles, Using Outline View

You might have worked on a long document before you even knew what a style was or how to format one. Now that you are aware of the power and flexibility of styles, you might want to format your document with some styles. A way that you can use the Outlining View of Microsoft Word to both format and structure your document follows.

STEP ONE

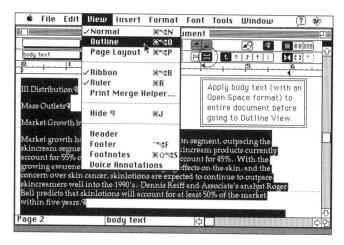

Figure 9.27

Use the techniques in the section preceding this one to define styles for body text and the various default heading levels. If there is a large body of text you want to format (that doesn't include tables or graphics), select the text and apply **body text** style from the Style Selection box on the Ruler. This basically "strips" your document of any formats you might have applied manually and saves you some valuable formatting time. Go to the **View** menu and choose **Outline** (Figure 9.27).

STEP TWO

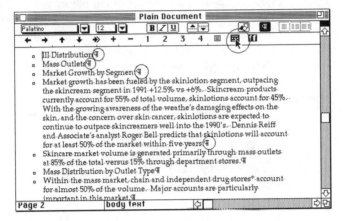

Figure 9.28

When in Outline View, you have a number of choices for the way you look at your document. If you see your entire document with large paragraphs of body text as shown in Figure 9.28, you'll want to collapse the text for easier viewing by clicking on the **Ellipsis** in the **Outline Ribbon**.

STEP THREE

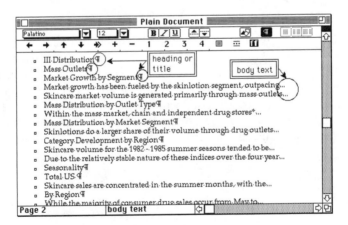

Figure 9.29

You'll easily be able to identify text that is meant to be a heading—versus body text that is part of a long paragraph—since most headings fit on a single line or paragraph. Your body text paragraphs will be followed by an ellipsis, as shown in Figure 9.29.

STEP FOUR

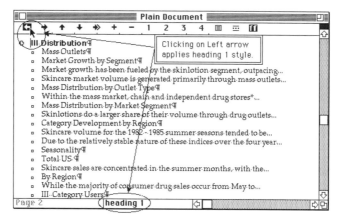

Figure 9.30

Position the flashing insertion point in the first heading paragraph. Click on the **Left** pointing arrow in the **Outline Ribbon**. This will reposition the text and also apply the **heading 1** style (Figure 9.30).

STEP FIVE

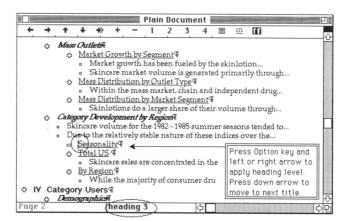

Figure 9.31

To apply various heading formats, rather than clicking on the Outline Ribbon bar, you can also use the arrow keys on your keyboard. Hold the **Option** key and press the **Left** or **Right** arrow to "promote" or "demote" a heading to level 1, 2, or 3. You'll know what level you're on because what you are actually doing is using the keyboard to apply a heading 1, heading 2, or heading 3 style (which you'll see displayed in the style indicator box in the bottom of the window). Once you've decided which level your heading belongs on and have applied the correct heading, press the **Down** arrow on your keyboard to move to the paragraph below (Figure 9.31).

> **NOTE:** *Don't press the Option key when you press the Down arrow or you'll end up moving the paragraph to a new location!*

See Chapter 10 for additional keyboard shortcut techniques for applying styles.

Viewing and Organizing the Structure of Your Document

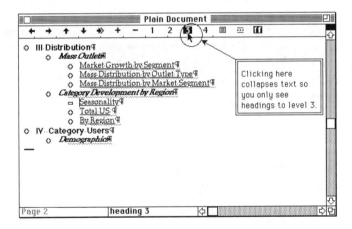

Figure 9.32

Applying default heading styles to your document text gives you access to the various outline heading level views. By clicking on the number **3** in the **Outline Ribbon bar**, you'll only view your heading text for levels 1 through 3 (Figure 9.32). Likewise, clicking on the number 1 or 2 will display even less text and give you a more streamlined Outline view.

If you are in the process of composing a document and not just keying in or formatting prewritten text, you can use the Outline View to structure your document as you are writing it. Use the arrows in the Outline Ribbon (or press **Option Left** or **Right** arrow on your keyboard) to apply the heading formats.

Numbering Paragraphs

While you are in the Outline View, you can make efficient use of the Renumbering function in Microsoft Word to automatically number the title paragraphs in your document. The numbering scheme will correspond to the various heading levels you had structured when you applied the default styles in the preceding section.

STEP ONE

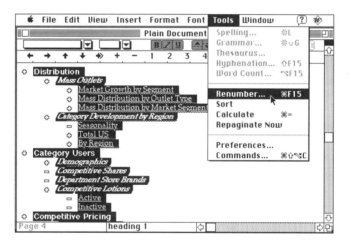

Figure 9.33

Collapse your document to the outline level you want to have numbered (for example, to the level of heading 3). Select the text and choose **Renumber** from the **Tools** menu (Figure 9.33).

STEP TWO

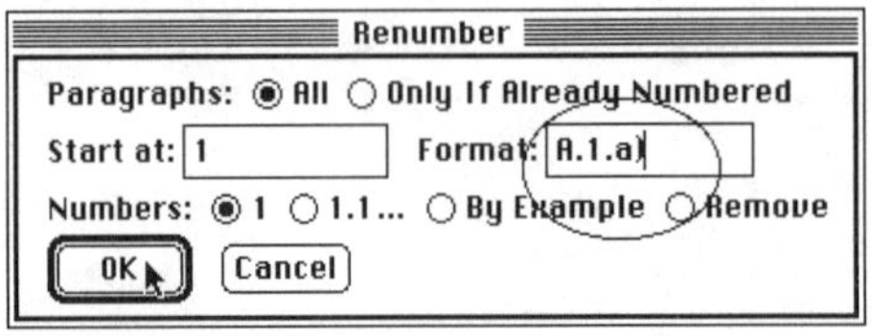

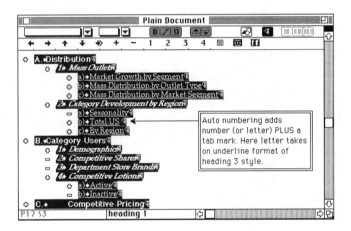

Figure 9.34

Enter the numbering scheme you want to use for your document, entering periods and parentheses where appropriate. Click on the **OK** button (Figure 9.34).

STEP THREE

Figure 9.35

If you had entered the numbering scheme illustrated in Figure 9.34, a tab would have been placed after the number and before the regular paragraph text. Additionally, the numbering would have taken on the characteristics of the paragraph heading style. If the format contains underlining, the number and tab mark will be underlined as well (Figure 9.35). You might want to put a **Tab** mark in the **Ruler** to control where the text will appear after the number, or set a **hanging indent** for your text and incorporate the setting into your style definition. (See Figure 4.40 in Chapter 4.)

STEP FOUR

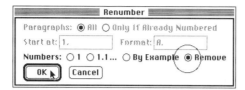

Figure 9.36

If you have made an error and this is not the formatting you want for your document, you can always choose **Undo** from the **Edit** menu if it is the next action you take. However, you might decide later to change or alter the numbering scheme. Select the correct heading level of text by clicking on the corresponding number in the **Outline bar** and choose **Renumber** from the **Tools** menu. There is a **Remove** option button that you can click to remove all the previous formatting (Figure 9.36). Click **OK**.

STEP FIVE

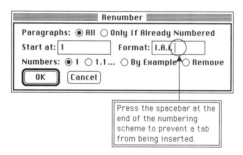

Figure 9.37

You can apply numbering so that a space rather than a tab mark will be inserted between the numbering and the paragraph title text. To do this, enter the numbering scheme example you would like and press the **Spacebar** once after the last example character (Figure 9.37). Click **OK**.

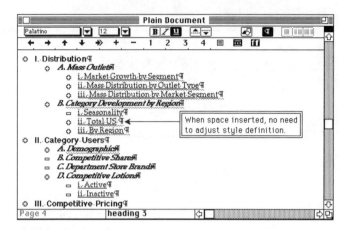

Figure 9.38

A space will appear after the numbers (Figure 9.38). When using spaces after numbers instead of tab marks, you won't need to make any adjustments to your heading style definitions. However, you might want to manually remove the underline format from the numbers or letters that appear before any heading text.

Merging Styles to Change Your Document Format

So far, you might have tried and successfully executed the definition and application of heading and body text styles explained in this chapter. However, what if you need to create a variety of report formats during the course of your business? You might consider building a library of style sheets. If you always use the same names for your style definitions (for example, heading 1, heading 2, body text, heading 3, hd3 text, etc.) but choose different font styles and formats, you can change the entire appearance of your document with a click of the mouse.

Style definitions are saved with the actual document. As you might realize, long documents can take up a considerable amount of hard disk space. A style sheet is nothing but an empty document that merely contains the definitions of all the styles and takes only about 2K of disk space. What follows are steps for creating a style sheet and how to merge styles to give any report document a totally different look.

STEP ONE

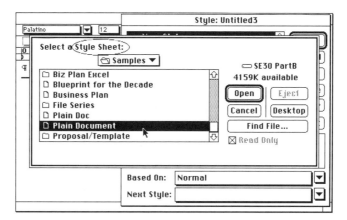

Figure 9.39

Go to the **File** menu and choose **New**. Choose **Style** from the **Format** menu. With the **Style** dialog box open, go to the **File** menu and choose **Open**. Navigate to the folder that contains your long document. Notice that the dialog box title says to "Select a Style Sheet" (Figure 9.39).

STEP TWO

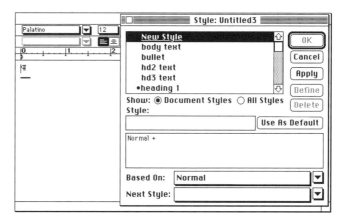

Figure 9.40

Double-click on the title of your long document. All the style names and definitions will now appear in the Style dialog box for the new untitled document. Click in the **Close box** (Figure 9.40). **Save** your document and name it appropriately (for example, Business Plan Style Sheet).

STEP THREE

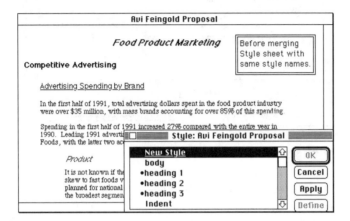

Figure 9.41

If you have a number of style sheets defined with different kinds of layouts and style variations but use the same style **names**, you can merge the style definitions from the style sheet of your choice with the document you are currently working on. The steps you follow to merge a style sheet are nearly identical to what you did in Steps 1 and 2 above. The example in Figure 9.41 shows a document formatted with the same style names as the style sheet it will be merged with.

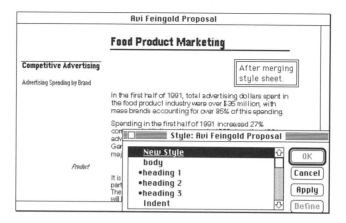

Figure 9.42

With your current document open on the desktop, choose **Style** from the **Format** menu. Choose **Open** from the **File** menu. Locate the style sheet of your choice and **double-click**. Because the style names are the same, the formats from the style sheet will override the document's style definitions. As you can see from the example in Figure 9.42, the results can be rather dramatic. You now have an economic and speedy method you can use to radically change the format of your documents.

Creating a Table of Contents or Figures

Though most long documents don't require a table of contents until you are somewhere near the final stages of its preparation, you can format your document in the early stages of production for where the table of contents will appear. Thus, when you are about to generate the final document, it is only a matter of replacing the existing table.

There are two different techniques for creating a table of contents. One method takes little effort on your part if you have defined and applied the default heading styles described earlier in this chapter. The second method requires that you code your headings so that they will appear in the table of contents (or TOC). You'll learn both techniques and understand the strengths and benefits of each one in what follows.

Generating a TOC from Outline Styles

Earlier in this chapter, you realized that once you had applied default heading styles you could go to Outline View and quickly obtain an overview of your document's structure. You can use these same outline styles to generate the table of contents. Executing the TOC is easier than you think!

STEP ONE

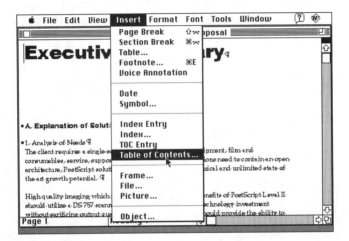

Figure 9.43

With your document open on the desktop, go to the **Insert** menu and choose **Table of Contents** (Figure 9.43).

STEP TWO

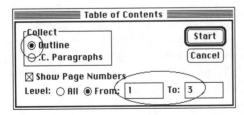

Figure 9.44

The Table of Contents dialog box has several options. The button next to **Outline** should be selected as you are using your "Outline styles" to generate the Table of Contents. (You can even choose not to show the page numbers if you simply want an outline of your document.) Click in the **Level** edit bars and enter **From 1 To 3**—or higher if you have defined a default style for heading 4 that you want included in the Table of Contents. If you only have three levels of heading styles, you can simply ignore the Level restrictions and keep the **All** button selected. Click on the **Start** button (Figure 9.44).

> **NOTE:** *When formatting your document for Figures you will generate a Table of Contents for a single Level, such as From 9 To 9.*

STEP THREE

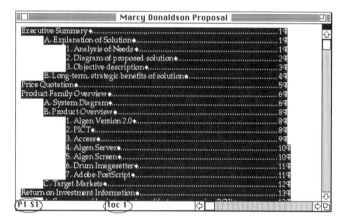

Figure 9.45

You'll see the page numbers in the lower left status bar of your window flash by and a Table of Contents will appear as highlighted text at the top of your document. Notice that the page status box now says **P1S1** (Figure 9.45). This means that a new section for the table of contents has been inserted into your document starting on page 1 (Page 1, Section1). You'll be examining page and section numbering later on in this chapter.

You should also notice that the "style" for the first entry in the table is indicated in the style indicator box as **toc 1**. Just as with heading 1, heading 2, etc., styles, Microsoft Word also has default table of contents styles. Whatever text you had formatted in the heading 1 style has now been placed in your table of contents and tagged with a "toc 1" style, and similarly for headings 2, 3, 4, etc.

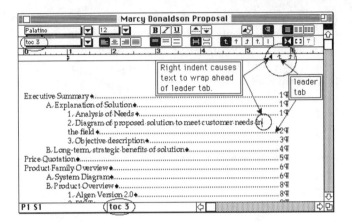

Figure 9.46

If you click in a level heading, you can examine the style formatting Microsoft used to define their "toc" default styles. The example in Figure 9.46 illustrates the logic behind the style format. The **Right indent** mark has been moved inward to accommodate "extra long" heading titles so that they wrap to a new line and don't exceed the length of the dotted leader tab mark. The **left aligned tab** mark in the Ruler formatted with a **leader tab** is positioned to the right of the Right indent mark. There is also a **right aligned tab** mark in the ruler.

Modifying TOC Styles

STEP FOUR

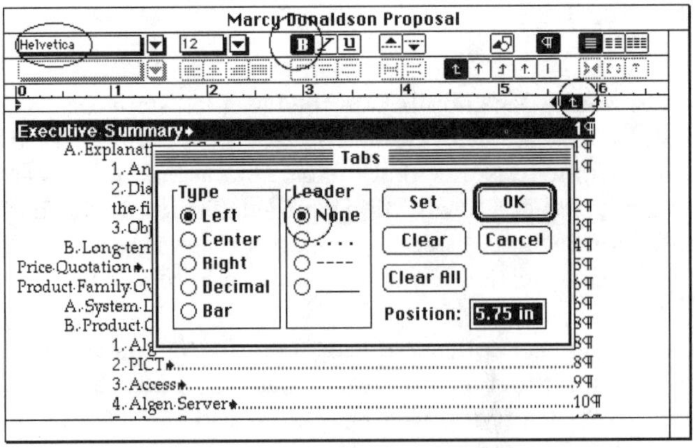

Figure 9.47

You can alter the default "toc" styles just as you did with Microsoft's default heading styles. You might want to make the **toc 1** style **Helvetica Bold** and remove the leader tab format (Figure 9.47).

STEP FIVE

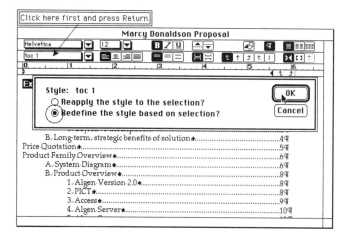

Figure 9.48

To redefine the toc 1 style (and all toc default styles) once you have made your formatting changes, simply click in the **Style Selection** box in the Ruler and press the **Return** key. A dialog box will appear showing choices either to reapply or to redefine the style. Click on the **Redefine** option and click **OK** (Figure 9.48).

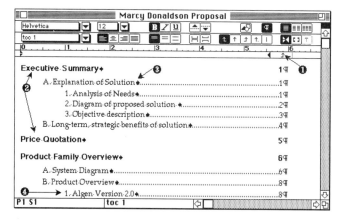

Figure 9.49

The diagram in Figure 9.49 indicates the following style formatting adjustments made to the default toc styles:

1. For all toc style levels, the left aligned Tab mark was removed and a **right aligned tab** mark was used. Right aligned Tab marks are the best format for accurately aligning numbers that might be formatted with different font and character styles (here **Helvetica Bold** and plain **Palatino**). Toc styles for levels 2 and 3 were formatted with a **dotted leader tab**.

2. Toc 1 style was redefined with **4 pt Before** and **8 pt After** spacing using the **Paragraph** dialog box.

3. Toc 2 style was redefined with **4 pt After** spacing.

4. Toc 3 style was redefined with **2 pt After** spacing.

Creating a TOC Title Style

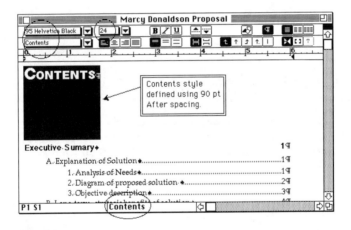

Figure 9.50

You will probably want to enter a title for your table of contents. Position the flashing insertion point at the very beginning of your document before the first character of text. Press the **Return** key for a new line then press the **Up** arrow on your keyboard to move the flashing insertion point into the blank paragraph. Press **Command Shift P** to clear the toc 1 formatting.

Enter your title text (Contents or Table of Contents) and apply all the character formatting you would like. Click in the **Style selection box** and name your style, pressing the **Return** key two times to define it (Figure 9.50).

The reason you define a separate style name for your table of contents title is that later on, when you replace your table of contents to update the page numbers, the contents title will be a separate item outside of the existing TOC.

Replacing Existing TOC

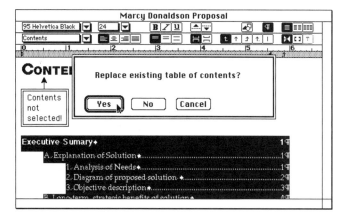

Figure 9.51

Be sure to save all the changes you've made to your document. To understand what will take place when you regenerate your table of contents later on, practice generating another table of contents now. Go to the **Insert** menu and choose **Table of Contents**. Choose the same options as you did in Figure 9.44.

Your existing table of contents will be highlighted (minus the Contents title!) and a dialog box will appear asking you if you want to replace the existing Table of Contents (Figure 9.51). Click on the **Yes** button. If you have made no changes or additions to your document, the table of contents should look the same as before.

Inserting TOC Entries

What if you have not defined and used default heading styles for your long document and you still need to generate a table of contents? And what if the table of contents entry descriptions are different from what your section headings are? You can use a special table-of-contents coding system to format text so that it will be placed in a table of contents.

STEP ONE

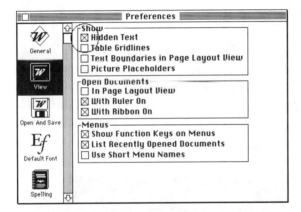

Figure 9.52

The TOC entry text "codes" you'll be inserting into your document are formatted with **Hidden Text** character format. (You might have seen this format on your visits to the **Character** dialog box and wondered what it was.) To make sure you can see the TOC entry, go to the **Tools** menu and choose **Preferences**. Click on the **View** icon. The **Hidden Text** option should be selected, as shown in Figure 9.52. If not, click in the box next to Hidden Text so that there is an **X** inside it. Click in the **Close** box when you are through.

STEP TWO

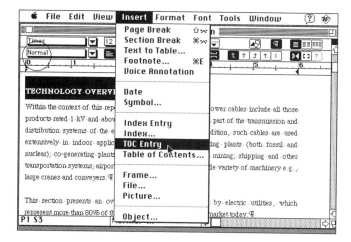

Figure 9.53

Select the text in your document that you want to appear in the table of contents. Go to the **Insert** menu and choose **TOC Entry** (Figure 9.53).

STEP THREE

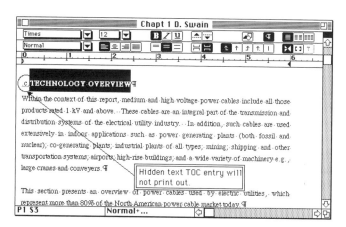

Figure 9.54

A ".c." text entry will be made into your document. It will appear to have a dotted line underneath it. The dots indicate the text is formatted as hidden text. This text will not print as long as you do not select the **Print Hidden Text** option from the **Print** dialog box when you print your document (Figure 9.54).

STEP FOUR

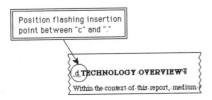

Figure 9.55

In order to indicate the "level" on which you want this entry to appear in the table of contents, you have to enter one more piece of information to the ".c." code. Position the flashing insertion point after the "c" and before the final period as indicated in Figure 9.55.

STEP FIVE

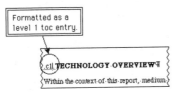

Figure 9.56

Enter the correct level number for the TOC entry (Figure 9.56).

> **NOTE:** *If you forget this step and fail to enter a level number, all your TOC entries will be treated as level 1 entries.*

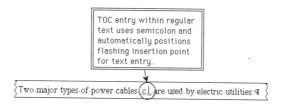

Figure 9.57

You can highlight and code existing text for your TOC entries as you did in steps 2 through 5. However, you can also create TOC entries for text not contained within your document. Position your flashing insertion point anywhere within the page you want the entry to appear (but within the ordered structure of your TOC entries).

Go to the **Insert** menu and choose **TOC Entry**. As illustrated in Figure 9.57, a TOC entry made within regular text inserts the hidden text ".c." followed by a hidden text semicolon. The flashing insertion point is automatically placed before the final semicolon so you can enter your text.

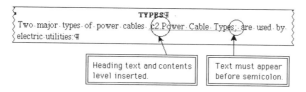

Figure 9.58

The example in Figure 9.58 shows a completed TOC entry.

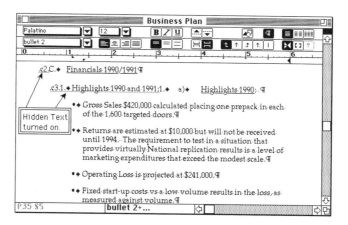

Figure 9.59

Depending on your document structure and where you need to insert the TOC entries, when Hidden Text is turned on your document may look rather confusing (Figure 9.59).

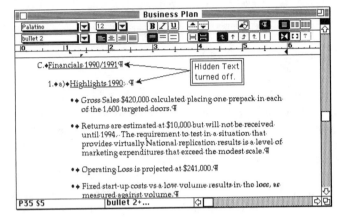

Figure 9.60

However, with Hidden Text turned off, the document will look and print like what is shown in Figure 9.60.

NOTE: *You can assign a keyboard shortcut to turn Hidden Text on and off and eliminate trips to the Preferences dialog box. See Chapter 10.*

Generating TOC from .c. Format

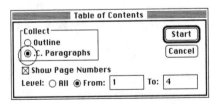

Figure 9.61

To generate the table of contents and insert it into your document, you would initiate the same steps as you did previously. Choose **Table of Contents** from the **Insert** menu. However, choose to **Collect** the **.c. Paragraphs** option and enter the correct level range for your table of contents (Figure 9.61). Click on the **Start** button.

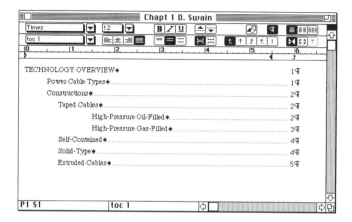

Figure 9.62

As you can see from Figure 9.62, the table of contents is formatted and inserted into your document just as it was using the outline styles. All the options for redefining the toc styles apply (see Figure 9.48).

Formatting and Generating a Table of Figures

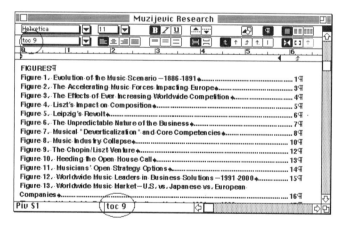

Figure 9.63

A Table of Figures differs from a regular Table of Contents only in that you would use a different level of heading style or .c. entry. Rarely would you have a long document that would have heading levels up to the maximum allowed in Microsoft Word (9 levels maximum). Therefore, you can make use of the heading 9 style to format your Figures and generate a Table of

Figures. As you can see in the example in Figure 9.63, all the figures have a **toc 9** style format indicating that these entries had an outline **heading 9** style (or **.c9.** format).

STEP ONE

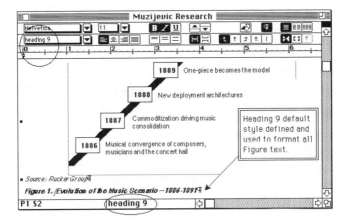

Figure 9.64

The Table of Figures example text is formatted with the heading 9 style, indicated in Figure 9.64. You can redefine the style attributes using the techniques you learned earlier in this chapter.

STEP TWO

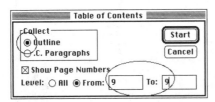

Figure 9.65

When it comes time to generate the Table of Figures, choose **Table of Contents** from the **Insert** menu, enter the Level **From 9 to 9** (Figure 9.65) and click on the **Start** button.

STEP THREE

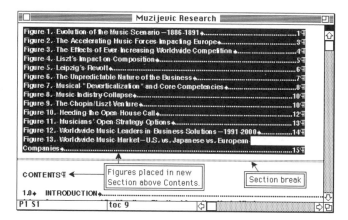

Figure 9.66

Since you are generating a table of contents using levels that were not previously included in your first Table of Contents, the Figures will be placed in a new section above your former TOC. A section break is indicated by a double dotted line, similar to a page break (Figure 9.66).

STEP FOUR

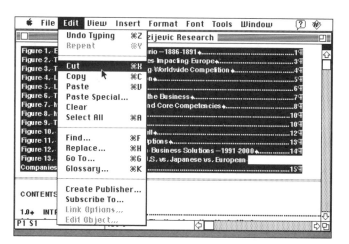

Figure 9.67

You'll most likely want to move your table of figures so that it follows your table of contents. Keep the text highlighted and choose **Cut** from the **Edit** menu (Figure 9.67).

STEP FIVE

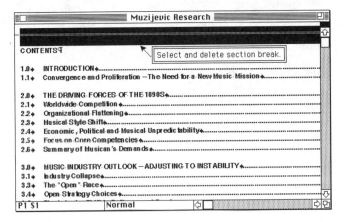

Figure 9.68

Select the **section break** (indicated in Figure 9.68) and press the **Delete** key to eliminate it.

STEP SIX

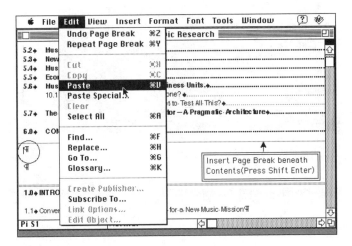

Figure 9.69

Scroll to the area underneath your table of contents and before the main body of your document. You should notice another section break there. Position the flashing insertion point after the final Table of Contents entry and enter a few blank paragraphs. You might also want to apply Normal text (press **Command Shift P**). Insert a Page Break by pressing **Shift Enter** (or choosing **Page Break** from the **Insert** menu). Go to the **Edit** menu and **Paste** in your Figures.

STEP SEVEN

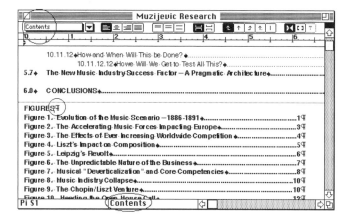

Figure 9.70

Create a new paragraph for your Figure title text and apply the **Contents** style you might have defined for the title of your Table of Contents (Figure 9.70).

STEP EIGHT

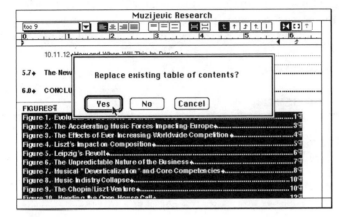

Figure 9.71

When it comes time to generate the table of figures for your final document production, you would choose **Table of Contents** from the **Insert** menu, enter **From 9 To 9** in the **Level** edit bars and click on the **Start** button. A dialog box will ask if you want to replace the existing table. Notice that only the Figures are included in the text to be replaced, shown in Figure 9.71.

It's a good practice in document structuring and management to set up, format and position your Figures and Table of Contents pages early on in your list of document formatting tasks—even if you only have one or two entries in your document. In this way, you will only need to replace the appropriate Table of Contents or Figures text when it comes time to generate the final document.

NOTE: *Rather than moving a Table of Figures after it has been generated, you could execute the Table of Figures first. Your next step would then be the generation of the Table of Contents.*

Creating a Title Page

Figure 9.72

Title and cover pages for proposals and reports can be formatted any number of ways. However, you probably will want to position the text for the title somewhere in the upper half of the page. Using a function of Microsoft Word called "framed text," you will discover how easy it is to move a block of text on a title page to the exact position you want it placed.

As you might have observed from the section on creating tables of contents and figures, information can be placed before the main contents of your document and separated by the insertion of a Section Break. Although the generation of a Table of Contents causes a section break to be inserted automatically as a part of that process, you can manually insert section breaks within your document to obtain a separate Title Page or Cover Sheet as well as a variety of other formatting options.

More specific applications of section formatting will be covered in the following section. However, to create and format a Title Page, you will first need to insert a Section Break at the top of your document.

Inserting Section Breaks and Frames

STEP ONE

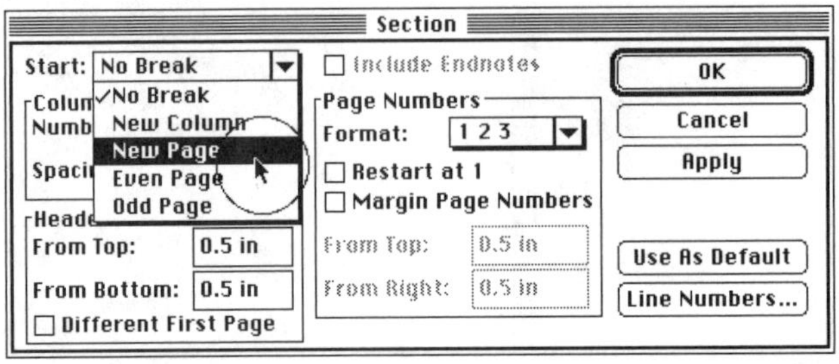

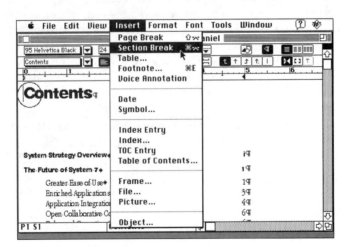

Figure 9.73

Before you insert the section break, you need to make certain that the title page will begin on a new page, separate from your table of contents information. Go to the **Format** menu and choose **Section**. Choose **New Page** from the **Start** list menu (Figure 9.73).

STEP TWO

Figure 9.74

Position the flashing insertion point at the very top of the document and go to the **Insert** menu and choose **Section Break** (Figure 9.74). (You can also press the **Command** and **Enter** keys.)

STEP THREE

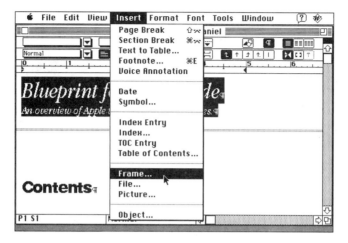

Figure 9.75

Enter the text for your title page and apply the font size and character formatting you want. Select the title page text and go to the **Insert** menu and choose **Frame** (Figure 9.75). You're going to use the "positioning" capabilities of the **Frame** command to move the title text on your page where you want it.

STEP FOUR

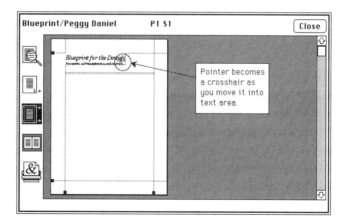

Figure 9.76

You will be taken immediately to the **Print Preview** mode. As you move your pointer over the text for the title, you should see the shape changes from an arrow to a cross hair (Figure 9.76).

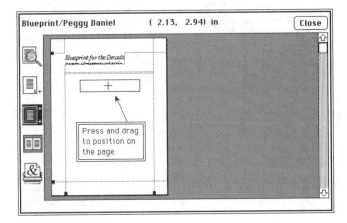

Figure 9.77

Press and drag with the cross hair to move your title text as a graphics block within the margins of your document (Figure 9.77). You can experiment with positioning it anywhere that suits your taste.

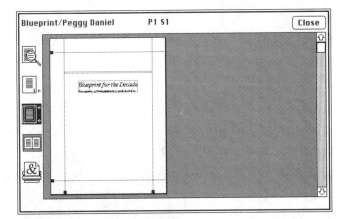

Figure 9.78

When you release the mouse button after moving the title text, your screen display will refresh and you'll see how the title text is positioned on the page (Figure 9.78). Click on the **Close** button when you are done.

STEP FIVE

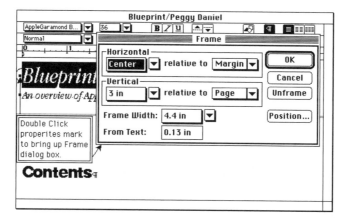

Figure 9.79

When you return to **Normal View**, you should see little black boxes next to your title text (if you have Show ¶ turned on). These **paragraph properties marks** indicate the paragraph's normal format has been altered. Move your pointer over the top of the black mark and double-click. The **Frame** dialog box should appear (Figure 9.79). This gives you more detail on the exact positioning of your framed text. You can obtain more "controlled" results with framed text by using this dialog box, which is explained in the next section.

Alternate Title Page Formats

Figure 9.80

Some title pages require formatting more information than just the title. As shown in Figure 9.80, you can have bordered text, indents, and a mixture of spacing formats within a given page.

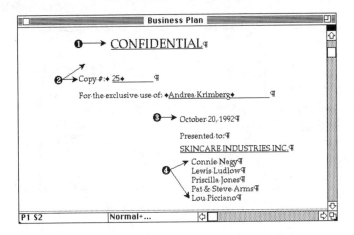

Figure 9.81

Some of the formats you might want to consider using for title page information are illustrated in Figure 9.81 as follows:

1. **Centered 18 point Palatino Bold Underline** with **12 pt Before** paragraph formatting.

2. **Left indent** set to **1.25 inches. 36 pt Before** paragraph formatting. Use of **underline tabs** in Ruler for fill-in-the-blanks. (See Figure 7.96 in Chapter 7 for directions.)

3. **Left indent** set to **3.5 inches** with **24 pt Before** paragraph formatting.

4. **Left indent** moved to **3.75 inches**. No space Before or After applied for text after first line.

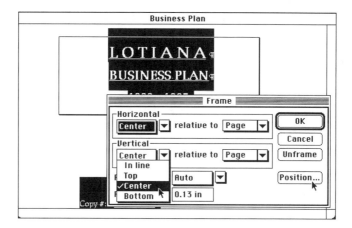

Figure 9.82

Once you've applied the various formatting to your title page text, don't worry about how it will be positioned on the page. Simply select all the text and choose **Frame** from the **Format** menu. You can use the various options in the **Frame** dialog box to position the text so it is aligned to the center of the page, both horizontally and vertically (Figure 9.82). When you've chosen your options, click on the **Position** button to view the title page in Print Preview.

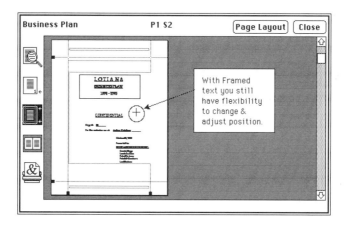

Figure 9.83

If you decide that you want to move the title text, you can still use the cross hair to press and drag the framed text to where you want it (Figure 9.83). Framed text gives you a lot of flexibility when aligning title text on a page.

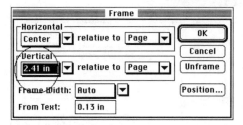

Figure 9.84

You might be using a report cover for your presentation that has a "cutout" window for the title of the document—similar to the border in the Figure 9.80 example. You can use a specific measurement in the **Frame** dialog box to align the border text with the cutout. Keep all the title page text selected and choose **Frame** from the **Format** menu. Enter the measurement taken from the top edge of the page to the top edge of the cutout in the **Vertical** edit bar (Figure 9.84). Click on the **Position** button to apply.

NOTE: *If you only select a part of your title text and then alter the Frame positioning, you might have a few formatting surprises when different pieces of the text align to different areas of the page.*

Page Numbering, Headers, Footers and Section Formatting

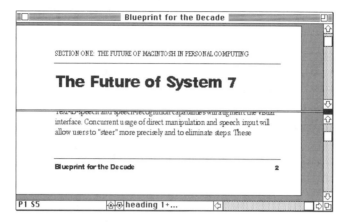

Figure 9.85

Page numbers and descriptive identification text on each page are essential organizational elements in any document. Among other purposes, they aid in the collection and insertion of any stray printed pages that might become detached from the document as a whole. Microsoft Word offers a rich palette of methods to assist you in organizing page numbering structures, and automating the page numbering process, as well as formatting the information that needs to appear at the top or bottom of each page.

Long documents are structured in a variety of ways. This section will address ways you can handle formatting a blank title page, numbering separate pages for a table of contents as well as the main body of your document. You'll learn how you can create multiple document "sections" and reformat text that should appear at the top of pages within those sections. There are also tools within Microsoft Word that you can employ to help you during the process of tracking multiple revisions during the creation cycles of producing a long document.

Page Numbering

If you have followed the topics presented thus far, you have now learned how to create a table of contents, a table of figures, and a title page. Each one of these have involved the insertion of section breaks. Though you might be unaware of it, with each section break you have inserted you have had options for determining at what point the page numbering should begin. Typically, a title page has no page number associated with it. Therefore, you will use the table of contents as your starting position for formatting page numbers so they will appear at the bottom of each page.

Typically tables of contents, prefaces, introductions, etc. use lower case Roman numerals as a numbering scheme to distinguish these pages from the main body of your document. These numbers are usually placed at the bottom of each page in an area known as a footer.

Formatting a Footer with Page Numbers

Click anywhere within a table of contents "section" of your sample document. If you have inserted a title page, your table of contents "section number" would most likely be section 2. (You can tell what section you are viewing by referring to the status box in the lower left corner of your window. However, make sure the section you are viewing is scrolled near the top of the document window for an accurate read-out. The section number would follow the "S," as in P1S2.) Because you want the page numbering to begin at page 1, you will use the **Section** dialog box to reset the page numbers as well as to determine the format the page numbers themselves will appear in.

STEP ONE

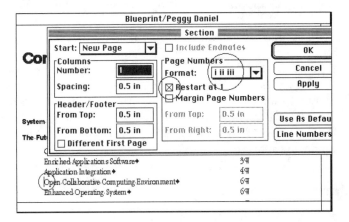

Figure 9.86

Position the cursor within the second section of your document (typically the table of contents). Go to the **Format** menu and choose **Section**. Select the lower case Roman numeral **Page Number Format** from the Format list menu (circled in Figure 9.86) and click on the **Restart at 1** option. Click **OK**.

> **NOTE:** *In order to easily access both the Section dialog box and the Footer window, you should work in Normal view. Page Layout View is best for making **modifications** to header and footer material and will be used later on in this section.*

STEP TWO

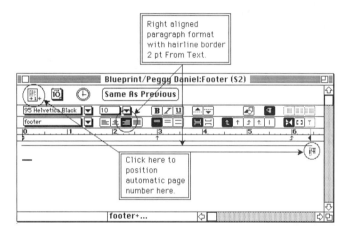

Figure 9.87

Go to the **View** menu and choose **Footer**. Since the **Ruler** and the **Ribbon** are not automatically displayed in headers or footers, you'll need to select them from the **View** menu. Click on the **Right aligned paragraph** icon and choose the font and character formatting you want for your page number. Click on the **Page numbering** icon to insert an automatic page number. You can apply a border by choosing **Border** from the **Format** menu (Figure 9.87). Click in the **Close box** when you are done.

STEP THREE

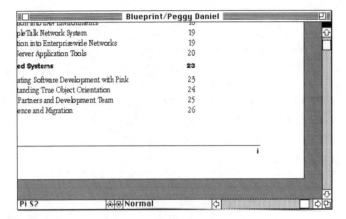

Figure 9.88

To view the results of your footer formatting, choose **Page Layout** from the **View** menu and scroll to the bottom of the page (Figure 9.88).

STEP FOUR

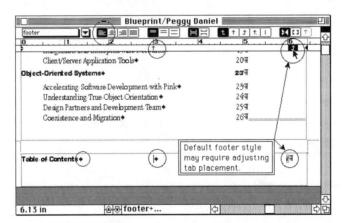

Figure 9.89

You might decide to add some additional text to your table of contents pages. You can do this from within **Page Layout** View. Click inside the footer. Although the text was previously aligned with **right aligned paragraph** format, you'll want to add text to the left side of your footer.

Therefore, click on the **Left aligned paragraph** icon in the Ruler. Microsoft Word has a default footer style which places two tab marks in the Ruler—one is a center-aligned tab mark at the 3-inch position and the other a right- aligned Tab mark at the 6-inch position.

Position the flashing insertion point in front of the automatic page number. Enter your footer text (e.g., Table of Contents) and press the **Tab** key twice (or remove the center tab mark from the Ruler and press the Tab key once). Depending on the margin setup for your document, you might need to reposition the right-aligned Tab mark in the Ruler (Figure 9.89).

STEP FIVE

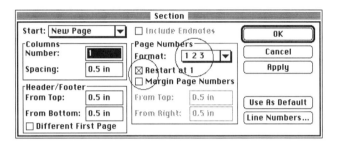

Figure 9.90

Scroll to the main body of your document and position the flashing insertion point somewhere within the section. Choose **Normal** from the **View** menu. Go to the **Format** menu and choose **Section**. Typically, you would want to restart your document's page numbering so that the main body of the document starts on page 1 and uses arabic numbers. Choose the arabic numbering scheme from the **Page Number Format** list menu and click on the **Restart at 1** option (Figure 9.90). Click **OK**.

STEP SIX

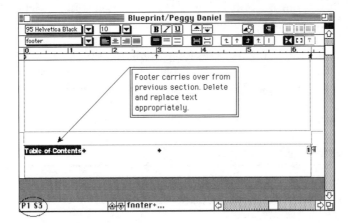

Figure 9.91

You can either return to **Page Layout** View or choose **Footer** from the **View** menu. You might be surprised to see that the footer has the identical formatting and text as the table of contents section. Microsoft Word carries forward any header or footer entries to the next section of your document. All you probably would have to alter is the replacement of the Table of Contents text with the title of your document (Figure 9.91).

Section Headings

Your long document might divide itself into distinct sections that you would like to indicate by placing text within a header. However, the page numbering is continuous throughout the document. You can have two sets of header and/or footer information per section but only one set will appear on the first page of the section. The other set of header and/or footer information will continue throughout the section. You also have the flexibility to create other sections and change the header information without disrupting the continuous page numbering of your document. You will undoubtedly get a clearer idea of what this means by examining the following example.

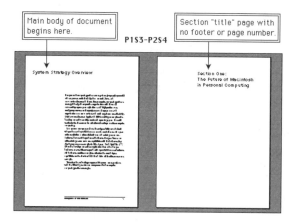

Figure 9.92

The example in Figure 9.92 displays the first page of the main document on the left which has an overall "strategy" or executive summary and has a footer with Page 1 indicated. On the right is a section "title page" that has no header or footer and does not display the page number of the document.

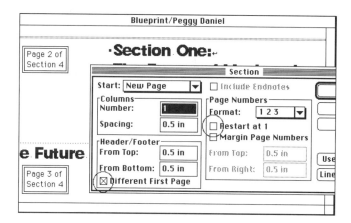

Figure 9.93

Though the main body has page numbering starting on Page 1, it is actually located in Section 3 of the overall Word document. The first two sections contain the title page, and table of contents. When the new section illustrated in Figure 9.93 was inserted, the **Section** dialog box was used to apply the **Different First Page** option and to turn off the **Restart at 1** numbering function. Therefore, the page numbering continues from Section 3 to Section 4 as indicated.

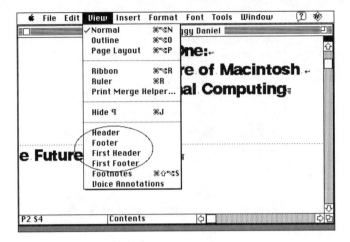

Figure 9.94

When the **Different First Page** option is selected in the **Section** dialog box, the **View** menu now has the option to view the **First Header** and **First Footer** in addition to the regular **Header** and **Footer** (Figure 9.94).

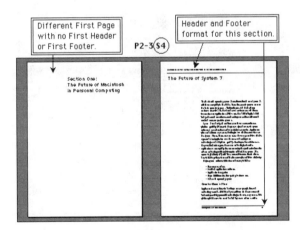

Figure 9.95

The illustration in Figure 9.95 shows that the **First Header** and **First Footer** have been left intentionally blank. The **Header** and **Footer** have been formatted with text and page numbering information.

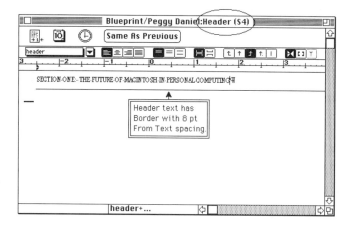

Figure 9.96

The Header formatting for this section (Section 4) is displayed in Figure 9.96. A **hairline** border has been applied beneath the text with **8 pt** of **From Text** spacing.

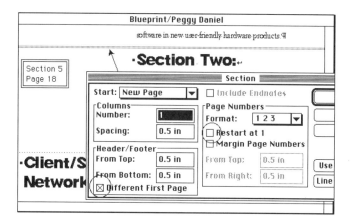

Figure 9.97

Further on in the document, there is another major section. A section break was inserted and the **Different First Page** option selected from the **Section** dialog box. Page numbering is continuous throughout (Figure 9.97).

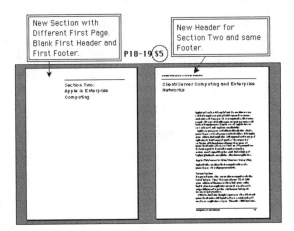

Figure 9.98

Similar to the formatting for Section 1, the illustration in Figure 9.98 indicates the blank header and footer of the "First Page." Only the Header text is different in this section while the Footer information remains constant.

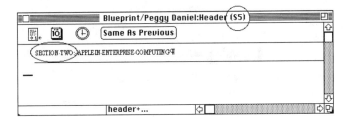

Figure 9.99

This final illustration displays the text for the new heading for Section 2 (Figure 9.99).

Other Kinds of Section Formatting

Figure 9.100

Your particular long document structuring may not require the section title pages discussed earlier. Perhaps all the formatting you might need to accommodate is new text in the header or footer for each section. In this circumstance, you would not need to apply the **Different First Page** option in the **Section** dialog box for every new section. However, you might want to activate the **Different First Page** option (in the **Section** dialog box) for the *first* page in your document and leave the header and/or footer blank. Typically the first page of a report wouldn't necessarily need to contain the title and page number information (Figure 9.100).

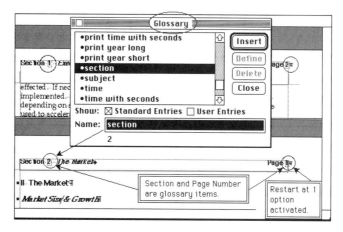

Figure 9.101

Each section might have its own unique heading. You can also choose to restart page numbering from 1 for each of these sections. There is a Glossary item for automatic section numbering that is similar to the automatic page numbering. To place this automatic section numbering in your document, choose the **Section** glossary item in the **Glossary** dialog box and click on the **Insert** button (Figure 9.101).

NOTE: *Because this section number is automatic, you would not want to incorporate it in long documents that use section breaks for title pages and tables of contents. The automatic section number would not accurately reflect the appropriate section of your main document.*

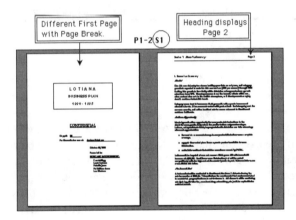

Figure 9.102

If you want to insert a title page but don't want it to be a separate section, consider using the **Different First Page** option (located in the **Section** dialog box) and deleting all First Header and/or First Footer information. However, the first page of your main document (that is, page 2) would contain the Header and/or Footer information (Figure 9.102).

Revision Tracking

When you are in the process of producing a long document, managing the cycle of printouts, reviews, and revisional editing can be an administrative nightmare if you don't develop some system for tracking which version is the current version.

This can be achieved by placing updated information within a footer. Though the **Summary Info** information (accessed through the **File** menu) can be modified to record which version you are working with, there is no way to have this revised version number inserted in your document and automatically updated. However, you can use the self-updating print time and print date glossary features of Microsoft Word to assist you.

Inserting Glossary Items

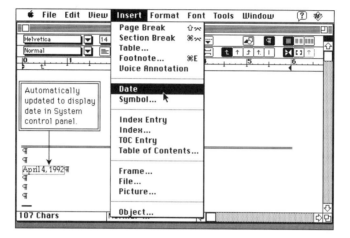

Figure 9.103

The **Date** function on the **Insert** menu is nothing more than a "quick menu access" to the **print time Glossary** item. This date is tied in with the date that is set in the general control panel of your Macintosh System software. If you insert the date in a document (as shown in Figure 9.103) and save it, the next time you open the document (which could be in several days, weeks, or months) the date will reflect the current date in your Macintosh system.

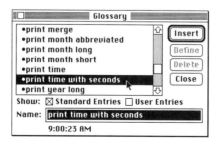

Figure 9.104

Choosing **Glossary** from the **Edit** menu and browsing through the list of **Standard Entries** reveals a number of "print" glossary items (Figure 9.104). Inserting combinations of these glossary items into a footer or header will record the exact time you printed out the document, therefore giving you an accurate means of coordinating the latest version of your document with the printed version.

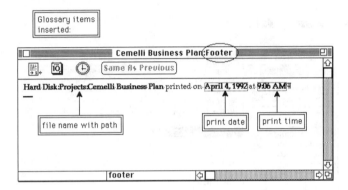

Figure 9.105

When placing this information in a footer, you can also use Glossary items to insert the document name and path name as to where the document is located on your hard disk to add further management controls. However, should you move your document or change its file name, the information will not be automatically updated in your document header or footer. Footer information can be inserted as shown in Figure 9.105 by choosing **Glossary** from the **Edit** menu, scrolling to the appropriate glossary name, and clicking on the **Insert** button for each item you want to place in your document.

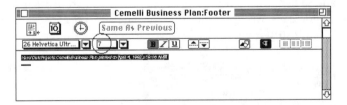

Figure 9.106

You probably would like this information to be as imperceptible as possible and not detract from the overall appearance of your document. Once you've inserted all the information you want, select your text and format it as **7** or **9 point** (or even 4 point!) text (Figure 9.106).

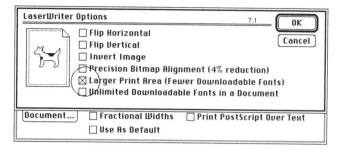

Figure 9.107

You might also want to have the text appear as close to the bottom margin as possible. If you have a LaserWriter, select the **Larger Print Area** option from the **Page Setup Options** dialog box (Figure 9.107). This will allow you to position the footer text within 0.25 inch of the paper's edge.

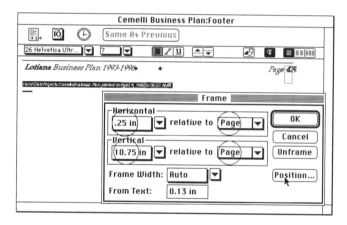

Figure 9.108

You can use the **Format Frame** function to position the footer information at the bottom of your page and away from other footer information you might have in your document. Select the version information and choose **Frame** from the **Format** menu. Enter the measurements shown in Figure 9.108 if you have a LaserWriter that allows you to print within 0.25 inches of the edge of your page. Otherwise, change the measurements so that they are 0.5 inches and 10.5 inches respectively. Be sure you select the **Page** option for both measurements and click on the **Position** button.

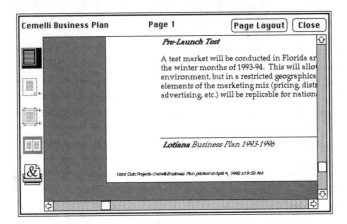

Figure 9.109

If you double-click on the footer area within the **Print Preview** window, you will see the placement of your revision tracking information (Figure 9.109).

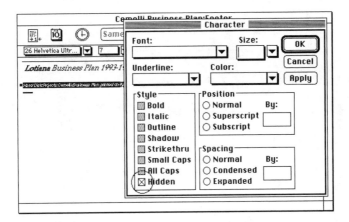

Figure 9.110

When you have finished all your revisions and are ready to print the final copy of your document, you can select your revision information and format it as **Hidden Text** using the **Character** dialog box (or press **Command Shift V**). As long as you don't select the Print Hidden Text option in the Print dialog box, this information will not print out (Figure 9.110).

Connecting a Series of Documents

You might have a team of people working on different sections or "chapters" of a long report. It would probably make good sense to have each chapter as a separate document on the appropriate team member's workstation so that they can work on it independently. However, you might wonder how you can generate a final table of contents and produce accurate pagination results in three separate documents without combining them into one main document. Not to worry! Microsoft Word has a "File Series" option that allows you to "chain link" documents so you can both generate a table of contents or print in one continuous operation.

As long as you have access to your teammate's hard drive where the various "chapters" are located, you can connect documents in a files series. (System 7.0 and AppleShare file servers allow you to "mount" drives and folders across a network on your own desktop as if they were additional drives.) The steps for linking a three-chapter report for generating a table of contents and printing follow.

Setting Up the Series

STEP ONE

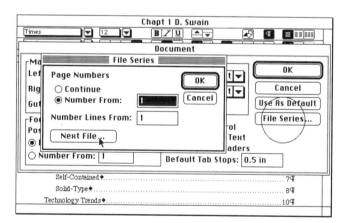

Figure 9.111

Start by opening the first document in the series (e.g., Chapter 1). Go to the **Format** menu and choose **Document**. Click on the **File Series** button and then click on the **Next File** button (Figure 9.111).

STEP TWO

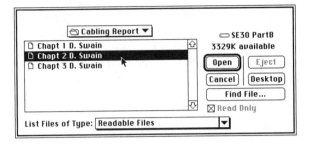

Figure 9.112

Navigate to the correct folder on the disk where the next "chapter" or document in the series is located. Double-click to **Open** it (Figure 9.112).

STEP THREE

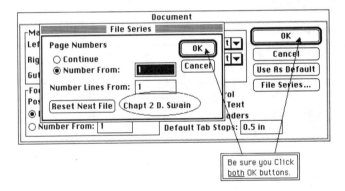

Figure 9.113

The File Series dialog box will indicate the document name and the Next File button will be changed to display "Reset Next File" (Figure 9.113). Click on the **OK** button for both the **File Series** dialog box and the **Document** dialog box or file series selection will not be "set." (You will also need to **Save** your document to retain this information.)

STEP FOUR

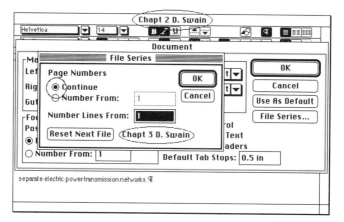

Figure 9.114

Open the second document in the series (e.g., Chapter 2) and choose **Document** from the **Format** menu. Click on the **File Series** button. Click on the **Continue** option for Page Numbers (Figure 9.114). (When it comes time to generate the final Table of Contents, you won't need to worry about where your page numbers end and begin from document to document.) Click on the **Next File** button, navigate to and open the next document in the series. Click on both **OK** buttons and **Save** your document. Repeat this step for all "chapters" *except* the last one in the series.

STEP FIVE

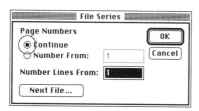

Figure 9.115

For the last file in the series, follow the same actions as in Step Four and select the **Continue** button in the **File Series** dialog box (Figure 9.115). Since it is the last document in the series, there will be no need to set a Next File. Save your document.

Generating a Table of Contents and Printing a File Series

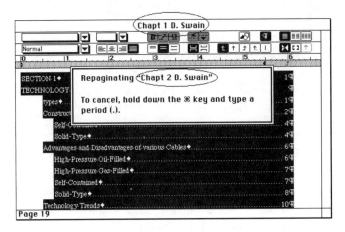

Figure 9.116

To generate the table of contents, you need to have the first document in the file series open on your desktop. If you had already created a "place holder" table of contents, you would merely be replacing and updating that information. Generate the table of contents in the normal way by choosing **Table of Contents** from the **Insert** menu. The only difference between generating a TOC from connected documents and a normal document is that there is a longer Repagination process as Microsoft Word goes through each document in the series and updates the page numbers (Figure 9.116).

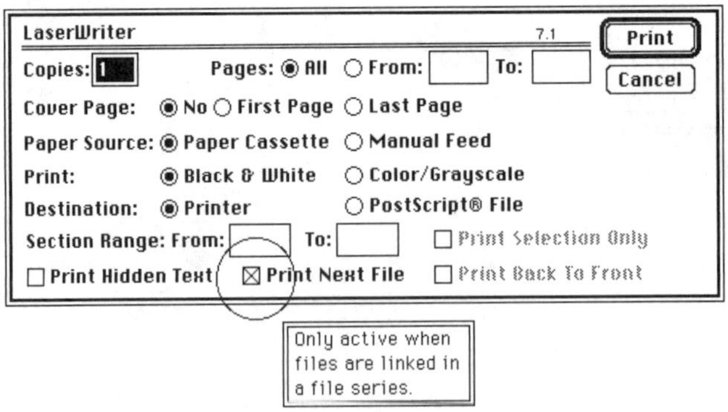

Figure 9.117

When printing documents linked in a file series, you need to execute the print process from within the first document in the series. Make sure the first document is the active window and choose **Print** from the **File** menu. The **Print** dialog box will have the **Print Next File** option automatically selected (Figure 9.117). If you only want to print pages from within a single document in the series, deselect this option.

> **NOTE:** *Whenever you print or generate a Table of Contents, the page numbers in the connected documents will be updated accordingly. However, if you choose Repaginate Now from the Tools menu once this process occurs, the page numbers in the connected documents will return to a starting page number of 1.*

Creating a Standard Report Format

Generating reports, contracts and business plans may be a function you execute regularly during the course of your business. After going to the trouble of setting up a great looking document, wouldn't it be wonderful if you could somehow automate the process to generate similar documents? You can use some features of the Print Merge language to "program" your document for key information that varies from document to document, such as the date, report name, company name, key personnel, etc. You can also "flag" text that you need to customize for the document and move quickly from flag to flag, using the Find capabilities of Microsoft Word.

What follows are a few examples of ways you can setup and customize a standard report format for your long document production needs.

Formatting a Contract Using the Print Merge Language

Though you might not have viewed the capabilities of Microsoft's Print Merge features as being classified a "language," you will soon realize that using the print merge language is a simple and direct way to gain powerful implementation of your document processing needs. There are print merge fields and keywords you can insert into a standard document which—when the Print Merge command is executed—will "prompt" the user through a series of dialog boxes. The information entered during this process will be placed throughout the document wherever you have inserted the appropriate "field."

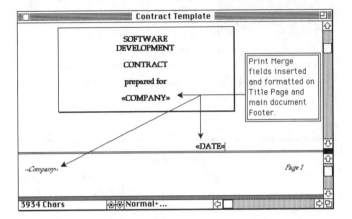

Figure 9.118

The example contract in Figure 9.118 shows some ways you can place print merge fields throughout your document—on the title page, footers, and elsewhere. To reformat your document to create a template, first Save a copy of a model contract and name it as your template document. Follow the steps below which will give you examples of ways you can begin to automate your document production tasks.

STEP ONE

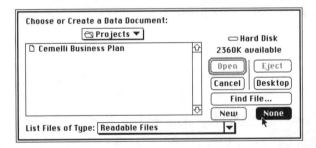

Figure 9.119

You're going to use the Print Merge Helper bar to assist you in "programming" your template. However, you do not need to associate the print merge with any data file. Choose **Print Merge Helper** from the **View** menu and click on the **None** button, as indicated in Figure 9.119.

STEP TWO

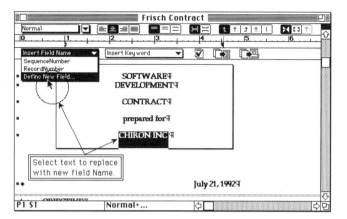

Figure 9.120

Select the example text from your model document. You are going to replace it with a defined field. Go to the **Insert Field Name** menu list in the Helper bar and choose **Define New Field** (Figure 9.120).

STEP THREE

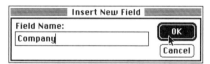

Figure 9.121

A dialog box will appear and ask you to name the new field. Enter the appropriate field name in the edit bar and click **OK** (Figure 9.121).

STEP FOUR

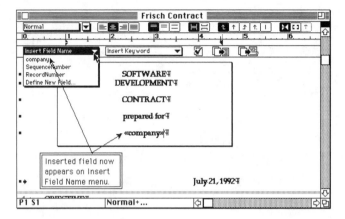

Figure 9.122

The field name will replace the text you had highlighted. It will also be formatted with the same characteristics as the text it replaced. The field name will now appear in the **Insert Field Name** list (Figure 9.122).

STEP FIVE

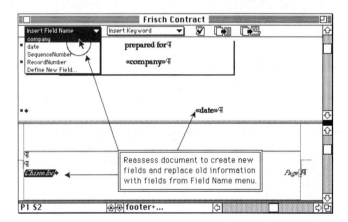

Figure 9.123

You will need to scroll though your document and reassess the information contained in it, looking for appropriate kinds of information that could be tagged as "fields" and automated. Execute Steps 3 and 4 for each new field that you ascertain is correct for your document. You can then highlight text where appropriate and choose the field name from the **Insert Field Name** list to replace it (Figure 9.123).

> **NOTE:** *If there is information in the footer that you want to create a field for, go to Page Layout View so that you still have access to the Print Merge Helper bar.*

STEP SIX

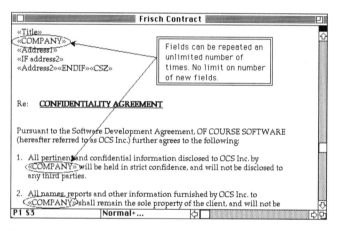

Figure 9.124

You can repeat fields as often as you like throughout the document (Figure 9.124) and create as many new fields as you need. The benefit of this method of automating your document production is that you will only enter the information once, and it will thereafter "find itself" in the appropriate places throughout your document where these print merge fields have been inserted.

STEP SEVEN

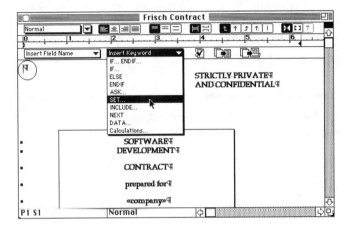

Figure 9.125

When you are done defining and inserting fields within your model document template, you will now invoke the SET Print Merge Keyword to "program" your document. Scroll to the top of your document and insert a new paragraph at the top. (You might also want to "clear" the formats by pressing **Command Shift P**.) Go to the **Insert Keyword** menu in the Helper bar and choose **SET** (Figure 9.125).

STEP EIGHT

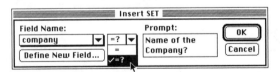

Figure 9.126

The **Insert SET** dialog box will appear. Choose the first field name in the **Field Name** list on the left then choose the **=?** operator. This sets up the keyword so that it delivers a "prompt" during the print merge process. Click in the **Prompt** edit bar and enter an appropriate question for the kind of information you are seeking. Don't worry if it is not complete. You can edit it once you click on the **OK** button (Figure 9.126).

STEP NINE

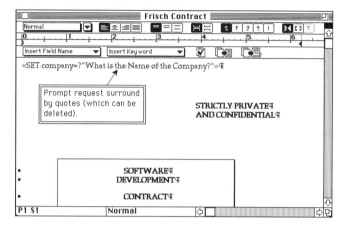

Figure 9.127

The information you entered in the **Insert SET** dialog box will be inserted into your document (Figure 9.127). The prompt text you entered will be surrounded with quotation marks (which you can remove).

STEP TEN

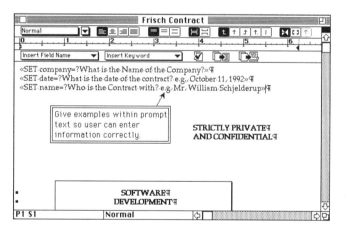

Figure 9.128

Continue to create more **SET** prompts following Steps 7 and 8 above. In order to help the user (who might well be you!), give yourself some good example text as a reminder (Figure 9.128). Be careful, though, with the length of your prompts. The maximum number of characters allowed for a prompt is 92.

STEP ELEVEN

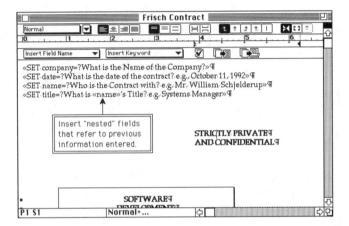

Figure 9.129

You can replace some of the text within your prompt with another print merge field (use the **Insert Field Name** menu list to do this). When you insert another field name within a prompt it is called a "nested" field (Figure 9.129). Nested fields will remind you of important information you might otherwise forget during the merge process (such as, "Who am I sending this to, anyway?").

STEP TWELVE

When you are setting up address information fields, don't forget the standard print merge conventions you learned in Chapter 6 (Figure 9.130). You can save yourself some time and effort by letting the user know that he or she can leave the edit bar empty and not have to worry about unnecessary blank paragraphs in an important contract or proposal.

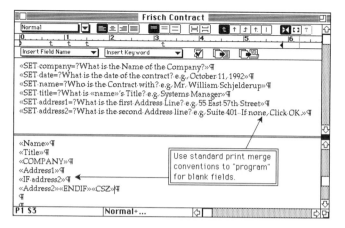

Figure 9.130

STEP THIRTEEN

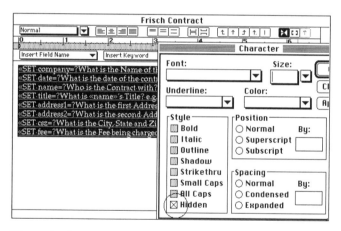

Figure 9.131

When you're through, you might want to format your **SET** prompts with Hidden text format so that they are out of sight when you work with the document. You might also want to click on the **Check Errors** button in the **Print Merge Helper** bar to see if you have any mistakes before continuing.

> **NOTE:** *To hide your SET instructions, you will need to turn the Show Hidden Text option off from the Preferences dialog box. You can set up a keyboard shortcut to do this if you refer to Chapter 10.*

Executing a Document Using Print Merge

Once your template document has been formatted and "programmed" for the print merge process you will be able to use it to generate documents on a regular basis. It's important to notice the distinction between using a template with Print Merge instructions and a regular document saved in "Stationery" format. The "Stationery" document brings up a replica of the original document into an Untitled window. If you wanted to make changes and adjustments, you might use the **Replace** dialog box to search and replace all the information you think is necessary. But there is no "tool" there to prompt and remind you as to what those changes might be on a consistent basis.

With the Print Merge template (saved as a Normal Word document), you are able to activate a series of prompts, which guide you through the process of constructing your document. Activating your template is a very simple procedure.

STEP ONE

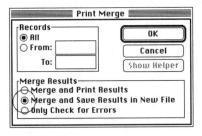

Figure 9.132

Open your report document template. Go to the **File** menu and choose **Print Merge**. The Print Merge dialog box will appear, the default of which is the option to "Merge and Save Results in a New File." To activate this choice you only need to click on the **OK** button or press the **Return** key (Figure 9.132).

STEP TWO

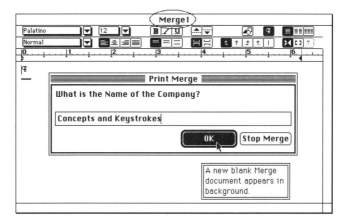

Figure 9.133

First of all, a new document window will appear in the background named "MergeX" with a Print Merge dialog box in front of it containing the prompt information you programmed earlier with the SET keyword (Figure 9.133). Enter the information in the edit bar. Make sure it is accurate before clicking the **OK** button (remember, this text will be placed in many locations throughout the document and will be time-consuming to correct). Click on the **OK** button or press the **Return** key when you are through. The entire series of prompts will appear in the order you entered them in your contract template document.

> **NOTE:** *If ever you have made a mistake or want to terminate the merge process, simply click on the Stop Merge button. You can always reexecute the Print Merge.*

STEP THREE

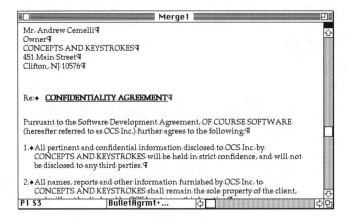

Figure 9.134

When you have finished entering information in the prompted dialog boxes, the body of your document will appear, filled in with the information you entered (Figure 9.134).

STEP FOUR

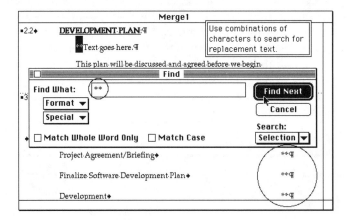

Figure 9.135

You might place text markers within your template document to indicate those areas where you have to insert text and refine your document. In Figure 9.135, the replacement characters are two asterisks. You only need to choose the **Find** command from the **Edit** menu, enter the place holder characters and replace or enter your text. Once you've initiated the first search, you can press the = sign on your numeric keypad to move on to the next occurrence of the place holder text.

NOTE: *You can also create glossary items to insert preformatted "blocks" of text into your document. See Chapter 10 for ways to implement this.*

Other Report Ideas

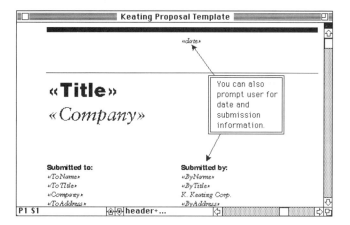

Figure 9.136

You can use print merge fields to prompt for title page information in reports you generate. In the Figure 9.136 example, rather than use the automatic print date, the user is prompted for the date the document will be submitted.

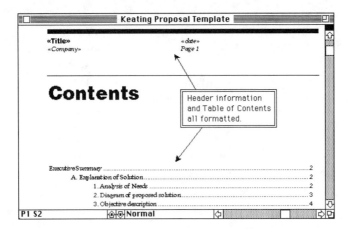

Figure 9.137

The same field names appear in the document header information as shown in Figure 9.137. A Table of Contents has been generated and formatted as a "place holder" for use when the document is completed.

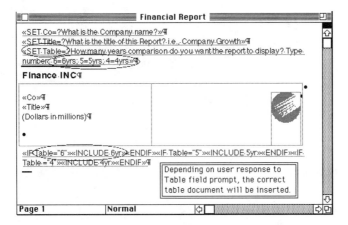

Figure 9.138

You can also use the Print Merge language to create a prompt that will ask you if you want to "include" information from another document in your report or proposal (Figure 9.138). As you might imagine, the combination of possibilities for programming and executing this kind of document automation are vast.

> **NOTE:** *See Chapter 6 following Figure 6.39 for more information on inserting INCLUDE statements.*

Conclusion

L ong document structuring and management will "push the enve lope" on your ability to work with a variety of tools and techniques inherent in Microsoft Word's powerful software. Whereas this chapter has explained and demonstrated how you might implement some of these methods, there is a lot of room for invention and creativity when designing and formatting long documents.

Productivity Solutions for Your Word Processing Environment

Many of the tasks involved in word processing go beyond keyboard skills for basic text entry. Formatting a document, deciding what information goes where and how it should look on the page all take time in addition to making sure the words are spelled correctly and in the right order.

Microsoft Word has some exciting tools you can use to boost your productivity when you need to get a lot done in a hurry or are even just tired of taking your hands off the keyboard and reaching for the mouse all the time. In this chapter, you'll learn some tricks for having your important documents open at your fingertips and see a few tips for ways you can format text from the keyboard and even insert blocks of preformatted text in your document by using a few simple keystrokes you'll invent yourself.

The final section in this chapter addresses cross-platform compatibility issues you might have if you share Word documents between Word 5.0 for the Macintosh and Windows Word 2.0.

How to Get to Your Important Documents Quickly

How much time do you waste in a day just trying to locate the documents on your computer's hard disk so you can get down to work? If you're well organized, perhaps only a few minutes. But wouldn't it be nice if those documents that you really need were easier to navigate to than the myriad of folders you dip into when you use the Open dialog box?

In this section you'll learn several different techniques you can use to swiftly open documents you use all the time, ones you've just put away or files you've not looked at for a long while.

Recently Opened Documents

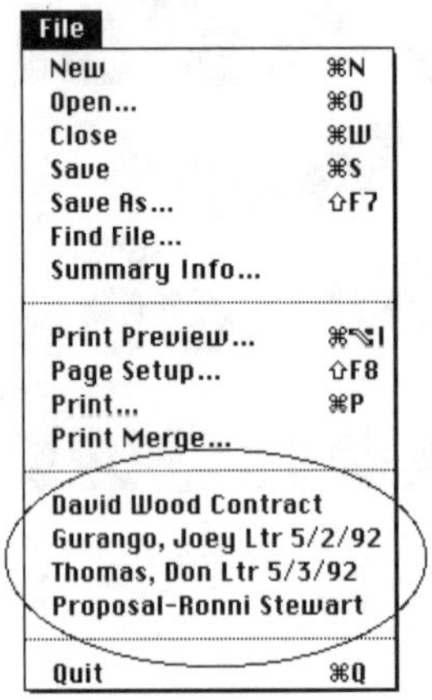

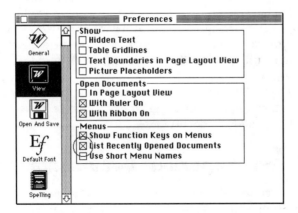

Figure 10.1

There is a Preferences function in Microsoft Word 5.0 that automatically lists the 4 most recently opened documents on the **File** menu (Figure 10.1). Selecting the document name from this list is a fast way to save some time when you need to get to important information quickly.

Figure 10.2

To make sure that this option is activated, go to the **Tools** menu and choose **Preferences**. Click on the **View** icon. The **List Recently Opened Documents** option should be selected. If it is not, click in the box next to it so that an **X** appears in the box (Figure 10.2). Click in the **Close** box.

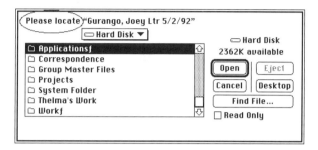

Figure 10.3

Now, every time you close a document, its name will be added to the File menu. However, if you move the document to another folder or change its name, when you select the file name from the **File** menu a **Please Locate** dialog box will appear (Figure 10.3). You'll then need to navigate to the folder it has been relocated in or click on the renamed document.

Adding Items to a Work Menu

In the first part of this book, there was some mention of a method you can quickly access so that documents you use everyday can be immediately available to you. Rather than going to the **File** menu, choosing **Open** and searching for that Envelope or Letterhead template, you can place these documents in a menu all their own called a **Work** menu. There are many other ways you can also make use of the **Work** menu which will be covered later on in this chapter.

STEP ONE

To begin with, you're going to place your letterhead and envelope stationery documents in a Work menu. Go to the **File** menu and choose **Open**. Navigate to the folder that contains your letterhead document. Press the following key combination: **Command** (next to the spacebar) **Option** and the + sign next to the Delete key (**Command Option** +). When you look up at your screen, your pointer will have changed into a large, bold + sign (Figure 10.4). Use the plus sign as a pointer and double-click on your Letterhead stationery template to select and open it.

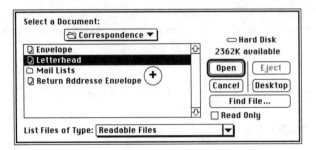

Figure 10.4

STEP TWO

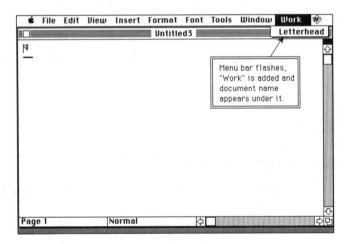

Figure 10.5

You should notice that your menu bar flashes and the word "Work" appears to the far right of the menu bar. Move your pointer over the **Work** menu item and press. You should see that your letterhead document is now an item on the drop down menu (Figure 10.5).

Having your document name appear in the Work menu merely acts as a pointer that Microsoft Word sets up to tell it where your document is located. Go to the **Work** menu and select your letterhead document. Since it is a stationery document, a blank Untitled document with your letterhead on it should appear on your desktop.

Continue to add documents to your Work menu by choosing **File Open**, pressing **Command Option +**, and double-clicking on the documents you feel are important daily files you need access to. Some of these documents might be your Envelope template, Labels template, Memo, Sales proposal template, or a standard report format.

> **NOTE:** *If ever you want to cancel out of the process above and return to a normal pointer shape, simply press Command period.*

STEP THREE

Figure 10.6

If you have been working on a document and it is open on your desktop now, you can also add it directly to your Work menu without making a trip to the Open dialog box. Press the `Command Option` + key combination and move the bold + sign into the `Title bar` of your document (Figure 10.6). Click on the title once and the document will be added to the `Work` menu.

> **NOTE:** *Similar to recently opened documents listed in the File menu, if you move or rename any of these files that appear in the Work menu, you will be asked to locate them. It might serve you better to remove the file name from the Work menu and then add the newly relocated or named document to the menu once again.*

Removing Items from a Work Menu

What if you accidentally click on a document you don't want to have
included on the Work menu, or you decide later you really don't want a
certain document on the list anymore? You can remove documents from
the Work menu very easily.

STEP ONE

Press the keyboard combination **Command Option -** (the minus sign is two
keys to the left of the Delete key). Your pointer will turn into a large, bold
minus sign.

STEP TWO

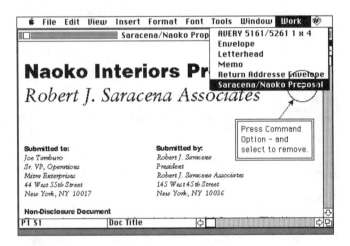

Figure 10.7

Go to the **Work** menu and use the pointer to choose the document name
you wish to remove (Figure 10.7). When you release the mouse button, the
menu bar will flash and the name will be gone.

Setting Keyboard Shortcuts to Open Documents or Switch Windows

Having your important documents listed in a **Work** menu saves time accessing dialog boxes and folders. However, if you had your wish, you'd probably
like not to have to even reach for the mouse to make a trip to the **Work**
menu. Here's how you can program your own keyboard shortcut for
opening up a document that appears on the **Work** menu.

Opening Documents

STEP ONE

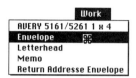

Figure 10.8

Press the key combination **Command Option +** (the plus sign above the **enter** key on the numeric keypad). Your pointer will turn into the shape of a large, bold Command sign. Using the pointer, select the document you access most often from the **Work** menu (Figure 10.8).

STEP TWO

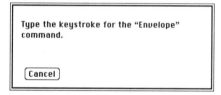

Figure 10.9

When you release the mouse button, a dialog box will appear asking you to type the combination of keystrokes you want to assign to this item (Figure 10.9). You have a variety of choices to make a selection from. However, because some keystrokes have already been programmed into Microsoft Word as "defaults," you probably wouldn't want to tamper with them just yet.

If you press the **Control** key in combination with most any other key (number, symbol or letter), chances are pretty high there will be no conflict with Microsoft's default settings. Since these are your most important documents, you might want to key them to Control 1, Control 2, etc.

> **NOTE:** *You can use any combination of the Command, Option, Shift and Control keys in combination with the other keys on the keyboard and numeric keypad. However, the combination must contain either the Command key or the Control key—unless you are combining them with the numeric keypad items. The numeric keypad numbers also allow the combined use of just the Option or Shift keys.*

Figure 10.10

Once you've entered your keystroke, it will appear next to your document name on the **Work** menu as a reminder in case you forget it (Figure 10.10). Press that key combination now and you should summon a blank envelope to your desktop. How's that for efficiency!

Switching Windows

There is a default keyboard command that will move you to the next open window on your desktop. By pressing **Command Option W**, you can cycle between all your open documents. If you only have one or two document windows open, this is fairly convenient. But what if you are manipulating between several documents and need to get to one or two documents without much trouble?

Follow the steps outlined above for setting a keyboard shortcut, only instead of selecting a document name from the Work menu, select it from the **Window** menu.

The keystroke will work for you as long as your document is open. Once you save and close the document, the next time it appears on your desktop the keystroke you assigned will not respond. This keystroke assignment is only a temporary work solution for documents appearing in the **Window** menu.

Working with Summary Info and Find File

The Summary Info and Find File features of Microsoft Word work hand in hand to help you access information in your documents. These features are designed for documents you might need to retrieve after some time has passed and probably won't be the kind of template or stationery documents you use every day.

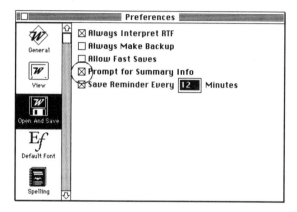

Figure 10.11

Summary Info is very much like an index card that is saved with your document. You can choose to be prompted for this function to appear when you first Save your document by activating the option from within the **Preferences** dialog box (Figure 10.11). However, if you don't plan to make use of Summary Info all the time, you might want to turn the prompt option off as it can become annoying.

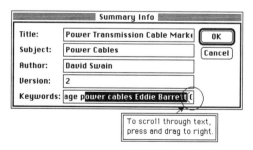

Figure 10.12

You can enter up to **255** characters in each of the five fields contained in the **Summary Info** dialog box. However, you won't be able to view all 255 characters at once. You'll have to use the mouse to select and scroll to view text (which isn't very convenient). For the most part, you might want to enter keywords for client information such as purchase order or invoice numbers, specific client names mentioned in the document, department numbers, subjects addressed—anything that you feel is important about the document (Figure 10.12). Be sure you click on the **OK** button and **Save** your document or the information will not be recorded for your search.

Just remember that in order to locate your document by the information you enter in these Summary Info fields, you will need to rekey this information exactly as it was entered. Unfortunately, you cannot Paste information into the Summary Info fields. (The Paste function is not active while the dialog box is open). To locate the document that contains this Summary Info, you will need to use the **Find File** utility.

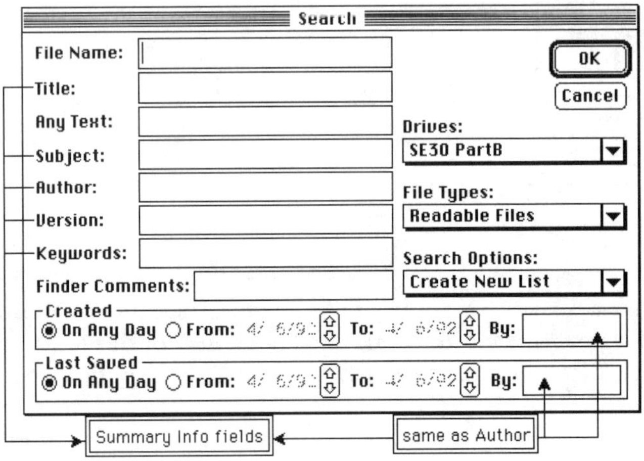

Figure 10.13

The **Search** dialog box (which appears when you choose **Find File** from the **File** menu) has a number of fields you can use for the search of any document. Figure 10.13 indicates those fields that use the information you enter and save in the **Summary Info** dialog box. Don't be misled with the By field that appears next to the date Created or date Last Saved information. The field only responds to information entered and saved in the **Author** field of the **Summary Info** dialog box.

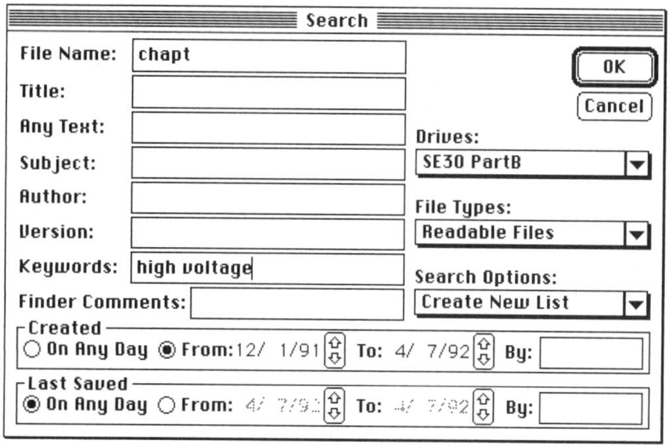

```
┌══════════════════════════ Search ══════════════════════════┐
  File Name:  │chapt                          │        ┌─────────┐
                                                       │   OK    │
  Title:      │                               │        └─────────┘
                                                       ┌─────────┐
  Any Text:   │                               │        │ Cancel  │
                                                       └─────────┘
  Subject:    │                               │    Drives:
                                                    │SE30 PartB      │▼│
  Author:     │                               │
                                                    File Types:
  Version:    │                               │      │Readable Files  │▼│

  Keywords:   │high voltage│                  │    Search Options:
  Finder Comments: │                          │      │Create New List │▼│
  ┌Created────────────────────────────────────────────────────────┐
  │ ○ On Any Day  ● From:12/ 1/91⬍  To: 4/ 7/92⬍  By:│           │ │
  └────────────────────────────────────────────────────────────────┘
  ┌Last Saved─────────────────────────────────────────────────────┐
  │ ● On Any Day  ○ From: 4/ 7/9⬍  To: 4/ 7/92⬍  By:│           │ │
  └────────────────────────────────────────────────────────────────┘
└══════════════════════════════════════════════════════════════┘
```

Figure 10.14

The fastest way to locate any document on your hard drive is to initiate a search by **File Name**. However, chances are you won't remember the file names of most documents. You can enter partial information in any of these fields; however, the number of documents that share that same information is increased if you search on File Name fragments. That is why you can combine File Name information with specific information you've entered in the **Summary Info** fields or the **Created** and **Last Saved** options to narrow your file searches (Figure 10.14).

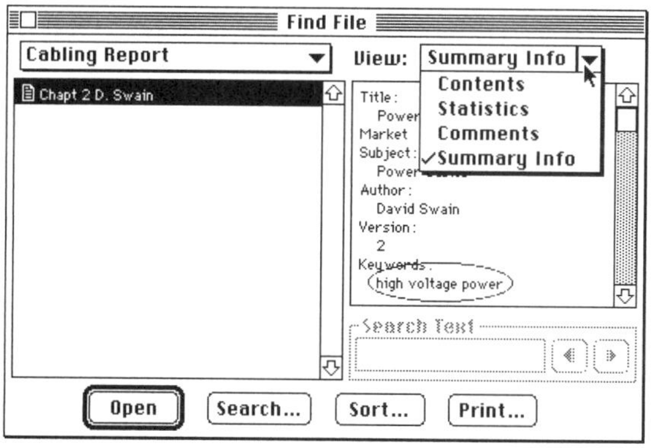

```
┌═══════════════════════════ Find File ═══════════════════════════┐
│ ┌─────────────────────┐              ┌──────────────────┐       │
│ │ Cabling Report     ▼│    View:     │Summary Info     ▼│       │
│ └─────────────────────┘              └──────────────────┘       │
│ ┌───────────────────────┐          ┌──────────────────────┐    │
│ │📄 Chapt 2 D. Swain   ⬆│          │ Contents            ⬆│    │
│ │                        │   Title:  │ Statistics           │    │
│ │                        │   Power   │ Comments             │    │
│ │                        │   Market  │✓Summary Info         │    │
│ │                        │  Subject:                         │    │
│ │                        │   Power                           │    │
│ │                        │  Author:                          │    │
│ │                        │    David Swain                    │    │
│ │                        │  Version:                         │    │
│ │                        │    2                              │    │
│ │                        │  Keywords:                        │    │
│ │                        │  (high voltage power)             │    │
│ │                       ⬇│                                 ⬇│    │
│ └───────────────────────┘          └──────────────────────┘    │
│ ┌Search Text──────────────────────────────────────────────┐    │
│ │ │                               │  ◀  ▶                   │    │
│ └──────────────────────────────────────────────────────────┘    │
│   ┌──────┐   ┌──────────┐  ┌──────┐  ┌──────┐                  │
│   │ Open │   │ Search...│  │Sort..│  │Print.│                  │
│   └──────┘   └──────────┘  └──────┘  └──────┘                  │
└══════════════════════════════════════════════════════════════┘
```

Figure 10.15

Once the document is located, you can view the contents of the document itself and also review the **Summary Info** information (Figure 10.15).

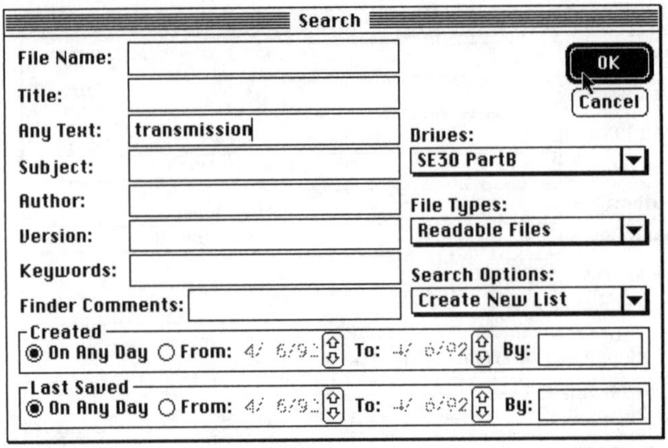

Figure 10.16

As a last resort, you can always use the **Find File Any Text** field to find information contained in a document (Figure 10.16). It is just a slower search process as every word of every document on your hard disk needs to be searched for matching criteria. However, there is a distinct advantage in using the **Any Text** field for searches.

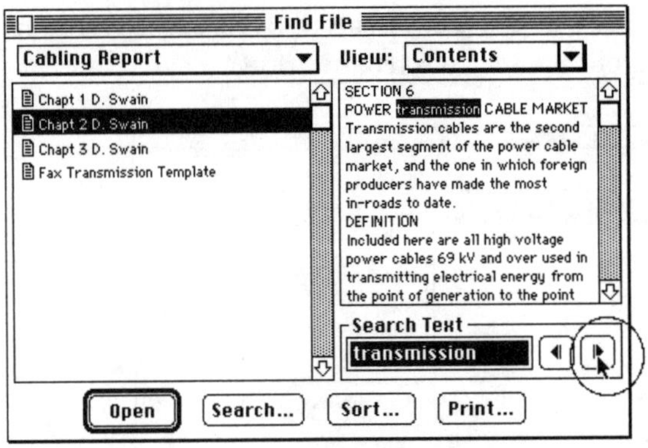

Figure 10.17

Once the document has been located, you can click on the **Search Text** arrow and the word will be highlighted within the document (Figure 10.17).

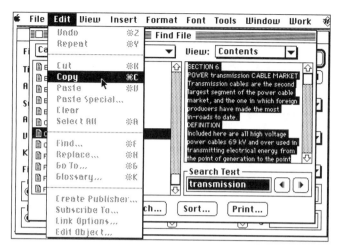

Figure 10.18

You can then **Copy** any text that is contained within the document into your Clipboard without even opening the document (Figure 10.18). You can also click on the **Open** button.

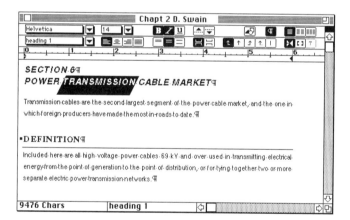

Figure 10.19

Once open, the document will be automatically scrolled to the location of the "Any Text" word(s) and the text will be highlighted (Figure 10.19).

NOTE: *Use a footer in your document to insert the File Name and the path name of the folders and hard disk where your document is located. This way, when you have a printed copy of the document you are trying to locate, you have a direct reference for locating it. See Chapter 9, the section called, "Revision Tracking."*

Creating Your Own Standard Keyboard Shortcuts

As you work with Microsoft Word, there will undoubtedly be some functions you use rather often and wish you could gain quicker access to through keyboard shortcuts. If the items already appear on menus, you can add a keyboard shortcut just as you did for the documents you added to the Work menu.

Applying Shortcuts from the Desktop

Figure 10.20

Press **Command Option** + (on the numeric keypad) and use the bold Command sign to select the command from the menu (Figure 10.20). You'll be prompted to type the keystroke. Don't worry if you end up trying a keystroke that is part of Microsoft Word's defaults. You will be warned if you do, and then you have the choice to remove it or not.

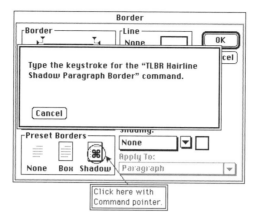

Figure 10.21

You can also add keyboard shortcuts to options within dialog boxes by pressing **Command Option** + (on the numeric keypad) within the specific dialog box and clicking on any option you see (Figure 10.21). This is often a more efficient method for assigning keyboard shortcuts because you might not know the proper name of the term that would describe the command you want.

In fact, you can change any commands within Microsoft Word that you want. You can even decide which menus they should appear on. (However, if you make too many changes, you might not be able to follow the directions in this book!) In order to change the **menu** position of standard commands and also add commands that don't appear on regular menus, you'll need to work with the **Commands** command located on the **Tools** menu.

Using the Commands Dialog Box

You can quickly scroll to a command name by pressing the first two characters of the command in rapid succession. One of the commands mentioned in Chapter 9 that would assist you in applying TOC entry codes as well as working with hidden-text print merge instructions is **Show Hidden Text**. Being able to toggle this option on and off with a keyboard shortcut will certainly eliminate trips to the View option inside the **Preferences** dialog box.

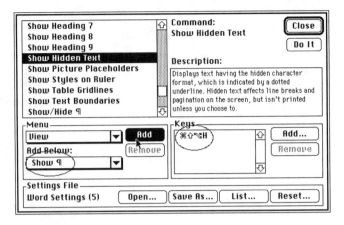

Figure 10.22

To create a keyboard shortcut, simply click on the **Keys Add** button. A familiar dialog box will appear asking you to type the keystroke.

Figure 10.23

You can also determine where the command will appear on any menu. The Menu options chosen in Figure 10.22 will cause **Show Hidden Text** to appear below the **Show ¶** command in the **View** menu (Figure 10.23).

Saving Settings (or Configuration) Files

One of the great opportunities for increasing your document production efficiency rests on your taking a few moments and analyzing repetitive kinds of tasks or commands you wish you didn't have to activate by reaching for the mouse. You also might want to customize a menu for specific tasks, such as those that you use often when you are working with tables and formatting borders.

When you quit Microsoft Word, all the changes you've made to any default settings as well as the keyboard shortcuts and menu placements are saved to a **Word Settings (5)** configuration file. This file is located in one of several places, depending on which system software you use. In System 6.0.x, it is in the System Folder; in System 7.0, it is inside the Preferences folder of the System Folder.

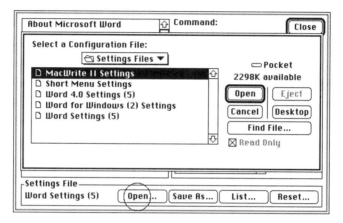

Figure 10.24

Microsoft Word ships with a number of settings files that alter placement of commands within menus to resemble other software programs, such as MacWrite II, Word 4.0, and even Windows Word 2.0. To access a configuration file, choose **Commands** from the **Tools** menu and click on the **Open** button (Figure 10.24).

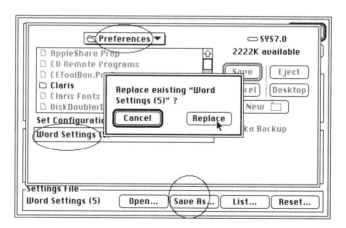

Figure 10.25

Your **Commands** dialog box will display which settings file you are currently using. However, if you load another settings file and want to return to the new settings you've just applied, you might run into some difficulty. As stated before, when you **Quit** from Word your changes are stored in the **Word Settings (5)** file. However, if you load other settings *before* saving changes to your **Word Settings (5)** file, you will lose those changes.

Rule of Thumb: Before you load any other configuration file, save the changes to your current Word Settings (5) file by clicking on the **Save As** button. Locate the **Word Settings (5)** file and **Replace** (Figure 10.25).

Format	
Paragraph Border...	^⌥B
Border...	^B
Table Cells...	⌘⌥C
Table Layout...	⌘⌥L
Insert Columns	^⇧I
Delete Columns	^⇧K
Insert Rows	^⌘U
Delete Rows	^⌘K
TB Hairline Cell Border	^⌥T
TLBR Hairline Cell Border	^⌥K
R Hairline Cell Border	^⇧R
Merge Cells	^⌥M
Split Cell	^⌥S
Frame...	^⌥F

Figure 10.26

Because you can save and name various kinds of settings files, consider creating "specialty" settings for working with tables, page layout, applying certain kinds of borders, or even settings that contain lists of Work menu items you only make use of for that kind of a project (Figure 10.26).

You can load a settings file by clicking on the **Open** button from within the **Commands** dialog box or you can also leave it on the **Finder** desktop and double-click the configuration to launch the Word application with your specific settings file (Figure 10.27).

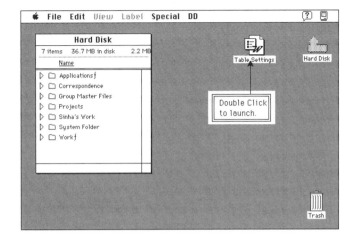

Figure 10.27

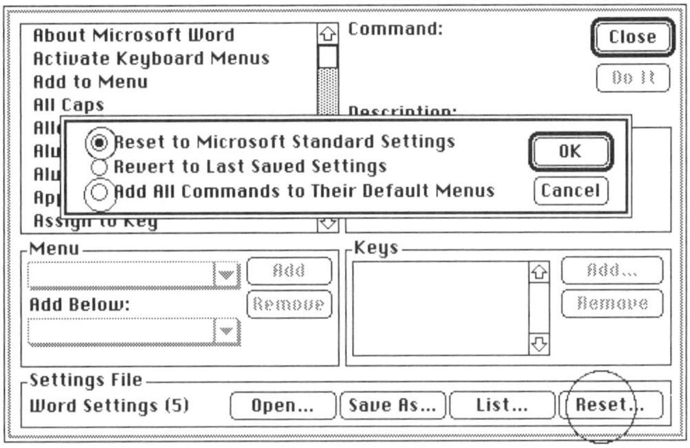

Figure 10.28

If you ever want to clear a settings file and start over, remember you can use the **Reset** button to load Word's default settings (Figure 10.28).

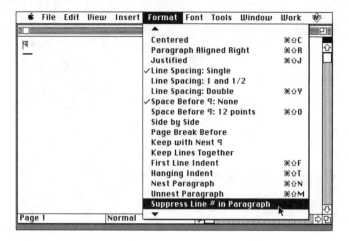

Figure 10.29

You might also consider loading all Microsoft's default settings into the menus and browsing through the menus to see and learn what various commands are available in Word. It's a bit of an adventure when you first look at the "loaded" menus, but you're sure to expand your knowledge for the time you invest in exploring (Figure 10.29).

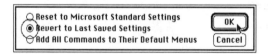

Figure 10.30

Once you've added all the commands to all the menus, you can get back to your normal settings by choosing the **Reset** button in the **Commands** dialog box and clicking on the **Revert to Last Saved Settings** option (Figure 10.30).

What if you are always forgetting those nifty keyboard settings you've created and you want to have some kind of a "reference sheet" you can place near your computer within eye distance? You can use the **List** button inside the **Commands** dialog box to generate a list of your menu commands (Figure 10.31).

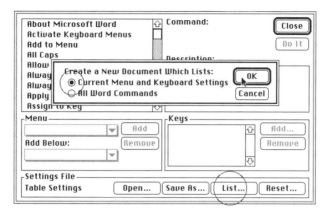

Figure 10.31

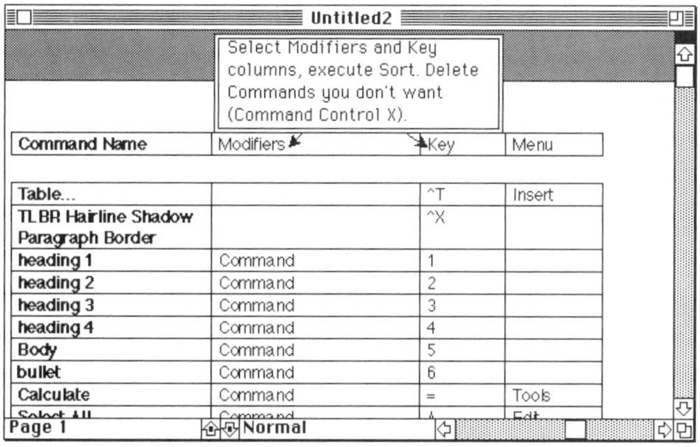

Figure 10.32

It will take a few moments to create the document. Once it appears on your desktop, you will see that the list is alphabetized by the Command Names. If you want to organize your list differently, choose the **Modifiers** and **Keys** columns by pressing the **Option** key and selecting them. Choose **Sort** from the **Tools** menu (this may also take a few moments). You might want to delete a number of functions placed in this list by pressing **Command Control X** (Delete Rows) and pare the list down to those specific commands you need access to (Figure 10.32).

Tired of Typing the Same Thing Over and Over Again?

Y ou've learned how to invent keyboard shortcuts to eliminate the necessity of reaching for the mouse every time you need to access menu options. How about some ways to help cut down on the time it takes you to enter text? It might be just a phrase (like your company name), a standard paragraph, or even a specific table setup you use time and again that you wish you could somehow automate.

This section will describe ways you can make use of Glossary entries and assign keyboard shortcuts to those entries. You'll also learn how to create specific glossary "files" that you can load into your word processing environment, files that are relevant to the specific kind of work you're executing on a particular day.

What Is a Glossary?

A glossary is a special type of Word document that saves coded "blocks" of text which can be quickly inserted into your document via the keyboard. There is no limit as to what you can place in a Glossary file. Entries are stored in a Standard Glossary file that is automatically loaded when you launch the Word application.

There are standard glossary entries that ship with Microsoft Word, such as the Date function you choose from the Insert menu and the automatic page number icon you click on when you are viewing a Header or Footer window. In Chapter 9, you learned about other kinds of standard glossary entries that you could insert into your document to assist you in your document revision tracking processes.

You're going to learn how to create, name, and save your own custom glossary items as well as how to rapidly insert these text blocks into your document (instead of typing!).

Creating, Defining, and Inserting a Glossary Item

It doesn't take much to create a glossary item—you merely select text (that you hope never to type again!) and give it a "code" name. The text might be your company name, a client company you always do business with, or the standard closure of a letter. What follows are the few short steps needed to work with glossaries.

STEP ONE

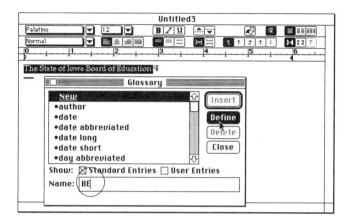

Figure 10.33

Select the text in your document. Go to the **Edit** menu and choose **Glos-sary**. The flashing insertion point will be located in the **Name** edit bar. Enter an appropriate code name you will find easy to remember and then click on the **Define** button (Figure 10.33).

STEP TWO

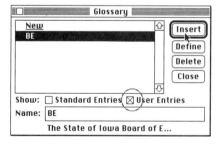

Figure 10.34

When it is time to insert your glossary item into a document, you have several techniques you can employ. You can select the **Glossary** dialog box from the **Edit** menu. When you click on the **User Entries** option, you should see listed the glossary items you defined. When you choose a glossary item from the list, you'll see the first line of text followed by an ellipsis displayed beneath the **Name** edit bar. You can click on the **Insert** button to have the text inserted at the location of the flashing insertion point in your document (Figure 10.34). However, there are more efficient methods you can use to insert a glossary item without making a trip to the **Edit** menu.

STEP THREE

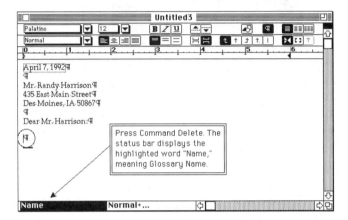

Figure 10.35

With your document open on the desktop, you can press a series of keys to insert the Glossary entry directly. Press the **Command** key with your left hand and tap the **Delete** key once with your right hand. The lower left status box should become highlighted with the word **Name** in it. This is a prompt that you are to enter the Name of your glossary item (Figure 10.35).

STEP FOUR

The text you enter from the keyboard will be displayed in the status box area (Figure 10.36). When you are finished entering the code name, press the **Return** key. Your glossary item will be inserted into your document.

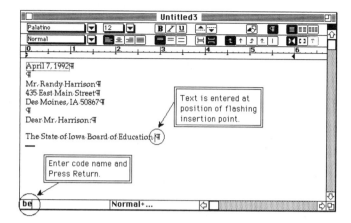

Figure 10.36

STEP FIVE

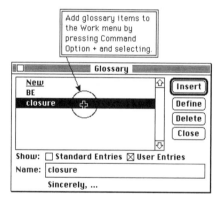

Figure 10.37

The method for inserting glossary items you just learned is effective *if* you remember the codes for your glossary entries. But what if your memory needs a little jogging? You can add the glossary items to your **Work** menu (along with your document templates) and use the **Work** menu to select the glossary item or as a reminder.

To add the Glossary item to the Work menu, go to the **Edit** menu and choose **Glossary**. Press **Command Shift +** (next to the **Delete** key). Click once on the glossary item (Figure 10.37). The **Work** menu will flash.

STEP SIX

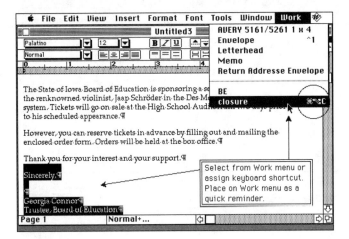

Figure 10.38

The example in Figure 10.38 shows documents listed in the Work menu separated from glossary items by a dotted separator line. You can also create your own unique keyboard shortcut for glossary items you use all the time (making it even more efficient to use the keyboard to insert large bodies of text). As with creating keyboard shortcuts for any menu item, press **Command Option** + (on the numeric keypad) and use the bold Command sign pointer to select the menu item. Enter the keystroke combination you want (Figure 10.38).

> **NOTE:** *You can also assign a keyboard shortcut to a Glossary Item from within the Glossary dialog box.*

You might wonder why you should go to the trouble of placing a Glossary item on a **Work** menu if you can make your own keystroke for it. The glossary listing on the **Work** menu serves as a reminder to you should you need it. It will also help others who might be working on your computer to understand how you've set up your document processing environment.

Saving and Loading Glossary Files

Figure 10.39

If you have added some glossary entries to your Glossary, when you **Quit** from Microsoft Word a dialog box will appear asking you if you want to save your changes (Figure 10.39). However, you don't necessarily have to wait until you terminate your Word session in order to save a Glossary file. You can always choose **Save** from the **File** menu while the **Glossary** dialog box is open on your desktop.

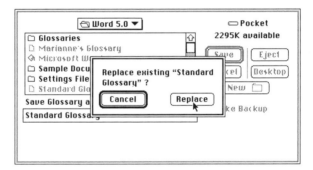

Figure 10.40

You'll be taken to a **Save** dialog box which asks you to save the Glossary with the **Standard Glossary** file name. Depending on which folder you decide to save the file in, you might be asked if you want to **Replace** the existing Standard Glossary file which ships with Microsoft Word (Figure 10.40).

> **NOTE:** *The Standard Glossary file needs to be located in the same folder as the Word application in order to be loaded automatically when you launch Microsoft Word.*

Creating a New Glossary File

You might want to create special glossaries for a variety of functions—addresses for clients, table layouts, phone number references, various bullet shapes—all of which do not need to be part of your Standard Glossary. These glossaries can be loaded in on an "as needed" basis.

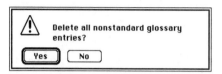

Figure 10.41

Before you create new entries for a special glossary, you should "clear" all existing user-defined glossary items. To do this, choose **New** from the **File** menu while the **Glossary** dialog box is open on the desktop. A warning dialog box will appear asking you to confirm that this is what you would like to execute (Figure 10.41). You then have a "fresh" glossary to make entries into which you can Save and name appropriately.

Loading Glossary Files

Just as you did before you created a New Glossary file, you might want to Clear the entries from an existing glossary before you open a new file. If you don't clear glossary items (Figure 10.41) then the glossary items will be "merged." Any glossary entries that have the same Names (or codes) will be overwritten by the incoming glossary item contents. This will be made clearer in the explanation for the illustration in Figure 10.45 below.

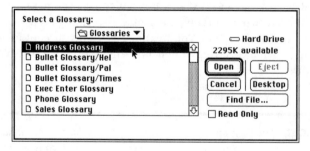

Figure 10.42

To load an existing glossary file, you first need to have the **Glossary** dialog box open on the desktop. Go to the **File** menu and choose **Open**. Navigate to the correct folder and double-click on the appropriate glossary file (Figure 10.42).

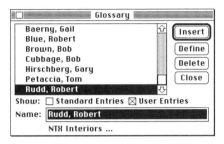

Figure 10.43

The particular glossary example in Figure 10.43 was constructed for client addresses. Using this glossary you have keyboard access to address information which you can use in conjunction with your letterhead template. Because the glossary was constructed with the last name first, you will probably need to key in only the first few letters of a person's last name (after pressing **Command Delete** and before pressing the **Return** key).

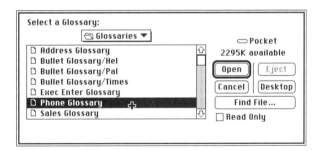

Figure 10.44

You can also add Glossary files to your **Work** menu which you can load directly. To add a Glossary file to the **Work** menu, make sure the **Glossary** dialog box is open. Go to the **File** menu and choose **Open**. Press **Command Option +** (next to delete key) and double-click on the glossary file name (Figure 10.44).

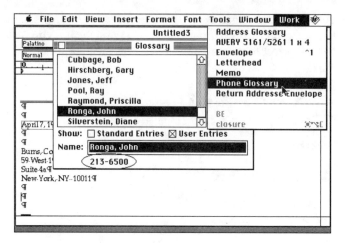

Figure 10.45

Figure 10.45 illustrates that you can select another glossary file—similar to your address glossary—which contains the telephone numbers of the same clients. Since the Glossary Entry names are the same, when the Phone Glossary is merged with the Address Glossary, the phone number information overrides the address information.

The **Glossary** dialog box has been kept open to demonstrate the merged information. However, you do not need to have the **Glossary** dialog box open in order to load in a glossary file from the **Work** menu. You can merge glossaries at any time by simply selecting the file name from the **Work** menu.

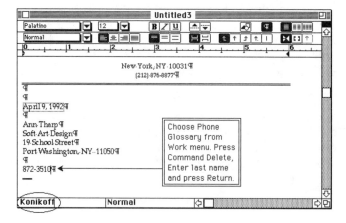

Figure 10.46

These address and phone glossaries can act as a "quick" reference file. Press **Command Delete**, enter the person's last name and, depending on which glossary is loaded, the information will be entered in your document (Figure 10.46). If you don't need to retain the information as document text, you can simply select the **Undo Insert Glossary Entry** function from the **Edit** menu or press **Command Z**.

Glossary Entry Ideas

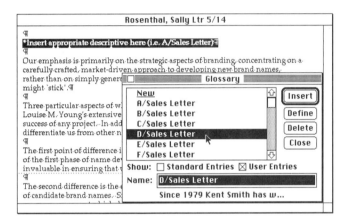

Figure 10.47

In the section on creating standard report formats within Chapter 9, it was suggested that you could insert "flags" within a document and use the **Find** dialog box to quickly move to text entry areas. The example in Figure 10.47 illustrates that you can use the same "flagging" idea in conjunction with glossary entries. Each glossary entry in the example represents a slight variation on a company's description with appropriate client examples for the industry they are pitching in the sales letter. The glossary entries were "coded" in such a way that the user had only to enter "A/" or "D/" and press the **Return** key (after pressing the standard **Command** and **Delete** keys) to insert the appropriate text block.

> **NOTE:** *You can print out a copy of your Glossary file to use as a quick reference. Simply choose Print from the File menu while the Glossary dialog box is open on the desktop.*

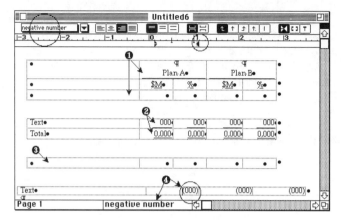

Figure 10.48

You might use a glossary file to quickly access a "palette" of standard table formats you can then insert into a document and use to begin text entry. As you press the Tab key at the end of each row, the new row will contain all the correct formatting. The example in Figure 10.48 indicates the following:

❶ Standard table heading with a blank first row so that text entry can be made by either inserting another blank row or entering directly into the existing blank row.

❷ A glossary entry for the same table format that is inserted for the row before and row containing the Total information. All paragraph border and spacing has been applied.

❸ A blank row for the same table format that can be inserted after a Total row. This glossary entry ensures that underline and border formats do not carry forward to the new row.

❹ Any style definitions you make for table cells (such as adjustment of the right indent mark for negative numbers) will be saved with the table glossary entry.

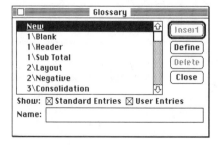

Figure 10.49

The coding for this particular Tables Glossary uses number prefixes for the various table "designs" and descriptive text for the table "parts" they refer to (Figure 10.49).

Glossaries are powerful tools that, once implemented, can reduce your document production time dramatically! The successful implementation of glossaries requires you to assess your document production tasks, determine what pieces can be defined as glossary items, intelligently code them, and assign them to the Work menu for automatic text entry.

How to Quickly Format a Document

Styles have been mentioned throughout this book in sections where it was an appropriate formatting tool to gain efficiency for the specific topic of document production tasks. What follows is a "round up" of time saving techniques you can execute to apply styles you've defined in your existing documents.

Working With Default Styles

Many users new to Microsoft Word and to the Macintosh are often confused by the word "default" and its use within this application. Most dictionaries define default as a failure to do something (such as failure to pay a bill). Within Word, default is used in conjunction with 9 preset dialog box or menu settings. When you first launch Word, many functions you initially execute are the result of "default settings"—such as the font, ruler settings, paragraph alignment, line spacing, and margins.

Many of these settings are contained within Microsoft Word's default style definitions for the default style named **Normal**. Normal will be part of every document you ever create in Microsoft Word. You also have the option to place other style names with formats you have defined into the default settings file (which is the Word Settings (5) file discussed earlier in the section on configuration files).

There are many advantages to setting default styles, particularly for heading 1, heading 2, heading 3, body text, and table of contents styles. When you first open a document the fonts, character styles, tab spacing, borders, etc., that you like to use on a daily basis are there for every new document you create without you having to do anything.

Setting Default Styles

Setting (and removing) default styles is a very simple process.

STEP ONE

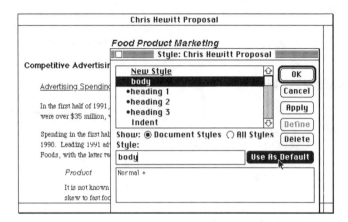

Figure 10.50

Open a sample document with style definitions you probably use for most of your document production needs. Go to the **Format** menu and choose **Style**. Select the style name and click on the **Use as Default** button (Figure 10.50).

STEP TWO

Figure 10.51

A dialog box will appear asking if it is OK to record the style in the Default Style Sheet (Figure 10.51). This default style sheet is the Word Settings (5) file in your System Folder. Click on the **Yes** button.

STEP THREE

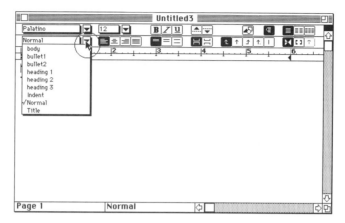

Figure 10.52

When you go to the **File** menu and select a **New** document, go to the **Style Selection box** on the **Ruler** and observe that all the styles you set as defaults are now part of any new document you create (Figure 10.52).

Removing Default Styles

You might decide that you don't want to have default style settings for every document. Or, perhaps you want to eliminate certain style definitions from just one document to avoid confusion. (Often if you see a style listed in a document, you might think it is being used somewhere within the document when indeed it is not.) Removing styles takes only the click of a mouse button.

STEP ONE

Select the **Style** dialog box from the **Format** menu. Click on the style you want to remove; then click on the **Delete** button (Figure 10.53).

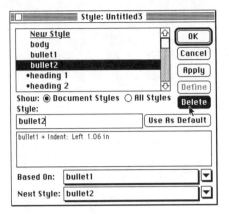

Figure 10.53

STEP TWO

Figure 10.54

A dialog box will appear asking you if you want to delete the style. Click on the **OK** button (Figure 10.54).

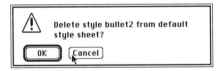

Figure 10.55

A second dialog box will appear for those styles you have defined as default styles (Figure 10.55). However, you might not want to delete the style from your default style sheet. At this point, you have the choice either to **OK** the action or to **Cancel** the action. Clicking on **Cancel** will still keep the default style in any new documents you create.

> **NOTE:** *Styles you define as default styles only appear in New documents. They do not affect any documents you have already created and saved.*

Creating Style Sheet Libraries

In the section on merging style sheets in Chapter 9 (see Figure 9.39), it was suggested that you could set up a style sheet library for different kinds of formats you might use when generating proposals and other long documents. Rather than defining default styles (discussed in the previous section), you might want to consider using style sheets as an alternate method for accessing styles you have already defined and used successfully in other documents. This section will basically review the concept of style sheets and how you create them.

Since styles are saved with the documents that define them, you can create blank documents that contain nothing but the definitions of your styles. This blank document is then termed a "style sheet." Creating a style sheet involves the merging of styles you have already defined in another document with a blank, Untitled document.

STEP ONE

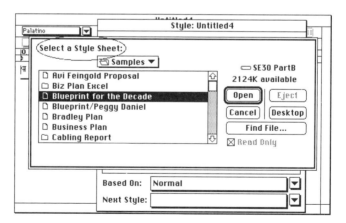

Figure 10.56

Go to the **File** menu and choose **New**. Choose **Style** from the **Format** menu. Remove any default styles that might have been incorporated into the new document. Go to the **File** menu and choose **Open**. Navigate to the document that contains the style definitions you want and double-click on it. Notice that the dialog box says "Select a Style Sheet" (Figure 10.56).

STEP TWO

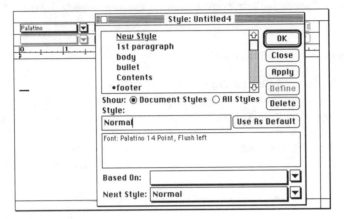

Figure 10.57

All the style names and definitions from that document will be merged into your Untitled document (Figure 10.57). Click on the **OK** button.

STEP THREE

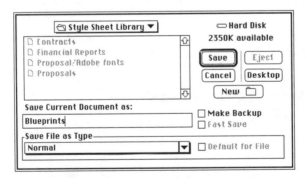

Figure 10.58

Save the document in a special **Style Sheet Library** folder. As you create different kinds of reports, proposals, and documents that use different style definitions or even font types, you have quick access for merging these files. Since the documents only contain style definitions, they take only about 2K of disk space.

> **NOTE:** *Make a backup floppy disk of your Style Sheet Library for safe keeping. You can also take it with you when you use other workstations for quick access to formats you are familiar with.*

Creating Style Keyboard Shortcuts

Just as you were able to set keyboard shortcuts for menu functions and glossary items, you can also speed the application of styles by assigning a keyboard shortcut to a style name. Used in conjunction with "Next Style" definitions (see Chapter 9, Figure 9.22), your hands will rarely have to leave the keyboard!

Just as you placed glossary items in the Work menu as a reminder, it's a good practice to also place styles that you assign keyboard shortcuts to on the Work menu. You will have a quick reminder for the key combinations you'll use to apply a style, as well as provide clarification of your particular custom settings for anyone else who might use your workstation.

STEP ONE

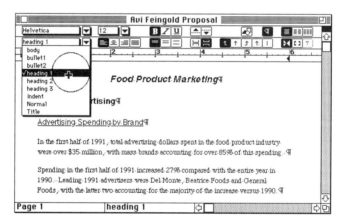

Figure 10.59

To add your style to the Work menu, press **Command Option** + (next to the **Delete** key) to change your pointer to a large, bold + sign. Go to the **Style Selection** box on the Ruler and choose the style (Figure 10.59). Your Work menu will flash and the style name will be added.

STEP TWO

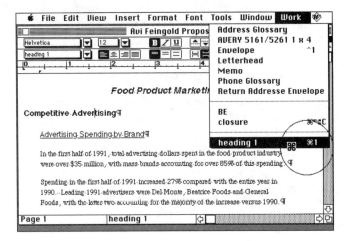

Figure 10.60

To create the keyboard shortcut for the style, press **Command Option** + (on the numeric keypad above the enter key). Go to the **Work** menu and choose the style name with the Command sign-shaped pointer (Figure 10.60). A dialog box will appear asking you to enter the keystroke. Consider using Command 1 for heading 1, Command 2 for heading 2, etc. This is an easy keystroke to remember and since the heading styles are default styles, it will work for any document you create.

> **NOTE:** *If you use a keyboard shortcut for a style that is not defined within a document, you will hear an alert beep. This signals you that the style is not contained within the document and therefore, it cannot be applied.*

Once you define keystrokes for your styles, they will be saved in the **Word Settings (5)** file (or the specific configuration file you determine through the **Commands** dialog box).

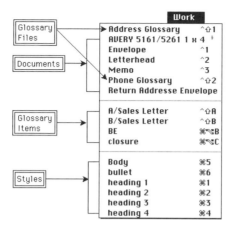

Figure 10.61

Style names listed on the **Work** menu are separated from glossary and document listings (Figure 10.61).

NOTE: *You can use the keyboard shortcuts for your default heading styles while you are working in Outline View since various heading levels are directly related to the application of heading 1, heading 2, etc., default styles.*

Sharing Documents Across Platforms

If you are working in a "mixed environment" between Macintoshes and PCs running Microsoft Windows, you might need to share Microsoft Word 5.0 documents with a colleague using Windows Word 2.0. There is a great deal of compatibility between the programs; however, here are some tips that will help you to identify and prevent possible formatting problems.

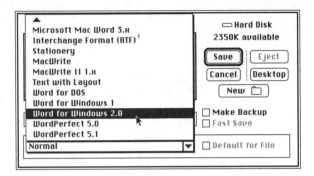

Figure 10.62

Save Macintosh created Word documents as **Word for Windows 2.0** documents. There is a **Save File as Type** pop-up list menu in the **Save** dialog box where you can select this format (Figure 10.62).

Users of Windows Word 2.0 should continue to save their documents in Windows Word 2.0 format. The Macintosh version of Word has conversion utilities that will read the document and convert it into a Macintosh document.

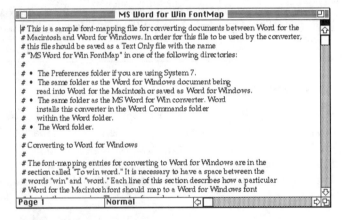

Figure 10.63

You will need to create a "font mapping file," as word processing fonts are dependent on the installed printers (Figure 10.63). Different fonts exist between printers on the Mac and PC platforms. The font mapping file ensures the correct font will be used on either platform. Detailed instructions for creating this font mapping file are contained in the **MS Word Conversion Options** file within the **Word Commands** folder created during the installation process.

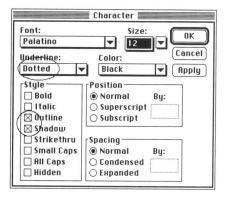

Figure 10.64

Outline, **dotted**, and **shadow** character formats exist on the Macintosh but not in Windows (Figure 10.64). These formats will not be converted and should be avoided. Also, most colors are converted between platforms—with the exception that dark colors on the Windows platform are converted to black on the Macintosh.

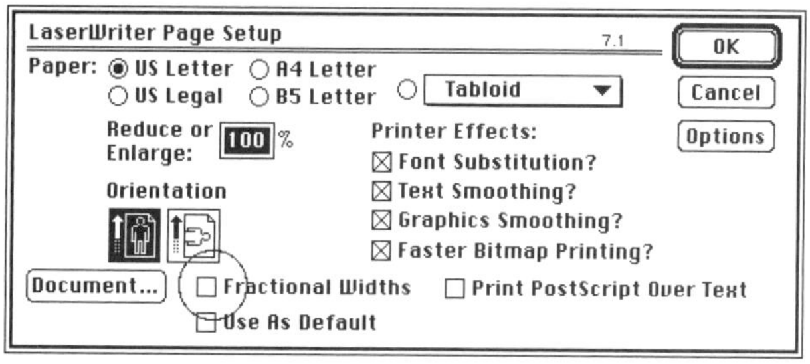

Figure 10.65

Text wrapping within Windows Word will wrap text some fractions of a point wider than the Macintosh will. Sometimes, this may cause a word in the Windows Word document to move to the next line in a paragraph; whereas on the Macintosh, the word would fit on the same line. To approximate consistent word wrapping between platforms, clear the **Fractional Widths** option in the **Page Setup** dialog box (Figure 10.65).

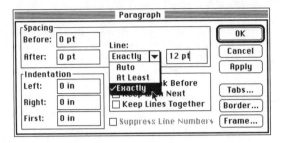

Figure 10.66

When using Auto line spacing, Windows Word 2.0 places more spacing above each line of text than the Macintosh does (approximately 0.5 points). This will create page break inconsistency between platforms. To achieve consistent results between platforms, you will need to apply fixed line spacing in your paragraph formatting. This should be adopted by users on *both* platforms.

To apply fixed line spacing, you need to choose the **Exactly** line spacing option from the **Paragraph** dialog box and enter a point size setting in the **Line** edit bar next to it (Figure 10.66). Generally, you should add two points of space to your Font size, for example, 10 point Times would have an exact line spacing of 12 points. You'll have to experiment on your own for results that satisfy your particular formatting needs.

Aside from the line spacing inconsistencies, all paragraph formats—including paragraph shading—will be converted between platforms with the following exceptions:

> Borders around pictures are not converted from Windows Word 2.0 to the Macintosh.

> Vertical line tab marks on the Macintosh do not appear in converted Windows Word 2.0 documents.

The following list summarizes other formatting compatibility issues:

- **Columns:** If a Windows Word 2.0 document contains a page break in a multicolumn section, the page break is converted to a column break in Word for the Macintosh. The Macintosh does not convert the Line Between formatting of columns created in Windows Word 2.0

- **Section Formatting: Odd only** header/footers in Windows Word 2.0 are converted to **every page** header/footers on the Macintosh.

- **Page Formatting:** The page orientation from the first section of a Windows Word 2.0 document is used for the entire document when converted to the Macintosh.

- **Annotations:** Annotations in Windows Word 2.0 are not supported or converted on the Macintosh. Any Voice Annotations inserted in Macintosh documents will appear in Windows Word 2.0 as a graphic.

- **Language:** Language formatting is a Windows Word 2.0 option and is not supported on the Macintosh.

- **Revision Marks:** These are a Windows Word 2.0 option and are not supported on the Macintosh.

- **Cross-References/Bookmarks:** These are not supported on the Macintosh though they will be preserved when a Windows Word 2.0 file is converted on the Macintosh and then saved as a Word for Windows 2.0 document.

- **Tables of Contents/Indexes:** In Windows Word 2.0 files, tables of contents and indexes are converted to text on the Macintosh. However, all entries are preserved and the table of contents or index can be regenerated.

- **Graphics:** The embedded graphic image within the document is converted, but the original graphic file is not. Therefore, an EPS graphic image is preserved but the original PostScript file is not converted. However, all bitmapped graphics and PICT files are converted between platforms. When creating rotated text on the Macintosh using the `Edit/Insert Picture` tool, the font used to create the text will be converted to a bitmapped graphic in Windows Word 2.0.

- **Object Linking and Embedding (OLE):** When converting from Word for the Macintosh to Windows Word 2.0, the Macintosh link information is ignored by Windows Word 2.0 but the linking result is preserved. However, all the information regarding the source of the link is retained when converting back to the Macintosh.

  OLE objects are converted and are editable if the same application exists on the other platform (for example, Excel). Although you can place another Word document as an object on the Macintosh, Windows Word 2.0 is not an "object server" and does not allow the user to edit the object. If the Windows Word 2.0 user double-clicks on a converted Macintosh Word object created in Word, the end result will be an "icon," and they will have lost the object information. Therefore, Word documents embedded on the Macintosh should not be edited on the Windows Word 2.0 platform.

- **Summary Info:** Certain summary information fields do not exist on both platforms. Macintosh Word has a version-number field that does not exist in Windows Word 2.0. Similarly, Windows Word 2.0 has a comments field that does not exist on the Macintosh. Once the document is converted and saved on either platform, the information in these fields is lost.

Conclusion

You'll find that an intelligent system of keyboard shortcuts, glossaries and style definitions as well as the effective placement of elements in a Work menu will streamline your document production tasks and free you from unnecessary repetitive actions. Devising a document production "system" will also save you and your company valuable time and money consistently on a daily basis.

Index

G

H

W

white text, 48-50
Windows, sharing
  documents, 525-530
windows
    splitting, 364
    switching between,
      keyboard shortcuts, 492
Word 5.0
    embedding objects,
      390-393
    linking Excel 3.0
      documents, 374-375
        System 6.0, 375-378
        System 7.0, 378-387
    sharing documents with
      Word for Windows,
      525-530
Work menus
    adding documents,
      487-489
    deleting documents, 490
    glossary items, adding,
      509-510
    styles, adding, 523
wrapping text, 60

X-Z

Zapf Dingbat font, 328-329
zooming documents, 29-31

Five Ways $15 Can Benefit Your Business:

1. *Save time* formatting necessary business documents.

2. *Enhance* your document processing productivity.

3. *Realize* the full value of your computer system.

4. *Get up to speed* in Microsoft Word immediately.

5. *Receive* over 100 preformatted business documents featured in
    Marianne Carroll's Super Desktop Documents.

As illustrated in this book, you can *save valuable time* and money every day by using documents already formatted to meet your needs in the normal course of business. Put Microsoft Word to work by using templates that *eliminate formatting errors* and *bring consistency* to your overall document production system.

On this companion disk you'll receive *bullet-proof* stationery documents for memos, faxes, letter-head stationery, envelopes, labels, expense reports, proposals, sales letters, invoices, as well as *time-saving* glossary files and much, much more!

Order now and realize how easily you can *become efficient* with Microsoft Word and *save* valuable administrative costs daily. Readers of **Marianne Carroll's Super Desktop Documents** can receive this companion disk for just $15* (plus postage and handling).

Use the coupon below to order — **and have Super Desktop Documents at your fingertips!**

☑ **Yes!** Send me *Marianne Carroll's Super Desktop Documents Companion Disk!*

Send your check or money order made out to *Marianne Carroll Enterprises* for $15 plus $2.50 for postage and handling (drawn on a US bank in US funds*) along with this coupon or a photocopy to: *Marianne Carroll Enterprises*, 51 West 86th Street, New York, NY 10024. New York residents add sales tax (total $18.95).

Name _____

Address _____

City _____ State _____ ZIP _____

Specify the printer model you use _____

Specify the Macintosh model you use _____

System Requirements:

*   Macintosh Plus, Classic, or above with a hard disk and 2 MB of memory running System 6.0.2 or later.
*   Microsoft Word 5.0.

Please allow 4-6 weeks for delivery.

*Foreign orders: add $5. No CODS or credit card orders.

Keeping Pace With Today's Microcomputer Technology

Available at your local bookstore, or order by phone (800) 428-5331.

College Marketing Group
50 Cross Street
Winchester, MA 01890

ATT: **Cheryl Read**